Ubiquitous Learning

Strategies for Pedagogy, Course Design, and Technology

Ubiquitous Learning

Strategies for Pedagogy, Course Design, and Technology

Edited by

Terry T. Kidd, PhD

Texas A&M University

Irene Chen, EdD

University of Houston–Downtown

INFORMATION AGE PUBLISHING, INC.
Charlotte, NC • www.infoagepub.com

Library of Congress Cataloging-in-Publication Data

Ubiquitous learning strategies for pedagogy, course design, and technology / edited by Terry T. Kidd, Irene Chen.
p. cm.
Includes bibliographical references.
ISBN 978-1-61735-435-9 (pbk.) – ISBN 978-1-61735-436-6 (hardcover) – ISBN 978-1-61735-437-3 (e-book)
1. Educational technology. 2. Ubiquitous computing. 3. Digital media. 4. Instructional systems–Design. 5. Education–Effect of technological innovations on. I. Kidd, Terry T. II. Chen, Irene.
LB1028.3.U355 2011
371.33–dc22

2011010598

Printed in the United States of America

CONTENTS

Acknowledgements ix

Preface xi

PART I

INTRODUCTION TO U-LEARNING: PROCESS, PEDAGOGY, AND PRACTICE

1 The Pedagogy of Things: Ubiquitous Learning, Student Culture, and Constructivist Pedagogical Practice 3
C. Edward Watson and William O. Plymale

2 A Process-Oriented Pedagogy for Ubiquitous Learning 17
Philip Bonanno

3 Ubiquitous Learning: Issues in the Australian Higher Education Context 41
Trish Andrews, Belinda Tynan, and Cherry Stewart

PART II

SOCIAL MEDIA + MOBILE LEARNING = U-LEARNING: CREATING CLASSROOM CONNECTIONS

4 Micro-Cycles: Course Design Model for Mobile Learning 63
Chris Haskell and Barbara Schroeder

5 Supporting Devices in Ubiquitous Learning 79
Victor Jengchung Chen and Andree E. Widjaja

6 Social Media, Story Stream + the University Classroom 107
Brad King

7 Social Networks: Pedagogical Tool or Pedagogical Threat?.......... 121
Keith J. Benson and Josephine A. Koster

8 Is the iPhone a Ubiquitous Learning Device? First Step Toward Digital Lecture Notes 137
Martin Ebner and Thomas Billicsich

9 Remote Laboratories and Mobile Devices...................................... 153
Javier Garcia-Zubia, Jaime Irurzun, Pablo Orduña, and Diego López-de-Ipiña

PART III

A NEW DIRECTION TOWARD TEACHING AND LEARNING: UBIQUITOUS LEARNING

10 A New Learning Environment Based on Reproducible Ubiquitous Computing: Experiences and Prospects...................... 179
Patrick Wessa, Ian E. Holliday, and Peter Reddy

11 The Good Teacher: Effective Teaching Strategies for a Ubiquitous Learning Environment 197
Torria Bond

12 Helping Your Lecturers to Creatively Introduce Ubiquitous Computing Technologies into Their Teaching: What Every Lecturer Should Know... 209
Lisa-Dionne Morris

13 Pedagogical Use of Video Podcast in Engineering: Teaching, Learning, and Assessment 229
Ying Xiong and Imin Kao

14 Ubiquitous Mathematics from South Africa to Finland: Does Reverse Transfer Work? 249
Teemu H. Laine, Eeva Nygren, Erkki Sutinen, Carolina Islas Sedano, Mike Joy, and Seugnet Blignaut

15 Case Study: Using Flickr in Design Education............................... 283
Diane Robbie and Lynette Zeeng

16 Global Perspectives of U-Learning 299
Dallas McPheeters

17 The Future as a Ubiquitous Learning Opportunity........................317
Kay E. Strong and Peter C. Bishop

About the Editors.. 329

Glossary of Terms.. 331

ACKNOWLEDGEMENTS

Completing a project of this magnitude is a great challenge and an opportunity many choose never to undertake. It's with the help of many individuals who have inspired and motivated me to complete this journey.

I would first like to take this opportunity to acknowledge the considerable time and effort the authors have invested in their respective publications included in this book. The authors presented within this book are intelligent and well-seasoned in their practice and respective areas. Without their hard work, dedication, and in some cases sacrifice, this book would not have been made into reality. Thank you for being gracious and patient under fire and accepting to my comments and ideas on your chapters. I would like to send a special acknowledgement and thanks to my co-collaborator on this project, Dr. Irene Chen from the University of Houston-Downtown.

Gratitude and acknowledgements go out to the reviewers who spent countless hours reading, proofing, and articulating their comments, from the proposal stage to the final chapter revisions.

Special thanks must also go to the Information Age Publishing team for their administrative support and in helping to bring this vision into reality.

I would also like to acknowledge and thank my good friend Ms. Peggy Powell at the University of Texas School of Public Health, as well as Dr. Ronald Peters, Dr. Carolyn Ashe from the University of Houston-Downtown, Dr. B. Stephen Carpenter and Dr. Trina Davis from Texas A&M University, and

Ubiquitous Learning, pages ix–x

Dr. Katy Greenwood from the University of Houston, and Dr. Curtis Bonk for their encouragement, advice, and mentorship in my career.

And lastly, to my ancestors, who were silenced and never saw freedom, this book is dedicated to them.

—Terry T. Kidd, PhD

I would like to express our appreciation to the number of people who have contributed in some way to this publication. These include the chapter authors as well as the editors and designers from Information Age Publishing; without them this publication would not have been possible.

—Irene Chen, EdD

PREFACE

INTRODUCTION

The arrival of the World Wide Web on the heels of the Internet opened new channels for communication and information delivery and retrieval. Recent advances in information, and communications technologies have led to advances in mobile devices that have nurtured the development of learning on-the-go and access opportunities for learning anywhere at any time. These new learning opportunities have been labeled *ubiquitous learning*—the intersection of mobile learning with e-learning. This new affordance of learning has allowed for access, integration, and interaction of resources regardless of time or location.

Ubiquitous learning—learning that is not constrained by time or physical spaces—is pervasive, dynamic, ongoing, and progressive, making learning current, relevant, prevalent, and interactive. This has led to learning being responsive to the learning needs of the public. Accessing information and learning opportunities are no longer confined by physical space or temporal conditions. Learners of all types have access and the opportunity to engage in formal and informal learning, whether at home, at work, or on-the-go. This type of learning can be powerful, personal, current, and situated, as learners and instructors can communicate, interact, and learn in real time.

As we move into the next decade of the 21st century, educators have an opportunity to engage in new technologies as a way of expanding their curricular and instructional options, engage their students in round-the-clock learning, and increase interactivity outside the bounds of the traditional classroom. Some use automated Web sites without human interaction, and

---

Ubiquitous Learning, pages xi–xx

others interact remotely through audio and video links, online discussion boards, e-mails, blogs, instant messages, chat rooms, texts, social networking sites, and even RSS or Twitter feeds. Additionally, smartphones, mobile communication devices, and handheld computing devices such as iPads and iPhones, provide more opportunities for learning. Moreover, with the convergence of e-learning with mobile learning devices, along with social media applications, the use of these tools in an educational context have given rise to ubiquitous learning.

The barrier of entry associated with ubiquitous learning may influence a variety of cultural norms that present powerful implications for education, while presenting a continuum that spans from blogging to classroom teaching to individual learning. The chapters assembled in this book serve as an introduction to ubiquitous learning in terms of pedagogy, process, practice, and its future directions for teaching and learning. Guiding this work is the theoretical assumption of grounding teaching and learning in an active learning process, where learners are engaged with the content, the learning environment, other students, the instructors, and themselves. Consider the possibilities of this new environment with constructivist theory, active learning strategies, and technology.

THEORETICAL FRAMEWORK GUIDING THIS BOOK

Constructivist theory supports learner-centered instruction during which the student is an active participant within a teaching and learning process. Learners construct, activate, and process prior knowledge and experiences to create new knowledge that can be applied to new situations. During lessons, students interact with their peers, their instructor, the course content, and with their previous knowledge. *Ubiquitous Learning: Strategies for Pedagogy, Course Design, and Technology* asserts a constructivist pedagogical assumption that outline practices that describe how the integration of various learning technologies within formal, nonformal, and informal environments creates a need to conceptualize and (re)conceptualize a different framework of how we look at a learning experience. This book takes the philosophical stance that supports constructivist, student-centered learning and instruction through the use of ubiquitous learning strategies and technologies.

While experts continue to bring the discussion of u-learning forward and to a larger extent, the discussion of teaching and learning practices, various stakeholders have been invited to contribute to the discussion on how teaching and learning can be (re)envisioned as we advance learning and development in the digital age. Experts in information and communication technology have been invited to explain hardware devices and the infrastructure of ubiquitous learning, such as WLAN, radio-frequency identification, GPS, and other technological trends. Educators have been invited to share their experiences as to how teaching and learning has been revolutionized by various technologies and associated teaching and assessment strategies. Policymakers have been invited to discuss the socioeconomic implications these technologies and strategies have for and within their societies. Future-studies experts have contributed a discussion that offers insight into the realm of possibilities and opportunities of ubiquitous learning. By anticipating possible outcomes of present actions based on past experiences and data, we are now able to predict future events with a certain degree of accuracy. Although great effort is needed to implement a ubiquitous teaching and learning environment, nonetheless, we are close. As human kind, we should be ready to feel comfortable living in a world where we learn what we want, whenever we want, and how we want, all with the touch of a device we can hold in our hands. Think of the possibilities and implications this has for of humanity.

PURPOSE

This book highlights issues and trends within ubiquitous learning from a global perspective and then provides more specific information on individual learning situations. Basically, this is a book about learning in the 21st century, illustrating dozens of learning options that combine aspects of mobile information and communication technology, constructivist instructional strategies, and social media with teaching and learning in formal academic settings and nonformal learning environments. Roughly half of the chapters focus on pedagogical, technical, process, and instructional design strategies, while the other half give concrete examples on how to implement, evaluate, and teach within a ubiquitous learning environment. Part I, "Introduction to U-Learning, Process, Pedagogy, and Practice," provides a vision and a foundation for u-learning that is grounded in emerging technologies, learning theory, and pedagogy. This section also provides commentary on ubiquitous learning that pushes our thinking and challenges our assumptions of learning in various contexts such as community-oriented learning, collaborative learning, problem-based learning, informal, and ad-hoc learning.

While college and university faculty seek to design instructional projects and courses to address the pervasive and growing use of ubiquitous learning devices, guidance and examples are needed. Part II, "Social Media + Mobile Learning = U-Learning: Creating Classroom Connections," provides insight and frameworks on how to create, enrich, distribute, and display instructional material for learning. Part III, "A New Direction Toward Teaching and Learning: Ubiquitous Learning," provides a rich discussion on (re)envisioning the teaching and learning process, where instructors are equipped with strategies for implementing u-learning.

Clearly, discussions and frameworks outlined and described in this book are in their early days, and their use suggests a certain amount of risk. The concepts, examples, and strategies outlined are fluid and emergent, and these practices will continue to evolve as technology advances, thereby moving teaching and learning practices forward. Additionally, this book clarifies where ubiquitous learning might find significant application given the vastly different opinions about the current state of technology integration into higher education. Clearly, a better understanding of the current state and the future direction of u-learning is warranted.

As u-learning progresses, many goals can be achieved through research, practices, and through forum discussions. This book provides such a forum to the possibilities of u-learning. For instance, this book is one of few books that covers ubiquitous learning situations and scenarios from around the globe. Second, this book is the first ubiquitous learning book to provide a broad picture of the applications of u-learning in an educational setting, specifically higher education.

Our goal with this book is to arouse interest and action plans to get those involved in adult learning, higher education, and in some cases, K–12 education to grasp the potential of u-learning and to implement u-learning associated practices. This book is meant to provide a connection between providers of learning and the learners themselves. As is apparent throughout this book, there are many examples of ubiquitous learning. Lastly, we hope this book will inspire others to create innovative and successful ubiquitous learning courses, programs, and events that discuss and debate findings and ideas reflected in this book and extend beyond them.

The models, examples, and strategies found here should provide a means to reflect on learning options and help foster decisions regarding ubiquitous learning. We hope that the examples and strategies included in this book can serve as a guide to others making similar journeys into ubiquitous learning. At the same time, we hope that those reading this book will continue to carry the discussion forward. We hope you enjoy this book, and we welcome your feedback and suggestions for follow-up volumes or themes.

AUDIENCE

This book can provide valuable information to higher education administrations, educators, researchers, instructional designers, educational technologists, and anyone else interested in how to design ubiquitous learning environments. In particular, this book will be valuable to higher education administrators struggling with issues of where to place valuable resources. Clarification on the various u-learning models and strategies can help administrators and staff of teaching and learning centers at college and university campuses train faculty for a wealth of formal and nonformal teaching opportunities. Teaching in a ubiquitous learning environment is a new experience for college faculty, so having a range of examples and strategies is vital. Instructional designers and educational technologists will need information on how to assist faculty in how to design and implement u-learning environments and situations.

Those conducting research in ubiquitous learning will benefit from reading chapters on the state of ubiquitous learning in a higher education setting. This book is for everyone interested in expanding their knowledge on the subject of ubiquitous learning.

BOOK OVERVIEW

The chapter authors were selected because of their leadership and knowledge within ubiquitous learning. With a wide range of perspectives covered in this book, there is something for everyone. The chapters are organized by three key themes: introduction and overview of u-learning for practice, making classroom connections with u-learning, and reenvisioning teaching and learning with u-learning. Brief descriptions of the chapters are outlined below.

Part 1: Introduction to U-Learning, Process, Pedagogy, and Practice

The first chapter, "The Pedagogy of Things: Ubiquitous Learning, Student Culture, and Constructivist Pedagogical Practice," written by Watson and Plymale, explores the interdisciplinary symbiosis that emerges between constructivism, student culture, and ubiquitous computing technologies and trends. Constructivist theory is summarized and integrated into various frameworks that highlight its relevancy to ubiquitous learning. Key ubiquitous learning technologies and practices that support students are also described and explored in this chapter.

In "A Process-Oriented Pedagogy for Ubiquitous Learning," Philip Bonanno suggests that the integration of a range of learning technologies in formal and nonformal education creates a need for a different frame of mind to conceptualize a learning experience. His chapter explores the detachment from models that emphasizes learning as a process of content transmission and moves on to a process-oriented pedagogy that reconceptualizes learning and knowledge-building in terms of dimensions and levels of interaction. A process-oriented methodology is proposed by Bonanno to analyze and manage ubiquitous learning systems. Using this framework as backdrop and inspired by a constructionist epistemology, this model categorizes interactions along the domain, technology, and community dimensions, and across three pedagogical levels. This process serves to develop protocols to be used in designing and evaluating ubiquitous learning.

Chapter 3, "Ubiquitous Learning: Issues in the Australian Higher Education Context," discusses how ubiquitous learning poses as an opportunity and a challenge to Australian higher education institutions, staff, and students. While the notion of "anywhere, any time, anyhow" learning can be seen to have obvious attraction and benefits for learners, u-learning also creates obvious challenges for higher education providers. These issues are explored, giving the reader detailed knowledge about the benefits and challenges of u-learning as one ventures to establish their own u-learning environment.

Part 2: Social Media + Mobile Learning = U-Learning: Creating Classroom Connections

Chapter 4, "Micro-Cycles: Course Design Model for Mobile Learning," describes how two instructors designed a mobile course about mobile learning. This course was among the first of its kind to be offered in the United States. This chapter addresses the pervasive and growing use of mobile devices by college and university students. Finally, this chapter details the goals and design of a mobile learning course, characteristics of mobile learning, methods for course evaluation, and challenges associated with designing for mobile learning.

Various hardware devices can be used to enhance ubiquitous learning. Chapter 5, "Supporting Devices in Ubiquitous Learning," presents hardware devices that support ubiquitous learning. These devices can be divided into three main categories: dedicated devices, mobile devices, and supporting technology. The chapter provides brief explanations on supporting devices, such as PCs, notebooks, PDAs, smartphones, RFIDs, GPS devices, and iPads. Future trends and conclusions are elaborated at the end of the chapter.

Chapter 6, "Social Media, Story Streams + the University Classroom," examines how the wisdom and collective intelligence of crowds can be paired with emerging technologies and social software tools to transform a university teaching environment. This chapter suggests that this transformation won't be driven by traditional research, as social technologies are evolving too quickly for these models to keep pace. This means education and instructional leaders must look toward more nontraditional sources to extrapolate innovative ways to use these technologies to create "living-learning" classroom environments that not only enable students to work more easily together to find solutions to problems, but also prepare them for an increasingly networked digital world.

The rapid explosion of social media platforms and their embrace by 18–25-year-olds has tremendous implications for college teaching. Today's 13–25-year-olds are "hypersocializers," used to constant communication via text, cell phones, and social networking sites. Since these young adults make up the largest percentage of students currently enrolled in colleges, it is imperative that college faculty assess the potential of using social media in their classrooms, and design and implement effective strategies for using this ubiquitous technology. However, not much attention has been paid to the role faculty play as facilitators in using these tools in a classroom rather than in purely social settings. Chapter 7, "Social Networks: Pedagogical Tool or Pedagogical Threat?" explores the potential benefits and pitfalls of using social networks in the classroom by detailing the experiences of two early adopters of Facebook as a pedagogical tool at a mid-sized comprehensive southern state university. This chapter describes the theories of engaged learning that have led faculty to adopt social networks in their classrooms, the successes, and the challenges faced. The authors conclude by discussing the rewards and consequences of using social networks as a regular part of collegiate academic instruction.

Chapter 8, "Is the iPhone a Ubiquitous Learning Device? A First Step Toward Digital Lecture Notes," suggests that students are among the first to adapt to and even accelerate the use of mobile devices for computing and communication. This not only opens new possibilities for teachers to reach and interact with their students, but also increases the amount of information a learner has to cope with. This chapter describes the idea and prototypical implementation of a method to use the Web and digital devices to ease the digitalization of lecture notes and thus the accessibility of information gathered in the course of learning.

Remote laboratories were born around the year 2000 as a learning tool that allows students to perform laboratory practices through the Internet, by avoiding the timing and availability constraints involved in physical labs. In "Remote Laboratories and Mobile Devices," Chapter 9 outlines how a group of engineering faculty developed one of the first remote labs of its kind based on Web 2.0 technologies. This chapter also discusses, from a software point of view, the possibilities of using remote laboratories from mobile devices, one of the most suitable tools for ubiquitous learning.

Part Three: A New Direction Toward Teaching and Learning: Ubiquitous Learning

Chapter 10, "A New Learning Environment Based on Reproducible Ubiquitous Computing: Experiences and Prospects," explains why reproducible computing is important and how it can be used as a socially constructivist learning technology with characteristics of ubiquitous computing. Based on reported experiences and objective measurements from two different statistics courses, authors present strong evidence that student perceptions and experiences are very positive toward this new type of technology and educational approach.

Chapter 11, "The Good Teacher: Effective Teaching Strategies for a Ubiquitous Learning Environment," details attributes of a good teacher in a ubiquitous learning environment. This chapter proposes that among learners, Web 2.0 tools are harnessed to foster community, facilitate collaboration, accommodate varying learning styles, and encourage professional discourse. The premise is that learner satisfaction and performance in the online course environment is enhanced by good course management, rapport building, and instructional methodology. The chapter offers suggestions and strategies for Web 2.0 technologies that can integrate the best attributes of traditional instruction into a ubiquitous environment.

Chapter 12, "Helping Your Lecturers to Creatively Introduce Ubiquitous Computing Technologies into Their Teaching: What Every Lecturer Should Know," suggests that while many lecturers acknowledge the push in higher education to improve their teaching practice through the use of educational technologies, many continue to struggle with these innovations in practice. This chapter offers insight into these challenges in addition to support strategies to equip instructors with the attitudes, principles, and skills they need to enjoy creatively introducing ubiquitous computing technologies into their teaching.

Wider adoption of podcasts in higher education has made it possible to create a learning environment where students can access learning materials and participate in active learning activities any time, anywhere. Chapter 13, "Pedagogical Use of Video Podcasts in Engineering: Teaching, Learning, and Assessment," illustrates applications of instructor-produced and student-produced video podcasts in engineering courses and how podcasting can be used as a method to assess student learning.

Ubiquitous learning spaces are inherently context-adaptive. Their context-aware features allow an educational system to be automatically configured to a set of aspects of a given context. Chapter 14, entitled "Ubiquitous Mathematics from South Africa to Finland: Does Reverse Transfer Work?" introduces concepts of UFractions. UFractions is a ubiquitous mobile game that combines a story line with manipulatives for learning fractions and in which context adaptation is limited to the set of manipulatives. For ubiquitous learning games, such as UFractions, findings indicate that learning contents and activities need to be recontextualized.

Chapter 15, "Case Study: Using Flickr in Design Education," describes a case study using ubiquitous learning for teaching and learning, specifically in the subject of photography in the design discipline. This innovative pedagogy has captured the enthusiasm of students and teachers alike. This approach has inspired student learning in first-year design discipline photography units resulting in collaborative communities of design practice and discourse. This case study identifies how a change in the millennial student's educational, institutional, social, and economic environment affects learning and teaching practices. The authors discovered that embracing the digital age and its expediential growth has encouraged student interaction, motivation, and peer learning.

Trends for integrating technology in education point to the same direction around the world. The localized goal of each country remains the same: to ensure its constituents are globally competitive in order to maintain each country's fair share of global resources. But how can localized goals be reached without sacrificing global needs and vice versa? In "Global Perspectives of u-Learning," Chapter 16 suggests that ubiquitous learning is a critical component needed to solve this complex puzzle because it offers the potential to flatten the dominant-versus-subordinate differences between economic regions. The author continues to explore the complexity that exists among the multitudinous perspectives toward education and identify principle forces that affect the formation of a framework for unifying global perspectives of ubiquitous learning.

The culminating chapter of future studies provides a forum for ubiquitous learning. Human fascination with the future reaches back millennia, yet few people have engaged in the formal study of the nature and the origin of the future. The elements of change, how change unfolds and impacts the evolution of possible, plausible, and preferable future outcomes are at the heart of future studies. Chapter 17, "The Future as a Ubiquitous Learning Opportunity," portrays u-learning opportunities from two perspectives. The first is a linear view. "What Time is This Place?" teaches lessons about the flow of time, the ubiquitous nature of change, and how we are all players in constructing (or destructing) the future. The second perspective is a complex view. Alternate-reality games that use the real world as a platform—a new context for informal ubiquitous learning—teaches players important lessons about unpredictability and uncertainty in complex environments, the dynamics of connectedness, and the possibility of producing a sustainable world and future in a coevolutionarily manner.

These chapters share specific information about what is taking place in u-learning from their respective organizations and countries. They provide data regarding trends, strategies for teaching, and techniques for assessing u-learning environments. Others provide models and frameworks for successful implementation, as well as problems and challenges faced. In the end, this book contains a wide variety of ideas, strategies, models, success stories, and solutions for engaging and implementing a successful ubiquitous learning environment.

PART I

INTRODUCTION TO U-LEARNING: PROCESS, PEDAGOGY, AND PRACTICE

CHAPTER 1

THE PEDAGOGY OF THINGS

Ubiquitous Learning, Student Culture, and Constructivist Pedagogical Practice

C. Edward Watson and William O. Plymale

ABSTRACT

This chapter explores the interdisciplinary symbiosis that is emerging between constructivism, student culture, and ubiquitous computing technologies and trends. Recent research regarding students highlights the value and need for constructivist pedagogies that utilize u-learning strategies. Constructivist theory is summarized and described in frameworks that show its relevancy to u-learning. Key u-learning technologies and exemplary practices that support today and tomorrow's students are described and explored in depth. This chapter ultimately provides a vision for the future of u-learning that is grounded in emerging technologies, learning theory, and relevancy to the rising generation of students.

Ubiquitous Learning, pages 3–15

INTRODUCTION

In 1991, Mark Weiser introduced the idea of ubiquitous computing: a world in which computers and associated technologies become invisible and thus indistinguishable from everyday life. This invisible computing is accomplished by means of "embodied virtuality," the process of drawing computers into the physical world (Weiser, 1991). Almost 20 years later, our technologies are redefining Weiser's impression of physical juxtaposition. Advances in sensing, computation, storage, and communications bring new meaning to terms like nearness and presence, and this evolution offers a range of pedagogical promise in an age where students are increasingly carrying devices that can interact with this emerging ubiquitous network of computing. This chapter explores current and future trends associated with the key components of these developments within the context of teaching and learning.

Providing a foundation for this exploration is a long-standing school of thought in educational psychology that argues, in short, that the student who talks, reflects, interacts, and engages the most, learns the most. This simplification of constructivist theory rings true with the intuition of most teachers and faculty, regardless of teaching philosophy and pedagogical approach, and is especially useful for those developing pedagogies employing these tools.

In concert with the emergence of research-informed ubiquitous learning strategies are ongoing narratives regarding today's millennial students. While much of the literature regarding today's youth is based upon generalizations, empirical data does exist that provides guidance for those engaged in learner analysis as a component of their larger instructional design. We know that the numbers of students using emerging technology (Web 2.0, convergence devices, etc.) are increasing, and today's students often use technology for social purposes. This chapter includes an examination of the literature surrounding millennials and offers clarity regarding how to incorporate our understanding of students into the development of u-learning strategies.

Emerging technologies provide the foundation for these strategies, and the most relevant of those will be explored. People-centric mobile applications, physical mobile interactions, and cross-reality are among the new ubiquitous computing trends that take advantage of the aforementioned synergy and will dramatically extend the capabilities of u-learning in the coming decade. Foundational among these is the cell phone, which now functions as a wireless sensor node. This omnipresent technology provides one of the keys behind an emerging people-centric global mobile sensing network, which is resulting in new application areas, such as personal, public, and social sensing, which enable different ways to sense, visualize, and share information about ourselves, friends, communities, the way we live, and the way we learn (Campbell, Eisenman, Lane, Miluzzo, & Peterson, 2006).

Just as the people-based global network is forming, so also is the Internet of Things. Tagging physical objects with RFID and Near Field Communication (NFC) extends these objects as digital resources associated with digital information or services. Physical Mobile Interaction (PMI) explores convenient and intuitive ways mobile devices can be used to interact with tagged physical objects. Cross-reality (x-reality) is the union of ubiquitous sensor/actuator networks and shared online virtual worlds. With x-reality, events in the real world drive phenomena in a virtual environment that is unconstrained by time, space, or physics. These technologies, applied with a clear understanding of today's students and relevant learning theory, provide an unambiguous path forward for u-learning.

BACKGROUND

Around the turn of the century, much was written concerning the then-current generation of students and their relationship with and usage of technologies (e.g., Arafeh & Levin, 2002; Duderstadt, 2000; Frand, 2000; Howe & Strauss, 2000; Oblinger, 2003; Prensky, 2001a, 2001b). A core theme within this scholarship was that learners were developing new learning styles and learning preferences as a result of their immersion in a variety of technologies throughout their formative years. Prensky (2001b) is likely the most well-known, as he coined the term *digital natives* and chronicled the technological immersion of students at that time. He estimated that children were being socialized by

> 10,000 hours playing video games; over 200,000 emails and instant messages sent and received; over 10,000 hours talking on digital cell phones; over 20,000 hours watching TV (a high percentage fast speed MTV); over 500,000 commercials seen—all before the kids leave college. (p. 1)

He posited that today's youth are so markedly different from past generations that our educational systems are a mismatch for these learners (Prensky, 2001a). This echoes similar calls for change in education around this time (e.g., Duderstadt, 2000; Tapscott, 1998); however, Prensky firmly rooted his call for change in issues of technology and student culture.

Around the same time, Frand (2000) provided a view of what he called the information-age mindset and argued that a growing number of students possessed these values and behaviors. He stated that this mindset reflected student self-perceptions and included their view of themselves as multitaskers, mistrustful of information, and so accustomed to computers that they did not perceive of them as technology. Oblinger (2003) echoed these observations and suggested instructional approaches that might best reach this new generation of students.

A second round of debate regarding student culture, digital natives, and learning emerged later that decade. Pletka (2007) echoed Prensky and framed the key issues in education as resulting from the digital technologies that have created a new generation of learners who have adapted to the new demands, tools, values, and expectations of an information age. Jenkins (2009), Palfrey and Gasser (2008), and Tapscott (2009) described a variety of student behaviors that they suggested provide evidence of significant generational differences, including youth using technology to meet people, create and exchange media content, engage in textual content creation (wikis, blogs, etc.), and stay connected. The rise of mobile convergence devices is a key emerging tool in these narratives. While these descriptions typically provide a positive view of today's students, concurrently, there are others who have provided less-flattering narratives.

In *The Dumbest Generation,* Bauerlein (2008) described today's youth as being challenged by a number of life's facets. He cites a variety of reports and research studies that suggest young adults have difficulty with memorization and understanding basic academic concepts. Neuroscientists Small and Vorgan (2008) provided related points, and frame high-tech immersion as contributing to increased social isolation, negatively impacting ADD, and resulting in Internet addiction for some young adults. Consistent with this view, Bauerlein (2008) framed the usage of social networking as a compulsive activity characteristic of today's youth.

In short, technology is being cited as the reason for a number of ills as well as many accomplishments associated with today's students, resulting in compelling arguments for new pedagogical practices associated with applications of technologies that students are believed to already be using. There is a perception that students are so immersed in technology in their private and day-to-day lives that any application of technology in the classroom will be well received. This argument resonates with faculty today because so many have had anecdotal experiences that are consistent with the aforementioned literature. Faculty see students with white ear buds, which are synonymous with the iPod. They observe students with cell phones. They have experienced students texting and Facebooking in class. Some students ask for notes to be placed online or for specific technologies to be used for course activities. Descriptive studies of student computer ownership and usage seem to provide further evidence in support of the ubiquitous digital native learner. The Educause Center for Applied Research (ECAR) completes a yearly study of college undergraduates and found that 87.8 percent of respondents owned a laptop, 51.2 percent carried an Internet-capable handheld device, 86.6 percent used social networking and spent an average of 21.3 hours online each week (Smith, Salaway, & Caruso, 2009).

Anecdotal personal observations, classroom experiences, and supporting descriptive data make the broad generalizations found in the literature regarding student culture all that more believable; however, a recent exhaustive review of this literature and the underlying data in support of the digital native claims call into question most of these assumptions. Bennett, Maton, and Kervin (2008) analyzed the educational research and the sociology behind these arguments to determine the efficacy of the current conception of students as digital natives. They found that the research evidence demonstrates that a number of young people are highly adept with a range of technologies; however, "a significant proportion of young people do not have the levels of access or technology skills predicted by proponents of the digital natives idea" (p. 779). They point out the lack of empirical evidence in support of new learning styles or learning preferences. They also conclude that "there is no evidence that multitasking is a new phenomenon exclusive to digital natives" (p. 779). Further, the latest empirical evidence regarding multitasking concludes that humans are unable to accurately perform more than two concurrent tasks at one time (Charron & Koechlin, 2010). This provides clear limitations on the reality of multitasking in practice. Bennett et al. (2008) conclude that the "digital natives literature demonstrates a clear mismatch between the confidence with which claims are made and the evidence for such claims" (p. 783). The evidence does support a view of students as incredibly diverse, and it is a mistake to select technologies and pedagogies based upon broad stereotypes fostered by digital natives mythologies. With that said, there is guidance regarding students for teachers and faculty planning to employ ubiquitous technologies in course settings.

The 2009 ECAR study reveals that less than half of students (45.9%) feel their instructors have "adequate IT skills for carrying out course instruction" (Smith et al., 2009, p. 17). As a broad strategy, faculty would be more successful with u-learning and instructional technology, in general, if they ensured a higher level of personal competency with the technologies in question before attempting to use them in course settings. This might require faculty to use fewer technologies to ensure greater success with a smaller set of approaches and technologies. Additionally, two thirds of students in this study reported that most or all of their instructors inadequately trained them to use the information technology employed in their courses. The assumption that all students have broad computing skills is clearly refuted by this finding and illustrates one of the dangers of progressing with that assumption. A more helpful practice would be for faculty to assume their students have a sparse understanding of the required technology. Faculty should be encouraged to provide copious guidance to ensure that students are able to focus on the learning goals of the activity without being distracted and frustrated by the technologies that are intended to facilitate learning.

While broad generational stereotypes are a problematic foundation on which to build u-learning pedagogy, the literature does provide guidance regarding students' cognitive development, which should inform choices when designing instruction. For instance, it was empirically determined that short-term memory capacity is different in different age groups (Cowan, Nugent, Elliott, Ponomarev, & Saults, 1999). Perry (1970) as well as Baxter Magolda and Porterfield (1988) identified intellectual development stages through which college students predictably pass. Knowles, Holton, and Swanson (1998) examined adult learners and found that they are quite self-directed, require clear relevancy in the instructional content, prefer experiential learning, and approach learning from a life-centered perspective. They also found that as adults age, the differences between them as learners increases (p. 40). This sampling of what we know about learners at different ages suggests a best practice wherein differentiated activities are employed based upon characteristics of learners at different stages of cognitive development. Contemporary learning theory, which leans heavily upon constructivist principles, provides additional guidance for those creating instruction for today's students. Fortuitously, the attributes of many u-learning technologies facilitate students' interactions as they actively participate in authentic learning environments, evoking many of the concepts and practices offered by constructivism.

While constructivism as a learning theory has a lengthy history, pedagogical practice associated with this theory has gained popularity only over the last 20 years (Richardson, 2003). Constructivism can be viewed as a philosophy associated with how we come to know or understand (Savery & Duffy, 1996), but it is also a multidimensional concept that has been applied to theory and teaching (Doolittle & Hicks, 2003). It is sometimes misunderstood due to a number of related perspectives that share the same name. They primarily include radical constructivism, social constructivism, and cognitive constructivism.

Foundationally, these schools of constructivism share several philosophical tenets, including a belief that the individual plays an active role in the construction of knowledge, social and individual experiences are key to the learning process, and that the accuracy of the knowledge obtained may vary when compared with an external reality (Doolittle & Hicks, 2003). Briefly summarized, philosophically, radical constructivism believes that reality is unknowable and is subjective to the individual (Piaget, 1973). As its name implies, social constructivism, emphasizes the role social interaction plays in the development of knowledge (Doolittle & Hicks, 2003). Web 2.0 technologies, such as wikis, u-learning concepts, and information residue, provide examples of social constructivism in practice. Unlike radical and social constructivism, cognitive constructivism, "embraces the notion that one can come to know reality, or truth, as it exists external to the individual" (Doolittle & Hicks, 2003, p. 80). The work of Russian psychologist Lev Vygotsky (1896–1934) has been significantly influential in the development of constructivist theory and practice, and his scholarship provides a framework for a learning theory for u-learning based primarily upon the social constructivist perspective.

Vygotsky posited a zone of proximal development for students as they learn. At the bottom of this zone is what an individual can learn or accomplish by him/herself. At the top of the zone is what an individual can learn or accomplish if aided by an instructor, peer, or classmate (Vygotsky, 1978). The emphasis on interaction in this educational model is clear; however, Vygotsky also states that the use of whole, authentic activities is required as well as an emphasis on processes to encourage individual change (Doolittle & Hicks, 2003; Moll, 1990). Let's now consider constructivism within the context of u-learning.

U-LEARNING PEDAGOGY

Ubiquitous learning (u-learning) is a learning paradigm offering the promise of support for teaching anything at any time in any place by using ubiquitous computing devices, software, and services. While this claim is unrealistic at this time, given the limitations of current implementing technologies (computational, networking, and storage), some have revised the definition of u-learning to that of teaching the right thing, at the right time, in the right place. Po-Sheng, Yen-Hung, Yueh-Ming, & Tzung-Shi (2008) developed the following list of u-learning characteristics after reviewing and synthesizing similar projects by other researchers (e.g., Chen, Kao, Sheu, & Chiang, 2002; Chen, Chang, & Wang, 2008; Hwang, 2006; Ogata & Yano, 2004; Yang, 2006). Note that these characteristics are presented in the framework of u-learning environments, though they have applications across many instructional contexts:

- *Urgency of learning need*—u-learning environment can be used for an urgent learning need. On-demand or just-in-time learning is an interpretation of this u-learning characteristic.
- *Initiative of knowledge acquisition*—u-learning system can provide information to a learner's request in a timely fashion.
- *Interactivity of learning process*—u-learning interfaces facilitate effective communications between learners and peers, teachers, and experts.

- *Situation of instructional activity*—u-learning involves situated interaction. Learning process is embedded deeply into the natural flow of everyday activities.
- *Context-awareness*—learners' interaction with u-learning environment is controlled by context—user, location, time, activity, etc.
- *Activity provides personalized services*—learners are provided personalized learning activities by the u-learning system based on surrounding context.
- *Self-regulated learning*—u-learning environment allows learner to actively control their learning progress and captures this behavior as learner context for future use.
- *Seamless learning*—learning activities can progress seamlessly as learners move from place to place.
- *Adapt the subject contents*—learner interaction with the u-learning environment can take place using various learning devices.
- *Learning community*—u-learning system can access networked content and services to enhance the learning interaction between learners and teachers.

These characteristics provide a current description of u-learning capabilities and evoke a variety of social constructivist instructional practices. For instance, like teachers and peers, u-learning technologies can provide guidance and information to learners as they progress through a learning activity. Vygotsky's emphasis on authentic activities mirrors the direction of u-learning technologies that are components within the physical world. Additionally, social interaction with other learners can be mediated by the technology, either through overt communications between learners or through information and data left behind by those who communicated with the technologies in question. Authenticity and interaction are key components of constructivist pedagogical practice and are, by the nature of the technologies under consideration, inherent to u-learning activities. As more u-learning technologies become available, the clear link to constructivist practice will play a key role in the development of pedagogy in this arena.

Current and Future Trends

There are a variety of technologies that will expand u-learning options in the future, and current research trends in ubiquitous computing are driven by related factors. One is the continuing refinement and convergence of personal mobile devices. Cell phones, like Apple's iPhone, Nokia's N900, and Google's Nexus One now run sophisticated operating systems and applications, contain fast CPUs, connect with multiple wireless interfaces, and incorporate numerous hardware sensors capable of collecting contextual information about the user and their environment. Another factor is the infusion of emerging computational and networking technologies that shape perceptions of reality. Earlier ubiquitous computing studies focused on augmented reality—a view of reality overlaid with various forms of additional computer-generated information. Essentially, this offers a combination of real and virtual elements to users. Current augmented reality research is in the area of cross-reality (x-reality). X-reality is the union of ubiquitous sensor/actuator networks positioned in the real world and in shared online virtual worlds. Millions of mobile wireless sensor nodes composed of people and their smartphones along with converging hardware applications like Intel Research's Wireless Identification and Sensing Platform (WISP) will impact x-reality studies and applications (Philipose et al., 2005).

A third contributing factor, in some ways related to augmented reality but far more significant, is the evolving Internet of Things. Embedding sensor, computational, and network hardware in everyday objects allows them to communicate with people as well as each other. In the Internet of Things, real-world objects have individual digital presences. These objects include people, places, things, and services uniquely identified, and defined in a standardized manner and capable of interacting with each other (Siorpaes et al., 2006). Implementation of a robust Internet of Things will be based on an infrastructure of ubiquitously networked sensors and actuators coupled with low-cost microcontrollers, wireless technologies, cloud services, and PMI interfaces. Environmental conditions and context data will further influence these exchanges. Next generation cross-reality environments are emerging as a result of the integration between Internet of Things technologies and the technology of massively shared online virtual worlds like Second Life (Paradiso & Landay, 2009). In cross-reality environments such as this, virtual worlds can be infused with real-world, real-time information provided by sensor networks. In addition, participants in virtual environments will be able to manifest their actions in the real world through a vast network of actuators and displays.

When considering these ubiquitous computing trends with respect to constructivist pedagogy, the number of opportunities for students to interact and engage with their environment and each other increase tremendously. Researchers at the University of Munich and Lancaster University are investigating ways to facilitate mobile interactions with the Internet of Things (Brollet al., 2009). Physical Mobile Interaction (PMI) is the use of mobile devices to physically interact with physical objects and places in a given context so as to facilitate access to associated information and services. At its simplest, for example, students visiting the La Brea Tar Pits could read the QR code affixed near their assignment, let's say the study of Pit 91, with their cell phones (Kato & Tan, 2007). This action would invoke a Web browser and connect it to the Pit 91 Web site, offering students additional detailed information related to the completion of their project. PMI actions include pointing as described, touching of RFID or NFC elements, or scanning a tagged object via Bluetooth. In addition to Web browsing, other types of services invoked through PMI could include context management, personalization, service discovery and composition, session management and migration, and privacy and security features.

CONCLUSION

As time passes, interaction and computation will become deeply embedded into the natural flow of everyday tasks, activities, and collaborations. Futurists predict 100 billion devices will be connected within the next 5–10 years, rising to trillions in the near future (Lucas, 1999). As more and more "things" become enabled in this fashion, new instructional opportunities and capabilities will emerge. Although it is unclear as to exactly how students and teachers will use and interact with the Internet of Things and cross-realities, it is certain that advances in technologies and access to computing devices will ensure this new ecology. Researchers in education, sociology, computer engineering, computer science, and other fields continue to be drawn to the study of u-learning and u-learning environments; however, a consensus opinion on a defining set of u-learning environmental criteria, functions, services, and implementations is far from clear. When comparing the above u-learning characteristics with traits of ubiquitous and pervasive computing, a number of commonalities emerge. They include collaborative interaction, user mobility, context awareness, ambient information, adaptive interfaces, event notification, and invisibility. These parallels should not be surprising as these fields are inextricably linked. In the future, those researching u-learning must have an eye toward emerging trends in ubiquitous computing, as those developments will ultimately impact the range of instructional options that become available. With that said, learning theory should ultimately guide practitioners as they implement these technologies in real-world instructional settings.

REFERENCES

Arafeh, S., & Levin, D. (2002). *The digital disconnect: The widening gap between Internet-savvy students and their schools.* Retrieved March 29, 2009, from Pew Internet & American Life Project Web site: http://www.pewinternet.org/Reports/2002/The-Digital-Disconnect-The-widening-gap-between-Internetsavvy-students-and-their-schools.aspx

Bauerlein, M. (2008). *The dumbest generation: How the digital age stupefies young Americans and jeopardizes our future.* New York: Penguin.

Baxter Magolda, M. B., & Porterfield, W. D. (1988). *Assessing intellectual development: The link between theory and practice.* Alexandria, VA: American College Personnel Association.

Bennett S., Maton K., & Kervin, L. (2008). The 'digital natives' debate: A critical review of the evidence. *British Journal of Educational Technology, 39*(5), 775–786.

Broll, G., Rukzio, E., Paolucci, M., Wagner, M., Schmidt, A., & Hussmann, H. (2009). Perci: Pervasive service interaction with the Internet of Things. *IEEE Internet Computing, 13*(6), 74–81.

Campbell, A. T., Eisenman, S. B., Lane, N. D., Miluzzo, E., & Peterson, R. A. (2006). People-centric urban sensing. *Proceedings of the second annual International Workshop on Wireless Internet, ACM.* WICON 2006, August 2–5, Boston, MA.

Charron, S., & Koechlin, E. (2010, April 16). Divided representation of concurrent goals in the human frontal lobes. *Science, 328,* 360–363.

Chen, Y. S., Kao, T. C., Sheu, J. P., & Chiang, C. Y. (2002). A mobile scaffolding-aid-based bird-watching learning system. *The proceedings for the IEEE International Workshop on Wireless and Mobile Technologies in Education.* WMTE 2002, August 29–30, 2002, Växjö University, Växjö, Sweden.

Chen, G. D., Chang, C. K., & Wang, C. Y. (2008). Ubiquitous learning Website: Scaffold learners by mobile devices with information-aware techniques. *Computers and Education, 50*(1), 77–90.

Cowan, N., Nugent, L. D., Elliott, E. M, Ponomarev, I., & Saults, J. S. (1999). The role of attention in the development of short-term memory: Age differences in the verbal span of apprehension. *Child Development, 70*(5), 1082–1097.

Doolittle, P. E., & Hicks, D. (2003). Constructivism as a theoretical foundation for the use of technology in social studies. *Theory and Research in Social Education, 31*(1), 72–104.

Duderstadt, J. J. (2000). *A university for the 21st century.* Ann Arbor: University of Michigan Press.

Frand, J. L. (2000). The information-age mindset: Changes in students and implications for higher education. *Educause Review, 35*(5), 14–24.

Hwang, G. J. (2006). Criteria and strategies of ubiquitous learning. *The proceedings of the IEEE International Conference on Sensor Networks, Ubiquitous, and Trustworthy Computing.* SUTC 2006, June 5–7, 2006, Taichung, Taiwan.

Howe, N., & Strauss, B. (2000). *Millenials rising.* New York: Vintage Books.

Jenkins, H. (2009). *Confronting the challenges of participatory culture: Media education for the 21st century.* Cambridge: MIT Press.

Kato, H., & Tan, K. T. (2007). Pervasive 2d barcodes for camera phone applications. *IEEE Pervasive Computing, 6*(4), 76–85.

Knowles, M. S., Holton, E. F., & Swanson, R. A. (1998). *The adult learner* (5th ed.). Woburn, MA: Butterworth-Heinemann.

Lucas, P. (1999). The trillion-node network. *MAYA Design.* Retreived May 12, 2010, from http://www.maya.com/portfolio/the-trillion-node-network

Moll, L. C. (1990). *Vygotsky and education: Instructional implications and applications of sociohistorical psychology.* New York: Cambridge Press.

Oblinger, D. (2003). Boomers, Gen-Xers, & Millennials: Understanding the new students. *Educause Review, 38*(4), 37–47.

Ogata, H., & Yano, Y. (2004). Context-aware support for computer-supported ubiquitous learning. *The proceedings of the Second IEEE International Workshop on Wireless and Mobile Technologies in Education.* WMTE 2004, March 23–25, 2004, Taoyuan, Taiwan.

Palfrey, J., & Gasser, U. (2008). *Born digital: Understanding the first generation of digital natives.* New York: Perseus Books.

Paradiso, J. A., & Landay, J. A. (2009). Guest editors' introduction: Cross-reality environments. *IEEE Pervasive Computing, 8*(3), 14–15.

Perry, W. G. (1970). *Forms of intellectual and ethical development in the college years: A scheme.* New York: Holt.

Philipose, M., Smith, J. R., Jiang, B., Mamishev, A., Sumit, R., & Sundara-Rajan, K. (2005). Battery-free wireless identification and sensing. *IEEE Pervasive Computing, 4*(1), 37–45.

Piaget, J. (1973). *To understand is to invent.* New York: Viking Press.

Pletka, B. (2007). *Educating the net generation: How to engage students in the 21st century.* Santa Monica, CA: Santa Monica Press.

Po-Sheng, C., Yen-Hung, K., Yueh-Ming, H., & Tzung-Shi, C. (2008). A meaningful learning based u-learning evaluation model. *The proceedings of the Eighth IEEE International Conference on Advanced Learning Technologies.* ICALT 2008, July 1–5, 2008, Santander, Spain.

Prensky, M. (2001a). Digital natives, digital immigrants. *On the Horizon, 9*(5), 1–6.

Prensky, M. (2001b). Digital natives, digital immigrants, part II: Do they really think differently? *On the Horizon, 9*(6), 1–9.

Richardson, V. (2003). Constructivist pedagogy. *Teachers College Record, 105*(9), 1623–1640.

Savery, J. R., & Duffy, T. M. (1996). Problem based learning: An instructional model and its constructivist framework. In B. G. Wilson (Ed.), *Constructivist learning environments: Case studies in instructional design.* Englewood Cliffs, NJ: Educational Technology Publications.

Siorpaes, S., Broll, G., Paolucci, M., Rukzio, E., Hamard, J., Wagner, M. et al. (2006). Mobile interaction with the Internet of Things. Retrieved May 12, 2010, from http://www.medien.ifi.lmu.de/pubdb/publications/pub/siorpaes2006pervasivelbr/siorpaes2006pervasivelbr.pdf

Small, G., & Vorgan, G. (2008). *iBrain: Surviving the technological alteration of the modern mind.* New York: Collins Living.

Smith, S. D., Salaway, G., & Caruso, J. B. (2009). *The ECAR study of undergraduate students and information technology.* Retrieved April 10, 2010, from the Educause Web site: http://net.educause.edu/ir/library/pdf/EKF/EKF0906.pdf

Tapscott, D. (1998) *Growing up digital: The rise of the net generation.* New York: McGraw-Hill.

Tapscott, D. (2009). Grown up digital: How the net generation is changing your world. New York: McGraw Hill.

Vygotsky, L. (1978). *Mind in society.* Cambridge, MA: Harvard University Press.

Weiser, M. (1991). The computer for the 21st century. *Scientific American, 265*(3), 94–104.

Yang, S. J. H. (2006). Context aware ubiquitous learning environments for peer-to-peer collaborative learning. *Educational Technology and Society, 9*(1), 188–201.

ABOUT THE AUTHORS

C. Edward Watson, PhD, received his doctorate in Curriculum and Instruction in 2007 from Virginia Tech. He is the associate director for the Center for Instructional Development and Educational Research at Virginia Tech. Dr. Watson teaches courses on change agency and visual media. His book, *Self-Efficacy and Diffusion Theory: Implications for Faculty Development,* was published in 2008. His research interests include the scholarship of teaching and learning, interdisciplinary pedagogy, social learning theory, learner motivation, and emerging technologies. Dr. Watson serves on Cengage Learning's advisory board, is the managing editor for the *International Journal of Teaching and Learning in Higher Education,* and is the co-executive editor of the *International Journal of ePorfolio.*

William O. Plymale, is the Director of Technology Applications for Research and Collaboration in Virginia Tech's Learning Technologies Division. He supports the university's research initiatives by coordinating and associating university research faculty and their projects with appropriate Learning Technologies areas. His current research interests include cross-reality and augmented physical environments, and tangible, presence-based messaging systems. He is also a PhD student in Virginia Tech's Bradley Department of Electrical and Computer Engineering. One of his responsibilities each semester is the supervision of an ECE undergraduate research project entitled "Application of Pervasive Computing Concepts to Teaching and Learning."

CHAPTER 2

A PROCESS-ORIENTED PEDAGOGY FOR UBIQUITOUS LEARNING

Philip Bonanno

ABSTRACT

Ubiquitous learning is emerging as the major mode of learning within the knowledge society and establishing itself as a lifelong and lifewide enterprise complementing initial formal education, which has also been radically transformed by emerging digital technologies. The integration of a range of learning technologies in formal and nonformal education creates a need for a different frame of mind to conceptualize the learning experience. It demands detachment from models that emphasize learning as a process of content transmission and move on to a process-oriented pedagogy that reconceptualizes learning and knowledge building in terms of dimensions and levels of interaction. Developments in various fields of research point to the importance of adopting process-oriented approaches in analyzing technology-enhanced learning contexts.

A process-oriented methodology is proposed to analyze and manage ubiquitous learning systems. Using this framework as a backdrop and inspired by a constructionist epistemology, the model categorizes interactions along the domain, technology, and community dimensions, and across three pedagogical levels. These levels progress in emphasis from the basic "acquisition," through "participation" to "contribution" modes of learning. The model or-

Ubiquitous Learning, pages 17–39

ganizes interactions at the experiential and metacognitive levels for each of the three dimensions. This scheme will serve to develop protocols to be used in designing and evaluating UL using the type, frequency, and direction of interactions as the fundamental design element. Interactions profiled along the three identified dimensions for different contexts of UL can be developed. Analysis of such profiles enables qualitative and quantitative evaluation techniques as well as formative and summative assessment mechanisms.

INTRODUCTION: THE NEED FOR PROCESS-ORIENTED APPROACHES

The pervasive use of digital technologies is triggering innovative ways of becoming knowledgeable in different domains of expertise. Explorations and experimentation with emerging digital technologies is leading to profound pedagogical reflection by learners and educational practitioners worldwide. Very small digital devices are becoming the norm among students, and are their preferred means of communicating and accessing learning resources. Content in every domain is becoming available globally and is free, so is knowledge building and sharing between experts and learners, making institutions rely on "cloud services" for more of their critical functions. Mobile and ubiquitous technologies offer opportunities for personally managed learning within and outside the classroom.

> The increasing performance and miniaturisation of technologies is allowing more objects and devices to become addressable (have a unique ID) and connected (usually wirelessly). This new "internet of things" could collect huge amounts of data, allow new interactions in the real world between people and things, people and places and between things and things. The web moves from being purely a virtual space to one that interacts with the real world and provides us with real time information, help and services at the time and place needed. (Becta, 2010)

Different categories of learning technologies are extending and transforming the learning experience beyond traditional transmissionist approaches, integrating more constructivist and constructionist epistemologies. Ubiquitous learning is emerging as the major mode of learning within the knowledge society. Technology-enhanced learning is establishing itself as a lifelong and lifewide enterprise, complementing initial formal education, which has also been radically transformed by these merging technologies. Learning has become a continual and connected process across a lifetime.

The integration of these technologies in formal and nonformal education creates the need for a different frame of mind to conceptualize the learning experience. It demands detachment from models that emphasize learning as a process of content transmission and move on to a process-oriented pedagogy that reconceptualizes learning and knowledge building in terms of dimensions and levels of interaction with the physical world, with conceptual artifacts (Bereiter, 2002) and with the intra-individual evolving learning experience.

> As more learners carry mobile devices the convergence between mobility, wireless connectivity and the internet, creates a permanent "info-cloud" that changes the way people learn, work and interact with other people and the world around them. (Becta, 2010)

Developments in various fields of research point to the importance of adopting process-oriented approaches in analyzing such contexts. Cognitive neuroscience (e.g., Frith 2007; Frith & Frith 2003; Frith & Wolpert 2003) emphasizes the importance of interpreting human behavior in whatever context from a social perspective, focusing on the dynamics of interactions that each member of a group triggers or reacts to. Connectionist and constructionist epistemologies advocate a process-oriented methodology that considers learning and knowledge-building as a process of interactions with the external world, with the intra-individual reality, with conceptual artifacts, and with communities of learning in different domains of expertise. Gaining competence and expertise in any field implies a continual process of establishing and elaborating interactions with the physical and conceptual artifacts of that field and with knowledgeable persons in that area.

U-learning is thus driven by key intrapersonal and psychosocial processes, which give rise to various levels of interactions. The underlying processes of skill imitation (Frith & Wolpert, 2003), negotiation, and argumentation (Dillenbourg, Baker, Blaye, & O'Malley, 1996) generate task-oriented interactions related to competence development along the domain and technology dimensions. On the other hand, the psychosocial processes of impression formation (Kreijns, Kirschner, & Jochems, 2003), mentalizing (Frith & Frith, 2003), social monitoring (Jost, Kruglanski, & Nelson, 1998), and interpersonal communication generate categories of person-oriented interactions that characterize technology-mediated group dynamics. In this way the online learning community is capable of promoting reflection about the interaction between the intra-individual reality and the external technology-intensive experience. Each member is challenged to accommodate or change one's attitudes, beliefs, behaviors, understandings, and skill level—the elements that constitute one's idiosyncratic experience with technology.

AN INTERACTIONS-ORIENTED MODEL

On the basis of this conceptualization of learning, a process-oriented methodology is here proposed to analyze and manage ubiquitous learning contexts. Using the above theoretical framework as backdrop and inspired by a constructionist epistemology, a model is proposed that categorizes interactions along three dimensions—domain, technology and community—and across three pedagogical levels that progress in emphasis from *acquisition*, through *participation* to *contribution* modes of learning. Individual, group, and task characteristics determine task and person-oriented interactions (Kreijns et al., 2003) occurring along these dimensions and pedagogical levels. The model will be contextualised and applied to the design description and development of a game-based ubiquitous learning experience that integrates a mobile-based game with ambient computing. The main objective is to provide an autonomous learning experience about the history of Valletta, the capital city of Malta. While moving through the city playing the game, adopting one of the historical roles provided, the game interacts with "hot spots" on key historical sites, which initiate interactions in the form of a virtual tour or tutorial.

Learning *from* Others

Learning *from* others through digital tools provides apprenticeship in cognitive, social, and psychomotor skills, thus addressing the need for competence along the three proposed dimensions. Along the domain dimension, declarative, procedural and conditional knowledge is acquired in a wide range of topics. Thus, facts and concepts about Valletta are learned, together with the procedures needed to acquire further knowledge and organizing it in idiosyncratic constructed models that resonate with those developed by history experts. Typical interactions at this level include learner-initiated actions such as imitations of skills used to acquire and organize domain knowledge, asking help to understand initial conceptualizations or procedures, and asking for clarifications while consolidating concepts and problem-solving skills through practice.

Viewing a domain from a gaming perspective would definitely trigger a comparative analysis between domain models promoted by didactical approaches and those proposed by a game. At the experiential level, this leads to the development of a complementary domain-assessment procedure based on new ways of representing and organizing domain knowledge and skills. For example, in history games, there is a shift from assessment procedures based on facts to those based more on developmental processes. Through this evolving experience and corresponding metacognitive activity, the game user develops new ways of interacting with domains employing a personal strategy based on a merger between previously constructed domain models and current game-based ones.

Thus, the metacognitive level involves monitoring and organizational interactions that systemize knowledge around domain core themes in the process of identifying or formulating a domain model and related skills regime. The game will integrate these dimensions of interactions in History as roles organized around different game characters. The game offers different levels of interactions. Besides the solitary gaming mode, where users can play these roles anywhere, the game will offer an "on-site" mode through which a player interacts with the game while moving in Valletta city. According to the role being played, the game will interact with wireless hotspots in particular buildings or sites that have historical significance to the role being played. The game will provide supplementary tutorials, simulations, or virtual tours to create an immersive location-based learning experience.

In ubiquitous learning, an important metacognitive activity when acquiring domain knowledge involves developing an awareness of natural propensities in information processing, mainly analytic versus holistic information processing and visual versus verbal information representation. A ubiquitous learning experience should offer a balance in information processing helping users, through appropriate feedback, integrate details within a bigger picture of the topic or theme being considered. This feedback should be both in verbal and pictorial formats. Individual propensities in information processing are also influenced by one's belief system about subject matter arising from previous positive or negative experiences developed mainly from didactical contexts. If designed from an interactions perspective, ubiquitous learning has the potential to challenge established negative attitudes and conceptualizations about history or, for that matter about any other subject or domain.

Acquisition along the technology dimension includes developing a working competence with the use of different tools, in this case understanding the surface structure of the portable gaming console or mobile learning device in other situations. On a portable gaming device, typical interactions will include identifying options provided by the game, testing game features, and imitating the use of such features as part of practicing basic gameplay gestalts. On a mobile learning device, these will include the options provided by the hardware and software to interact at different levels with any domain, with the surroundings, and with others through communication or knowledge-sharing tools. Metacognition involves rationalizing one's personal belief systems about the use of such portable devices, controlling for attitude to technology-mediated learning, and developing affective strategies to manage anxiety. Competence along the community dimension entails acquiring interpersonal skills, especially through imitations of how others make use of the different features and options offered by such ubiquitous learning environments. This will eventually lead to the identification and adoption of particular roles that boost one's sense of affiliation with real or virtual learning groups invoked within the learning experience. In this regard, metacognition implies rationalizing and controlling individual propensities related to perception, beliefs, and reactions (approach versus withdrawal behaviors) to social interactions in a contiguous and virtual groups, and reflecting on any contrasting behaviors manifested in these diverse social contexts.

Learning *with* Others

Experienced gamers show interactions characterized mainly by participatory learning. This level addresses the need for relatedness, affiliation, and intimacy with contiguous and online groups, together with any domain-related "communities of practice." Participation in learning and knowledge building involves mainly negotiation and argumentation. These processes widen the "zone of proximal development" (Vygotsky, 1978) along the domain and technology dimensions that lead to the joint construction of distributed knowledge and skills through task and person-oriented interactions. Thus, the group serves as a forum for negotiation and argumentation along all dimensions. Participants assess and refine their knowledge and skills through further imitation, guided practice, and negotiation. The group provides apprenticeship in developing advanced technology-mediated learning schemas and understanding the deep structure of the ubiquitous learning experience. The deep structure (Gredler, 1996) defines the levels of interactions, not only with the digital device, but most importantly with the mode of interaction with the domain, the surrounding environment, and other learners within the network. Along the community dimension, negotiation and argumentation manifest themselves in sharing impressions about the technology-mediated learning experience, sharing domain-related biography, negotiating roles, suggesting goals, and promoting interpersonal communication.

For more experienced gamers, metacognition involves monitoring interactions in the process of developing distributed knowledge and skills along the three dimensions. The domain model is further elaborated through discussion and negotiation, while the deep structure of the ubiquitous learning experience is further understood through the identification, categorization, and schematization of the interactions mediated by the mobile device. Along the community dimension, technology-mediated communication and monitoring skills are identified and practiced. Individuating impressions are challenged, while the goals and beliefs of other colleagues are evaluated by comparing incoming impressions with past experience and established interaction patterns.

Mediating Others' Learning

The highest level of competence, the expert level, is characterized by contributory and mediational forms of learning and knowledge building that addresses the need for self-actualization. Domain experts (like historians) communicate their highly refined knowledge and skills through discourse increasingly based on digital conceptual artifacts. They mediate the learning of less-competent learners through mentoring, modeling, and evaluation of domain models and skills together with technology-mediated domain-related learning systems. These activities are an expression of their stature in the field and the corresponding leadership role that satisfies their need for self-actualization and professional authority. Thus, highly competent participants show higher levels of interactions involving evaluation and modification of domain and technology-enhanced learning systems, together with those interactions arising from negotiation characterizing mentoring and modeling.

Along the community dimension, contribution by expert gamers implies monitoring and managing group interactions by challenging impressions and beliefs, problematizing established behavioral patterns, evaluating group goals, and suggesting alternative roles. Metacognition involves developing insight into domain and technology-mediated learning models with the necessary skills for using these models as conceptual artifacts that can be further modified and elaborated. Insight into community functioning is shown by interactions related to nurturing group affinity, anticipating others' behavior, and proposing alternative relationship models for the learning community.

Figure 2.1 summarizes the major categories of interactions underlying this theoretical framework. These cab serve as a guide in designing ubiquitous learning experience based on identified dimensions and levels of interactions.

DESIGNING A UBIQUITOUS LEARNING EXPERIENCE

Guided by the model described above, the following section elaborates on the different dimensions and levels of interactions that have to be considered when designing ubiquitous learning experiences including any form of digital technology. For each of the identified dimensions (domain, technology, and community), interactions at the experiential and metacognitive level are proposed. The experiential level includes all those interactions between an individual and the surrounding physical environment. Interactions at the metacognitive level refer to all those internal reflections initiated by an individual to clarify, organize, elaborate, and utilize his/her idiosyncratic experience. It is considered as the intra-individual interaction

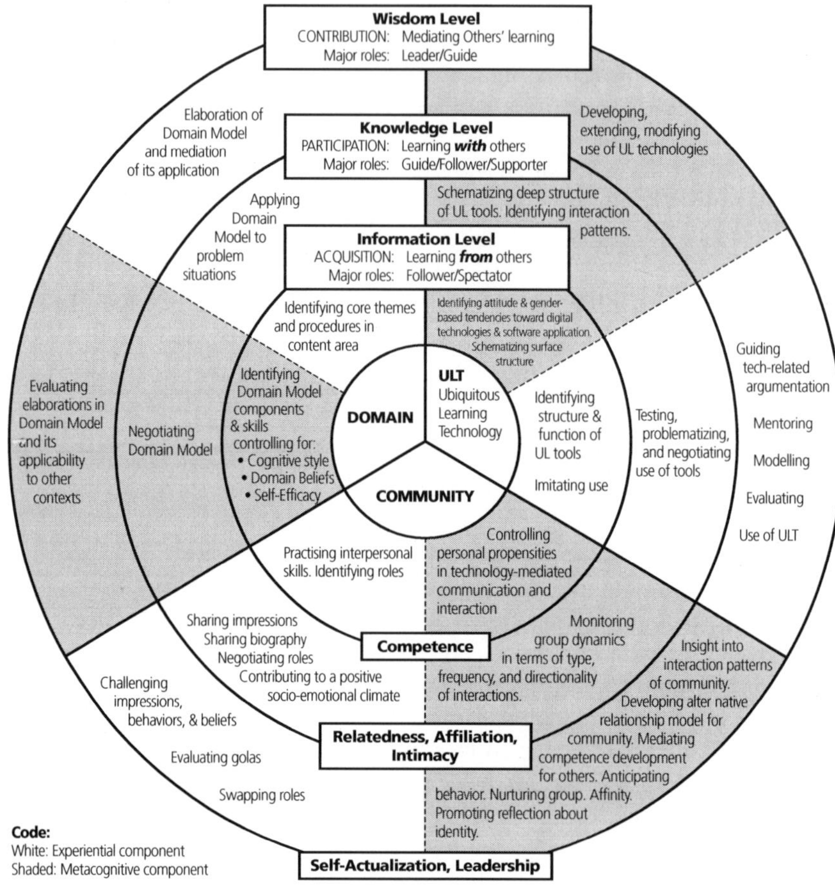

Figure 2.1 Model of interactions for ubiquitous learning.

between the sensory, cognitive, affective, conative, and social components of one's experience. Reflection is thus considered as one's conscious interaction with these internal subsystems.

Designing the Mode of Interaction with the Domain

Designing a ubiquitous learning experience from a process-oriented approach demands the identification of those categories of interactions that propose a particular experience for the learner with the identified domain. The level of interaction within a subject comprises the hierarchy of learning outcomes ranging from basic facts, concepts, relational and procedural rules, problem solving, and attitude formation about the domain. The basic level of interaction with the history game about Valletta is to present categories of facts about different aspects of Valletta. A higher level of interaction would be the discussion of concepts evident in the development and structure of the city. The fundmental concept adopted by the Knights of Malta for designing the city was "a city from gentlemen for gentlemen." At the time this implied innovative approaches for designing the city's infrastructure, defense system, recreational facilities, communication system, and all other services. Building these facilities involved the application of procedural and relational rules, which gave the solution to problem-solving situations. In interacting with these levels, one may develop a personal attitude toward the city that determines how the individual reacts to this place and its history.

An effective pedagogical strategy to deal with such complexity is to organize these interactions around core themes that represent expert ways of organizing knowledge and behavior. In the game about Valletta city, these levels of interaction with domain will be presented in relation to the core history themes. An *evolutionary perspective* organizes facts and events along a timeline, giving detailed descriptions of the different eras of the city, starting from a barren peninsula in medieval times through the various historical layers that are now evident. Knowledge can also be organized around how *structure relates to function*, considering the range of architectural features and buildings that constitute the city. Another organizing theme is *universality versus diversity*, or how universal social, economic, and religious rules are evident in the development of the city and how these differ to accommodate local circumstances. Knowledge about Valletta can also be organized using a systems approach, which describes how *equilibrium* is achieved in the Valletta/Maltese historical and environmental systems. This elaborates on the checks and balances that existed over time to maintain harmony and functionality among the geographical, administrative, economic, and religious elements of the social system.

These core themes are transformed into modes of interaction through personification in game characters: explorer, architect, archbishop, and grandmaster. Core themes are thus acquired in an implicit way as they are embedded in the action of the character with which and through which the learner is continually interacting. Thus, a game employs a different pedagogical strategy based on a particular mode of interaction. The learner will acquire the same domain knowledge and skills, not through representation, as in instructional contexts, but in this case through simulation. The game determines the mode of interaction with the domain according to the roles adopted. Facts, concepts, and skills are acquired while playing a particular role and thus form an integrated component of the whole experience.

Gaming modes offer yet another form of interaction with the particular domain in question. Some games offer the possibility of playing a game in default settings or in more open scenarios. When playing a default scenario or character, the gamer has to think and act in a preset environment to execute an assigned mission. In other open gaming modes, such as campaigns in history games, the user is responsible for developing and organizing the setting, thus assuming a deeper level of reflection and interaction with the environment considering a more complex system of cause-and-effect relationships. The latter gaming option is based on an evolving situation, so the mode of interaction is much more dynamic and engaging.

A mobile gaming format, which integrates the console-based game with the surrounding environment, provides a further dimension of interaction. Acquisition of domain knowledge and skills is further mediated through "enactment," besides representation and simulation. The pedagogy in context provides an immersive experience that complements cognitive and affective processing with embodiment, a direct multisensory experience that tags new elements with previous, relevant sensory experience.

The design of the experiential level of interaction with the domain involves

- Determining learning outcomes related to domain. Consider these as levels of interaction with domain.
- Determining core themes of domain. Consider these how an expert interacts with domain.
- Determining pedagogical approaches to be used in the ubiquitous learning experience. Consider this as a mode of interaction with the identified domain content and projected learning experience.

Designing the Metacognitive Level of Interaction with the Domain

Reflection about the learning process along any of the proposed dimensions is a fundamental component of any underlying pedagogy. Reflection can be considered as the introspective interaction between a learner's internal and external reality that maximizes the pedagogical value of a ubiquitous learning experience (ULE). Through reflection, knowledge and skills acquired during the experiential component of the ULE serve to identify and organize an underlying unifying structure—the domain model. Ubiquitous learning leads to the development of a more valid organizing model as it integrates interactions between virtual and real-life learning contexts.

Analysis of the metacognitive activity related to the domain dimension enables the development of a more holistic pedagogical strategy relevant to the learner's competence level. With learners having entry knowledge of the domain, and thus still in the phase of developing basic awareness and competences, emphasis will be more on reflection about the instructional component of the experiential level. So the main activity would be to organize the acquired knowledge and skills around core themes controlling for intervening individual propensities. The task-related reflection focuses on the identification and description of core themes and how these may help in the formulation of an organizing model.

Yet one must consider the individual affective and cognitive processes that determine the construction of the inner experience and how one should become aware and manage them during the learning process. In practical terms, learners should appreciate how cognitive style, considered as one's preferred mode for acquiring, processing and communicating information, influences their interaction with subject matter and technology-mediated learning. This reflection about one's default mode of interacting with incoming information should make learners aware of how to control and balance natural tendencies in processing information. In most ULEs, many factors have to be monitored and controlled simultaneously. Focusing continuously on one single factor or just one organizing core theme might distort the learning experience of individuals with analytic tendencies and proves to be detrimental at the end. The skill of parallel thinking and multitasking must be developed. The opposite may apply for learners with a more global tendency. Their globetrotting mode of interaction might lead to the construction of a superficial cognitive structure, which lacks essential details and anchoring. Learners should also appreciate how these strategies directly influence the use of tools in acquiring domain-related knowledge. Focusing on just one such information-acquisition tool without referring to or using collaboration tools will not develop a comprehensive understanding of the theme on which the ULE is focused.

The use of communication and collaborative tools is determined by the social tendencies of individuals. Technology-mediated learning may offer a form of interaction that is more conducive to the needs of socially withdrawn persons, which would manifest restrained behavior in contiguous learning contexts. For those equipped with approach skills, this pedagogical approach enhances learning and knowledge building through communication and sharing.

One should also control for beliefs and attitudes about the domain in question and how to learn relevant knowledge and skills. Learners should adopt an open attitude that ubiquitous learning might provide a totally different experience from typical didactical classroom contexts. Attitude about a domain comprises learner's perceived confidence in acquiring knowledge about topics and domain-related skills, perceived control on organizing this knowledge into a systematic framework, perceived use of the acquired knowledge and skills, and the evoking of positive emotions coming from a sense of mastery when interacting with the subject content. At this stage, it is important to reflect on each of these attitudinal components to develop a good conception of the domain and how technology, combined with real-life contexts, influences the general learning experience.

With more-competent learners, emphasis will shift to the role of collaboration in elaborating the knowledge and skills acquired through solitary learning. Within collaborative contexts, metacognition along the domain dimension involves interactions with others through which different conceptions of domain models are compared and contrasted. Negotiation of meaning with colleague learners enables each participant to refines his/her conception of the domain and how knowledge is organized. This will lead to elaborations made on the previously constructed model and about the possibilities that exist to apply it in other contexts. Reflection should also be about the best learning approach to adopt in this constructive process by evaluating the strengths and weaknesses of the different modes of interactions that involve or exclude the use of digital tools.

In designing the metacognitive level of interaction with the domain one should

- Organize domain-related interactions around core themes and an overarching model.
- Identify the best pedagogical strategy, adjusting the degree of interaction according to the level of domain-competence shown by the learner.
- Identify natural tendencies in processing and organizing information, guiding learners to reflect about the impact that these natural tendencies have on domain learning and about the need to develop effective (compensating) strategies.
- Reflect on the different components that constitute one's general attitude to a particular domain, subject, or topic. Identify and control for acquired personal beliefs and perceptions.
- Suggest interactions that promote negotiation of domain organizing themes and model.
- Evaluate different modes of interaction with the domain considering various combinations of digital tools and learning contexts.

Designing the Mode of Interaction with Technology

Complementary to the design process along the domain dimension, levels of interactions with digital tools used in a ULE are determined by a learner's technological competence. Different scenarios may arise in u-learning.

Learners may be novice both in the domain and in the use of technological tools. Other situations may involve learners competent in a domain aspect but unskilled in employing digital tools for learning, learners who are highly skilled in ICT but novice in a particular domain, or learners who are highly skilled in both domain and learning technologies. Ubiquitous learning adds yet another component: that of learning through technology on the move, which might demand other competencies, in both solitary or collaborative contexts.

The design of a u-learning experience for learners with basic technology-related know-how focuses on interactions with the surface structure of the tool. A user has to identify and start using the different search, communication, design and knowledge-sharing tools. At this stage, instructional tools in the form of demos, tutorials, or examples of good practice will address the need for developing competence, especially through apprenticeship, the basis of which is imitation of expert behavior. The metacognitive activity complementary to this experiential level of interaction is related to the analysis of one's personal feelings with technology. At this critical entry level, it is very important for novice users of tools to reflect and control for their attitude toward digital tools and technology-mediated learning. One must become aware of possible gender-related tendencies toward digital technologies and software applications. Several international reports point to male task orientation and female relationship orientation when using online tools. Practice develops in a user a working confidence that, together with reflection, enables the schematization of the tool surface structure. An overarching conception is thus developed through which the various tool features and options are related to specific task demands. The interaction between the experiential and metacognitve components of this level leads to the development of task-related schemata, or built-in intuitive patterns of interaction that definitely enhance task efficiency.

Beyond the predominantly solitary novice level, ICT-competent learners adopt a more collaborative approach through communication and knowledge-sharing tools. The idiosyncratic conceptions of tool features and the personal way these are used become challenged and elaborated through social monitoring, negotiation, and reflection. New combinations of features and possibilities of tool use are identified while interacting with colleagues. These are then tested and adopted if found relevant to task execution. This analysis of the use of tools actually problematizes every aspect of the personal experience with the tool so that more refined and efficient interactions result.

Such collaborative competence development leads to the schematization of the tool's deep structure. The deep structure comprises the interactive potential of the tool, that is, the levels and degrees of interactions mediated by the tool. Besides "within tool interactions," the deep structure adresses more the "beyond tool interactions" that is the mediation of interactions with the external environment, between users, with online communities, and within affinity spaces (Gee, 2007: Web sites where competent users share information and personal experience about use of tool), and how much the tool is "shareable." Another aspect of the deep structure is the degree of "shareability" it allows between users. Interaction with the external environment involves both the physical form of interaction, which is more related to the surface structure of the tool, and the pedagogical mode of interaction that relates more to the deep structure. The use of Bluetooth, radio-frequency identification (RFID), or geolocalization through GPS are physical forms of interaction. The deeper mode of interaction with the external environment can take various forms, ranging from a quiz, a tutorial, a virtual tour, a physical tour based on an identified itinerary, a full-fledged location-based investigation, a game within a game if using an ambient game or any other combination of environment–tool interactive process. The "shareabilty" aspect of the deep structure describes the possibilities supported by the tool to share both the content integrated in the tool and also the group process. The latter shows the type and degree of group communication supported, together with the type and degree of synchronous activity that is supported. The overarching outcome of this reflection about the collaborative use of the tool is the identification of patterns of interactions either mediated by the tool or manifested by fellow users while using the tool.

The most sophisticated form of the deep structure of a tool consists of a pedagogic agent that is capable of monitoring, analyzing, and managing interactions within and beyond the system. In collaborative learning, it is typical that learners' interaction evolves into a highly differentiated form creating difficulties for external moderation and for providing guidance and support. Pedagogical agents can be developed to track learners' interaction patterns and provide valuable support. A pedagogical agent comprises a set of autonomous units, each having a specialized function in storing or processing information about learner's activities. These include learners' physical interaction with the digital tools or with the external environment, together with use of communication and knowledge-sharing tools. The system automatically gathers information about interactions. These are then analyzed, categorized, recorded, and evaluated against an itemized interactions-based knowledge repository. It identifies interactions gaps between individuals or groups, proposes lines of action, records emerging individual and group interactions profiles, and enters into another evaluation-action cycle.

Based on the process-oriented model discussed above, profiles are constructed to record acquisition, sharing, and contribution at the experiential and metacognitive levels. Interactions characterizing the experiential level include two categories. The "Ask" function is used to obtain information or guidance for acquiring a particular competence. Through the "Report" function, one shares a particular competence. The metacognitive component represents the reflections on competence and performance of learners as part of the evolving learning experience. This will be tracked by a "Comment" function in the system, assuming that learner comments are a product of their reflection on a task or a joint construction between colleagues. These three modes of interactions will be provided as options in the tool's surface structure. The pedagogical agent monitors, categorizes, and records all these interactions.

The pedagogical agent will also record the directionality of group-based interactions. For learners engaged in a ubiquitous learning context, direction of interactions will include participant to participant (p–p) and participant to all group (p–g). But since group activity may lead to task-related subgrouping, other possible interactions will include participant to two colleagues (p–2p), participant to all subgroups (p–sgs), subgroup to subgroup (sg–sg). There is also the possibility of one group interacting with other groups (g–gs), the latter involving other groups within other ubiquitous learning systems, online communities, or learning groups. If a human tutor is included to monitor and manage the learning system, then a more complex system of interactions results. Besides the above directions of interactions, there will also be participant to tutor (p–t), subgroup to tutor (sg–t), subgroups to tutor (sgs–t), tutor to participant (t–p), tutor to all group (t–g), and tutor to subgroups (t–sgs).

When various ubiquitous learning systems are interacting from different physical locations and each has an assigned human tutor, then the system has to record the interactions of tutors with participants and between tutors. The system thus has to also record participant to tutors (p–ts), tutors to participant (ts–p), tutor to participants (t–ps), tutors to group (ts–g), tutors to groups (ts–gs), tutor to tutors (t–ts), and tutors to tutor (ts–t).

The socioemotional climate comprising person-oriented interactions can also be captured in two ways. One is by recording the interactions mediated through a communications toolbar equipped with a range of emoticons, personalized audio and video clips showing different emotional expressions, and through text-based communication. The other is to capture facial expressions through a Web cam and corresponding audio expressions through a computer-based integrated system that analyzes facial and audio expressions and records these as emotional states.

Thus, through the analysis of the frequency and directionality of task and person-oriented interactions captured during collaborative sessions, individual or group interactions profiles will be developed by the system. The interactions profile will be broken down according to the above-identified categories and directions of interactions. These can then be analyzed, compared, and contrasted with built-in pedagogical templates or with different stages of the evolving individual or group experience. Through such analysis, underlying factors that determine the type, frequency, and directionality of group-related interactions are identified, and corresponding pedagogical interventions are activated. For example, a low frequency in the asking and sharing categories can be interpreted as a sign of lack of competence along the domain dimension. A consistent pattern of low interaction with other participants or with a restricted number of participants might show a withdrawal tendency in social contexts. So the necessary intervention would be activated, suggesting the widening of the circle of communication and sharing. When these profiles are used to prescribe pedagogical suggestions they establish a mechanism of formative assessment. If they are categorized, recorded, and quantified, they will form a summative assessment mechanism.

Along the technology dimension, the role of technologically competent learners is to help less-competent colleagues to understand the deep structure of the tool and develop relevant competences. They model to others the different roles and interactive possibilities offered by the system and evaluate the role of technology in mediating individual and group processes during the ubiquitous learning experience. They might also have the role of monitoring, updating, and elaborating the adaptive system based on the pedagogic agent discussed above. The learning system serves as a conceptual artifact that they can further develop and adapt.

The two levels of the design process along the technology dimension will include

- Designing the experiential level:
  - Identify the structure and function of UL tools, including online tutorials that describe the structural design of the virtual learning environment or mobile learning tool being used.
  - Explain the function of the different options included in the tool and give enough practice in the use of these functions.
  - Provide examples of good practice in using the tools to be followed by less-experienced users.
  - Create activities to share experiences in using digital tools for the ubiquitous learning experience.
  - Make users identify potential problems and their solution when using digital tools.
  - Provide peer-to-peer tutoring by more-experienced users.
  - Evaluate the use of tools, considering ease of use and the degree of interaction provided with the domain and among learners.
- Designing the metacognitive level:
  - Include attitude-monitoring activities, checking for reactions to digital tools from different participants. With hesitant or apprehensive participants, use support activities to address negative perceptions about the use of tools and perceived control.

- Create discussion and sharing activities to identify links between different tool options, commonalities, and differences in using the different options.
- Include activities to analyze dimensions and levels of interaction mediated by the tool, including different ways of interacting with subject matter, the interaction possibilities offered by different applications and digital tools, the levels of interactions between participants, and with other online learning communities.
- Identify interaction patterns comprising frequency and directionality of interactions from and to different participants, subgroups, or different learning communities.
- Develop design activities that provide solutions to the difficulties encountered during use of the tool or to include added functionalities that elaborate or customize the tool more for the current use.

DESIGNING THE SOCIAL EXPERIENCE IN UBIQUITOUS LEARNING

As in the other dimensions, interactional competence along the community dimension is seen to progress along three levels. The first level describes the process of developing personal social competence for a newcomer through interaction within a group. Basic communication and group interaction skills are acquired and refined through the specific mediating technology. The next level of this model focuses on developing participatory skills as part of the process of becoming an efficient participant in contiguous or online learning groups that include "communities of practice" or experts related to the particular digital tool being used (e.g., community using a particular VLE) and to the domain invoked by the ubiquitous learning experience. The highest level of social competence will be that of a "contributor" in animating, managing, and leading learning communities. Learning *from* others addresses the need for competence; learning *with* others fulfills the need for relatedness, affiliation, and intimacy; while *mediating* others' learning satisfies the highest social need, that of self-actualization through leadership.

The basic experiential level of this technology-mediated socialization process provides the context for helping novice users of the tool imitate and practice interpersonal skills through a range of multimodal tools. This might involve a process of affective engagement starting from the rather impersonal text messaging, going through audio communication, and culminating in video conferencing as the most powerful form of technology-mediated human communication. The shift in media usage is motivated by the evolving need for affiliation the stronger this becomes, the more engaging medium is used. This process of communication serves to familiarize novice members with the various roles possible in a learning group across the receiver–contributor continuum.

At the metacognitive level, this evolving technology-mediated social experience presents a number of intrapersonal challenges. Technology-mediated communication invokes built-in cognitive and affective propensities in using technology for interacting within and between the learning groups. Any negative perceptions or inhibiting factors have to be controlled through a process of rationalization arising from a comparative analysis of one's experience in communicating through technology with the more positive attitudes and skillful use by competent colleagues. A similar process of reflection should counteract natural tendencies in social comportment. In shifting from passive to more-active roles, one has to deal with technology-induced approach or withdrawal behaviors that can be substantially different from, if not opposite of, those manifested in contiguous contexts. They should become aware that in technology-mediated interaction, extrovert and introvert tendencies are manifested as different interaction patterns (Bonanno, 2008). Extrovert behavior involves higher frequencies of person-to-person interaction, while introvert tendencies are characterized by lower frequencies of anonymous interaction; that is, interactions addressed to the whole group, not directed specifically to any particular participant.

The second level along the community dimension shifts the focus onto the social participatory aspect of collaborative technology-mediated learning. The group experience has to be managed to develop competence for collaborating in learning communities and to promote domain learning through the social processes of negotiation and argumentation. The experiential level involves sharing one's impressions about technology-mediated learning and participation in task-related discussions. It also involves all those actions that promote each participant's sense of relatedness, affiliation with the learning community, and increased levels of intimacy with particular members.

This sense of community arises from the definition of roles and from those actions that promote friendship and a positive affective socioemotional climate. A sense of community and friendship is developed both by task-related activities and off-task ones specifically provided by the learning system to develop the social component of a community. A ubiquitous learning system should thus provide tools through which participants share their biographies, interests, plans, and other themes aimed at developing this complementary humane dimension of the community.

Besides off-task interactions, the socioemotional climate is also promoted through task-related positive feedback and person-oriented interactions in the form of encouragement and performance-related compliments. The UL system should thus include tools that facilitate person-oriented interactions very much like the range of communication and sharing tools found in social networking environments. Toolbars equipped with a range of feedback symbols and expressions, together with emoticons and short animation clips to provide encouragement or approval, should be available and easily accessible in environments mediating the ULE.

In technology-mediated learning environments, two approaches may be used to assess group involvement, cohesion and needs satisfaction. Through the use of audio- and video-based online conferencing, one's relationship with the group can be assessed through the type of body language, voice tonality, and facial expressions. This enables the intra-individual social-monitoring process of mentalizing through which individual impressions are formed about the group processes and the evolving learning experience. The availability of these auditory and image-based communication tools makes the learning process much closer to real face-to-face communication, considered as the highest form of human interaction.

But in technology-mediated learning environments, the level of communication is also expressed by the type, frequency, and directionality of person-oriented interactions (Bonanno, 2008). The socioemotional climate in a technology-mediated learning community can thus be quantified through the degree of interaction with the various communication and sharing tools. An fulfilled engaged participant will definitely show a higher variety and frequency of interaction through these tools than a detached, uncommitted member. Their interactions profile would definitely contrast. Constructing individual and group interaction profiles based on task and person-oriented interactions is a very effective way to get insight into group dynamics and evolution.

Using the information obtained from these interactions profiles, specific pedagogical interventions should be identified for different individuals or groups. Some group members might need someone to challenge their goals for participating in the learning community. Others have to be prompted to revise their role in the group or might need guidance to change their strategy for interacting within the group. Community members should be made aware of how to assess group activity through the type, frequency, and directionality of interactions promoted by the the UL system.

Actually, the type of task and person-oriented interactions occurring in a group, and the roles that evolve, manifest the degree of influence the ULE had on the group. In-depth analysis of interactions will reveal perceived competence facilitation (Ryan, Rigby, & Przybylski, 2006) by the tools included in the UL system and participation facilitation along the domain and community dimensions. Improving one's sense of competence and range of participatory skills leads to the development of more positive attitudes about the ULE and thus its adoption as an effective way of learning.

The third level of the proposed pedagogical model focuses on how participants use the UL system to develop and refine their mediational and contributory skills. This "wisdom" level is concerned with the ability to use knowledge for motivating and helping less-competent community members understand and develop domain-related competences and the skillful use of digital tools.

Through meditational and generative activities, highly competent members of the learning community satisfy the higher-order needs for affiliation and self-actualization in contiguous and virtual communities. Their task and person-oriented interactions are an expression of leading and guiding roles. Their insight into the domain models and mediating technological tools puts them in a position to anticipate interaction patterns by individual members or the whole group. They are able to quickly evaluate group activity and propose relevant guiding or corrective measures. On an individual level, they might challenge negative impressions and beliefs about collaborative technology-mediated learning. They model the use of tools for enhancing collaboration, provide guidance, support, and encourage members lacking in confidence and challenging them to take more active roles. On a collective level, their role is to nurture group affinity by addressing both task-related processes and the socioemotional climate of the group. Through their analysis of the group goals and the prevalent interaction patterns, they will be able to guide group strategy, challenge inefficient approaches, and suggest alternative group structure through change of roles.

One of the most important metacognitive activities along the community dimension is the promotion of reflection through the contiguous group or virtual community promotes reflection about a participant's evolving identity. Collaborative technology-mediated learning promotes reflection about mature identities, which motivates participants to identify a strategy for upgrading various competences in an attempt to bridge the gap between current and more-evolved identities. The role of experienced participants is to mediate this process by continually challenging less-competent participants or those showing low levels of interactions to adopt more assertive and active group roles. This shifts their comportment from that of a passive participant to a more leading and contributing one. At the group level, they should encourage rotation of roles and control in-group formations arising from exclusive patterns of interaction. At the same time competent participants should encourage a more inclusive approach by interacting with all group members and habitually addressing the whole group.

The two levels of the design process along the community dimension will include:

- Designing the experiential level of the community dimension:
  - Develop activities to familiarize oneself with different communication and knowledge-sharing tools.

 - Include situations for imitating and practicing interpersonal skills.
 - Identify and describe different group roles.
 - Develop off-task activities to promote the socioemotional climate within a learning community.
 - Use tools that provide and use task-related feedback tools to promote a positive socioemotional climate.
- Designing the metacognitive:
 - Identify and control negative perceptions and inhibiting factors regarding technology-mediated communication.
 - Include activities to identify and counteract natural tendencies in social comportment.
 - Identify interaction patterns manifesting personal tendencies of colleagues.
 - Devise pedagogical intervention according to information from interactions profiles.
 - Create reflection about the degree of perceived competence facilitation and participation facilitation promoted by the community.

CONCLUSION

Ubiquitous learning extends our conception of learning to a more sophisticated level by integrating real with virtual environments, which creates networks of learners socially interacting in space and time. The complexity of such contexts arises from the myriad processes interacting and influencing each other. Simplistic models that give snapshot descriptions are not valid for analyzing human activity in such contexts. The model proposed above tries to address a need established by leading researchers who consider collaborative learning from a process-oriented approach.

This approach organizes technology-mediated collaborative learning around a pedagogical model inspired by constructionist and connectionist epistemologies. The current design trend for virtual learning environments is to integrate course-management systems with ePortfolios and social networking tools. Ubiquitous learning systems will have to operate exploiting such technological infrastructures. Such systems need to be conceptualized through models that integrate the range of underlying processes and interactions. This demands nothing less than a paradigm shift that promotes the design, analysis, and evaluation of ubiquitous learning through task- and person-oriented interactions.

The draft National Educational Technology Plan 2010 points to the need for adopting new methods of assessment that give detail about the evolving learner experience:

> The model of 21st century learning requires new and better ways to measure what matters, diagnose strengths and weaknesses in the course of learning when there is still time to improve student performance, and involve multiple stakeholders in the process of designing, conducting, and using assessment. In all these activities, technology-based assessments can provide data to drive decisions on the basis of what is best for each and every student and that in aggregate will lead to continuous improvement across our entire education system. (O.E.T., 2010, p. 6)

One valid method for assessing the complexity of technology-mediated learning through the quantification of interactions has been proposed here. Customized forms of assessment can be developed in the form of interactions profiles. Saving such profiles in databases can be exploited by pedagogic agents to give adaptive learning and assessment tools. This is how the plan conceptualizes learning experiences:

> The model of 21st century learning described in this plan calls for engaging and empowering learning experiences for all learners. The model asks that we focus what and how we teach to match what people need to know, how they learn, where and when they will learn, and who needs to learn. It brings state-of-the art technology into learning to enable, motivate, and inspire all students, regardless of background, languages, or disabilities, to achieve. It leverages the power of technology to provide personalized learning instead of a one-size-fits-all curriculum, pace of teaching, and instructional practices. (O.E.T., 2010, p. 5)

A process-oriented pedagogy is definitely the way forward!

REFERENCES

Becta. (2010). *Emerging technologies.* Retrieved from http://schools.becta.org.uk/upload-dir/downloads/page_documents/research/emerging_technologies/ET_key_trends_timeline.pdf

Bereiter, C. (2002). *Education and mind in the knowledge age.* Mahwah, NJ: Lawrence Erlbaum Associates.

Bonanno, P. (2008). *Learning through collaborative gaming: A process-oriented pedagogy.* Joensuu, Finland: Publications in Education, University of Joensuu.

Dillenbourg, P., Baker, M., Blaye, A., & O'Malley, C. (1996). The evolution of research on collaborative learning. In E. Spada & P. Reiman, (Eds.), *Learning in humans and machine: Toward an interdisciplinary learning science* (pp. 189–211). Oxford, UK: Elsevier.

Frith, C. D. (2007, January 24). The social brain? *Philosophical Transactions: Biological Sciences, 362,* 671–678. London: The Royal Society.

Frith, U., & Frith, C. D. (2003). Development and neurophysiology of mentalizing. *Philosophical Transactions: Biological Sciences, 358*(1431), 459–473. London: The Royal Society.

Frith C. D., & Wolpert D. M. (2003). Decoding, imitating and influencing the actions of others: The mechanisms of social interaction. *Philosophical Transactions: Biological Sciences, 358*(1431), 431–434. London: The Royal Society.

Gee, J. P. (2007). *Good video games and good learning.* New York: Peter Lang Publishing.

Gredler, M. E. (1996). Educational games and simulations: A technology in search of a (research) paradigm. In D. H. Jonassen (Ed.), *Handbook of research for educational communication and technology* (pp. 521–540). New York: Simon & Schuster Macmillan.

Jost, J. T., Kruglanski, A. W., & Nelson, T. O. (1998). Social metacognition: An expansionist review. *Personality and Social Psychology Review, 2*(2), 137–154.

Kreijns, K., Kirschner, P. A., & Jochems, W. (2003). Identifying the pitfalls for social interaction in computer-supported collaborative learning environments: A review of the research. *Computers in Human Behavior, 19,* 335–353.

O. E. T. (2010, March 5). *Transforming American education: Learning powered by technology.* Draft National Educational Technology Plan 2010. Washington, DC: U. S. Department of Education, Office of Educational Technology.

Ryan, R. M., Rigby, C. S., & Przybylski, A. (2006). The motivational pull of video games: A self-determination theory approach. *Motivation and Emotion, 30,* 347– 363. Springer Science + Business Medi, LLC.

Vygotsky, L. S. (1978). *Mind in society.* Cambridge, MA: Harvard University Press.

ABOUT THE AUTHOR

Dr. Philip Bonanno graduated from the University of Malta (UoM) as a science teacher with a BEd (Hons) in 1992. He obtained an MPhil in Instructional Design in 2001 from the Centre for Communication Technology, UoM. Since 2006, he has been a full-time lecturer in Technology-Enhanced Learning at the Faculty of Education, UoM. He holds a doctorate in Instructional Psychology and Technology from the University of Joensuu, Finland. His PhD thesis was entitled “A Process-Oriented Pedagogy for Game-Based Learning.” He is the coordinator of the Educational Technology, Design and Innovation Program at the Faculty of Education at the University of Malta. Lastly, he was the coordinator of the Centre for Educational Technology, Research and Innovation, and from 2007 to 2009 he coordinated the EU (Grundtvig) project PAVE: Promoting Audio-Visual Education (http://projects.um.edu.mt/pave/).

CHAPTER 3

UBIQUITOUS LEARNING

Issues in the Australian Higher Education Context

Trish Andrews, Belinda Tynan, and Cherry Stewart

ABSTRACT

The notion of ubiquitous learning is one that poses both opportunity and challenge to Australian higher education institutions, staff, and students. Pervasive technology ownership, reliable broadband networks, changing students' expectations, and government policy are all fuelling a push toward more ubiquitous learning. While the notion of "anyhow, anywhere, anytime," learning can be seen to have obvious attractions and benefits for learners, it also creates obvious challenges for higher education providers. In most cases, institutions are ill-prepared for the level of flexibility required to provide and support ubiquitous learning. Appropriate infrastructure can be lacking, and staff and students demonstrate considerable diversity in their digital literacy. This chapter explores the opportunities and challenges of ubiquitous learning in the Australian context.

Ubiquitous Learning, pages 41–59

INTRODUCTION

The digital age provides access to information previously unknown in history. The pervasiveness of mobile technologies and ubiquitous computing has created both opportunities and concerns for students and teachers alike as they mesh the use of devices in and beyond the classroom. The refocus on the learner being mobile responds clearly to a population that is wired in the widest possible meaning of the word, making the notions of mobility and ubiquity possible in previously unthought-of ways (Barnes & Tynan, 2007; Katz & Aakhaus, 2002; Kukulska-Hulme, 2009; Kukulska-Hulme & Traxler, 2007; Naismith, Lonsdale, Vavoula, & Sharples, 2004; Traxler, 2008, 2009b). The ability of populations to contribute information to the global masses rather than just assimilate it is made possible by the technologies supporting the creation of borderless Web-based communities.

The introduction of portable devices from laptops, e-readers, personal organizing devices, gaming consoles, and the mobile phone, to name but a few, are integrated into our everyday activities for work, learning, and managing our personal lives. Higher education has in many contexts only experimented with the affordances of potentially new learning environments enabled by this ubiquitous access and has been slow to fully theorize and introduce scaled solutions.

The trend toward the use of mobile devices is without boundaries. In Western higher education environments, few teachers or their students are without a mobile phone or laptop at their disposal. However, designing for learning using technologies has predominantly been led by technology rather than by pedagogy and expert knowledge of teaching and learning. A ubiquitous learning focus creates a disruption to both teacher-led and technology-led learning. To truly respond to the world that our students now live in, we need to reconsider institutional issues of strategy, policy, and infrastructure that will support a realignment of teaching and learning with social imperatives. This chapter will explore how ubiquitous learning intersects with the elements of student learning, the state of academic perspectives toward changing technologies, and policy issues associated with change in higher education learning provision.

BACKGROUND

Ubiquitous learning is commonly described as learning that is sensitive to context and able to support individual learner needs for "anyhow, anywhere, anytime" learning (Ramaprasad, 2009). Notwithstanding this common thread, there are many and diverse definitions of ubiquitous learning.

Jones and Jo (2004) take the view that ubiquitous learning enables total immersion by students in their learning environment.

> So, a ubiquitous learning environment (ULE) is a situation or setting of pervasive (or omnipresent) education (or learning). Education is happening all around the student but the student may not even be conscious of the learning process. Source data is present in the embedded objects and students do not have to DO anything in order to learn. They just have to be there. (p. 469)

Cope & Kalantis, 2009, present an expanded understanding of ubiquitous learning that includes knowledge construction:

> Ubiquitous computing can mean using technology to bridge distance and time, the merging of physical and virtual, and bringing computing off the desk into social and public spaces through wearable and handheld devices. A focus on learning, and on the increasing prevalence of knowledge construction activities being conducted in online environments by experts and novices alike, however, suggests that the definition of ubiquitous be expanded to include the idea that learners can engage with knowledge about "anything," and that this learning can be experienced by "anyone."

However it is understood, ubiquitous learning implies reliable access to wireless networks and mobile devices capable of connecting to the Internet. Further, drawing on the definitions of ubiquitous learning outlined above, it expands the notion of learning space outside of physical classrooms and virtual learning spaces to include an endless range of other spaces The consequences of ubiquitous learning mean substantially changed roles for institutions, students, and teachers.

For higher education institutions in Australia, there are numerous issues to contend with in relation to the adoption of ubiquitous learning and providing a viable and sustainable approach to "anyhow, anywhere, anytime," learning. Student populations are becoming increasingly diverse. Updating and keeping up with new technologies is a major cost. Governments drive policy impacting institutional organization both internally and in relation to external factors. Higher education is becoming global, and quality assurance is increasingly related to external funding imperatives.

Furthermore, the diverse student population poses additional concerns around their own expectations of what constitutes a "higher education" experience, and while some students have the expectation that their teachers can and will use technology in a sophisticated way, it remains that for others, their own use of technology is not as good as teachers might expect (Kennedy et al., 2009). This is no doubt similar to other international contexts (JISC, 2009).

The availability of appropriate infrastructure is a key component of ubiquitous learning. While high levels of broadband access are available to higher education institutions in Australia, reliable access outside that network can be problematical in some areas. Australia is a vast country, and supporting access and connectivity to enable ubiquitous learning remains a challenge.

However, appropriate infrastructure to support ubiquitous learning is only one part of the ubiquitous learning issue. Academics in the Australian higher education system (we use the term *academics* for persons who determine the elements of the student's learning environment and guide the processes of learning) require comprehensive professional support, sometimes referred to as "academic development," so they can keep up with technologies and new approaches to pedagogy and thus participate in the potential of ubiquitous learning. Maintaining busy teaching, research, and service commitments impacts on their ability to engage with new ways of learning with technology, and for many it is easier to keep doing what they do in the way they know how to do it (Kirkup & Kirkwood, 2005). Beyond the early adopters, there is a high level of unwillingness to participate in ongoing professional development, especially when there is poor resourcing, competing demands, and a fear of the unknown, as well as having serious implications for their already bulging workloads (Oomen-Early & Murphy, 2009).

At the institutional level, in spite of the pervasiveness of technology and extensive institutional adoption of tools such as learning management systems, many Australian universities lack any policy for wholesale, systematic, and sustainable adoption and implementation of existing and emerging technologies (Smyth, Caladine, & Andrews, in press). Figure 3.1 attempts to display the factors as described here for the successful adoption of ubiquitous learning.

It will be critical for the Australian higher education sector to consider how government policy, national infrastructure, institutional policy, diverse student populations, professional development, and the pervasive nature of mobile devices might each come together to create new ways of learning that respond to enabling the "anyhow, anywhere, anytime" learning promise.

Students: Diversity and Voice

The possibilities and opportunities created by the notion of ubiquitous learning are ones that have profound implications for the ways in which students engage in teaching and learning activities and for the approaches taken by academic staff to provide teaching and learning in higher education. Ownership of mobile devices in Australia is high (Andrews, Davidson, Hill, Sloane, & Woodhouse, in press; Litchfield, Dyson, Lawrence, & Zmi-

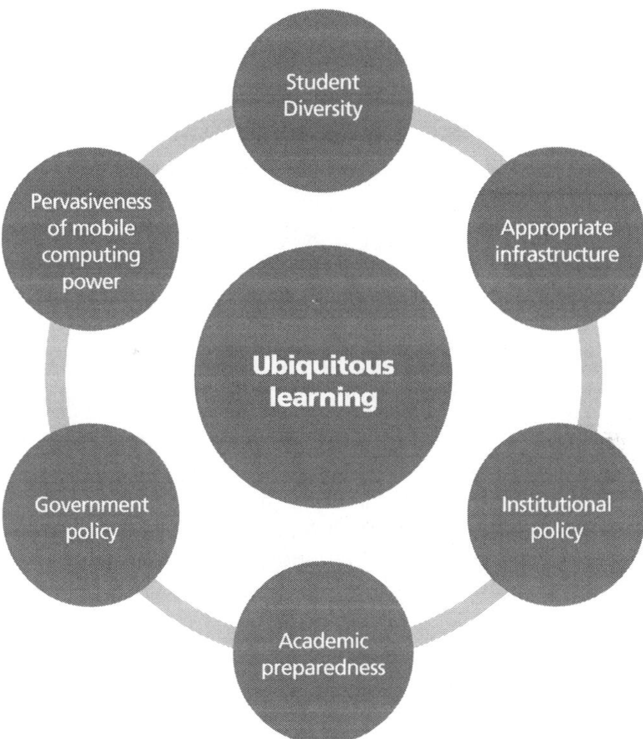

Figure 3.1 Factors to be considered for successful adoption of ubiquitous learning.

jewska, 2007), with many university students owning at least three mobile devices that they use in different ways for different activities (Andrews & Smyth, 2010). The ongoing and competitive development of new mobile devices such as the Apple iPad and other tablet technologies and the continuing enhancement of existing tools, such as super phones (GigaOM, 2009), mp3 players, tablets, laptops, and gaming consoles, will continue to impact on the ways in which mobile devices are utilized by their owners for a range of personal, work, and learning activities. In keeping with the Cope & Kalantis (2009) definition of ubiquitous learning as involving knowledge construction as outlined previously, this ubiquitous access to computing power means that

> Students no longer need to engage with information and discussion at the expense of real life but can do so as part of real life as they move about the world, using their own devices to connect them to people and ideas, ideas and information of their own choosing, perhaps using their own devices to generate and produce content and conversation as well as store and consume them.

> This is changing how students relate to technology. It is also changing how they relate to other students and to the content and conversation facilitated by the technology, so consequently it is changing how they relate to learning and to education. (Traxler, 2009b, p. 70)

Today's students are generally busy people with work, study, and personal lives creating potential conflicts. Students are aware of the opportunities offered by their technologies (Andrews et al., in press) and value the ability to access learning in ways that suit their needs and enable them to be flexible about how they engage with learning, other learners, and teachers (Garrison & Anderson, 2003). While there are currently technologies highly utilized by many higher education institutions such as lecture recording and learning management systems that can enable flexibility in the ways learning is accessed (Gosper et al., 2008), there is considerable variation in how these technologies are made available to students, both institutionally and individually. Indeed, in many cases, the use of new technologies does not translate into any pedagogical changes to best utilize these tools (Gosper et al., 2008; Kirkup & Kirkwood, 2005). Institutions frequently struggle to implement policies in relation to the use of these technologies (Smyth et al., in press), and many individual lecturers resist the changes required to adopt these technologies for teaching and learning activities, as discussed further below.

From the perspective of the student, a danger in the adoption of ubiquitous learning by institutions is treating all students as a homogeneous group regardless of their mode of learning, their location, and the nature of their individual circumstances. As JISC (2009) points out, not all learners are the same, and they have different needs. Mature-aged working learners and young on-campus learners experience their learning programs differently. Work by Holt and Challis (2007) found that merging on-campus and off-campus learners together could result in disappointing experiences for both groups. Additionally, while ownership of computing power might be high, there is considerable diversity in how people use their technologies as well as in relation to levels of technological literacy. A recent study by Kennedy et al. (2009) strongly refutes the notion of digital natives and digital immigrants fostered by Prensky (2001). Prensky makes the assumption that all Gen Y students (digital natives) have high levels of technological literacy, while the remainder of the population (digital immigrants) have lower levels of technology skills. Indeed, the study by Kennedy et al. (2009) found that both digital immigrants and digital natives varied greatly in their use and competency in relation to a range of technologies.

However, the adoption of students' own technologies threatens many teachers, and a common response is to ban such devices from classrooms. This is a move that students reject as being counterproductive (Van Der

Werf & Sabatier, 2009). Increasingly, the push by students for ubiquitous access to learning will require institutions and teachers to productively consider how such tools might be used to support ubiquitous learning in spite of the potentially disruptive nature of these technologies.

Further, while recent studies show that students are willing to use their own technologies for teaching and learning activities (Andrews & Smyth, 2010; Andrews et al., in press) particularly if there are no or low costs. There are some indications emerging that students want more direction in how to utilize these technologies for teaching and learning (Andrews et al, in press; Kennedy et al., 2009). There are increasing expectations that these technologies can be used by students to access learning how, when, and where it best suits them (Van Der Werf & Sabatier, 2009).

The potential of ubiquitous learning is also complicated by the diversity of the tools owned by students. As Traxler (2009b) points out:

> There is no standard footprint or format. The devices come in all sorts of shapes and sizes, from slim matchbox to sturdy paperback book, landscape or portrait. They may open out, slide open or neither; they have all sorts of keyboards (some virtual, some real) and screens; they may respond to touch, gesture or stylus, they may capture or play various media and connect to various networks and peripherals. They run various operating systems, applications, networks and connectivity, any of which will change overnight, even if those are supposedly stable and standard. (p. 71)

A growing perception by students is that many lecturers lack the skills to utilize technologies appropriately (JISC, 2009), and that much needs to be done to improve and develop teacher skills in this regard (JISC, 2009; UNE, 2009).

CHANGING HIGHER EDUCATION ACADEMICS' PEDAGOGIES

Many academics find their conventional understandings of teaching and learning significantly challenged when asked to teach "anyhow, anywhere, anytime" students with access to ubiquitous technologies. While academics may be receptive to change, the degree of change and the complexities associated with it are often too confounding. There is repeated concern over the structures and strategies that support the implementation of changes leading to facilitation of ubiquitous learning opportunities (Oomen-Early & Murphy, 2009; Stewart & Adlington, 2009; Vlachopoulos, 2009). As institutions begin to experiment with new learning tools and more ubiquitous approaches to teaching and learning, it becomes evident that it is not possible to do what has always been done, and that existing practices and/or policies become irrelevant (Van Der Werf & Sabatier, 2009).

The milieu identified above leads to the possibility of new principles and practices for learning and teaching (Seely-Brown, 2008; Siemens, 2006). Ubiquitous technologies are rapidly going beyond simple dissemination of information and forcing new interactions where people engage collaboratively with others and engage in activities that include knowledge construction. This is evident with Web 2.0, which has "blurred the line between producers and consumers of content and has shifted attention from access to information toward access to other people. New kinds of online resources—social-networking sites, blogs, wikis, and virtual communities—have allowed people with common interests to meet, share ideas, and collaborate in innovative ways" (Seely-Brown, 2008, p. 1).

When academics are engaging with new technologies, they need access to people with a variety of perspectives and expertise, as well as diverse sources of information when considering learning designs and resources. It appears that few academics find this easy to grasp (Stewart & Adlington, 2010). Quite often, there is concern that existing discipline-based traditions might be eliminated (Vlachopoulos, 2009), yet this may be what needs to occur. It is unlikely that higher education institutions will see much wide-scale engagement with ubiquitous learning until academics come to terms with the changed social environments that require new learning habits (made possible by the technologies). The role of an educator is different in the ubiquitous environment. The academic becomes a "connector"; a person who understands where and how learners can find the resources and access the expertise. In addition to their own discipline expertise, they must understand more fully the basis of human learning (Zull, 2002), how people access information, and how individuals turn information into knowledge.

Many studies (Bonk, 2002; Mishra & Koehler, 2006; Moore, 2006; Prebble et al., 2005; Snyder, Marginson, & Lewis, 2007; Zhen, Garthwaite, & Pratt, 2008) have demonstrated that academics need many forms of professional development and support to adopt new approaches to teaching and learning. The adverse impact on staff workloads has been one of the greatest disincentives to the take-up and use of the previous generation of Web-based teaching systems. Fortunately, there are now alternatives. Tynan and Barnes (2010) argue that the Web 2.0 world has provided academic staff with a new generation of easy-to-use, swift, and powerful tools. Unlooked for, and unasked for, they may well be exactly what many academics need.

At the institutional level, many policymakers are also feeling disconnected. Technology, pedagogy, and student cohorts change quickly, and quite often higher education institutions are bureaucratic and unable to respond appropriately to the new learning needs. They also tend to have little flexibility, and resources are spread thinly. While many researchers have reported time as a key issue for academic involvement with ubiquitous learning design and strategies, a quantitative study conducted by Zhen et al. (2008) disputed this. Instead, they identified issues of *self-efficacy* and *philosophy* as being more problematic. Stewart and Adlington (2009) articulated similar findings as related to Senge et al.'s (2000) concept of *personal mastery*. Workshops in either pedagogy or technology are unlikely to gain academic commitment to the ubiquitous learning paradigm (Mishra & Koehler, 2006); nor will institutionally led projects or the provision of technical support and educational design expertise alone. It is not an easy task to learn about the Web and all the potential tools and strategies that are expanding exponentially. The task becomes even more difficult if, as individuals, we find we cannot *learn* these new ways of doing; or perhaps, do not view the world of higher education through a more complex understanding of what might be the 21st-century learning paradigm.

Academics who direct their personal motivation and engagement in ubiquitous learning design as an intellectual challenge are often at the leading edge. Kegan and Lahey (2009) believe inhibiting factors are overcome by the will to find a better way of teaching students—by the person recognizing her own immunity to change and dealing with it directly. Other studies appear to confirm this idea (Bartone, Snook, & Tremble, 2002; Benay, 1997; Eigel, 1998). Lack of support, time restraints, or inexperience in learning design and technologies are often quite unknowingly used to conceal and reinforce more deeply held beliefs that new tools and strategies are too difficult, create more work, or are fads. It is not just academics who teach who need to engage with these changes, but the whole of the higher education institution; not one segment, but everything in unison. Such a change process begins with deep personal change (Quinn, 1996), that of finding the leader within.

Engaging the emotional life of the higher education organization requires skillful leaders who can facilitate and overcome individual aversions to changing ideas about how, when, and where the learner gains access to information, and what type of connections are required to support the process of transforming that information into personal knowledge. While for some it may be unpalatable, universities could draw upon the change-management practices adopted in the business world in order to reframe how they go about change (Leonard & Swap, 2005). Transforming universities from teaching organizations to learning organizations (Friedman, Friedman, & Pollack, 2005) is imperative if ubiquitous learning is to occur.

Australian Higher Education: Context

On March 4, 2009, the Australian government responded to the Bradley (2009) Review of Higher Education, which was a comprehensive analysis undertaken for the then-new incoming Labour government of the Higher Education sector. Among the recommendations was a public commitment to the rapid expansion of student numbers and the improvement of access for students from low socioeconomic status (SES) backgrounds. The Commonwealth's targets include:

- 40 percent of 25–34-year-olds to attain a qualification at bachelor level or above by 2025; and that
- 20 percent of higher education enrollments at undergraduate level should be people from low SES backgrounds by 2020.

The ambitious nature of these goals is clear. Currently, only 32 percent of 25–34-year-olds in Australia have degree-level qualifications. Reaching the target figure of 40 percent will involve an extra 544,000 graduates by 2020, or the equivalent of 20 new institutions of around 12,000 students each (Massaro, 2009). Clearly, the use of technology to provide teaching and learning activities appropriate to the needs of these groups and to support more-flexible and ubiquitous learning will be an important strategy in achieving these goals.

These proposals are in part a response to the relative neglect of the higher education sector during the previous decade. In 2008, Australia was the only OECD country not to have increased public funding for universities over the preceding 12 years. For most of the period, public funding per university student failed to keep up with inflation. The result was chronic underfunding, which compromised the capacity of all universities to meet the needs of the Australian community and the changing expectations and demands of new generations of students (Van Der Werf & Sabatier, 2009).

At the same time, the school sector is undergoing a digital revolution (DEEWR, 2010)—a revolution that has recognized the pervasive force of technology and the need for students and their teachers to engage in understanding how learning might be enhanced with its use. With a budget of $2.2 billion over a 6-year period, the investment outstrips the higher education arena significantly. It will

- provide for new information and communication technology (ICT) equipment for all secondary schools with students in years 9 to12 through the National Secondary School Computer Fund;

- support the deployment of high-speed broadband connections to Australian schools;
- collaborate with states and territories and Deans of Education to ensure new and continuing teachers have access to training in the use of ICT, which enables them to enrich student learning;
- provide for online curriculum tools and resources that support the national curriculum and specialist subjects such as languages;
- enable parents to participate in their child's education through online learning and access;
- support mechanisms to provide vital assistance for schools in the deployment of ICT.

This investment in changing teaching and learning practices in the school sector to more ubiquitous approaches will have a significant impact on the expectations of students entering higher education. There is emerging evidence that a strong predictor of students' expectations regarding higher education is based on their school earning experience (JISC, 2009). Consequently, new generations of "wired students are arriving at University with expectations of 'anyhow, anytime, anywhere' learning depending on their particular needs, interests and circumstances" (Van Der Werf & Sabatier, 2009).

The Commonwealth is additionally developing a National Broadband Network (NBN), which promises that 90 percent of Australian's will be able to access and connect to high speed broadband. The Commonwealth has

> established NBN Co Limited to build and operate the network, with the objective of providing 90 per cent of homes, schools and workplaces with "fibre to the premise" delivering speeds of 100 megabits per second and connecting all other premises with next generation wireless and satellite technologies, offering speeds of 12 megabits per second or more. (DBCDE, 2010)

Furthermore, as part of its package of reforms for the higher education sector, the Commonwealth is moving toward a "student-centered funding model." From 2012, Australian universities will be funded on the basis of actual enrollments. There will be no limits on the number of students that they will be able to admit, and institutions will be able to set their own entry standards. In part, this move reflects the priorities of the Bradley Report (2009) in terms of flexibility and the quality of the student experience.

The next decade will also see a rapid turnover in the Australian academic workforce, propelled by looming retirements and low satisfaction levels among academics. Almost half of full-time academic staff at Australian universities are 50 years of age or over. During the next 5 years, almost a quarter of senior academics in Australia will retire, and a further 23 percent will follow by 2019 (Coates et al., 2009). Moreover, dissatisfaction with increasing workloads is causing a slow exodus of academics from the system. Almost a third of Australian academics have reported taking concrete steps to find work overseas. Another third have sought jobs outside the sector.

These trends are all the more challenging in that they are occurring at a time when the system is on the brink of rapid expansion, along with the increasing pervasiveness of technology within our universities. The increase in the demand for teaching staff will not be restricted to the junior academics needed to teach a fresh wave of undergraduates after 2012. Recent projections show that jobs requiring doctorate-level qualifications are growing at a faster rate than that for jobs at any other qualification level (Coates et al., 2009).

The staffing crisis in the Australian higher education system presents a tremendous challenge to all institutions that are seeking to enhance or expand their use of technologies to support the "anyhow, anywhere, anytime" learning creed. There are fears that the recruitment of new staff will lag behind the expansion of the higher education system, further compromising student staff ratios and the ability of universities generally to respond to the diversification of student cohorts—globalization. If these anxieties are realized, such a trend might well impose fresh obstacles to the spread of new ubiquitous learning and teaching approaches. Faced with rising workloads, academics are more likely to fall back on traditional pedagogies than to experiment with new forms of learning. To truly respond to the world that our students now live in, there is a need to reconsider institutional issues of strategy, policy, and infrastructure that will support a realignment of teaching and learning with social imperatives. Figure 3.2 attempts to capture four dimensions of the issues influencing the adoption of ubiquitous learning that are explained in this chapter. The blue center is not static, but rather each quadrant can be placed against each static corner for consideration of higher education institutions.

The issues outlined above suggest that a multifaceted approach involving governments and institutions is required to develop an environment that will be conducive to supporting ubiquitous learning.

FUTURE TRENDS

There is no doubt that government policy within the Australian higher education sector and technology arena, economic pressures, and societal attitudes will impact on how ubiquitous technologies, learning, and computing will be engaged with. The success or otherwise of the Australian NBN will not stop the "anywhere, anyhow, anytime" sensibility of our current and next generations. Public demand and enterprise will assist in driving the demand for access and connectivity. There is little doubt that ownership of

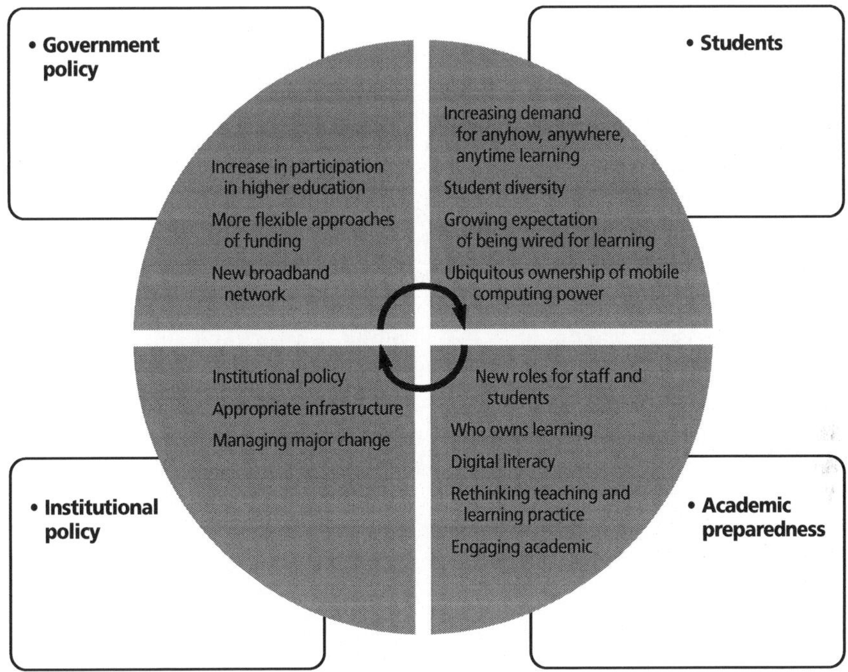

Figure 3.2 Issues influencing adoption of ubiquitous learning.

computing power, particularly in the form of mobile devices, by students will continue to grow, and that students will increasingly seek ways to use these devices for their teaching and learning activities. In a recent posting to the EduTech World Bank blog on education, Hawkins (2010) identified ubiquitous learning as a one of 10 major trends in education. The ongoing adoption and upgrade of wireless networks in institutions will provide a viable network to support ubiquitous access to learning. The rapid development of small tablet computer—heralded by the Apple iPad and copied by many other companies—with large screen sizes, and 3G and super phones means that emerging technologies will better support a wide range of teaching and learning activities.

There are strong indications that students are looking for more flexible ways to access learning (Andrews et al., in press; Van Der Werf & Sabatier, 2009), and this will further drive the need to adopt more ubiquitous approaches to learning. Evolving understandings of what constitutes learning and knowledge construction is a further trend that will challenge institutions (Cope & Kalantis, 2009).

CONCLUSION

To capitalize on the opportunities of ubiquitous learning, much needs to change. A decade ago, Spratt and her colleagues at Deakin University in Australia posed the question: "What kinds of professional development strategies can meet the real-world, just-in-time professional development needs of busy academics?" (Spratt, Palmer, & Coldwell 2000, p. 459). Unfortunately, it is widely recognized that the solution to this dilemma has yet to be developed. In one sense, this is hardly surprising, as the resources required for effective academic staff development far exceed those that university decision makers have been willing to provide in the past. Additional research into the staff-development needs of academics is therefore urgently needed before new generations of academics replicate the habits of the past, which may not allow for the possibilities for learning.

The optimizing rich media project (Smyth et al., in press) found that, in general, institutions are still ill-prepared for wholesale adoption of technology and lack the policies and procedures to enable wholesale successful adoption of such notions as ubiquitous learning, and to effectively support the new ways of thinking about teaching and learning required to support this. As Barnes and Tynan back in 2007 proposed in drawing attention then to many of the issues observed in this chapter, in Miranda's Brave New World, there remains much that needs to be done:

> The most important of these is the need to rethink teaching and learning within higher education. University teaching has fallen behind changes in social technologies. Whereas universities are still struggling to assimilate the first wave of Web-based teaching tools, an increasing number of students have already arrived in a Web 2.0 world. To meet the needs of these students, universities must reconsider their priorities. The latest social technologies have the potential to deliver truly student-centered learning environments, to create a University 2.0. However, this will not happen overnight or without sustained effort.

Further, they concluded that there was a need

> to develop alternative ways of viewing university learning and to rethink the concept of a university itself. Such a discussion must involve all those working within the higher education sector, particularly the decision-makers who shape institutional policies on teaching and learning. The authors do not presume to provide the answers. Miranda's narrative is intended to do no more than provoke, to open the door to new ways of thinking. And there is no time like the present. Social technologies are already shaping the private and social worlds of millennium students. The task for educators and policymakers is to bridge the existing digital divide before it becomes wider, and a generation of opportunities is lost. (Barnes & Tynan, 2007, p. 198)

REFERENCES

Andrews, T., Davidson, B., Hill, A., Sloane, D., & Woodhouse, L. (2011). Using students' own mobile technologies to support clinical competency development in speech pathology. In A. Kitchenham (Ed.), *Blended and mobile learning across disciplines: Models for implementation.* IGI Global.

Andrews, T., & Smyth, R. (2010). Utilising students own mobile devices and rich media: Two case studies from the health sciences. In P. Dini (Ed.), proceedings *The second international conference on Mobile, Hybrid, and On-line Learning: el & ml 2010.* St Maarten, Netherlands Antilles.

Barnes, C., & Tynan, B. (2007). The adventures of Miranda in the brave new world: Learning in a Web 2.0 millennium. *ALT-J, 15*(3), 189–200.

Bartone, P. T., Snook, S. A., & Tremble, T. R. (2002). Cognitive and personality predictors of leader performance in West Point cadets. *Military Psychology, 14*(4), 321.

Benay, P. (1997, January 1). *Social-cognitive development and transformational leadership: A case study. ScholarWorks@UMass Amherst.* Retrieved April 14, 2010, from http://scholarworks.umass.edu/dissertations/AAI9721431

Bonk, C. (2002). *Current myths and future trends in online teaching and learning.* Retrieved September 2, 2008, from http://www.courseshare.com/cjbonk/myth_trend.html

Bradley, D. (2009). *Review of Australian Higher Education* (p. 100). Canberra: DEEWAR. Retrieved July 15, 2008, from http://www.dest.gov.au/sectors/higher_education/policy_issues_reviews/reviews/highered_review/

Coates, H., Dobson, I., Edwards, D., Friedman, T., Goedegebuure, L., & Meek, L. (2009). *The attractiveness of the Australian academic profession: A comparative analysis.* Melbourne: L. H. Martin Institute.

Cope, B., & Kalantis, M. (Eds.). (2009). *Ubiquitous learning.* University of Illinois Press. https://apps.lis.illinois.edu/wiki/display/sp09lis590ul/Another+Definition+of+Ubiquitous+Learning

Department of Broadband, Communications and the Digital Economy (DBCDE). (2010). *National Broadband Network.* http://www.dbcde.gov.au/broadband/national_broadband_network

Department of Education, Employment and Workplace Relations (DEEWR). (2010). *Digital education revolution—Overview.* http://www.deewr.gov.au/SCHOOLING/DIGITALEDUCATIONREVOLUTION/Pages/default.aspx

Eigel, K. (1998). *Leader effectiveness: A constructive developmental view and investigation.* Unpublished Dissertation.

Friedman, H. H., Friedman, L. W., & Pollack, S. (2005, Fall). Transforming a university from a teaching organisation to a learning organisation. *Review of Business,* 31–35.

Garrison, D. & Anderson, T. (Eds.). (2003). E-Learning in the 21st century: A framework for research and practice. London: Routledge/Falmer.

GigaOM. (2009). *The summer of the superphone.* http://gigaom.com/2009/06/07/the-summer-of-the-superphone/

Gosper, M., Green, D., McNeil, M., Phillips, R., Preston, G., & Woo, K. (2006). *The impact of Web-based lectures on current and future practices in learning and teaching,*

Final report, ALTC http://www.altc.edu.au/project-impact-webbased-lecture-macquarie-2006

Hawkins, R. (2010). 10 global trends in ICT and education. *EduTech: A world bank Blog on ICT use in Education.* http://blogs.worldbank.org/edutech/10-global-trends-in-ict-and-education

Holt, D., & Challis, D. (2007). From policy to practice: One university's experience of implementing strategic change through wholly online teaching and learning. *Australasian Journal of Educational Technology, 23*(1), 110–131.

JISC. (2009). *Transforming curriculum design and delivery through technology.* http://www.jisc.ac.uk/whatwedo/programmes/elearning/curriculumdelivery.aspx

Jones, V., & Jo, J. H. (2004, December 5–8). Ubiquitous learning environment: An adaptive teaching system using ubiquitous technology. In R. Atkinson, C. McBeath, D. Jonas-Dwyer, & R. Phillips (Eds.), *Beyond the comfort zone: Proceedings of the 21st ASCILITE Conference* (pp. 468–474). Perth, Australia. http://www.ascilite.org.au/conferences/perth04/procs/jones.html

Katz, J., & Aakhus, M. (2002). *Perpetual contact: Mobile communication, private talk, public performance.* Cambridge, UK: Cambridge University Press.

Kennedy, G., Dalgarno, B., Bennett, S., Gray, K., Judd, T., Waycott, J. et al. (2009). *Educating the net generation: Implications for learning and teaching in Australian universities.* Final report. Sydney: Australian Learning and Teaching Council. http://www.altc.edu.au/system/files/resources/CG6-2

Kegan, R., & Lahey, L. L. (2009). *Immunity to change: How to overcome it and unlock the potential in yourself and your organization* (1st ed.). Boston: Harvard Business School Press.

Kirkup, G., & Kirkwood, A. (2005). Information and communications technologies (ICT) in higher education teaching—A tale of gradualism rather than revolution. *Learning Media and Technology, 30*(2), 185–199.

Kukulska-Hulme, A. (2009). Understanding the value of mobility and movement in learning. In D. Metcalf, A. Hamilton, & C. Graffeo (Eds.), *Proceedings Mlearn2009, 8th world conference on Mobile And Contextual Learning,* Orlando, FL.

Kukulska-Hulme, A., & Traxler, J. (2007). Designing for mobile and wireless learning. In H. Beetham & R. Sharpe (Eds.), *Rethinking pedagogy for a digital age: Designing and delivering e-learning.* London, New York: Routledge.

Leonard, D., & Swap, W. C. (2005). *Deep smarts: How to cultivate and transfer enduring business wisdom.* Boston: Harvard Business Press.

Litchfield, A., Dyson, L., Lawrence, D., & Zmijewska, A., (2007). Directions for m-learning research to enhance active learning. *In proceedings ASCILITE,* Singapore.

Massaro, V. (2009, March 9–10). *A new start for policy and funding.* Paper presented at the Australian Financial Review Higher Education Conference, Sydney. from http://www.lhmartininstitute.edu.au/research_publications_consultancy/publications/A_New_Start_Policy_Funding.pdf

Mishra, P., & Koehler, M. (2006). Technological pedagogical content knowledge: A framework for teacher knowledge. *Teachers College Record, 108*(6), 1017–1054.

Moore, M. G. (2006). Faculty professional development. *American Journal of Distance Education, 20*(2), Editorial.

Naismith, L., Lonsdale, P., Vavoula, G., & Sharples, M. (2004). *Literature review in mobile technologies and learning.* Future lab Series, Report 11. University of Birmingham.

Oomen-Early, J., & Murphy, L. (2009). Self-actualization and e-learning: A qualitative investigation of university faculty's perceived barriers to effective online instruction. *International Journal on E-Learning, 8*(2), 223.

Prebble, T., Hargraves, H., Leach, L., Naidoo, K., Suddaby, G., & Zepke, N. (2005). *Impact of student support services and academic development programmes on student outcomes in undergraduate tertiary study: A synthesis of the research* (p. 165). New Zealand Ministry of Education. Retrieved November 19, 2009, from http://www.educationcounts.govt.nz/publications/tertiary_education/5519

Preensky, M. (2001). Digital natives, digital immigrants. *On the Horizon, 9*(5), 1–6.

Quinn, R. (1996). *Deep change: Discovering the leader within* (p. 235). San Francisco: Jossey-Bass.

Ramaprasad, A. (2009, February 16). Ubiquitous learning: An Ontology. *Ubiquitous Learning: An International Journal, 1*(1), 57–65. Available at SSRN: http://ssrn.com/abstract=1305686

Seely-Brown, J. (2008). How to connect technology and passion in the service of learning. *The Chronicle of Higher Education, 55*(8). Retrieved March 18, 2010, from http://find.galegroup.com.simsrad.net.ocs.mq.edu.au/gtx/retrieve.do?contentSet=IAC-Documents&resultListType=RESULT_LIST&qrySerId=Locale%28en%2CUS%2C%29%3AFQE%3D%28JN%2CNone%2C31%29%22Chronicle+of+Higher+Education%22%3AAnd%3ALQE%3D%28DA%2CNone%2C8%2920081017%3AAnd%3ALQE%3D%28VO%2CNone%2C2%2955%24&sgHitCountType=None&inPS=true&sort=DateDescend&searchType=PublicationSearchForm&tabID=T002&prodId=EAIM&searchId=R1¤tPosition=33&userGroupName=macquarie&docId=A186906138&docType=IAC

Senge, P. M., McCabe, N. H. C., Lucas, T., Kleiner, A., Dutton, J., & Smith, B. (2000). *Schools that learn: A fifth discipline fieldbook for educators, parents, and everyone who cares about education.* New York: Broadway Business.

Siemens, G. (2006). *Knowing knowledge.* Lulu.com.

Smyth, R., Caladine, R., & Andrews, T. (in press). Viability, sustainability, scalability and pedagogy: Investigating the spread of real-time, rich media technologies in Australian universities. In D. Surry, T. Stefurak, & R. Gray, (Eds.), *Technology integration in higher education: Social and organisational aspects.* IGI Global.

Snyder, I., Marginson, S., & Lewis, T. (2007). An alignment of the planets: Mapping the intersections between pedagogy, technology and management in Australian universities. *Journal of Higher Education Policy and Management, 29*(2), 187–202.

Spratt, C., Palmer, S., & Coldwell, J. (2000). Using technologies in teaching: An initiative in academic staff development. *Educational Technology and Society, 3*(3) 455–461.

Stewart, C., & Adlington, R. (2009). Shall we dance? Managing change from print-based to interactive networked learning. *The International Journal of Knowledge, Culture and Change Management, 9*(9), 93–104.

Stewart, C., & Adlington, R. (2009). Changing direction with teacher educators in distance education provision. *Journal of the International Society for Teacher Education, 13*(2), 62–70.

Stewart, C., & Adlington, R. (2010). The dance of change: From print-based distance education to creative networked learning. In W. Kinuthia & S. Marshall (Eds.), *Cases 'n' places: Global cases in educational and performance technology* (vol. 2, pp. 59–70). Charlotte, NC: Information Age Publishing. Retrieved June 20, 2009, from http://theorganisation.com/conference-2009/sessions/

Traxler, J. (2008). *Mobility, modernity and development.* Paper presented at first M4d Karlstadt, Sweden. Retrieved July 2, 2009, from http://wlv/academia.edu/JohnTraxler/Papaers/83101/Mobility—Modernity—Development

Traxler, J. (2009b). Learning in a mobile age. *International Journal of Mobile and Blended Learning, 1*(1), 1–12.

Tynan, B., & Barnes, C. (2010). Web 2.0 and professional development of academic staff. In M. Lee & C. McLoughlin (Eds.), *Web 2.0-based e-learning: Applying social informatics for tertiary teaching* (pp. 365–379). doi:10.4018/978-1-60566-294-7.ch019

UNE. (2009). *Students experience of learning at UNE.* Armidale, Australia: University of New England.

Van Der Werf, M., & Sabatier, G. (2009). *The college of 2020: Students.* Chronicle Research Services. http://research.chronicle.com

Vlachopoulos., D. (2009). The challenges of introducing new technologies in humanities: A case study of the perceptions of academic staff of classics. *Ubiquitous Learning: An International Journal, 1*(2), 51–60.

Zhen, Y., Garthwait, A., & Pratt, P. (2008). Factors affecting faculty members' decision to teach or not to teach online in higher education. *Online Journal of Distance Learning Administration, 11*(4). Retrieved January 4, 2010, from http://www.westga.edu/~distance/ojdla/fall113/zhen113.html

ABOUT THE AUTHORS

Trish Andrews is Senior Research Fellow with DEHub at the University of New England (Australia). Trish has extensive experience in teaching and curriculum development in higher education and has been involved in numerous projects relating to the integration of technology into teaching and learning. Her current research interests include mobile learning, rich media, learning spaces, and the student experience of using technology for teaching and learning.

Belinda Tynan is the director of DEHub at the University of New England (Australia). She also serves as the Academic Director for the Flexible & Online Program. Previously, she was Academic Director, Faculty of the Professions (2008–2009) and leader, Academic Unit, at the University's Teaching and Learning Centre (2006–2008). She held the position of Dean in

the Faculty of Flexible Learning, Lasalle-Sia, College of the Arts, Singapore (2004–2005). Professor Tynan has held numerous teaching positions in the UK, Australia, and Japan. She has demonstrated experience in the management of large projects in the higher education sector, both in Australia and overseas. She is on the leadership team for the ALTC Developing Our Staff project, which is an eight-university collaboration for mapping and delivery of a shared professional development program for tertiary educators. Her latest major initiative, DEHub, received $3.544 million in Commonwealth funding in 2008. Lastly, Professor Tynan has authored and co-authored almost two dozen journal articles and book chapters, in addition to many peer reviewed conference papers. Her research covers areas such as music teaching, distance education, academic staff development, and collaboration. Belinda was also previously the treasurer and hosts the Secretariat of the Open and Distance Learning Association of Australia (ODLAA).

Cherry Stewart is Research Fellow with DEHub: Innovation in Distance Education at University of New England (Australia). She has extensive experience in teaching and management in a wide range of educational environments in both the public and private sectors. Following a career in primary teaching, and NSWTAFE, more recently, she has provided advice and guidance in educational design and academic development to the staff at UNE.

PART II

SOCIAL MEDIA + MOBILE LEARNING = U-LEARNING: CREATING CLASSROOM CONNECTIONS

CHAPTER 4

MICRO-CYCLES

Course Design Model for Mobile Learning

Chris Haskell and Barbara Schroeder

ABSTRACT

Two instructors from the Department of Educational Technology at Boise State University, Chris Haskell and Barbara Schroeder, designed a mobile course about mobile learning to address the pervasive and growing use of mobile devices by college and university students. This course, called "Mobile Learning: Devices, Applications, and Pedagogy," was designed to work with an Internet-enabled mobile device as the primary means of interaction. The instructors researched mobile learning, identified key characteristics, and constructed a mobile learning design model, which includes a unique delivery and interactive design model they named "micro-cycles." This chapter details the goals and design of the course, characteristics of mobile learning, methods for course evaluation, and the challenges of designing for mobile learning.

Ubiquitous Learning, pages 63–78

INTRODUCTION

Two instructors from the Department of Educational Technology at Boise State University (http://edtech.boisestate.edu), Chris Haskell and Barbara Schroeder, designed a mobile course about mobile learning to address the pervasive and growing use of mobile devices by college and university students (Smith, Salaway, & Caruso, 2009). This course, called "Mobile Learning: Devices, Applications, Pedagogy" (Haskell & Schroeder, 2010), was designed to work with an Internet-enabled mobile device as the primary means of interaction. The course was designed for an 8-week summer session.

In order to create a course where students could interact with, research, design, and integrate effective and innovative mobile learning environments, the instructors researched mobile learning, identified key characteristics, and created a design model they named "micro-cycles." Through this micro-cycle model, they were able to facilitate learning within the unique environment of mobile learning.

This chapter begins with a brief overview of mobile learning research, characteristics of informal learning, and the micro-cycle approach. Next, the instructors discuss the progression of the course design, the tools they used to implement their design model, and their evaluation of the course using the FRAME model (Koole, 2009). The chapter ends with a discussion of what was learned, suggestions for integrating mobile learning into face-to-face and online courses, and the need for continuing research in this rapidly expanding field.

MOBILE LEARNING RESEARCH

The instructors started the process of course design by reviewing the literature on mobile learning and reflecting upon their own experiences learning with mobile devices. Current research about mobile learning includes various evaluation methods (Ally, 2009; Attewell, 2005; Traxler & Kukulska-Hulme, 2005), illustrating the importance of evaluating mobile learning across various aspects, such as access, changes in teaching and learning, or alignment with institutional goals. In fact, new systems of evaluation may be required for mobile learning, to address its unique aspects.

Traxler and Kukulska-Hulme (2005) write, "Mobile learning takes place in a wider social context and evaluation must also recognise this" (p. 3). Therefore, the instructors recognized the review of literature in the field as evolving and fluid, providing guidance and ideas, but also including opportunities for experimentation and the development of mobile learning design models and instructional strategies. Haskell and Schroeder, therefore, applied and and adapted concepts about mobile learning for their course, recognizing that the design of the course would evolve through multiple iterations.

Starting with a good definition of mobile learning was key to the process of designing the course. Mobile learning was defined as

1. occurring anytime, anywhere;
2. informal, occurring in tandem with and as an offshoot of formal instruction;
3. initiated by the learner's curiosity;
4. authentic;
5. accessible;
6. situated;
7. personal; and
8. time-dependant (Ally, 2009; Brown & Diaz, 2010; O'Malley et al., 2003; Traxler & Kukulska-Hulme, 2005;).

INFORMAL PATTERNS OF MOBILE LEARNING

Vast differences exist between informal and formal learning. While both types of learning can utilize the same tools, similar resources, and appear very similar on the surface, they are quite unique. In order to understand how informal and formal learning diverge, it is important to first analyze mobile learning that occurs within the informal, or social context.

Informal learning occurs spontaneously and is directed by personal inquiry. A study by Vavoula (2005) of everyday adult learning found that 51 percemt of the reported learning took place at home or in the learner's own office at the workplace. Mobile learning occurs in many settings, fueled by need and accessibility. Here is an example: You are out with your special someone having a nice dinner before going to a movie. It's a warm summer evening and you have just finished your meal when a discussion about calories and nutritional content leads you to a question. How many calories did I just consume?

This question is simple but represents several of the fundamental tenets of mobile learning: a need for knowledge that is authentic, personal, and situated. Unlike facts about major battle dates, formulas, or ordered structures, the knowledge you are seeking has an immediate impact on your understanding and can be applied, in this case, in a social context. This new information can validate beliefs about your health and healthy eating habits, inform suggestions or recommendations you might make to others, and even influence your decision about whether to have dessert or not.

Before the age of mobile learning, it was still possible to answer this question, but in different ways. A number of resources may have been available to help you glean information and other nutritional characteristics about the food you ate, but the path to this information might have been more convoluted. It might require information such as a nutritional card provided by the restaurant or a detailed search of a number of printed resources.

In many cases, the stigma, time constraints, or hassle in obtaining such information would dissuade one from the search. Smaller restaurants seldom spend the time to research such information, and some simply have no interest in providing it. However, in the age of mobile learning, the tools exist for you to seek answers that are authentic, personal, and situated.

Let's return to the restaurant scenario. In the true fashion of a mobile-empowered learner, you pull out your smartphone and begin a search. As it is Internet-enabled, you do a simple browser search for the keywords "steak gorgonzola" and "calories." Among the results, you see listings for general recipes as well as dishes served by major restaurant chains. This allows you to solve initial question in a manner that satisfies your need and provides additional information you did not expect, such as sodium content and other nutritional details.

When we look at the three primary characteristics of informal mobile learning, we may not make a connection to the effort of self-directed informal learning being the combination of three important conditions. This learning experience can be described as the amalgamation of authentic, personal, and situated. Understanding the value of these characteristics helps us to identify critical elements of mobile learning, which can support learning in both traditional and informal educational structures.

THREE CHARACTERISTICS OF INFORMAL LEARNING

Authenticity in self-directed, informal learning is essential. If the knowledge we seek applies directly to us and is a real situation, the likelihood of its successful assimilation increases (Burke & Burke, 2009; Newmann & Wehlage, 1993, 1995; Wiliam, Lee, Harrison, & Black, 2004). Informal learning is initiated through everyday activities, and the need for learning occurs when a person must solve a problem (Vavoula & Sharples, 2002).

While putting together a piece of furniture from a box full of parts, we rely heavily on the instruction sheet provided. It contains information helpful to the task at hand. The learning that takes place by referencing the sheet influences an authentic task, and often the successful completion of the furniture depends on the learning that takes place.

Assume for a moment that step-by-step instructions were not available for this project, and a formal learning environment was responsible for preparing us to build the furniture. In a traditional classroom setting, we would be shown the finished product as part of an anticipatory set or other lesson introduction. We might be introduced to each of the parts and complete a worksheet identifying various screws, clasps, panels, and various components. We might participate in group projects to assemble a mock-up of the furniture. The goal of formal education is to help an entire group reach the same standard of completion. This type of learning does not normally address the different levels of knowledge, skill, and experience of the individual learners. Traditional instructional strategies include everything that must be done by all students through a process of learning objectives.

However, when using authentic learning through an individualized instruction sheet, we find we approach teaching and learning in a much different way. Most amateur furniture builders will simply spread all of the supplies out on the floor. We tend to look at the first step and collect those pieces. Once laid out in some sort of visual pattern, we begin to assemble the basic structure. If we are unfamiliar with some fastener, part, or tool, we will return to the instructions and find the answer. We are looking for knowledge, in this case, that is authentic and meets an immediate need. We are drawn to this knowledge because it serves us at that moment. Having a tool, such as an instruction booklet, allows us to capture and apply authentic knowledge, which is also personal and situated.

Mobile learning, therefore, can be viewed as existing within an authentic, personalized, and situated context, with learners accessing, networking, and creating content and knowledge in their own Personal Learning Environments (PLEs) (Ally, 2005; Brown & Diaz, 2010; Koole, 2009; Wilson et al., 2000; Sharples, 2002; Vavoula, Sharples, Lonsdale, Rudman, & Meek, 2007; Wilson, Liber, Johnson, Beauvoir, Sharples, & Milligan, 2007). Our instruction booklet is authentic, because it would apply this to something that we want or need to know; personalized, because we find the information that is valuable and meaningful to us; and situated, because it exists at the point of the need for knowledge.

Our previous restaurant example also demonstrates all three characteristics. The desire to know the calories and nutritional content was situated. It applied to the meal that was eaten and the dessert being considered. The need for knowledge was expressly personal and applied immediately. And finally, learning about the nutritional content of the food was authentic.

What makes this exchange unique and valuable to our concept of mobile learning is the learner's experience. The learner can search for, access, and apply this information using an Internet-enabled mobile device (or smartphone). A smartphone differs from our printed furniture instruction sheet because it taps a number of resources immediately; might provide additional links or resources, such as instructional videos; and is individualized by the learner. It also enables the learner to extend the learning or maybe divert her attention based upon new inquiries. Mobile, informal learning can be conceptualized as a continual cycle of inquiry, access, learning, sharing, and reflecting.

MOBILE LEARNING MICRO-CYCLES

Based upon the evolving theories of mobile learning and the recognition that mobile learning is authentic, personal, and situated, the authors developed a unique design for their mobile learning course, a design model they named "micro-cycles" (see Figure 4.1). These micro-cycles included formal elements of viewing, reading, sharing, completing assignments, and reflection during 48-hour cycles. However, included in the student experience would also be elements of informal learning, with learners being driven by their own inquiry.

The rationale behind the micro-cycle design model was to emulate the experience of learning with mobile devices, delivering updates and communication throughout the day, accessible wherever and whenever the student wanted. Instead of presenting information, assigning interactivity, and providing course resources through a Web-based course, the mobile course was designed to mimic mobile learning opportunities, delivering the information directly to the student.

For instance, online courses are typically designed around modules or weekly activities, with students accessing content posted on the course site. This type of interaction tends to be mostly asynchronous, inconsistent, and passive. In the mobile environment, however, users experience and expect simultaneous feedback and interaction, using various applications such as text messaging (SMS), multimedia messaging (MMS), instant messaging, access to social networks, and mobile apps. Therefore, the micro-cycle approach creates an inherently different experience with course access, com-

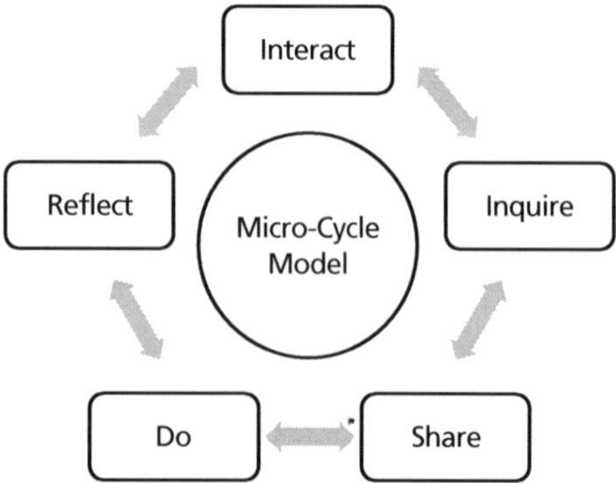

Figure 4.1 Elements of the micro-cycle for mobile course design.

munication, and time-on-task than a traditional online course. Students actively engage in the real-time and immediate nature of mobile learning by interacting with short, intermittent updates, links, and assignment information received through the mobile device.

If students become concerned about missing micro-cycle updates and communication, they could always access the Web-based version of the course, finding the same information and more resources to help with the activities and assignments. By using both a mobile and Web-based Moodle course site along with mobile device course updates, the students could easily verify all activities and assignments.

Although micro-cycles might seem rigid and time dependant, learners always have the option of reading and responding to messages during times that are convenient for them, an essential aspect of mobile learning. By using mobile devices to communicate, learners can receive timely responses from classmates and instructors, experiencing just-in-time and helpful feedback within the mobile learning environment. The concept of anytime, anywhere learning is supported through the micro-cycle design, allowing the learners to respond more timely to messages and other activities.

The instructors used easily available tools to enable micro-cycles: creating communication alerts within short time-frames, directing learners to participate in various course activities, and providing links to mobile content. Communication and updates were sent to students through a course Twitter feed, with students directed to follow the Twitter account and enable updates on their mobile devices. Thus, almost all of the course activities could be completed using a mobile device, with students receiving updates throughout the 48-hour cycles.

To simplify the process of sending Twitter feeds, the instructors used Twuffer, a Twitter scheduler, to set up the notices ahead of time, to be delivered at specific dates and times. An example of a typical day's Twitter feeds is outlined below:

- June 11, 2010 @ 9:00 a.m. Finish reading Chapter 1, Ally http://bit.ly/allychapter1 pages 19–21.
- June 11, 2010 @ 11:00 a.m. Review Participation Rubric as needed: http://docs.google.com/View?id=dfp69sx9_208fpbxn2dv
- June 11, 2010 @ 12:00 p.m. Tweet one important idea/concept from videos watched (remember to include #et597 hashtag)
- June 11, 2010 @ 1:00 p.m. Subscribe to the Cool Teacher Podcast http://bit.ly/ctpodcast and listen to a recent episode. Listen throughout the course.

Detailed instructions are provided to students, especially at the beginning of the course, to help them set up their mobile devices to receive Twitter feeds, and students quickly assimilated into this cycle of learning. Students are also advised to install a Twitter aggregator, such as Tweetdeck, on their mobile device, in order to organize and respond to tweets and other messages. Additionally, student learning and participation in the course is supported by weekly Adobe Connect meetings, which can also be accessed through a mobile app. These weekly meetings are optional, but can help students connect with their instructors and classmates, increase their sense of course presence, and provide them with another method of communication.

MOODLE LMS AND MLE MOODLE

The instructors needed a robust LMS that would include mobile access. They decided to use Moodle (http://moodle.org), since it was already being used by the Department of Educational Technology and offered various mobile plugins and options. Mobile Learning Engine (MLE) Moodle was selected to provide the mobile interface needed for the course. MLE Moodle (http://mle.sourceforge.net) is free and open-source and can be easily installed on any Moodle site. It adds mobile learning functionality to a Moodle site and can be accessed from any Internet-enabled mobile device. The MLE Moodle plugin creates a unique and different URL, rendered for mobile devices. The instructors created a shortened URL for the MLE Moodle site so it would be easy to remember and access: http://bitly.com/mlemoodle.

Screen shots comparing the Moodle Web-based and mobile sites are shown below in Figures 4.2, 4.3, 4.4, and 4.5, to demonstrate the different renderings needed for each type of presentation.

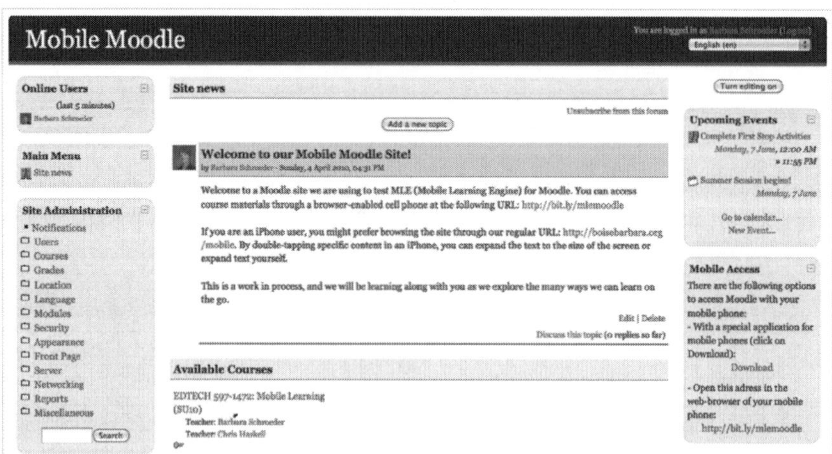

Figure 4.2 Front page of Moodle Web-based course site.

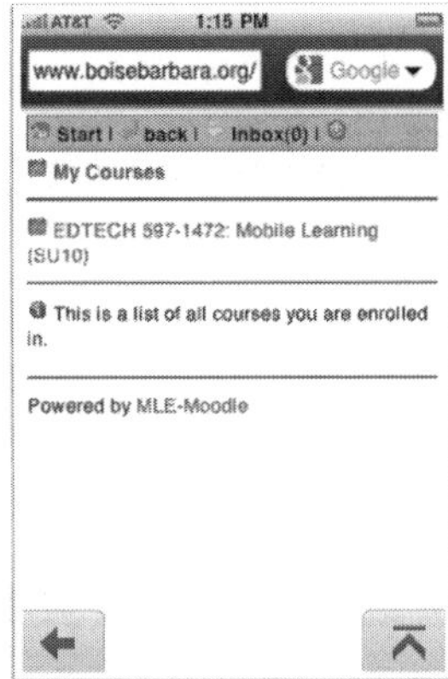

Figure 4.3 Front page of Moodle MLE (mobile) site (viewed on iPhone with Opera mini browser).

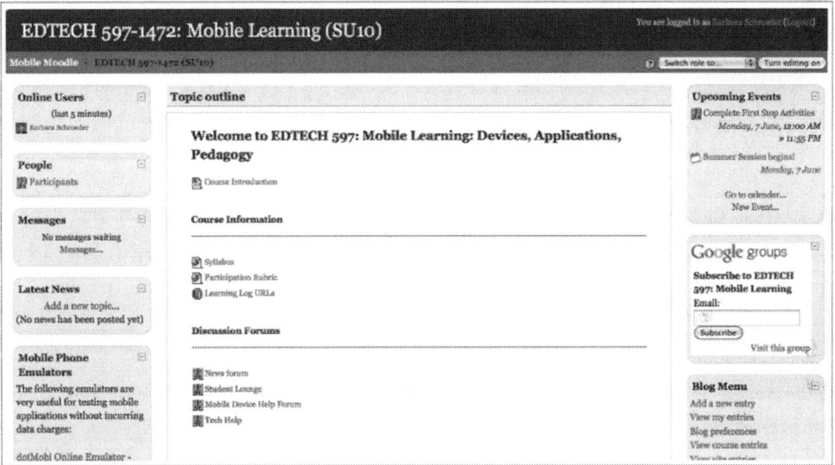

Figure 4.4 Home page of course site in Moodle.

Figure 4.5 Home page of course site in MLE Moodle.

Figure 4.6 MLE Moodle on Sony K70 device (Web emulator).

As can be seen from comparing the images, each Moodle site is designed to maximize the technology and learner needs. For instance, on the Web-based Moodle site, more information is available, such as blocks of information on the left and right sides. The MLE Moodle site, on the other hand, includes just the most important information, rendered in a way that can be better viewed on the device. Although many new phones, such as the iPhone and Android models, also enable viewing of the Web-based Moodle site, the MLE Moodle site has more capabilities across multiple mobile devices and operating systems.

For instance, when viewed in a Web-based mobile emulator for a Sony K70 phone, the site looks as shown in Figure 4.6.

COURSE DESIGN AND COMMUNICATION

Once the Moodle site design was underway and the MLE Moodle plugin was installed, course design proceeded from the syllabus and the micro-cycle design model. A course Twitter feed was created (http://twitter.com/et597) to serve as the main communication portal and provide updates and resource links for students. These updates were scheduled through Twuffer (http://twuffer.com) and timed for automatic release during the micro-cycle periods (48 hours), providing an easy way for students to stay in touch and up-to-date on activities and assignments.

A YouTube channel for the course was also created to upload video and multimedia prepared for the course and to subscribe to feeds and link to favorites: http://www.youtube.com/user/ET597. Students would also be required to provide their cell phone numbers for SMS and MMS and could also contact instructors immediately through SMS.

Moodle provides additional ways to communicate. One very easy method is the messaging system, which can be used on the MLE Moodle site. However, a student needs to be logged in to Moodle to view or send messages. Discussion forums are another way Moodle provides communication, but this would be more of an asynchronous activity too. The course instructors plan on using the Moodle blogs for student reflections, which can also be accessed and updated on a mobile device.

It took much experimentation and checking back and forth between the Web-based Moodle site and the MLE Moodle site to make sure the mobile site rendered as well as the instructors wanted. For instance, when using ordered or unordered lists in the Web-based Moodle site, the MLE Moodle site rendered them as hashmarks (#). This was not visually pleasing, so the instructors modified the design of the Web-based site to render as well as possible in the MLE Moodle site. As can be expected, when designing for mobile devices and Web sites, design can never be perfect, but a focus of the MLE Moodle learning environment was to make it as visually appealing and easy to read as possible.

The instructors discovered some pleasant surprises along the way. They found out that Google Docs renders very well on a mobile device, so some of the documents and resources were placed and published in Google Docs and linked from the Moodle course site. Forms can be created in Google Docs Forms and render very well on a mobile device, allowing collection of online surveys and other forms. Also, more and more Web sites recognize mobile devices and render content for them very well. WordPress (http://wordpress.com) provides a very nice interface for the iPhone and Android devices.

The course textbook was available as a PDF online book, so these files were also made available to students to read either through the Web-based Moodle site or the mobile site. However, viewing a PDF file on a mobile device may not be the best use of this device and will require more study and feedback from students. Of course, reading from the book is always another option.

USING FRAME TO EVALUATE COURSE DESIGN

Haskell and Schroeder used the Framework for the Rational Analysis of Mobile Education (FRAME) (Koole, 2009) as an evaluation tool for their mobile learning course. This framework describes mobile learning as a "process resulting from the convergence of mobile technologies, human learning capacities, and social interaction" (p. 25) and is composed of three aspects that intersect: device, learner, and social. A visualization of this model is provided in the Venn diagram in Figure 4.7.

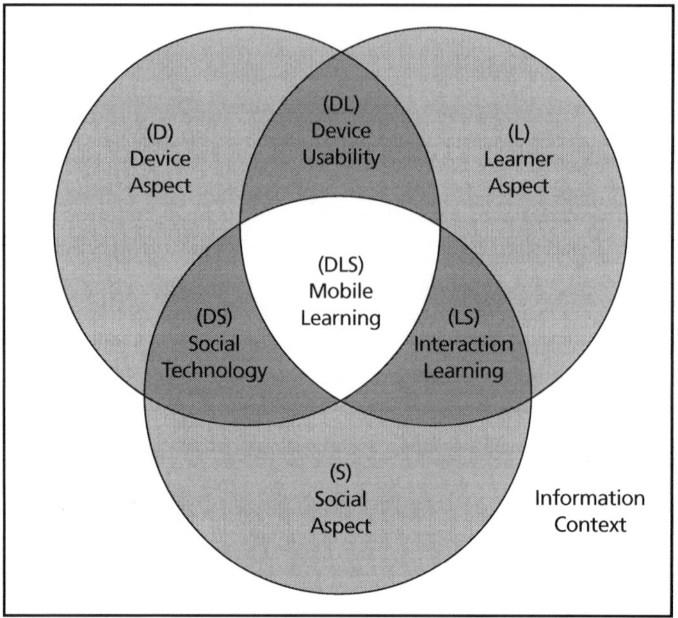

Figure 4.7 Koole's FRAME model (used with permission of the author).

Underlying this model is a constructivist epistemology: "collectively and individually, learners consume and create information" (Koole, 2009, p. 26). The purpose of this model is to guide instructors in developing excellent mobile learning materials and courses, helping them to reach the center intersection of the three circles in the Venn diagram, where ideal mobile learning occurs. This FRAME model proved to be very easy to use and helpful in evaluating the course both formatively and summatively through using the checklist provided in the Appendix (Koole, 2009). Students also will use the checklist in the course, to help them self-evaluate their culminating mobile learning activity.

CHALLENGES

Haskell and Schroeder experienced many challenges in designing a mobile course to teach mobile learning—from brainstorming and categorizing the mobile learning environment, identifying course objectives and hardware requirements, deciding upon the LMS and mobile component—to the final development of the course in Moodle.

For instance, much time was spent on analyzing and identifying key features of mobile learning, resulting in the micro-cycle model for course design. Student progress and experiences needed to be evaluated throughout the course, with instructor support available through the mobile interface. The instructors also had to view, confirm, and edit the MLE Moodle site multiple times to verify that it rendered well on mobile devices and included the required content.

Assessing student learning in a mobile environment has its own set of challenges. Hakell and Schroeder designed student pre- and postsurveys to be administered and analyzed, providing information about student skill improvement on mobile devices, student learning, and student success compared with the amount of mobile participation. This information will be used to evaluate course design and disseminate future research in the field of mobile learning.

CONCLUSION

How important is mobile learning? Mobile learning has the potential to improve face-to-face and online courses, providing the sense of presence that improves student satisfaction and success (Gunawardena & Zittle, 1997; Picciano, 2002; Richardson & Swan, 2003). Internet-enabled mobile devices are now powerful minicomputers, allowing users to access online resources and communicate from any location with cell phone service. The growth and popularity of mobile apps has also demonstrated the acceptance of accessing information on these portable devices (Kumar & Zahn, 2003; Siau & Shen, 2003).

Mobile learning can provide students with more options, from accessing course materials to communicating with instructors and classmates. Mobile learning can increase opportunities for those who lack a computer and Internet connection at home. Mobile learning can be interactive, self-initiated, and inquiry-based, promoting higher order thinking (Alexander, 2004; Ally, 2009; Sharples, 2000).

Is it difficult to integrate mobile learning in a course? The instructors suggest starting in small increments, first providing quick and easy ways for students to communicate with the instructors and classmates. For instance, instructors could provide a class Twitter feed that students could subscribe to, receiving up-to-date and instant alerts on their mobile devices. Another easy instant communication method is to set up a Google Voice number, allowing students to send text messages (SMS) to this number rather than giving out a personal cell phone number. After this, experiment with online components available through your school's LMS or use other options, such as a WordPress blog to post materials and encourage comments and feedback. As more and more sites offer mobile options, instructors will be able to use these for course communication and many other purposes. Enabling students to access a course using a mobile device could be a huge advantage over a course that only provides Web-based access.

How might we assess learning in a mobile environment? Since much learning is informal and situated, this is a challenging aspect of mobile learning. However, the authors empowered the students in the course by requiring self-assessments and the sharing of all coursework, to further enable self-assessment and progress. All assignments included rubrics, and were assessed by either a peer or instructor, or were self-assessed. A collaborative, iterative process of assessment and the ability to use personal inquiry for other avenues of learning should be an essential element of mobile learning.

Using mobile devices for learning is already happening. As the mobile ecosystem continues to develop, accessing information and learning with mobile devices will become more and more common. If universities and schools offer mobile portals and courses, they will be better positioned to tap into this expanding market.

REFERENCES

Alexander, B. (2004). Going nomadic: Mobile learning in higher education. *Educause Review, 39*(5), 28–35.

Ally, M. (2005). Using learning theories to design instruction for mobile learning devices. In J. Attewell & C. Saville-Smith (Eds.), *Mobile learning anytime everywhere: A book of papers from MLEARN 2004,* (pp. 5–8). London: Learning and Skills Development Agency.

Ally, M. (2009). *Mobile learning: Transforming the delivery of education and training.* Edmonton, AB: Athabasca Press.

Attewell, J. (2005). *Mobile technologies and learning.* London: Learning and Skills Development Agency.

Brown, M., & Diaz, V. (2010). Mobile learning: Context and prospects. A Report on the ELI Focus Session. Educause Learning Initiative. Retrieved from http://www.educause.edu/Resources/MobileLearningContextandProspe/204894

Burke, K. B., & Burke, K. (2009). *How to assess authentic learning.* Thousand Oaks, CA: Corwin Press.

Gunawardena, C. N., & Zittle, F. J. (1997). Social presence as a predictor of satisfaction within a computer-mediated conferencing environment. *American Journal of Distance Education, 11*(3), 8–26.

Haskell, C., & Schroeder, B. (2010). EDTECH 597: Mobile learning: Devices, applications, pedagogy. *Syllabus.* Retrieved from http://docs.google.com/View?id=dfp69sx9_48chs36tcz

Koole, M. L. (2009). A model for framing mobile learning. In M. Ally (Ed.), *Mobile learning: Transforming the delivery of education and training* (pp. 25–47). Edmonton, AB: Athabasca Press.

Kumar, S., & Zahn, C. (2003). Mobile communications: Evolution and impact on business operations. *Technovation, 23*(6), 515–520.

Newmann, F. M., & Wehlage, G. G. (1993). Five standards of authentic instruction. *Educational Leadership, 50*, 8–12.

Newmann, F., & Wehlage, G. (1995). *Successful school restructuring* (pp. 30–32). University of Wisconsin-Madison, Center on Organization and Restructuring of Schools.

O'Malley, C., Vavoula, G., Glew, J. P., Taylor, J., Sharples, M., & Lefrere, P. (2003). Guidelines for learning/teaching/tutoring in a mobile environment. *MOBIlearn deliverable D, 4.*

Picciano, A. G. (2002). Beyond student perceptions: Issues of interaction, presence, and performance in an online course. *Journal of Asynchronous Learning Networks, 6*(1), 21–40.

Richardson, J. C., & Swan, K. (2003). Examining social presence in online courses in relation to students' perceived learning and satisfaction. *Journal of Asynchronous Learning Networks, 7*(1), 68–88.

Sharples, M. (2000). The design of personal mobile technologies for lifelong learning. *Computers & Education, 34*(3–4), 177–193.

Sharples, M. (2002). Disruptive devices: Mobile technology for conversational learning. *International Journal of Continuing Engineering Education and Life Long Learning, 12*(5), 504–520.

Siau, K., & Shen, Z. (2003). Mobile communications and mobile services. *International Journal of Mobile Communications, 1*(1), 3–14.

Smith, S. D., Salaway, G., & Caruso, J. B. (2009). *The ECAR study of undergraduate students and information technology, 2009.* Boulder, CO: EDUCAUSE Center for Applied Research.

Traxler, J., & Kukulska-Hulme, A. (2005, October 28). Evaluating mobile learning: Reflections on current practice. *Proceedings of mLearn 2005: Mobile technology: The future of learning in your hands*, Cape Town, South Africa.

Vavoula, G. N. (2005). *D4.4: A study of mobile learning practices*: Internal report of MOBIlearn project.

Vavoula, G. N., & Sharples, M. (2002). KLeOS: A personal, mobile, knowledge and learning organisation system. *IEEE International Workshop on Wireless and Mobile Technologies in Education* (pp. 152–156). Los Alamitos, CA: IEEE Computer Society. doi: 10.1109/WMTE.2002.1039239

Vavoula, G., Sharples, M., Lonsdale, P., Rudman, P., & Meek, J. (2007). Learning bridges: A role for mobile technologies in education. *Educational Technology Magazine: The Magazine for Managers of Change in Education, 47*(3), 33–37.

Wiliam, D., Lee, C., Harrison, C., & Black, P. (2004). Teachers developing assessment for learning: Impact on student achievement. *Assessment in Education: Principles, Policy & Practice, 11*(1), 49–65.

Wilson, S., Liber, O., Johnson, M., Beauvoir, P., Sharples, P., & Milligan, C. (2007). Personal learning environments: Challenging the dominant design of educational systems. *Journal of e-Learning and Knowledge Society, 2*(3).

ABOUT THE AUTHORS

Chris Haskell serves as a special lecturer in the Department of Educational Technology at Boise State University; he specializes in instructing preservice teachers in methods and applications of technology integration in the classroom. In addition to instilling fundamental skills, Chris focuses on the use, adaptation, and implementation of emerging technologies in teacher education, including mobile communication devices, portable media players, social networking tools, virtual worlds, and gaming. Chris is a regular conference presenter in these emerging areas and continues to research and explore tools used by millennial students.

Dr. Barbara Schroeder is a clinical associate professor at Boise State University. She designs and teaches online courses for the Department of Educational Technology and is a strong advocate for digital equality in the schools and the workplace. Barbara co-hosts the Cool Teacher Podcast, authors her Technology Teacher blog, and leads the Moodle initiative for the Department of Educational Technology at Boise State.

CHAPTER 5

SUPPORTING DEVICES IN UBIQUITOUS LEARNING

Victor Jengchung Chen and Andree E. Widjaja

ABSTRACT

Various supporting devices can be used in ubiquitous learning. This chapter will present various devices that support ubiquitous learning. These devices can be divided into three main categories: dedicated devices, mobile devices, and supporting technology. Some examples of supporting devices and supporting technology covered in this section are considered from previous study conducted by many researchers on ubiquitous learning. Each supporting device is discussed in brief and illustrations are provided. The chapter will cover brief explanations on supporting devices such as PCs, notebooks, PDAs, smartphones, RFIDs, GPS, and other devices. Future trends and conclusions will be elaborated upon in the last part of chapter.

INTRODUCTION

Like a coin's two sides, both supporting devices and software are indispensable in conducting ubiquitous learning. Even though software seems very

Ubiquitous Learning, pages 79–105

important to an effective ubiquitous learning system, supporting devices also play a significant role in making it available. Various supporting devices, particularly computer devices, whether dedicated or mobile, can be used for ubiquitous learning. Other technology, such as positioning systems can be embedded in supporting devices for providing a more advanced and sophisticated ubiquitous learning system. This chapter's objective is to briefly discuss various devices that can support ubiquitous learning.

The first section begins with a background that discusses the several ubiquitous learning studies on the use of various supporting devices. The second section will discuss the various devices in more detail, for instance, the general introduction of those particular devices. Illustrations are also provided to visualize the device. The last section will elaborate on the future trends of the device along with the conclusion. In addition, references and definitions are also given.

Background

Recent developments in technology for computers for supporting learning has created many options in using varieties of ubiquitous learning supporting devices. These devices should fulfill main characteristics of computer supported ubiquitous learning (CSUL), which include permanency, accessibility, immediacy, interactivity, and situating instructional activities (Chen, Kao, Sheu, & Chiang, 2002). Initially, the use of technology to support learning may first come out of using computer devices such as personal computers (PCs) or television. However, as the most recent technology development has shifted to become mobile, mobile learning has become more popular. The term *ubiquitous learning environment* refers to allowing learning with various mobile devices such as PDAs, WebPads, Tablet PCs, or laptops in indoor, outdoor, individual, and group situations (Chen, Chang, & Wang, 2008).

Mobile technology in learning brings new paradigms for extending learning far beyond classroom walls without being limited by a school schedule (Huang, Lin, & Cheng, 2010). Compared with traditional classroom learning, mobile learning overcomes the limitations of learning time and space (Chih-Ming & Yi-Lun, 2009). In general, mobile technology advancement such as wireless communication, sensor, and mobile technologies provide new learning opportunities in both the real and digital worlds (Chu, Hwang, & Tsai, 2010). For example, a study called the Ambient Wood Project employs a novel approach to the designing and building of pervasive environments that are able to integrate both indoor and outdoor ubiquitous learning experiences (Rogers et al., 2005). Furthermore, this "nondesktop" technology opens a wide variety of opportunities for developing activities and interaction among learners (Fallahkhair, Pemberton, & Griffiths, 2007). We call this mobile learning (M-learning), which allows learning anywhere and anytime with ease of use (learning on the move) (Roschelle, 2003).

Mobile learning can also use audio devices such as an audio interpretation guide or a portable mp3 player using podcasting facilities (Gebbensleben, Dittman, & Vielhauer, 2006; Lee & Chan, 2006) to deliver digital audio content to learners. Even though it holds tremendous potential as a low-cost, low-barrier tool for mobile ubiquitous learning (Lee & Chan, 2006), audio itself may not be sufficient to promote learners interactivity with the devices or other learners in one environment. Therefore, incorporating sophisticated technology embedded in particular supporting devices such as mobile devices, learners are able to study real situations with computer support and sensor technology to be used for positioning services that are transmitted through a wireless signal, IrDA, GPS, Bluetooth, or radio frequency identification (RFID).

Several studies have used mobile technologies, mainly PDAs, to augment ubiquitous learning environments, for example, scaffold learning bird watching using handheld devices (Chen, Kao, & Sheu, 2003); musex PDA and RFID systems to support collaborative learning by children in museums (Yatani, Sugimoto, & Kusunoki, 2004); ubiquitous learning on pocket PCs using SCORM (Chang et al., 2005); a prototype for a zoo information system using PDAs containing RFID readers and WLAN cards (Hlavacs, Gelies, Blossey, & Klein, 2005); the development of Educational Resources (EULER) using PDAs based on RFID for outdoor teaching (Tan-Hsu, Tsung-Yu, & Chi-Cheng, 2007); personalized Knowledge Awareness Map (PERKAM) based on RFID technology to detect learners' environmental objects and location (El-Bishouty, Ogata, & Yano, 2007); ubiquitous learning environments with Educational Resources (ULEER) based on RFID and the Internet to assist school students (Ying & Yang, 2008), using mobile telephones for mobile learning to increase environmental awareness (Uzunboylu, Cavus, & Ercag, 2009); and PDAs equipped with the Mobile Plant Learning System (MPLS) to access plant information in facilitating student learning in an elementary school level botany course (Huang, et al., 2010).

In addition, some researchers are more concentrated on innovative language-learning support, such as the CLUE system as a computer-supported ubiquitous language-learning environment (Hiroaki & Yoneo, 2004), mobile-based (PDA) interactive language-learning environments for elementary school children learning English as a second language (Tan & Liu, 2004), cell phones to assist language learning (Collins, 2005), TAMALLE (television and mobile phone assisted language learning environment) (Fallahkhair et al., 2007), mobile English learning by PDA (Chen & Chung, 2008; Chen & Hsu, 2008), and development of personalized context-aware ubiquitous learning systems (PCLUS) implemented in PDAs for learning English vocabulary based on a Wireless positioning system (Chih-Ming & Yi-Lun, 2009). Other experimental studies designed a ubiquitous learning Web site, which is a Web-based learning system that can be accessed by various devices such as a desktop PCs, laptops, PDAs, or cell phones. This system can be used by learners to access any resources to improve their learning outcomes (Chen et al., 2008).

Up to now, many researchers agreed that mobile devices as well as wireless communication have become the most convenient way to access digital content from the Internet (Chu et al., 2010). Nevertheless, still there are many design challenges for this mobile learning concept, foremost concerning the limitation of mobile devices themselvees such as small screen, less powerful and less immersive content (Fallahkhair et al., 2007). Based on several studies on ubiquitous learning, it can be shown that various devices are used to support ubiquitous learning. This chapter discusses some ubiquitous learning supporting devices in three main parts. First is the dedicated device, second the mobile device, and third is the supporting technology device.

DEDICATED DEVICES

Interactive Television

Interactive television (iTV) is not a new concept (Gawlinski, 2003). Since the 1950s, although it was very limited, television production has striven to create dynamic environments where viewers have some interaction with the programs they watch. Thus, interactive television can be defined as anything that allows viewers and the people providing the show, channel, or service to engage in a more active experience such as making choices or taking actions (Gawlinski, 2003). Interaction needs the active participation of the viewers so that a dynamic environment can be created.

In the past, there were many ways to create interactivities. For example, by asking the viewers to be involved in the program. Another way is using phone calls to interact with viewers in real time. However, sophisticated technology development nowadays has made interactive television more real. For instance, digital transmission allows transmitting more bandwidth for broadcasting, hence delivering much more information as well as sending back information to the television company. Therefore viewers can directly interact in new and exciting ways with television producers. There are different types of interactive television, such as electronic program guides (EPGs), Teletext-style services, walled gardens, Internet on television, enhanced television, video on demand, and personal video recorders (Gawlinski, 2003).

One of the most important and useful types of interactive television is EPGs (Gawlinski, 2003). This service provides complete menu listings of various programs to the viewer. Viewers can select the program they want to watch by clicking on their television remote. The service usually includes the schedule and the program information, which can replace TV magazines or newspapers. The other important type is enhanced television. In this type, viewers would have more options for the program they watch. For example, the viewer can choose whether they want to have full narration on the program or not. Besides, it is also possible to jump into particular scenes that viewers wants to watch.

Compared with mobile devices, iTV provides rich multimedia presentations of authentic as well as immersive content, which is consistently renewed (Fallahkhair et al., 2007). Such programs provided in iTV would certainly enhance the learning experience. The term *t-learning* refers to TV-based interactive learning (Pazos-Arias, 2007). Little research on iTV for supporting learning has been conducted. One project developed is called TAMALLE (television and mobile phone assisted language-learning environment) (Fallahkhair et al., 2007). Figures 5.1 and 5.2 shows the TAMALLE system proposed in the research. This research aims to develop a cross-platform ubiquitous learning service via iTV and mobile phones, and results show that it is a usable, useful, and desirable tool to support informal language learning. Other research tried to build frameworks for developing and deploying t-learning services, which promote interoperability as well as reusability in using Interactive Digital Television Medium (IDTV) (Pazos-Arias, 2007).

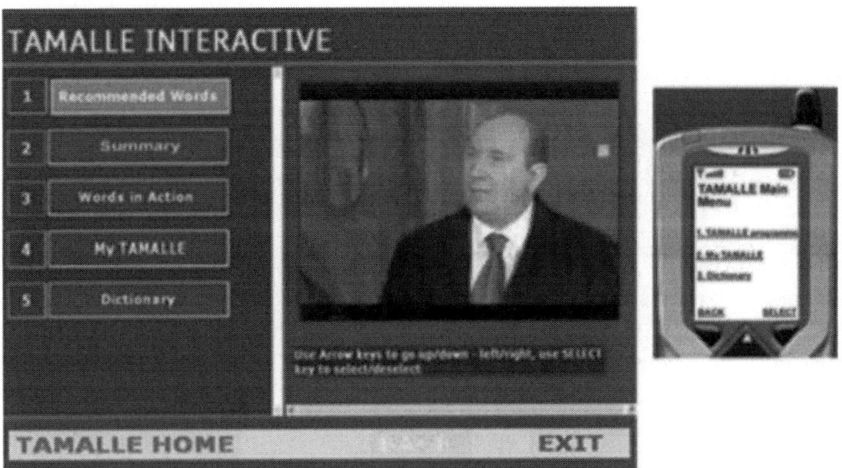

Figure 5.1 TAMALLE main menu (Fallahkhair, et al., 2007).

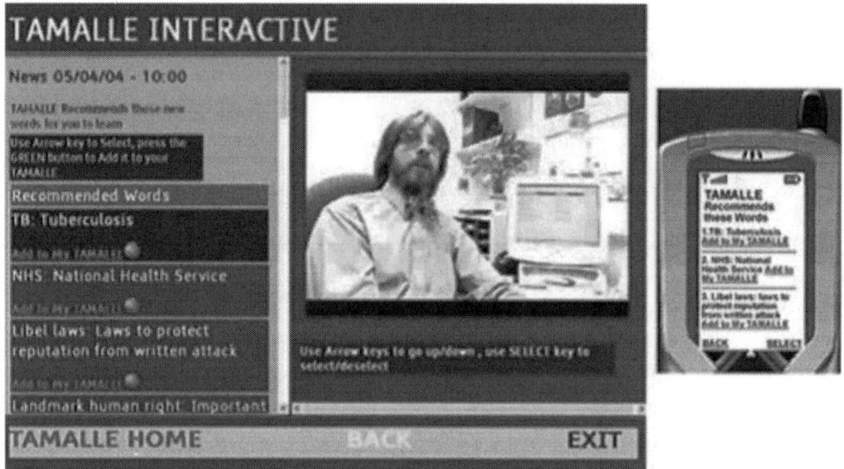

Figure 5.2 TAMALLE interactive system (Fallahkhair, et al., 2007).

Apple Computer

Apple Computer, Inc. is an American computer technology corporation and has been a major player in the evolution of personal computing since its founding in 1976. The Apple I (1976) was the first computer with a single circuit board. The first home computer with a graphical user interface (GUI) was known as Apple Lisa (Bellis, 2010; Fact-index, 2010). In the 1970s, Apple developed the very first graphical user interface in conjunction with the Xerox Corporation at their Palo Alto Research Center (PARC). Products from Apple range from operating systems such as Pro DOS, Mac OS, and A/UX networking products such as AppleTalk and the multimedia program QuickTime. Discontinued products include the Apple Power Mac G4 Cube and the Apple Newton handheld computer (David, 2010; Evans, 2010). More recent products include the Apple AirPort, which uses Wireless LAN technology to connect computers of different brands to the Internet without wires. There is also the iBook and G4 Personal Desktop Computer. In early 2002, Apple unveiled its one-piece designed iMac. It has a hemispherical base and a 15-inch flat panel all-digital display, supported by a shiny neck that serves as the handle. More recently, Apple introduced the Mac OS X, a new version of their operating system that finally marries the stability, reliability, and security of Unix with the ease of use of the Macintosh interface in an OS targeted at professionals and consumers alike. Apple no doubt can be used as an excellent ubiquitous learning platform. Figure 5.3 shows an Apple computer.

Figure 5.3 iMac 27 inch.

Personal Computer (PCs)

Personal computers, popularly known as PCs, are considered the most common computer device for personal use. The principle characteristic of PCs is the single-user system based on microprocessor technology, which enables an entire CPU on a single chip (Webopedia, 2010). Its functions include word processing, desktop publishing, spreadsheets, games, and an excellent platform for u-learning. The first PCs were introduced by Apple in the late 1970s, with the Apple II, introduced in 1977. It was the first and the most popular model of the time. Then, in 1981, IBM launched its first PC products, the IBM 5100, which later became the standard for the next generation of personal computer.

Though PCs are not mobile, they are largely used for u-learning at certain dedicated places such as the home, office, school, university, and elsewhere. They can also be connected through Local Area Network (LAN) and the Internet to access material needed for u-learning. In general, PCs have more computing power, higher performance, as well as incredible visual graphics presentation as compared with other devices, say notebooks, PDAs, or smartphones. However, it also depends on the particular specifications required. There are a lot of options to make our own PCs depending on budget and desires. There is a variety of supporting devices for custom PCs, starting from very cheap to extremely expensive products that have excellent quality. Moreover, built-up PCs are also an option, though they are generally more expensive.

PCs can be composed of many components that integrate well together. Nowadays, there are rapid developments in PC supporting devices, especially as far as central processing units (CPU), random access memory (RAM), and graphics processing unit (GPU). The CPU is the most important part of a PC. It is the central brain, doing complex calculations. There are two major brands available: Intel (www.intel.com) and AMD (www.amd.com). Both companies offer high performance CPUs. The latest Intel innovation is known as the Core i7 and i5 platform, which is a brand new multicore processor design with incredible processing speed compared with its predecessor. AMD offers the latest AMD Phenom II platform. This platform is the multicore processor upgrade from its predecessor, AMD Phenom. However, other than this flagship CPU, both brands also offer various cheaper platforms that are considered still adequate to be used for conducting u-learning. For example, Intel Pentium or Celeron are acceptable CPUs, but budget priced. Meanwhile, AMD also offers the Athlon64 and Sempron64 series for the budget CPU.

Along with CPUs, RAM technology has developed quite fast. The function of RAM is as a buffer memory to store data temporarily before and after it has been processed in the CPU. Large-capacity buffers and high-speed RAM are crucial to making sure that data flow in and out of the CPU is not impeded. Currently, the most-used RAM technology is DDR3. It has the fastest speed as well as a large capacity to accommodate enormous data flow. The GPU is also important in presenting stunning graphics on your monitor. The technological development of GPUs is also very fast. In the market, at least each year there are new products equipped with the most current sophisticated technology available. Two major GPU manufacturers are NVidia and ATi. Both companies have done extensive research on GPUs for delivering the best visual experience, particularly in presenting u-learning multimedia material. NVidia, with its GeForce series has dominated the market for a long time. The GeForce series' durability and technological innovation has been trusted to deliver the best graphics among its competitors. In ATi products, Radeon is also famous for its performance, product ranges, and budget prices. PCs equipped with adequate specifications can run many applications required for u-learning. Figure 5.4 shows a desktop personal computer.

Figure 5.4 Personal computer.

MOBILE DEVICES

Audio and Multimedia Interpretation Guide

Audio and multimedia interpretation guides are commonly used for guiding activities or explaining something in the real world, both indoors and outdoors. These guides have been particularly designed for educational or learning purposes, the need of interpretation, as well as enriching visitors' experiences on the site. They can be used in various places, and they don't require the purchase or extensive installation of any additional components in or around objects (Gebbensleben et al., 2006). In general, it is composed of interpretive audio tours or other self-guided audio and audio-visual experiences, depending on which system package is chosen. Museums, historic sites, and cultural attractions are a few of the many places that use this device to enhance the visitor's learning experience. Furthermore, multimedia enrichment may also be embedded in the system, such as music, images, video, sound effects, as well as archival audio or audio-visual material. Besides that, if visitors own mobile smartphones, they can experience learning by uploading an audio guide at a single point of entry and store it on their personal devices (Gebbensleben et al., 2006).

For example, in a museum, audio and multimedia are very useful tools to guide visitors, delivering short or comprehensive explanations of various museum collections. The audio explanations are prerecorded in high-quality audio, which is transmitted through high fidelity earphones. Besides, if the tour is guided, the device also can function as a wireless device for transmitting audio explanations directly from the tour guide in real time. This group-tour function uses multiple frequencies so that you can choose any program you want.

In addition, it can also come with different languages that can be set according to the user's preference. Its mobility as well as ease of use make it comfortable to use anytime an explanation is needed on certain objects or places. Therefore, this device has become an excellent tool for u-learning when visiting particular places, providing knowledge on the objects or places visited. Some of the systems are Antenna Audio (www.antennaaudio.com) and accousticguide (www.acousticguide.com). Many famous places use audio and multimedia guides, such as the Taipei 101 Observatory, the National Palace Museum, and the Chimei Museum in Taiwan. Figures 5.5 and 5.6 show these devices.

Figure 5.5 Antenna Audio used at National Palace Museum and Chimei Museum, Taiwan.

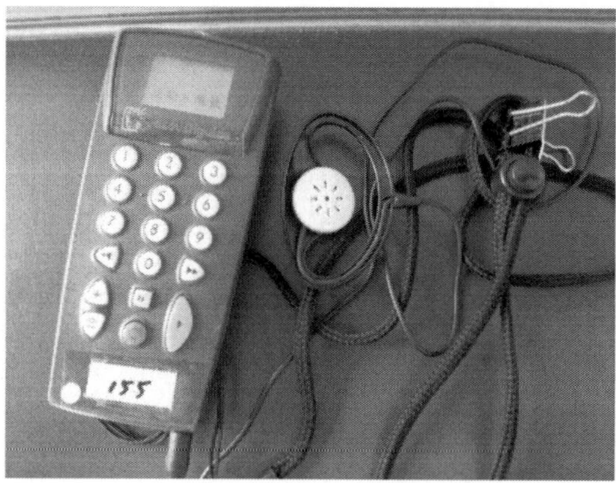

Figure 5.6 Accoustiguide used at National Palace Museum, Taiwan.

One of the most advanced products developed by acousticguide is called the Opus series. It has been specifically designed for on-site presentation equipped with newly sophisticated technology. It provides rich digital multimedia resources such as video, images, and animation rather than traditional audio. Opus is also equipped with excellent computing capabilities and easily operated functions. It can play high-resolution graphic images and digital movies. The more advanced Opus series came out with new touch screen series. Certainly, stunning graphics as well as CD-quality sound would enhance a visitor's learning experience.

Podcast (Portable mp3 Player)

Mp3 technology was designed in the early 1990s and first appeared on the market in 1998. Through technology advances, it enabled minimal storage capacity, however during the 2000s, flash-drive memory was replaced with hard drives in portable mp3 players. This allows for storage of thousands of songs on one device. An mp3 file is a way for encoding musical files in a format that can be played on other supporting devices such as the computers or on a portable player, even the iPod.

Some functions of mp3s are the same as a regular CDs, however, with an mp3, the music is compressed to a much smaller size. The advantage of compression allows the user to store a relatively larger amount of music compared with a traditional CD. To the same extent, it impacts the audio quality. The iPod, coupled with iTunes, led the market and revolutionized portable mp3 player style and technology. Mp3s create a compromise between the size of the file and quality of the sound. More compression gives the user smaller file sizes, but also sacrifices audio quality.

Due to emerging trends in portable information technology, such as iPod and smartphones, e-users can easily download their favorite audio/video programs from popular content management and distribution software such as iTunes. The ease of publication, ease of subscription, and ease of use across multiple environments, typically over computer speakers, over a car stereo, and over headphones, drives the popularization of podcasting. The Web address of the media file is contained in the enclosure tag of an item in the XML file. The enclosure tag was added to the RSS 2.0 standard in 2004, making podcasting possible. iTunes acts as a content aggregator as well as media player, where users can download desired content and synchronize it with their iPod. Podcasting is not limited only to iPod, but can be used with other portable mp3 devices as well as traditional computers (Cosper, 2010; Orden, 2008; Rosenberger, 2010). Podcasting can be an alternative way to support ubiquitous learning. Figure 5.7 shows a portable mp3 player.

Figure 5.7 Portable mp3 player.

Cell Phone

Cell phones were born through the combination of radio and technology. It enables communication not limited by location. The basic principal of the cell phone is the same as a CB radio or a walkie talkie. Cell phones have low-power transmitters. Moreover, through the cellular approach, which requires a large number of base stations in a city of any size, a typical large city can have hundreds of towers, and because so many people use cell phones, costs remain low per user. Each carrier in each city also runs one central office called the Mobile Telephone Switching Office (MTSO). This office handles all of the phone connections to the normal land-based phone system and controls all of the base stations in the region (Brain, Tyson, & Layton, 2008).

The FCC approved the analog cell phone standard called AMPS (Advanced Mobile Phone System) in 1983, which enables AMPS to use a range of frequencies between 824 megahertz (MHz) and 894 MHz for analog cell phones.

A version of AMPS,.known as Narrowband Advanced Mobile Phone Service (NAMPS), incorporates digital technology to allow the system to carry about three times as many calls as the original version. AMPS and NAMPS operate only in the 800-MHz band range and do not offer many of the fea-

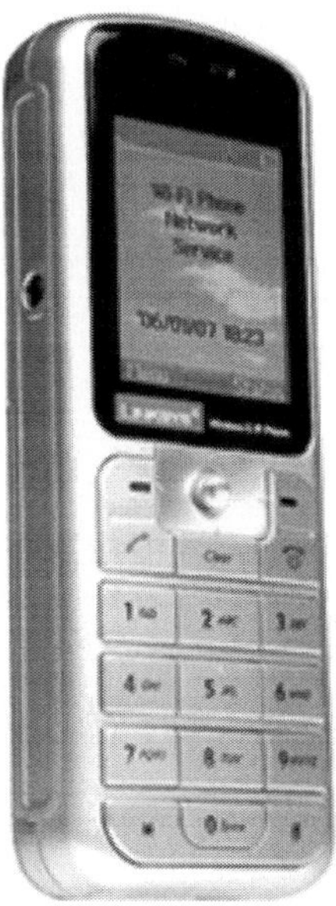

Figure 5.8 Typical cell phone.

tures common in digital cellular service, such as e-mail and Web browsing. Digital cell phones are the second generation (2G) of cellular technology (Brain et al., 2008).

Up to now, cell phone technology has developed rapidly. Many models with different bands embedded with various sophisticated technology such as Nokia, Sony Ericsson, and Samsung, are the major players in cell phone world. Moreover, the "generational" level has rapidly expanded into 3G, 3.5G, and even 4G, which offer unprecedented data transmission. With this high bandwidth data transmission, cell phone functions are not only merely communication devices, but also support many other functions, such as ubiquitous learning. Figure 5.8 shows a typical cell phone.

Personal Digital Assistance (PDA)

The original type of PDA, Palm Pilot, was designed by Jeff Hawkins in the late 1980s. However, the term *personal digital assistant* was generally promoted by Apple CEO John Sculley in January 1992, during the introduction of the Apple Message Pad (which later became known as the Newton). In the initial stage of PDA development, Apple Newton was the most famous model. However, some weaknesses such as its large size, short battery life, and poor handwriting recognition had to be taken care of (BAPCO Journal, 2008; freepatentsonline, 2010; Freudenrich & Carmack, 2010).

Originally, PDAs were designed as organizers, but to date, many features have been added to cater to the demands of a modern world, for example to retrieve or send e-mail, download information from the Internet, and in general do word processing and play music or video games. PDAs sold at a record-breaking rate—20 million—mostly from one company, Palm Computing. Basically, handheld devices run on one of two operating systems: the Palm OS and Hand-spring Visor devices, and the Windows CE used by the Compaq IPAQ and HP Jornada. Palm machines are less expensive than those that operate with the Pocket PC. All handheld devices come with a basic suite of programs: a diary, address book, to-do list, and memo pad.

In general, the PDA is a handheld device that provides electronic versions of the functions one would expect of a paper-based personal organizer, such as a diary, calendar, address book, to-do lists, note and memo pads, and clock. PDAs based on standard operating systems have become popular for mobile information systems (Hlavacs et al., 2005). PDAs can be used in various situations, for example, for providing general information about displayed items at museums or exhibitions from large companies or universities, or navigational assistance (Hlavacs et al., 2005). Moreover, PDAs have been widely used to support ubiquitous learning. Some of them combined PDAs with RFIDs or wireless technology and even cameras. Figure 5.9 shows a PDA ubiquitous learning system, equipped with RFIDs and cameras to support outdoor learning. Meanwhile, Figure 5.10 shows how a PDA system works in amobile plant learning system.

Figure 5.9 Ubiquitous learning device that consist of a PDA, RFID reader, camera, and RFID tags (Tan-Hsu, et al., 2007).

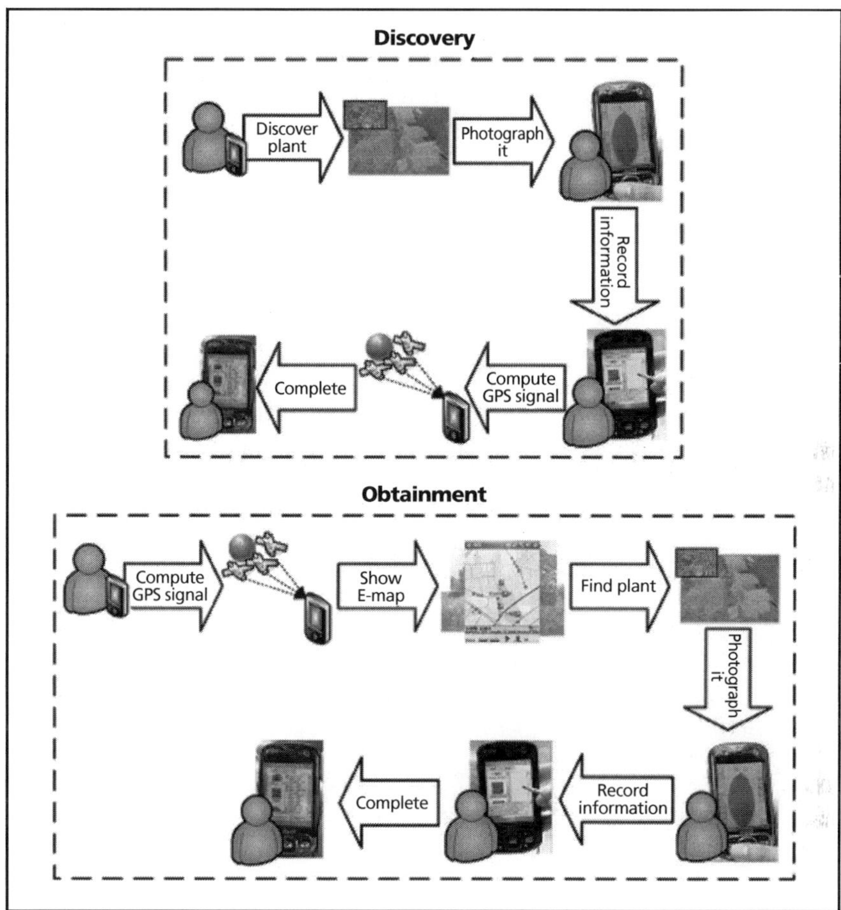

Figure 5.10 Mobile plant learning system uses a PDA (Huang et al., 2010).

Smartphone

The smartphone is an emerging mobile phone technology that supports Java program execution and provides both short-range wireless connectivity (Bluetooth) and cellular network connectivity through which the Internet can be accessed. Besides traditional voice communication and messaging functionality, in terms of personal communication, it enables the user borderless access to information. Simply put, it adds phone functions—"smart" capabilities—to already capable PDAs. Smartphones provide a rich set of tools, enabling control and interaction with varied environments by embedded systems located in their proximity (Ballagas, Borchers, Rohs, & Sheridan, 2006; Iftode, Cristian, Ravi, Kang, & Zhou, 2004).

There are four modes of interaction between a smartphone and the surrounding environment, namely universal remote control, dual connectivity, gateway connectivity, and peer-to-peer. However, each of these modes has different characteristics. Due to the hybrids of mobile phones and PDAs, smartphones have many similarities with PDA devices and use some of the same technologies. Like PDAs, smartphones can also be connected to wireless Internet, GPRS, or RFIDs to support ubiquitous learning systems. Figure 5.11 shows a smartphone.

Another excellent example of the smartphone is the iPhone from Apple (Figure 5.12). It is best known as the smartphone line released in 2007 by Apple Inc., based in Cupertino, California. Apple's iPhone popularized the use of touch screens as a primary interface for a mobile phone. Beyond the

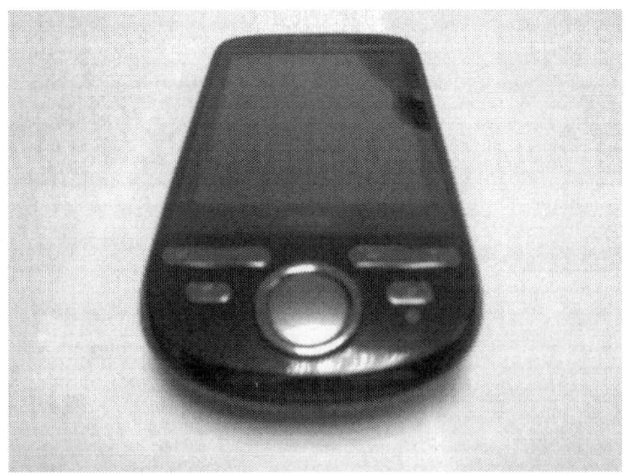

Figure 5.11 HTC PDA.

Figure 5.12 Apple iPhone.

aspects standard in most smartphones such as Internet connectivity and messaging, the iPhone's features can be divided into three main groups: supporting device, media, and applications. The iPhone's supporting device has been one of its biggest draws. Based around touch screen technology, the iPhone does not have a keypad, instead, a virtual keyboard and keypad are displayed on the touch screen when required (roseIndia, 2008; wiseGEEK, 2010). Figure 5.12 shows an Apple iPhone connected to Internet accessing e-learning Moodle.

Blackberry

Blackberry is one leading smartphone, developed by Canadian company Research in Motion (RIM), which has many unique features, including its ability to always connect wherever and whenever, as long as it is withn proximity of the surrounding network. This sophisticated device features many variants, such as the Pearl, Bold, Curve, Tour, and Storm (www.blackberry.com). Current Blackberry key technology features are its support of Wi-Fi, 3G, and also GPS, depending on the model.

There are also various software applications embedded in a Blackberry device for daily tasks, whether personal or business. Moreover, the software can also be personalized with games, social networking applications, themes, personal productivity, and many more. Like PDAs or other smartphones, it can be connected online to Internet resources without time or place constraints (Chen et al., 2008), Blackberry can be a very good device to support ubiquitous learning. Figure 5.13 shows a Blackberry.

Figure 5.13 A Blackberry device.

Notebook or Laptop

A notebook computer is a battery- or AC-powered personal computer, smaller than a briefcase, which can easily be transported and conveniently used in temporary spaces such as airplanes, libraries, temporary offices, and at meetings. A notebook computer, sometimes called a laptop computer, typically weighs less than 5 pounds and is 3 inches or less in thickness. Among the best-known makers of notebook and laptop computers are IBM, Apple, Compaq, Dell, Toshiba, and Hewlett-Packard (Alpert-Sandler, 1999; Articlesbase, 2007; About.com, 2010).

Somehow, the terms *laptop* and *notebook* are quite confusing. The history of it began in 1979–1980, when Bill Moggridge of GRiD Systems Corp. designed one of the first laptops and named it the GRiD Compass 1101. In 1989, Compaq introduced Compaq LTE, which was a smaller model, about the size of an A4 sheet of notebook paper, and later on came to be known as a notebook computer or notebook. Thereafter, the terms laptop and notebook began to be used interchangeably. Nevertheless, notebook and laptop are incorrect terms, as due to the heat, many laptops cannot be placed on top of the lap, and most notebooks are not the size of an A4 sheet of notebook paper. However, what manufacturers usually call a notebook, end-users prefer to call a laptop, hence, both the terms are used.

Notebook computers generally cost more than desktop computers with the same capabilities because they are more difficult to design and manufacture. A notebook can effectively be connected into peripheral input/output devices such as a printer or a desktop-style monitor. More conveniently, the less capable port replicator allows connection to a number of peripherals through a single plug. Notebooks usually come with displays that use thin-screen technology. The thin-film transistor, or active-matrix screen, is brighter and views better at different angles than the STN or dual-scan screen. Notebooks use several different approaches for integrating a mouse into the keyboard, including the touch pad, the trackball, and the pointing stick. A serial port also allows a regular mouse to be attached. Notebooks are commonly used for ubiquitous learning. Figure 5.14 shows a notebook.

Apple iPad

The Apple iPad is a half inch thin, weighing 1.5 pounds, with a 9.7-inch IPS display; therefore it is in between a laptop and a multimedia digital mobile phone device or between an iPhone and an Apple MAC laptop. It is available in six models, with 16GB, 32GB, and 64GB capability, with or without 3G connectivity. All models offer WiFi. The various applications in-

Figure 5.14 Acer notebook.

clude browsing the Internet, manage and store photos, watch movies, listen to songs, access iTunes, download apps and games, play games, browse Web sites, watch YouTube videos, and much more. Safari, Internet, mail, photos, videos, YouTube, iTunes, AppStore, iBooks, maps, notes, calendar, contacts, search, and lots more are the key features of an iPad.

Thanks to Multi-Touch technology, the larger iPad surface was completely reengineered, making it extremely precise and responsive. With its lithium-polymer battery, the iPad can be used for up to 10 hours while surfing the Web on Wi-Fi, watching videos, or listening to music. The iPad runs a version of the iPhone operating system and, as a result, can run programs from the AppStore. Another application is an upscale of its size to fill its entire screen (newer apps can be written to fit its larger dimensions). The iPad is the first Apple product to employ the A4, a new processor developed by Apple. The iPad's processor runs at 1 Ghz. The iPad is possibly more attractive to general users than to more dedicated e-readers. As to the ease of formatting and typography on the system, it might also be more attractive to publishers. The iPad is no doubt a transformative device, though it's left itself some room to grow in future versions (Costello, 2010; Hiroshi, 2010; Naone, 2010; Truong, 2010). Furthermore, the iPad can also be comfortably used for ubiquitous learning. Figure 5.15 shows an iPad, which can access e-learning systems.

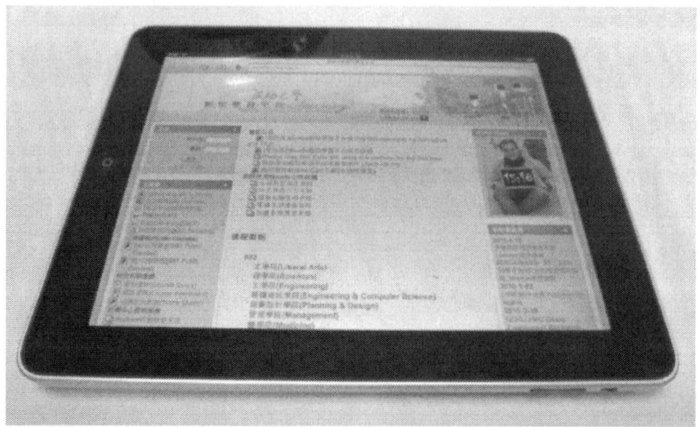

Figure 5.15 Apple iPad.

SUPPORTING TECHNOLOGY

Wireless LAN

Regarding aspects of design, extension, and default, 802.11 Wireless Local Area Network (WLAN) is a critical element in all enterprise networks. To be part of the overall network design, it requires office workers to have a wireless option. Mobile users can extend their reach by using wireless networks wherever they are available, including in public places, in a prospect's conference room, or at home. One of the advantages of 802.11 WLANs is their ability to dynamically adjust to changing conditions and to configure themselves to make the best use of available bandwidth. These capabilities work best, however, when the problems they address are kept within limits. The WLAN technology is defined by the IEEE 802.11 family of specifications. There are currently four specifications in the family: 802.11, 802.11a, 802.11b, and 802.11g (Network dictionary, 2010; Javvin, 2010; WildPackets, 2010). Wireless LAN is used by mobile devices or computers to connect to the Internet or LAN for supporting ubiquitous learning. Figure 5.16 shows a wireless LAN device system.

RFID

RFID (Radio-Frequency Identification) refers to small electronic devices that consist of a small chip and an antenna. By providing a unique identifier for that object, an RFID device functions as a bar code or a magnetic strip on the back of a credit card or ATM card. The chip typically is capable of

Figure 5.16 Wireless LAN system.

carrying 2,000 bytes of data or less. The bar code or magnetic strip must be scanned to get the information, then the RFID device retrieves the identifying information (Technovelgy, 2010).

Many types of RFIDs exist, but at the highest level, we can divide RFID devices into two classes: active and passive. Active tags require a power source—they're either connected to a powered infrastructure or use energy stored in an integrated battery. Passive RFIDs are of interest because the tags don't require batteries or maintenance. A passive tag consists of three parts: an antenna, a semi and protects the antenna and chip from environmental conditions or reagents. The tags also have an indefinite operational life and are small enough to fit into a practical adhesive label. An RFID is generally used to provide location service in ubiquitous learning systems. Figure 5.17 shows an RFID tag.

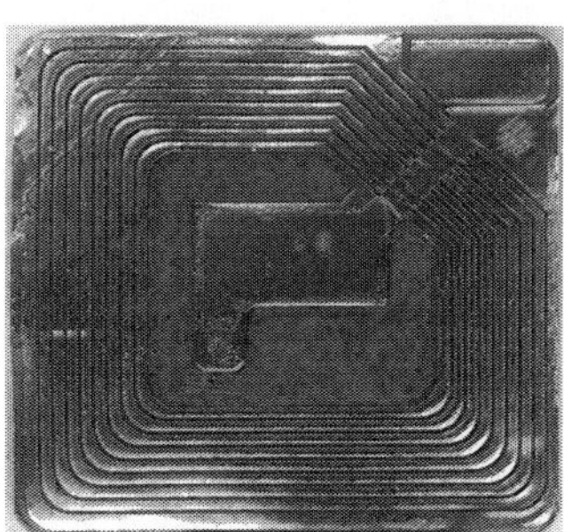

Figure 5.17 RFID tag.

Figure 5.18 A GPS device.

Global Positioning System

The Global Positioning System (GPS) is a navigation and precise-positioning tool. Developed by the Department of Defense in 1973, the purpose of the original design was to assist soldiers, military vehicles, planes, and ships in accurately determining their locations worldwide. Currently, the uses of GPS have extended to include both the commercial and scientific worlds. Satellites (SVs) transmit a signal deploying their own unique ID code, ephemeris data, and almanac data. The ephemeris data contains information about the position of the satellite, along with the current date and time. The signal is an important part to determine a position. The almanac data indicates where all the SVs are supposed to be in orbit at that given moment.

The GPS receiver takes this information and, making dozens of calculations per second, finds your position. Individuals may purchase GPS handsets, which are readily available through commercial retailers. Equipped with these GPS receivers, users can accurately locate where they are and easily navigate to where they want to go. A GPS can be used to assist ubiquitous learning systems for giving location service (Glasscoe, 1998; gpscity, 2010; Smithsonian, 1998). Figure 5.18 shows a GPS device.

FUTURE TRENDS

As the technology has shifted from dedicated to mobile, we can consider that it is already a common way to achieve ubiquitous learning using mobile devices, for example PDAs, smartphones, or notebooks. Undeniably, the growth of mobile technology is very rapid. We can see many new technologies that have been used in mobile devices introduced to the market. For instance, Apple launched its breakthrough iPad. Soon thereafter, it became one of the most popular portable computer on the market. With its capability to connect to the Internet as well as run various application software programs, it is one supporting device that is very suitable for conducting ubiquitous learning. As research has advanced ubiquitous learning through the use of PDAs, pocket PCs, cell phones, television, and many other supporting devices, in the future, these mobile devices will replace the dedicated device such as television or PCs for conducting ubiquitous learning, since the capabilities of these mobile devices have become better and better. Therefore, ubiquitous learning through mobile devices is no longer a realm of research, but a reality that will only grow over the next several years. In researching ubiquitous learning, more emphasis will be placed on using new supporting devices as they are introduced to the market.

CONCLUSION

This chapter presents various devices, both dedicated and mobile, that can be used to support ubiquitous learning. Based on studies, and as mobile technology has become more popular, mobile devices seem a more common support for ubiquitous learning. However, dedicated devices such as PCs or television can still be a good alternative, even though research proves the trend toward mobile devices such as PDAs to promote ubiquitous learning systems. This trend will become more apparent in the next several years as many new mobile supporting devices will be introduced to the market. Moreover, other supporting technology like RFID, wireless, or GPS will become more mature and can be embedded in the supporting devices as well as other software in order to create sophisticated ubiquitous learning systems. Indeed, learners will have more options to do their learning with the aid of supporting devices with more advanced technology.

REFERENCES

About.com. (2010). *History of laptop computers.* Retrieved from http://inventors.about.com/library/inventors/bllaptop.htm

Alpert-Sandler, B. (1999). *Notebook computer.* Retrieved from http://searchmobilecomputing.techtarget.com/definition/notebook-computer

Articlesbase. (2007). *Types of notebook computers.* Retrieved from http://www.articlesbase.com/computers-articles/types-of-notebook-computers-162303.html

Ballagas, R., Borchers, J., Rohs, M., & Sheridan, J. G. (2006). *The smart phone: A ubiquitous input device. IEEE Pervasive Computing, 5,* 1.

BAPCO Journal. (2008). *PDAs for everyday use.* Retrieved from http://www.bapco-journal.com/news/fullstory.php/aid/1198/PDAs_for_everyday_use.html

Bellis, M. (2010). *The history of Apple computers.* Retrieved from http://inventors.about.com/od/cstartinventions/a/Apple_Computers.htm

Brain, M., Tyson, J., & Layton, J. (2008). *How cell phones work.* Retrieved from http://www.howstuffworks.com/cell-phone.htm

Chang, H.-P., Chang, W.-C., Sie, Y.-L., Lin, N. H., Huang, C.-H., Shih, T. K. et al. (2005). Ubiquitous learning on pocket SCORM. *Lecture Notes in Computer Science, 3823*: Springer Berlin.

Chen, C. M., & Chung, C. J. (2008). Personalized mobile English vocabulary learning system based on item response theory and learning memory cycle. *Computers & Education, 51,* 624–645.

Chen, C. M., & Hsu, S. H. (2008). Personalized intelligent m-learning system for supporting effective English learning. *Educational Technology & Society, 11*(3), 153–180.

Chen, G. D., Chang, C. K., & Wang, C. Y. (2008). Ubiquitous learning Website: Scaffold learner by mobile devices with information-ware techniques *Computers & Education, 50*(1), 77–90.

Chen, Y. S., Kao, T. C., &, Sheu, J. P. (2003). A mobile learning system for scaffolding bird watching learning. *Journal of Computer Assisted Learning, 19*(1), 347–359.

Chen, Y. S., Kao, T. C., Sheu, J. P., & Chiang, C. Y. (2002, August 29–30). *A mobile scaffolding-aid-based bird-watching learning system.* Paper presented at the proceedings of the International Workshop on Wireless and Mobile Technologies in Education, Los Alamitos, CA.

Chih-Ming, C., & Yi-Lun, L. (2009). Personalised context-aware ubiquitous learning system for supporting effective English vocabulary learning. *Interactive Learning Environments, 18*(4), 1–24.

Chu, H.-C., Hwang, G.-J., & Tsai, C.-C. (2010). A knowledge engineering approach to developing mindtools for context-aware ubiquitous learning. *Computers & Education, 54,* 289–297.

Collins, T. G. (2005, July 5–8). *English class on the air: Mobile language learning with cell phones.* Paper presented at the proceedings of the Fifth IEEE International Conference on Advanced Learning Technologies, Kaohsiung, Taiwan.

Cosper, A. (2010). *The history of portable mp3 player.* Retrieved from http://www.ehow.com/about_5409458_history-portable-mp-players.html

Costello, S. (2010). *What is the iPad?* Retrieved from http://ipod.about.com/od/glossary/g/ipad-defintion.htm

David, N. (2010). Apple computer: A new trend setter in computer world. *Computer Full.* Retrieved from http://www.computerfull.com/173/apple-computer-a-new-trend-setter-in-computer-world/

El-Bishouty, M. M., Ogata, H., & Yano, Y. (2007). PERKAM: Personalized knowledge awareness map for computer supported ubiquitous learning. *Educational Technology & Society, 10*(3); 122–134.

Evans, J. R. (2010). *Advantages and features of Mac computers.* Retrieved from http://www.ideamarketers.com/?Advantages_and_features_of_Mac_computers&articleid=449807

Fact-index. (2010). *Apple computer.* Retrieved from http://www.fact-index.com/a/ap/apple_computer.html#Pre-history

Fallahkhair, S., Pemberton, L., & Griffiths, R. (2007). Development of a cross-platform ubiquitous language learning service via mobile phone and interactive television. *Journal of Computer Assisted Learning, 23,* 312–325.

freepatentsonline. (2010). *Method and apparatus for a virtual display/keyboard for a PDA.* Retrieved from http://www.freepatentsonline.com/6266048.html

Freudenrich, C., & Carmack, C. (2010). *How PDAs work.* Retrieved from http://electronics.howstuffworks.com/gadgets/travel/pda.htm

Gawlinski, M. (2003). *Interactive television production.* Oxford, UK: Focal Press.

Gebbensleben, S., Dittman, J., & Vielhauer, C. (2006, January 15–19). *Multimodal audio guide for museums and exhibitions.* Paper presented at the 18th annual IS&T/SPIE Symposium on Electronic Imaging, San Jose, CA.

Glasscoe, M. (1998). *What is GPS?* Retrieved from http://scign.jpl.nasa.gov/learn/gps1.htm

gpscity. (2010). *What is GPS?* Retrieved from http://www.gpscity.com/support/whatisgps

Hiroaki, O., & Yoneo, Y. (2004). CLUE: Computer supported ubiquitous learning environment for language learning. *Transactions of Information Processing, Society of Japan, 45*(10), 2354–2363.

Hiroshi (2010). *What is iPad.* Retrieved from http://www.techmynd.com/ipad/

Hlavacs, H., Gelies, F., Blossey, D., & Klein, B. (2005, November 30–December 2). *A ubiquitous and interactive zoo guide system.* Paper presented at the INTETAIN 2005, Madonna di Campiglio, Italy.

Huang, Y.-M., Lin, Y.-T., & Cheng, S.-C. (2010). Effectiveness of a mobile plant learning system in science curriculum in Taiwanese elementary education. *Computers & Education, 54,* 47–58.

Iftode, L., Cristian, B., Ravi, N., Kang, P., & Zhou, P. (2004, May 26–28). *Smart phone: An embedded system for universal interactions.* Paper presented at the 10th IEEE International Workshop on Future Trends of Distributed Computing Systems (FTDCS'04), Suzhou, China.

Javvin. (2010). *WLAN: Wireless LAN by IEEE 802.11, 802.11a, 802.11b, 802.11g, 802.11n.* Retrieved from http://www.javvin.com/protocolWLAN.html

Lee, M. J. W., & Chan, A. (2006). Exploring the potential of podcasting to deliver mobile ubiquitous learning in higher education. *Journal of Computing in Higher Education, 18*(1), 94–115.

Naone, E. (2010). *The iPad: Like an iPhone, only bigger.* Retrieved from http://www.technologyreview.com/computing/24423/?a=f

Network dictionary. (2010). Wireless LAN (WLAN) security problems and technologies. Retrieved from http://www.networkdictionary.com/wireless/WLANSecurity.php

Orden, J. V. (2008). *How to podcast.* Retrieved from http://www.how-to-podcast-tutorial.com/what-is-a-podcast.htm

Pazos-Arias, J. J. (2007). Provision of distance learning services over interactive digital tv with mhp. *Computers & Education, 50*(3), 927–949.

Rogers, Y., Price, S., Randell, C., Fraser, D. S., Weal, M., & Fitzpatrick, G. (2005). Ubi-learning integrates indoor and outdoor experiences. *Communications of the ACM, 48*(1), 55–59.

Roschelle, J. (2003). Unlocking the learning value of wireless mobile devices. *Journal of Computer Assisted Learning, 19*, 260–272.

roseIndia. (2008). *iPhone advantages and disadvantages.* Retrieved from http://www.roseindia.net/iphone/iPhone-advantages-disadvantages.shtml

Rosenberger, E. (2010). *Advantages and disadvantages of mp3 technology.* Retrieved from http://www.helium.com/items/819811-advantages-and-disadvantages-of-mp3-technology

Smithsonian. (1998). *How does GPS work?* Retrieved from http://www.nasm.si.edu/gps/work.html

Tan-Hsu, T., Tsung-Yu, L., & Chi-Cheng, C. (2007). Development and evaluation of an RFID-based ubiquitous learning environment for outdoor learning. *Interactive Learning Environments, 15*(3), 253–269.

Tan, T., & Liu, T. (2004, August 30–September 1). *The mobile interactive learning environment (MOBILE) and a case study for assisting elementary school English learning.* Paper presented at the 4th IEEE International Conference on Advanced Learning Technologies (ICALT 2004), Joensuu, Findland.

Technovelgy. (2010). *What is RFID?* Retrieved from http://www.technovelgy.com/ct/Technology-Article.asp

Truong, T. (2010). *iPad, the good and the bad.* Retrieved from http://www.theepochtimes.com/n2/content/view/33554/

Uzunboylu, H., Cavus, N., & Ercag, E. (2009). Using mobile learning to increase environmental awareness. *Computers & Education, 52*, 381–389.

Webopedia. (2010). *Personal computer.* Retrieved from http://www.webopedia.com/TERM/P/personal_computer.html

WildPackets. (2010). *Wireless LAN analysis.* Retrieved from http://www.wildpackets.com/elements/whitepapers/Wireless_LAN_Analysis.pdf

wiseGEEK. (2010). *What is an iPhone?* Retrieved from http://www.wisegeek.com/what-is-an-iphone.htm

Yatani, K., Sugimoto, M., & Kusunoki, F. (2004, March 23–25). *Musex: A system for supporting children's collaborative learning in a museum with PDAs.* Paper presented at the proceedings of the IEEE International Workshop on Wireless and Mobile Technology in Education, Los Alamitos, CA.

Ying, J., & Yang, X. (2008, March 23–26). *RFID-based ubiquitous learning environment for school students.* Paper presented at the Fifth IEEE International Conference on Wireless, Mobile, and Ubiquitous Technology in Education, Beijing, China.

ABOUT THE AUTHORS

Jengchung Victor Chen (PhD in CIS, University of Hawaii) is an Associate Professor in the Institute of International Management at National Cheng Kung University (NCKU), Taiwan. Dr. Chen's research interests are Information Ethics, Project Management, IS Service Quality, and Electronic Commerce. His research outcomes have been published in journals such as *Information & Management*, *European Journal of Information Systems*, *Decision Support Systems*, *CyberPsychology & Behavior*, and *Journal of Database Management*. He serves as the Program Chair for the 21st International Conference on the Pacific Rim Management and President–Elect at the Association for Chinese Management Educators (ACME) 2011–2012. He is the President of the International Chinese Information Systems Association (ICISA). He is also the Secretary-Treasurer for the Taiwan Association for Information Systems (TWAIS).

Andree Emmanuel Widjaja is a graduate student in the Institute of International Management at National Cheng Kung University (NCKU), Taiwan. He earned Bachelor of Informatics Engineering from School of Computer Science, Universitas Pelita Harapan (UPH), Indonesia. Before joining NCKU, he had worked as Systems Analyst and assistant lecturer for computer science courses. Currently, he is working as research assistant and teaching assistant in NCKU.

CHAPTER 6

SOCIAL MEDIA, STORY STREAMS + THE UNIVERSITY CLASSROOM

Brad King

ABSTRACT

This chapter examines how the wisdom of crowds and collective intelligence can be paired with emerging technologies and social software tools to transform the university teaching environment. This is no small task; current classrooms (even technologically advanced classrooms) still resemble 18th-century learning environments. This transformation won't be driven by traditional research either, as social technologies are evolving too quickly for these models to keep pace. This means we must look toward more nontraditional sources to extrapolate innovative ways to use these technologies to create "living-learning" classroom environments, which not only enable students to more easily work together to find solutions to problems but also prepare them for an increasingly networked, digital world.

INTRODUCTION: THE WISDOM OF CLASSROOMS

On May 21, 1967, the U.S.S. Scorpion, a nuclear submarine, went missing in the Atlantic Ocean. Losing a ship at sea is bad enough, but losing a nu-

Ubiquitous Learning, pages 107–120

clear-powered submarine is worse. The potential biohazard it could create was enough to send the Navy scrambling to try to do the impossible—locate a single ship lost in the ocean without any data that could effectively narrow the search. With little hope of finding the wreckage, the Navy turned to Dr. John Craven, the Chief Scientist of the Navy's Special Projects Division, who had helped pioneer the Bayesian search theory, a mathematical construct that requires the collection of theoretical "locations" that are used to create a "probability" search area. His theory, in essence, would try to glean a specific location from educated guesses.

Craven's idea was conceptually simple: gather a "distributed" team of experts who studied the ocean from different perspectives (e.g., an oceanographer, a ship captain, etc.), give each person the same basic information (e.g., last location, submarine speed, etc.), and allow each person to come up with his or her "best guess" about the Scorpion's location. Each of those location points was run through the theorem, narrowing the search area and offering up a "find" probability. In other words, Craven was trying to develop a way to quantify *The Wisdom of Crowds,* an idea James Surowiecki would write a book about, using Craven's story (Surowiecki, 2004).

But college students aren't submarines and professors aren't looking for search probabilities. So how does Craven's theory help to explain the modern learning environment?

The answer to that question lies in understanding what happens in college classes. Ideally, professors work with students to create learning environments within their classrooms. These environments take on different looks, but the goal is the same—enable students to transfer the bits of data delivered by the professor into practical information and knowledge owned by the student. How the bits are delivered is irrelevant. What's important is that students, oftentimes working together through study groups, discussions, and help sessions outside of class, make that transfer.

What Craven's story, and Surowiecki's book, teaches us is that under the right circumstances—and make no mistake, *The Wisdom of Crowds* doesn't work in every situation—there are some basic rules to follow to enhance the probability that students can form these living-learning class environments.

To do this, it's imperative that professors create a digital environment for students using social media software applications (e.g., wikis, mobile text streams such as Twitter, rewriteable documents such as Google Docs), which allow a ubiquitous environment to form outside the classroom. These environments, if they are set up using some of the basic principles designed by Craven and described by Surowiecki, become a "story stream" of information that can be used to create a collective class knowledge. That knowledge can then be used in future classes, creating a story stream that cuts across semesters and academic years.

Those principles—creating a place for diversity of private opinion, independent thought, decentralized knowledge acquisition, and aggregation—are essential for students to take what happens in the classroom into the virtual space. If it is set up properly, the real-life classroom becomes a discussion place for the work that happens within the digital classroom—an area that has neither hours nor walls.

This chapter will explore how social media can be used within a university environment to create a living story stream, tapping into the wisdom of the collective.

BACKGROUND: THE LIVING-LEARNING CLASSROOM (700)

The ideas Surowiecki referenced in his book are discussed in a wide range of seemingly unrelated fields, reaching across the technological landscape stretching back to the dawn of the modern computer age through the evolution of modern social media. This is instructive, particularly as software tools have, generally speaking, become ubiquitous enough for people to easily publish, search, archive, and share without a deep technical knowledge. The originators of the modern digital networks envisioned these tools as a way for people to think and learn better, a fact sometimes forgotten in today's digital landscape.

The idea that ubiquitous environments could foster better human thinking is rooted in the work of Vannevar Bush, the father of the National Science Foundation. Bush wrote that our world, if networked, would quickly grow beyond our capacity to comprehend all of the data, making it imperative that such data be stored and made searchable so that we could retrieve the information we need when we need it. What that would enable, he postulated, is the opportunity for human creativity to be unleashed. We would spend less time sifting through information and, instead, use technological tools to parse through the data stream to find the knowledge that would allow us to craft answers using a wider information field (Bush, 1945).

The idea was carried forward by J. C. R. Licklider, the man in charge of the Information Processing Techniques Office at the Advanced Research Projects Agency (ARPA). Licklider oversaw the project that would, over time, evolve into the Internet. Along the way, he wrote that the data on this emerging distributed network of computers, as Bush predicted, would quickly overwhelm humans. Honing Bush's arguments, Licklider wrote that software agents should do more than parse the data stream. These bits of technology should both act on our behest (e.g., the way of directed search) and act on our behalf (e.g., the way of collaborative filtered recommendations) (Licklider, 1960).

Eventually, according to Licklider, humans would be able to better communicate using advanced software tools and cheaper hardware (as Bush predicted) than they could in person. The reason is a greater access to information.

The growing data stream created by researchers and universities, along with software tools that enable people to access great storehouses of knowledge, would lead to advances in human knowledge heretofore unknown before the advent of the digital network. For Licklider and Bush, the concept was always grounded in the idea that it was humans, using these software and hardware tools, who added the informational context to these bits of data (Licklider, 1968).

At various times, this philosophy would extend into the educational environment. The most applicable example of the creation of a Bush-Licklider classroom setting came at the Georgia Institute of Technology using the idea of the "Living Educational Environment," an experimental approach that deployed technologies to capture and retrieve all of the multimedia information created within a lecture environment. This enabled students to easily parse through analog data (e.g., lecture, discussion) by digitizing it (e.g., audio, video, digital notes) (Abowd, 2000).

This approach raises an interesting question, one that seems to run counter to the idea of emulating the data stream on the Internet by creating a data stream within a classroom: What data is really important for students? The real learning may not come from the Living Educational Environment, but instead from a student-driven technologically enhanced environment that teaches students how to transform the data from lectures and discussions into useful information.

The goal of this living-learning classroom, as Kansas State University professor Dr. Michael Wesch writes, is to teach students to "find, sort, analyze, share, discuss, critique and create" because that is the world—the networked world described by Bush and created by Licklider—that students will enter (Wesch, 2009).

We no longer live in a passive, memorized world. Instead, we are in a read/write culture created by software tools that allow us to publish out (e.g., blogs, wikis) and search and gather (e.g., Google search, RSS readers). The goal is to create an educational environment that supports both the accumulation of data and its transformation into information and knowledge, and supports students as they explore social technologies that allow them to acquire data from multiple sources (Valjataga & Fiedler, 2009).

MAIN FOCUS OF THE CHAPTER: SOCIAL MEDIA, STORY STREAM + THE UNIVERSITY CLASSROOM

Part 1: How Students Study

One of the worst ideas to emerge in the last few years is that of the "digital native," the concept that students today think and process information fundamentally differently than students who came before the networked, digital age (Prensky, 2001).

Certainly there are some students who have a deep, and sometimes profound, understanding of aspects of networked technology and communication. But much of that is localized to singular events, not extrapolated across different environments. They are, for instance, more likely to have used emerging forms of technology such as starting a social networking profile, uploading a video of themselves, or using Twitter than older generations (Pew Research Center, 2010). But the modern students' use of emerging technolgy is largely limited to their personal experiences. To demonstrate, let's examine how university students study.

The Ball State University Center for Media Design, a research and development facility for media that is used at home, in school, and at work, ran a local study to examine how students operated within their learning environment. While not a cross-section of the country, this university, equipped with state-of-the-art technologies, smart classrooms, open computer labs, mobile classes, and online classes, has the generic qualities of a modern university.

The study asked 111 students to submit photo essays and journals describing how and where they studied. Only three of the top 10 study habits involved the use of technology, and two of those involved Blackboard (an online tool for teachers and students to share information) to retrieve an assignment, or using a search engine. A small handful of students used their computers to take notes or scan Wikipedia, and a few listened to podcasts.

Predominantly, students read texts (number 1), wrote papers (number 2), took notes by hand (number 3), read their notes (number 4), underlined passages in the reading (number 6), did memorization drills (number 8), and scanned printed PowerPoint slides (number 10) (Holmes, Martinsen, & Reichlin, 2009).

In other words, the modern student's university experience still basically resembles that of an 18th-century student's. Lecture. Drill. Repeat. The few bits of technology the students use were not designed to encourage collaboration; they were extensions of the lecture (Blackboard) or drills (computer note-taking, search).

It's important to understand that, despite the immersion in technology, students still perceive school as a directed-learning environment where books, notes, highlighting, memorization, and response are the "right way."

The extent of their learning "collective" is working in groups, which are simply smaller versions of the directed environment. There is no "process sharing" with a class-only product as the end.

The point is that simply setting up a social media-based learning environment within the classroom isn't enough. We must train students how to operate within a free, open, technologically enabled environment where knowledge isn't a "thing," but part of a process.

Part 2: Transforming the Classroom

The challenge, then, is to create a living-learning classroom that incorporates some of the basic frameworks for *TheWisdom of Crowds* while also training students (without overwhelming them) on collaborative processes. Teachers need to help students reconfigure the ways in which they approach the learning process. And all of this needs to be done in conjunction with the actual bits of data that need to be taught in the class.

The idea is to combine the "traditional" classroom environment with "emerging" software tools and virtual spaces. What this living-learning classroom can do is allow the virtual space to become a cybertraining ground, where students work with each other to understand and work through the data delivered in the class. The in-class experience becomes a combination of short, directed lessons (e.g., lectures) and analysis of what has happened within the cyberenvironment. The in-class experience becomes more focused and the cyberenvironment becomes more experimental.

To create a living-learning classroom, it's important to remember the four ideas extrapolated from Craven's work: creating a place for diversity of private opinion, independent thought, decentralized knowledge acquisition, and aggregation. Then couple that with some directed and explicit instruction within the physical classroom environment, which will help drive the implicit motivation for the collaborative environment. This combination, creating a virtual environment and meshing that with in-class instruction, helps do three things:

1. **End the Expert Era:** This collaborative environment, which is student-driven and ungraded, creates a sense of autonomy among the class. It becomes a fertile ground for students to explore the bits of data and transform them into knowledge while the professor observes their progress. These lessons can then be corrected or discussed in the classroom.
2. **Learn to Learn:** It encourages students to struggle with each other in a read/write forum. Left on their own, the environment oftentimes

develops slowly until students understand it is theirs. Once this happens (through direct instruction within the class), they will begin to construct their own arguments and treat the bits of data delivered in class as building blocks and not memorized facts.

3. **Teach Skills:** This collaborative environment forces the professor to remove him/herself from the experience, using directed learning to deliver information (e.g., lectures), training (e.g., how wikis work) and discussion (e.g., ideas that emerge from the collaborative environment). The classroom becomes both a directed teaching environment and a discussion driver for the collaborative environment.

What this environment does, like Craven with the U.S.S. Scorpion, is allow the professor and the students to aggregate the discussions and thinking that happens outside of class. It allows students to incorporate emerging technologies into their study habits, an idea that is important for two reasons: the tools allow for search-and-archive capabilities, which make information retrieval easier than physical note-taking, and it implicitly prepares students for a world that is increasingly networked and searchable.

Here's a basic example of what this looks like: For two semesters of the author's Introduction to Social Media courses, the class used a group wiki and a Twitter stream. As part of the class, students were not allowed to ask the instructor technological questions. This may seem problematical on the surface since the class was learning how to use software tools (e.g., WordPress blog software, etc.) to launch their own Web sites. The reasoning behind not directly answering student questions was to force them to rely upon each other, along with the data streams of information that already existed, before looking to the professor for an answer.

Throughout the course of the two semesters, there were 734 interactions between students using the Twitter stream (see Figure 6.1), or approximately 23 interactions per week. Those students continued to use that stream after the class was finished, so former students were helping current students. And for a time after, they continued to ask questions, all under a shared hashtag, a system Twitter uses to organize conversations. Eventually, they just added each other as friends, creating a back channel and eliminating the need for the hashtag.

Through the course of the year, 25 student-to-student questions were answered, a number that may seem small, but consider this: the 25 questions represent only the formal interactions that were tracked through one service (we will get to the wiki interactions later), and it represents 25 answers that were archived for future use by students outside of class. That's 25 questions a professor didn't need to answer while also giving the other students the opportunity to see (and search for) those answers.

min186 - Twitter Search » Show: Expanded - **List**

Show: 1 new item - **all items** | Mark all as read | Refresh | Feed settings... | show details

@brad king, #min186, confused on why my google analytics ain't working!!!?? any suggestions??? - @brad king,	Jul 27, 2009
I've just received my first spam message on my blog...... YES! #min186 - I've just received my first spam message on	Jul 24, 2009
@vwthumper Speaking of which, I'm Mieko-Kaida, or search my name #min186 - @vwthumper Speaking of which, I'm	Jul 24, 2009
Hey #min186 I'm on skype! username is audiofire - Hey #min186 I'm on skype! username is audiofire	Jul 24, 2009
#min186 finally got my audio working on The Dudeman. #EpicInstructorFail. Changed domain names; DID NOT update	Jul 23, 2009
#min186 if you want access to The Soho Theater project wiki we discussed in class today, DM me + I'll send ya the link -	Jul 23, 2009
@Brad_King it was all good until you let the crazy chick sing with her revised Still Alive lyrics. Painfully not amusing.	Jul 23, 2009
We are currently listening to different versions of Still Alive in #min186, I am a ridiculous professor I realize this - We are	Jul 23, 2009
#min186 is bad for my caffeine addiction, good for my brain. Plus I meet cool people. Now to figure best to integrate SM	Jul 21, 2009
RT @Brad_King: RT @jim_clark23: Best Buy pulls job ad #min186. http://shar.es/JOge - RT @Brad_King: RT	Jul 21, 2009
New Job Requirement: Be Popular In Social Media - http://shar.es/JOge #min186 - New Job Requirement: Be Popular In	Jul 21, 2009
RT @jim_clark23: Best Buy pulls job ad #min186. http://shar.es/JOge - RT @jim_clark23: Best Buy pulls job ad	Jul 21, 2009
I love space so much... all of this anniversary stuff is exciting- now we're watching an awesome video in #min186	Jul 21, 2009
#min186, I forgot my paper @ home!!!!, Thank You God for givin me a super GF... - #min186, I forgot my paper @	Jul 21, 2009
@beckyrasch @Klopfstein make sure you spend time with the trade organizations, NUMBERS, describing the industry	Jul 20, 2009
@beckyrasch I'm thinking the movie industry. You? #min186 - @beckyrasch I'm thinking the movie industry. You?	Jul 20, 2009
@Klopfstein what'd you end focusing on for your paper? #min186 - @Klopfstein what'd you end focusing on for your	Jul 20, 2009
Writing a paper and playing Sims 3 - all in the name of school and Social Media #min186 - Writing a paper and playing	Jul 20, 2009
@LilBigBen yuppers, but if you remember last spring, I also did what I'm doing now :) which is reminded you to catch on	Jul 19, 2009
@Klopfstein the point of the twitter stream is to discuss with each other as you go #min186; cluetrain=conversations, yo	Jul 19, 2009
@Brad_King or perhaps we're all just winging it to see how bad we screw up - then learn to worry about it #min186 -	Jul 19, 2009
#min186 is strangely silence while writing their first reports; either have forgotten this is a social media class OR they are	Jul 19, 2009
RT @Jason_Pollock: "Anyone who has never made a mistake has never tried anything new." Albert Einstein via	Jul 17, 2009

Previous item | Next item more than 60 items

Figure 6.1 Teachers can use Twitter to aggregate conversation. By using Twitter Search to find a hashtag (in this case, #min186) and create an RSS feed, an instructor can collect and follow a discussion using RSS readers, such as Google Reader.

Part 3: Creating a Classroom Story Stream

Building this living-learning classroom, engaging Bush and Licklider's philosophy of integrating technology with the human experience, can transform the way students' experience learning and prepare them for life in a networked world.

That was the challenge faced when the author created the Media Ethics class at Ball State University. Students in this senior-level class delve into a series of case studies cutting across journalism, advertising, public relations, and marketing. The students must develop an ethical framework for decision making through writing, discussions, and presentations. This type of upper-division discussion class is not uncommon, although it's difficult to maintain a strong dynamic in these classes as students can easily fall behind in the readings as more project-oriented and directed-learning classes take precedence.

Instead of relying upon out-of-class reading to spur in-class discussion, a collaborative learning environment was built, giving students the chance to have their discussions in an ungraded atmosphere, in this case on private wikis through PBWorks, a privately owned business that provides these read/write environments. By allowing students the opportunity to clarify thinking in an asynchronous way outside of class, in-class time could be spent discussing relevant information that bubbled up from the virtual discussions. Using the Twitter stream and a hashtag (#bsuME), a public place was developed where students could easily share information—links, articles, thoughts, and questions.

Students receive one day of training on wiki software and Twitter (a decidedly non-Media Ethics-related task), and each class is divided into groups, with four to five people per group. The divisions are based on an arbitrary system using gender, race and, major. The idea is to, superficially, create a diversity of opinion, a necessity for *The Wisdom of Crowds.*

Once groups are divided up, each one is given a wiki page (see Figure 6.2) and assigned a case study each week for 13 weeks. They receive their assignment on Tuesday (after a short in-class lecture and discussion) and must have a 10-minute presentation prepared on Thursday.

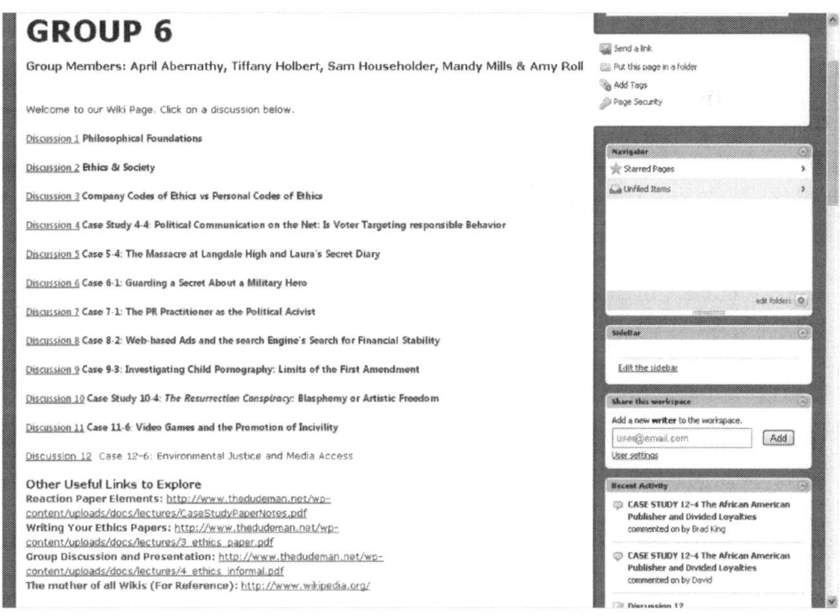

Figure 6.2 Each student group has a wiki page dedicated to its Media Ethics class, which they can use however they see fit. This particular group designed its main page as a Table of Contents for each case study.

To complete these presentations, students quickly find that asynchronous, non-geolocated collaboration through wiki software is the most practical way to gather information, parse out assignments, create a multimedia presentation, and finalize the group's decision (see Figure 6.3). The wiki is programmed to send an e-mail to the instructor any time there is a change to the site, enabling the professor the opportunity to monitor the virtual discussions. Students can also use the Twitter stream and class hashtag to get more immediate answers to questions, either from other class members or the professor. These conversations can be aggregated in a Google Reader by using Twitter Search to find the hashtag and create an RSS feed for it.

The e-mail alerts and the RSS feed following the hashtag allow the changes and conversations the students have to be tracked through an RSS reader. Short, directed lessons are culled from these conversations and can be done in class as problems arise, or more immediate intervention can occur if the group is going off topic. Class, then, is about work and outside-of-class time is about discussion.

While aggregating this may seem to contradict the independent thinking necessary in *The Wisdom of Crowds*, in fact the diversity of thinking within the groups helps individuals think through ethical problems in ways they

Case 12-6: Environmental Justice and Media Access

Case Definition Amy	The Nirvtech Corporation is a multinational corporation specializing in the production of chemicals and pesticides. Nirvtech proposed building a chemical plant in LaFitte Parish, two miles from Rev. Jeremy Washington's church, in a predominantly black neighborhood. The proposal is said to be an economic stimulus for the state at large and for LaFitte Parish as well. Washington sees Nirvtech's initiative as environmental racism. Because of his leadership in the community, Washington became the leader of the black opposition to Nirvtech's proposal. Washington sought out Abecrombie and Associates, a PR firm, in order to gain favor and support in the court of public opinion.
Ethical Dilemma Amy	Should Abercrombie represent Washington as a pro-bono cause in order to be socially responsible and serve as an outlet for the voices of underprivileged members of the community to heard by the media and government officials or should Abercrombie not represent Washington as a responsibility to the firm to avoid a financial loss and protect their image as it stands?
Philosophical Foundation Tiffany	Social Contract- "The purpose of morality is to enable us to live together. Unbridled individualism is antithetical to communal living. Society's inhabitants must reach agreement on a set of principles that is conductive to peaceful harmony. We are free to do as we please as long as we do not harm others or cause serious social disruption." Egalitarian because the voice of each member of the moral community is represented. All individuals should be treated equally in terms of rights and opportunities-there should be no double standard of ethical treatment unless there is an important and morally defensible reason to discriminate. The ethical norms are respected as a long as society agrees on their value or utility. (Day 59-60) Utilitarianism-when making a decision we should attempt to promote the greatest good, with the most favorable consequences, for the greatest number of people. When confronting an ethical dilemma, moral agents should analyze the benefits and harms to everyone (including themselves) affected by the decision and then choose the course of action that results in the most favorable outcome for the greatest number. Minimize harm. (Day 63)
Meta-Ethics Mandy	**Responsibility (to society)** (Corporate Social Responsibility)- aligning a company's activities with the social, economic and environmental expectations of its stakeholders. (It has become a multi-billion dollar public relations specialty in the business world). **Responsibility (to the company)**- an obligation to protect their image against being seen as radical or antiprogressive. (Day pg. 413) We rank the responsibility to society above the responsibility to the company in this case. Although Abercrombie would not directly benefit financially from this client, the company must consider that if they were to choose not to take on the pro-bono client, they may lose other potential clients offended by their refusal to participate in corporate social responsibility to other competing pr firms who do support it. Representing Reverand Washington would instill in society a sense of trust and committment toward

Figure 6.3 This group created a wiki page for each case study. Here, the group aggregates its collective thinking about a particular case study.

hadn't thought of before. And it's always instructive to remember that professors aren't looking for lost submarines.

This type of aggregation system—using RSS feeds and e-mail alerts—is similar to the Just-in-Time Teaching (JiTT) methodology, which uses blogs and directed instruction to gather student responses before class in order to facilitate discussion (Higdon & Topaz, 2009).

One main difference with the living-learning classroom approach is how this author approaches grading. The JiTT methodology approaches information collection by assigning substantial grade percentages to the assignments; the living-learning classroom requires ungraded spaces. Instead, after each set of group presentations, there is a directed lesson on the wikis, examining and discussing how different groups approached gathering their information as well as examining how past classes gathered information. The idea is to model how groups might use collaborative environments and introduce them to the story streams created by previous groups that worked on the same case studies. Each student then uses the group's wiki for an individual assignment (e.g., a paper on each case study, where students argue their ethical reasoning in comparison or contrast with their group's) that can be used for additional assessment.

The students responded to this collaborative environment by making several hundred substantial changes to the wiki during the 17-week course. They also formed informal "study" groups on Facebook and Twitter to collaborate on their individual papers, ensuring a basic continuity of work through which the instructor could monitor and answer questions.

The highlight, though, came when 19 students created a five-page "ethical case study" to suggest the elimination of written papers, to be replaced by more interactive, group presentations. The 19 students created the five-page document by making 57 substantive changes in 2 days. They had, in essence, taken the tools and lessons in class and applied them to a student-driven solution to a problem they had with the class.

FUTURE TRENDS: STORY STREAMS, COLLECTIVE WISDOM, AND TEACHING

Increasingly, college instructors will need to deploy emerging collaborative technologies within their classrooms as students grow to expect more interactive engagement with the materials. As this happens, instructors need to examine how pervasive educational environments should be administered in the classroom to promote learning.

While there is no standard approach to these environments, there are solid foundations upon which collaborative environments can be built. This can be done by using ideas such as creating ungraded "sandbox" environments and personal spaces for students, creating a practical use for the spaces, spending classroom time teaching social interactions in collaborative environments, and integrating various social technologies within the classroom to give students different entry points into the class (Twu, 2009).

Those environments, and the living streams of information created within classrooms, have the potential to transform the way we think about education. If Wesch is correct in his analysis of teaching—that we should focus on activities such as finding information rather than memorizing, for instance—and universities are truly engaged in bringing the classroom environment from an 18th-century model into the 21st century, then teachers might begin reevaluating how they evaluate students.

Instead of using memorization quizzes to gauge the retention of knowledge in the Introduction to Magazine Writing class, a class wiki with a series of questions was created. Answering the questions required information from readings, lectures, and outside sources. The wiki was broken up into two parts: individual responses and group responses. Some 60 percent of the grade came from students pulling answers from outside sources (e.g., find an example of a narrative introductory lead, post it with a link, and explain how the author used it to set up the story theme) and 40 percent came from collaborative answers (e.g., create a database of Web sites that track political spending nationally and statewide). A total of 20 students took the first wiki-test, creating a 15-page document with 128 substantive changes.

That learning document became the jumping-off point for the next class, which built upon the student-created knowledge. The integration of social technologies such as Twitter and shared RSS readers (e.g., Google Reader) enable former students to connect with current students. This builds a directed back-channel for students to work with each other in an asynchronous way. These types of evaluation methodologies help teachers model the importance of learning how to navigate collaborative environments and the importance of shared knowledge, which is, as Bush and Licklider wrote, a fundamental part of the digital, networked age.

CONCLUSION: LIVING STREAMS

In 1945, Bush predicted that the cost and size of technology hardware would soon transform the ways in which people interacted with the world. Licklider explained, 15 years later, that software tools would soon allow us to retrieve data more efficiently.

Another technologist, Gordon Moore, famously predicted that advances in technology would rapidly shrink computing devices while computing power grew (Moore, 1965). The most fascinating prediction, the one that has the most relevance to the future of learning and education, comes from

Ray Kurzweil, who posits that the progression of technological leaps is reaching a point where digital networks are so connected, the power of computing so great, and the mobility of devices so pervasive, that we will soon lose the ability to truly comprehend what will come next (Kurzweil, 2001).

These are hefty technological concepts to be sure, yet they are the very ideas that drive the ways in which we share, store, retrieve, and access information. Our world has been transformed from one of analog atoms into digital bits 20 years after Tim Berners-Lee released the Web protocols. Today's students, the Millennials, view advances in technology as simplifying their lives. More importantly, they use mobile technologies more than other generations (Boyd, Casey, & Lenhart, 2010). In other words, we are watching the evolution and expansion of these networks speed up with every generation.

With each iteration of technology, software upgrade, or processor advancement, our devices become smarter. As we integrate these technologies into our lives, as our children will surely continue to do, it's imperative that our educational environment strive to not only keep up with this pace, but reach out as far ahead as possible. Classes can no longer be viewed simply as analog gathering places where directed learning takes place. We must create information story streams, bits of data that extend from one semester to the next, from one year to the next. Teachers must reach beyond the classrooms to where students live, work, think, and share.

REFERENCES

Abowd, G. D. (2000). Classroom 2000: An experiment with the instrumentation of a living educational environment. *IBM Systems Journal*, 508–530

Boyd, D., Casey, D., & Lenhart, A. (2010, February 24). *Millennials, media and information.* (J. Woodruff, Interviewer). http://pewresearch.org/pubs/1516/millennials-panel-two-millennials-media-information

Bush, V. (1945, July). As we may think. *The Atlantic Monthly, 176*(1), 101–108.

Higdon, J., & Topaz, C. (2009). Blogs and wikis as instructional tools. *College Teaching, 52*(2), 105–109.

Holmes, M. E., Martinsen, J., & Reichlin, S. (2009, November). *"Show Us How You Study": Student perspectives on locations and resources for studying.* Paper presented at the 2009 Annual Educause Conference, Denver, CO.

Kurzeil, R. (2001, March 7). *The law of accelerating returns.* Retrieved April 12, 2010, from http://www.kurzweilai.net/articles/art0134.html?printable=1

Licklider, J. (1960). Man-computer symbiosi. *IRE Transactions on Human Factors in Electronics*, Vol. HFE-1, March 1960, pp. 4–11.

Licklider, J. (1968, April). The computer as a communication device. *Science and Technology.*

Moore, G. E. (1965, April 19). Cramming more components onto integrated circuits. *Electronics*, 4–7.

Pew Research Center. (2010). *Millennials: A portrait of generation next.* Washington, DC: Pew Research Center.

Prensky, M. (2001, October). Digital natives, digital immigrants. *On the Horizon, 9*(5).

Surowiecki , J. (2004). *The wisdom of crowds: Why the many are smarter than the few and how collective wisdom shapes business, economies, societies and nations.* New York: Doubleday.

Twu, H.-L. (2009). Effective wiki strategies to support high-context culture learners. *TechTrends, 53*(5), 16–22.

Valjataga, T., & Fiedler, S. (2009). Supporting students to self-direct intentional learning projects with social media. *Educational Technology & Society, 12*(3), 58–69.

Wesch, M. (2009, January). *From knowledgable to knowledge-able: Learning in new media environments.* Retrieved April 11, 2010, from Academic Commons: http://www.academiccommons.org/commons/essay/knowledgable-knowledge-able

ABOUT THE AUTHOR

Brad King, PhD, is an assistant professor of journalism and an Emerging Media Initiative fellow at Ball State University, Muncie, Indiana. His research examines how emerging technologies are changing the ways we tell and share stories. He is the co-author of *Dungeons & Dreamers: The Rise of Computer Games from Geek to Chic* and is currently finishing *The Cult of Me: How Social Technologies Have Changed Storytelling.* He is also on the advisory boards for South by Southwest Interactive (www.sxsw.com) and Carnegie Mellon's ETC Press (www.etc.cmu.edu/etcpress/).

A journalist since 1994, King earned his master's in 2000 from the Graduate School of Journalism at the University of California, Berkeley. He then worked for Condé Nast's *Wired* magazine and then its sister Web site, Wired News, covering the convergence of technology and culture. In 2002, he co-authored *Dungeons and Dreamers,* a book on the history of computer games, virtual worlds, and their effects on American culture for McGraw-Hill. In 2004, he was hired as the senior editor and producer for MIT's *Technology Review.*

Along with his academic and journalism work, King has kept close to his Net roots. He helped launch blogs at *Variety* magazine and MIT. He also sat on the advisory board for the first Austin Game Conference in 2004.

CHAPTER 7

SOCIAL NETWORKS

Pedagogical Tool or Pedagogical Threat?

Keith J. Benson and Josephine A. Koster

ABSTRACT

The rapid explosion of social media platforms and their embrace by the 18–25 age group have tremendous implications for college teaching. Today's 13–25 year olds are "hypersocializers," used to constant communication via text, cell phones, and social networking sites. Since these young adults make up the largest percentage of students currently enrolled in colleges, it is imperative that college faculty assess the potential of using social media in their classrooms and design and implement effective strategies for using this ubiquitous technology.

Social networks such as Facebook, MySpace, EdModo, and the like, have been the subject of only a handful of few recent studies that assess their effectiveness as pedagogical tools. In one recent article, Lisa Dawley argues persuasively that "It is important to acknowledge that credibility and expertise in social networking comes from the extent of [faculty] involvement in the network, including the amount of participation, frequency, and the usefulness of the information provided." However, not much attention has been paid to the role the faculty member plays as facilitator in using these tools in a classroom rather than in purely social settings.

Ubiquitous Learning, pages 121–135

Our chapter explores the potential benefits and pitfalls of using social networks in the classroom by detailing the experiences of two early adopters of Facebook as a pedagogical tool at a mid-sized comprehensive southern state university. We describe the theories of engaged learning that have led us to adopt social networks in our classrooms and the successes and challenges we have faced. Based on our observations, we conclude by discussing the rewards and consequences of using social networks as a regular part of collegiate academic instruction.

INTRODUCTION

Shakespeare wrote, "To be or not to be: that is the question." If Shakespeare were a faculty member today, his question might be rephrased, "To Facebook or not to Facebook: that is the question." Social network sites (SNS) have become endemic to the environment on university campuses. According to a March 2009 Nielsen survey, 67 percent of global online users link to a social network, and social networks and blogs are more popular than personal e-mail; and in 2008, scholars estimated that as many as 79 percent to 95 percent of all undergraduates had Facebook accounts (Lampe, Ellison, & Steinfield, 2008). That percentage has held steady for the past 3 years. The popular culture tool Wikipedia currently lists over 150 active major social network sites covering a divergently wide spectrum of topics and issues, as well as many more private social networking sites.

Much of this growth is driven by the millennial generation, for whom technology is a way of life. Today's 13–25-year-olds are hypersocializers, used to constant communication via text, cell phones, and social network sites (Zaslow, 2009). A 2009 Intel Harris Interactive Survey of 2,695 adults ages 18 and older found that 62 percent agree "that mobile devices, such as laptops, netbooks and cell phones, are part of our daily lives and society needs to adapt to the fact that people use them at all times" (Intel, 2009). The average American child has grown up with multiple electronic media and is both comfortable and proficient in using these multiple media (Brooks-Gunn & Donahue, 2008). The typical undergraduate student has a cell phone, access to the Internet and social networking sites, e-mail, music player, and the capacity to send/receive instant or text messages in his or her dorm room. For some, one single mobile device offers all of these applications. According to a Pew Research Center report released in February 2010, 75 percent of millennials have a social network site profile. Many belong to multiple social network sites, with 44 percent reporting they visit such a site at least once a day. Moreover, 83 percent report sleeping with their cell phones at their bedsides. The typical millennial sends 20 text messages in a 24-hour period, believes that technology makes life easier and more efficient, and 41 percent have abandoned land-line phones in favor of wireless communication only. These numbers represent all millennials; the percentages increase for millennials with some college education, showing the significant impact that social networks and technologies have in the lives of our current and future students (Pew Research Center, 2010).

These millennial learners come to the college campus expecting entirely different kinds of experiences than did students of the previous few generations. Not only is the classroom different from when many faculty were undergraduates, but the interactions among students and between students and faculty are different as well. The days of lingering after class, talking with fellow students about the subject or a related topic in the classroom or hallway, are gone. Students rarely come to a professor's office hours and seem reluctant even to check their official campus e-mail messages. Their orientation has shifted from face-to-face contact to virtual communication. It is not uncommon to see students, as soon as the professor concludes class, whipping out a mobile device to reconnect to their circle of friends and acquaintances while barely noticing the students in the classroom or hallways around them, or to observe them walking across campus texting madly, iPod earphones in place, while ignoring the people or physical spaces they encounter. In the university environment, students have often been the first to adopt social networks, then admissions or athletics, and finally, reluctantly, faculty. Part of this is due to the fact that most undergraduate students are digital natives, whereas most faculty can at best be described as digital immigrants, immersing themselves in a world that is not innately familiar to them (Prensky, 2001). This chapter explores the potential benefits and pitfalls of using social networks in the classroom by detailing the experiences of two early adopters of Facebook as a pedagogical tool at a small comprehensive southern state university. In it we describe the theories that led us to adopt Facebook in our classrooms, the successes and challenges we have faced, and speculate about the consequences of using social networks as a regular part of collegiate academic instruction.

LEARNING STYLES AND SOCIAL NETWORKING

A significant and ongoing challenge for most faculty members is finding ways to engage students in learning activities that promote retention and engagement, what is usually described as "active learning" (Jones, Harmon, & O'Grady-Jones, 2004–2005). This challenge has become even more pronounced as students have adapted to the essential egocentrism of the mobile communications device. Electronic media offer opportunities to both engage and disengage students (Brooks-Gunn & Donahue, 2008). David Sousa has estimated that 24 hours after instruction takes place, student retention rates for information presented in class vary greatly depending on the strategy of instruction used. Traditional instructional methods such as lectures have only a 5 percent retention rate, and reading has a 10 percent retention rate. More interactive activities, such as audio-visual presentations (20% retention rate) and demonstrations (30% retention rate) foster better recall of information among students. But the most successful activities in terms of recall are those that actually engage students in active participation, such as group discussion (50% retention rate), practicing what is learned (75% retention rate), and teaching fellow students (90% retention rate) (Sousa, 2005). Such results fly in the face of traditional practices in college classroom environments, in which a professor or expert lectures, students dutifully take notes, and all is focused on "coverage" of a certain amount of content. The challenge for the instructors of digital natives, then, is to find ways wherein such students can productively and actively engage with the materials presented through reading and lecturing. One way to do this is to consider the differences between the learning styles of students and teachers.

Two of the most influential theorists of learning styles, Jerome S. Bruner and Jean Piaget, have described how humans assimilate knowledge about their environment through four sensory modalities: visual (observing pictures, symbols, or diagrams), auditory (listening, discussing instructional material), visual/iconic (reading and writing), and kinesthetic (using tactile sensory abilities such as smell and touch). New Zealand educator Neil Fleming created the VARK survey to assess these learning preferences; VARK is an acronym for visual, aural, read/write, and kinesthetic (Fleming, 1992). He contends that visual learners prefer to use graphs, flow charts, hierarchies, models, and arrows that represent printed information. They may also explain a concept to others by drawing a diagram or picture. Read/write learners prefer lists, glossaries, textbooks, lecture notes, or handouts and frequently make outlines, paraphrase class notes, and study old exams. Aural learners, in Fleming's taxonomy, concentrate on what lecturers say; they would prefer to listen rather than take notes and to discuss material with classmates as a means to clarify their understanding. Kinesthetic preference refers to learning achieved through the use of experience and practice. In other words, the kinesthetic learner has to feel or live the experience in order to learn it, through hands-on practice, demonstrating to others, student teaching or presentations, and other engaged experiences (Fleming, 1992).

Fleming's research suggests that there are significant differences in learning style by age, gender, and discipline. For instance, men are more likely to show kinesthetic preferences; women are more likely to show read/write preferences. Teachers are more likely to be read/write learners than students are and are less likely to be kinesthetic learners than students. Students are more frequently multimodal learners than are faculty; they often demonstrate a blend of learning preferences. And learning styles vary greatly by disciplines; students in mathematics and the natural sciences, for instance, are more likely to be read/write learners, while education majors may be more visual learners, musicians predominantly auditory, and art majors predominantly kinesthetic learners (Fleming, 2009). Although student learning styles may vary, they all show a benefit from instruction that focuses on engaged, active learning that appeals to their learning preferences. And this is where social networks, which require participants to interact, can be extremely useful for pedagogy.

Social networks such as Facebook, MySpace, EdModo, and the like have been the subject of a handful of recent studies that assess their effectiveness as pedagogical tools. However, not much attention has been paid to the role the faculty member plays as facilitator in using these tools. In one recent article, Lisa Dawley (2009) argues persuasively that

> It is important to acknowledge that credibility and expertise in social networking comes from the extent of involvement in the network, including the amount of participation, frequency, and the usefulness of the information provided. Teachers and students in virtual worlds must gain "avatar capital" (Castronova, 2006) (QA: There is no reference for this citation. Please provide.)through ongoing participation in networks to develop their credibility as a network member. What does this mean for a teacher in virtual worlds? A teacher must become a facilitator in the network, integrate these tools into their [sic] teaching, and learn to model, facilitate, and assist students in the successful use of networks to achieve learning goals. (p. 112)

FACEBOOK IN THE CLASSROOM

Social networking sites were primarily developed to allow friends and those with common interests to stay in touch. This quickly evolved into staying connected with constant updates. Facebook was originally designed to be a social network for Harvard students and alumni, then expanded to students at other colleges, and eventually to anyone over the age of 13 (Carlson, 2010). Almost since its inception, Facebook has offered a "Groups" application, which allows users with shared interests to create sites for mutual discussion. There are currently nine different categories of groups, ranging from businesses to student groups to common interests, and for purposes from profit making and policy influence to simply fun. For example, President Obama raised $55 million without ever attending a fundraiser by leveraging his social networks and raising the money online (Peddycord, 2008). The Ottawa Health Research Institute in Ontario, Canada, launched the Facebook decision-making application iShould to provide teenage Facebook users a framework for rationally making everyday life choices (Wilcox,

2009). Public libraries have used Facebook to create digital communities (King, 2009). In both of our cases, Facebook allowed us to reconnect with high school classmates as we celebrated reunions—30th and 35th, respectively. These potentials suggest that Facebook is a tool that can be leveraged into the college classroom to achieve some of the same outcomes—development of learning communities, exchange of information and ideas, opportunities for discussion, students teaching students, and growth in a number of intellectual categories.

Already, a number of primary and third-party applications have been developed to help use Facebook in the classroom, at both the K–12 and college levels. One Facebook application, Courses, provides a classroom management utility similar to Web CT and Blackboard, located entirely within the Facebook environment. Other Web portals, such as CollegeDegree.com and OnlineCollege.org, make more than 100 classroom applications available for Facebook, from slide sharing to discussion to foreign language editing and practice. One can now find Facebook groups for K–12 educators, for science educators, for history educators, for writing instructors, and so on, showing that faculty are beginning to use the connective powers of social networking to discuss, proselytize, and share resources. These tools and trends point out that since Facebook is where the students are, we as educators can productively go to Facebook to reach them. But how do they react to our use of Facebook in the classroom?

SOCIAL NETWORKS IN CLASSROOM SETTINGS

As professors, we are very different. Though we have been both early adopters of Facebook for personal use and then migrated into using Facebook in the classroom, our disciplines—health care management and medieval studies—are literally worlds apart. Both of us have been recognized by students and peers as being engaging professors and have won teaching awards. Our university is a mid-size comprehensive state-supported university in South Carolina, with an ethnically integrated student body. While the campus offers a number of computer labs and wireless computer access in most campus buildings, in reputation and in fact, we are not a "tech school." Our students, we believe, represent a spectrum of typical collegiate attitudes toward technology and social networking, from enthusiastic to Luddite. Thus, our experiments with using social networking tools in the classroom have been carried out on a wide variety of learners, from freshmen to Executive MBA students. This cross-section of our enrollment gives us confidence that the results we have seen are, in fact, typical of our student body. In the section that follows, we describe individually our varying experiences in using Facebook as a learning tool and then collectively discuss the advantages and disadvantages we have experienced in using social networking tools in the classroom.

Keith Benson

In summer 2008, I had recently read an article on how many businesses had to develop Facebook policies. I had to miss class to present a paper at a conference and wanted to give students in my EMBA-level Management Information Systems class a valid pedagogical assignment, even though I was not physically present. A survey at the start of class showed that 18 out of 27 students (67%), already had Facebook accounts. So I created a Facebook student group, posted YouTube videos on the relevant topic, and set up questions on the discussion board. All students joined the Facebook group and participated in the exercise. This class was a graduate-level class, and there was mixed feelings about the use of Facebook as a pedagogical tool. Some of the students felt that Facebook was a time-waster, whereas, other students commented that they already spent time on Facebook, so the ability to incorporate school work while visiting a social network was a positive benefit. My next use was in HCMT 200 (Introduction to Health Care Management), where the students were required to post links to *Wall Street Journal* articles and then lead a threaded discussion about the article they had posted. In fall semester 2009, all questions related to an upcoming exam were posted on the course Facebook group. What I discovered is that students were answering each others' questions before I could. What happened next surprised me, because students started asking independent questions about President Obama's proposed health reform and having discussions about it. We had similar discussions in class, but these discussions extended those conversations much further. Reviewing the threaded discussions of the students, I realized the amount of student engagement was increasing. Students were posing questions and then replying to the responses of other students. The number of student interactions was greater, and there was more collaboration using Facebook as a tool. This is consistent with the engaged-learner definition posited by Jones, Valdez, Nowakowski, and Rasmussen (1994), which argues that engaged learning occurs where there are more student interactions, more connections, and a greater emphasis on technology as a tool.

Some of the most revealing experiences I have had with Facebook, however, have come not in my discipline but in our second-semester freshman general education course, HMXP 101. In the course, titled "Who Am I: The Human Experience," the course Facebook group is primarily used for carrying on an extension of classroom discussions. Using Facebook has allowed students to add, clarify, modify, or even change their viewpoints after reflection and reading of other viewpoints. The newest way I am using Facebook is for an Executive MBA Leadership Class. In this group, the primary focus is leadership development. The Facebook group is being used to post relevant Youtube videos, blogs, and RSS feeds; to ask and answer questions; and to share results. Whereas in my disciplinary courses, membership in the Facebook group was limited to current students, and students who dropped the class were manually removed from the Facebook group, the Executive MBA group is open to current and previous members. The purpose of this group is to transcend the normal semester-long Facebook group and keep the leadership development process ongoing. The group is slowly growing as the content posted grows. One discovery from this group is that for a group to be an effective pedagogical tool, the content must be actively managed with frequent updates. Because of the volume of social network sites and competing Web-based sites, a Facebook group that is not actively managed will allow engaged learners to become disengaged.

Jo Koster

Though my academic specialty is medieval literature, I have long had an interest in technology in the classroom and was introduced to blogging as early as 2000. When Winthrop revised its General Education curriculum in 2004 and created a sophomore-level required Critical Thinking, Reading, and Writing course, CRTW 201, I decided to incorporate class and personal blogs into the class. Though I kept the requirement for nearly 3 years, it was not an unqualified success; those students who were comfortable around technology and who were fairly extroverted usually embraced blogging in the class, while introverted and/or technophobic students tended to resist it. Most of them were not bloggers, did not consider blogging to be "real" writing, and thus felt the class requirement was make-work rather than essential for their intellectual progress in the class. Therefore, blogging increased engaged learning for only a small subset of the class. In 2007, after a particularly resistant CRTW 201 class rebelled against the blogging requirement, I eliminated it in favor of the more traditional reading journal, kept on paper and submitted for a grade three times a semester. In the next year, however, I began to hear students talking about something called Facebook, and when I explored the site, I believed it might create the kinds of engaged learning opportunities I had originally sought with the blogs.

In fall 2008, I began incorporating a Facebook group restricted to class members into my CRTW 201 class, requiring students to start topics on the Facebook wall or discussion forum at least twice a week and to respond to two other students' posts that week. In the subsequent four semesters, I have used similar groups in almost a dozen CRTW classes. On average,

17–18 students (out of 22) will have Facebook accounts coming into the class, and almost all have joined the class groups. I have had two students who had previously been banned from Facebook, and one whose parents objected to her using the network. In all three cases, students e-mailed their contributions to me, and I posted them for others to see, but these three students were obviously handicapped as to being able to participate in the discussion.

The results, like the blogs, have been mixed. As with the other technology, some students are more comfortable and willing to use it than others, and they are the most frequent posters. Some students who are quiet and reluctant to talk in class have developed into regular posters; apparently the ability to reflect on their words and posts in privacy has freed them to become part of discussions in ways they are not comfortable with in class. Several have posted videos and added pictures to the group site, making it a more multimodal learning experience; it is often, in fact, the videos that generate the best discussion among students. Others, however, remain less communicative, either simply clicking the "Like" button to agree with a classmate's post or refraining from starting discussions of their own. In this sense, the Facebook group has been neither more nor less successful than traditional tasks like journaling or the requirement to blog. Furthermore, some students have expressed resentment that I, as a teacher, am co-opting what they perceive to be "their" space, and am turning Facebook from something fun into just another school assignment. While this resentment hasn't been widespread—or at least not widely expressed—it raises issues that subsequent research will have to address.

But using the Facebook groups has led to more engaged learning, especially with students teaching other students. When a CRTW student has a question, she or he will post it on the Facebook group (and usually receive an answer) before choosing to e-mail or call me; the students seem to trust each other to provide accurate information and to assist classmates, which has lessened their dependence on me as the sole authority figure in the class. This has strengthened the sense of community in several of the sections of CRTW where Facebook groups have been used. Moreover, students working on group projects have switched almost entirely to Facebook for working on group projects and presentations; they seem to prefer meeting online and using tools like chat, supplemented by the e-mailing of documents, to actual face-to-face interaction. As we see with students and mobile communication devices, they sometimes seem to favor the mediation of technology to actual human interaction, a factor that will have considerable consequences for our pedagogy in the future.

Noting these dynamics, I have also experimented with alternatives to Facebook in my specialization courses. In several courses, I have now tried using private social networking sites like www.ning.com to set up private social networks that enable multimember chat and the posting of documents and slide shows, with considerable success. In a Chaucer class, students have made and shared recordings of recitations in Chaucer's Middle English to assist with the class pronunciation requirement, added videos of interpretations of the *Canterbury Tales* for discussion, and even uploaded the PowerPoint slides for their class presentations for comment and suggestion. Students routinely use the chat room for discussion of assignments and exam study sessions, from which they text or message me to ask questions and float ideas. In my Writing for New Media class—one where the students were mostly far more tech-savvy than I am—they created videos and multimedia presentations, uploaded drafts of their graphic novels, swapped pictures and cartoons, and generally converted the class site into something much more like a multiuser environment than the more static Facebook allows. On two occasions, we had guest speakers who could not physically attend the class (which met at night) join us in the chat room, and the classroom dynamic where students were talking back and forth to each other while typing furiously at the same time was an exciting and enlightening experience that showed how social networking tools could transform the pedagogical experience for students and teacher alike. Both of these classes were small and consisted of upper-division students who mostly knew each other before the class began; this friendly and intimate dynamic certainly contributed to the success of the in-class networks. By contrast, the CRTW students, frequently strangers to each other, have been slower to generate that sense of community.

CONCLUSIONS

No educational technology is totally neutral, and Facebook is no exception. While, as our experiences have shown, there are numerous benefits to student engagement and learning when using social media in classroom situations, there are also significant consequences and pitfalls. The first is the time required for faculty to engage students in Facebook. It requires an almost-daily presence to engage students, usually at least 20 minutes a day for one small-to-medium-sized class. If an instructor is using multiple Facebook groups, this can take up to 30–60 minutes per day. While faculty members are evaluated on traditional measure such as contact hours and observing office hours, few college or university roles and rewards systems recognize the time instructors might spend interacting with students in social networking venues, which may have long-term consequences for a faculty members' professional advancement.

While many students are comfortable using Facebook, there are a few students who are overwhelmed by or unsure using social networks. Additionally, some students are worried about the permanency of their viewpoints being in writing. In HMXP 102, the Facebook group discusses sensitive issues such as religion, sexual orientation, and issues of race. Some students have expressed a concern that a post made to stimulate discussion could be misconstrued and become viral, posted all over the Web. Also, there is a concern that parents or others may find out that a student's beliefs are different than that of their parents, and that could cause problems. Discussion of the complexities of social networking and privacy has helped the students develop their critical evaluation skills with relation to the medium, but it of course does not solve the potential problem; faculty must be given significant consideration to the possible consequences of such postings as they plan assignments and suggest (or require) discussion topics for online communities.

From the faculty perspective, a significant concern is the development of appropriate boundaries between faculty and students. Facebook groups do not require that instructors and students share personal information through the process Facebook calls "friending," but students routinely expect that their instructors will friend them, since this is the social convention of Facebook interaction. Is it appropriate for faculty to accept friendship requests from current students? We both have had students who thought that because we were their friends on Facebook, they should have special privileges; other, unfriended students have wondered if we were playing favorites. Occasionally, students with friend privileges (and therefore able to see our full profiles, not just the limited information we share with all Facebook users) have made derogatory comments about our political affiliations, religious beliefs, or the like. We have addressed such concerns by telling students we will friend them when the course is over, so that none need to have any concern about our fairness, but are aware that this issue is fraught with potential conflict. Many faculty anecdotally have told us that they won't use Facebook in the classroom because they want to preserve the boundaries between their personal lives (where they may be active Facebook participants) and their professional spaces; for such faculty members, private social network class sites like Ning.com or EdModo.com might allow them to experiment with social networking while protecting their personal privacy. This is a subject we are continuing to explore.

Another concern is that even though the Facebook groups set up for class use are private and limited only to enrolled students and their professors, comments can and will be copied and posted elsewhere on Facebook and other networks. This could be potentially damaging to a professor if he/she is playing devil's advocate to stimulate student discussion and might inhibit a faculty member from making such comments or using the site to its full potential for fear of what a promotion and tenure board might think if the comment was conveyed to it. The consequences of using Facebook in the classroom could literally develop into a case of academic freedom. Moreover, there have already been cases where information a faculty member has posted on Facebook could be used interpreted incorrectly or out of context. For instance, in spring 2010, Gloria Gadsden, an African American associate professor of sociology at East Stroudsburg University, Pennsylvania, was suspended by the university for a month after she made two joking wall posts about possibly killing students (Miller, 2010). Students filed the protest against Ms. Gadsden, who had previously complained of racial harassment at the university, and she was allowed to return to the classroom only after passing a psychological evaluation. Some students also protested her reinstatement. In a time when the possibility of violence in the college classroom has become real, institutions must take such student complaints seriously, but they reflect how dangerous it can be for faculty members to vent their frustrations through social media, as students routinely do. Many educators could sympathize with the kinds of experiences and days that made Ms. Gadsden post that she "didn't want to kill even one student.:-) Now Friday was a different story..." (Miller, 2010), but the extreme consequences must certainly remind faculty that in social networks, nothing is really private.

Searches of "professor suspended Facebook" and "professor fired Facebook" on Internet search engines like Google will bring up a number of other consequences of using Facebook, from being tagged in photographs beyond one's control to opposition to links the faculty member had posted to being censured for inviting controversial speakers to the classroom and mentioning it on a Facebook page. At the K–12 level, firings and lawsuits have become common enough that some school districts are establishing social media participation policies, requiring parents to sign permission slips before their children are tagged in Facebook photos, and even prohibiting Facebook use by employees. While such policies have not yet penetrated deeply into higher education, it is clear that our current litigious climate may make them necessary in the future, and faculty using Facebook in the classroom would do well to have a clear policy statement about what kinds of interaction, language, and behavior is acceptable in their class Facebook encounters as guidelines for student participation.

Thus, our conclusions about Facebook use in the college classroom are mixed. We both have seen enough positive outcomes to recommend its use (or use of sites like Facebook) in college instruction, but we are also aware that issues of time, faculty roles and rewards, acceptable teacher/student boundaries, and appropriate and/or free speech may have significant impact on how these social networking sites can be used in the classroom. Future research will include surveys of student perceptions of Facebook use in the classroom, surveys of faculty attitudes toward social media, and deeper investigation of how the use of social media can be integrated into systems of faculty roles and rewards. We remain convinced and enthusiastic users of social media, but ones who are fully aware that this is teaching on the edge, and are awake to its challenges and potential pitfalls.

REFERENCES

Brooks-Gunn, J., & Donahue, E. H. (2008, Spring). Introducing the issue. *The Future of Children, 18*(1), 3–10. Retrieved from http://futureofchildren.org/futureofchildren/publications/docs/18_01_01.pdf

Bruner, J. S. (1967). *Toward a theory of instruction.* Cambridge, MA: Harvard University Press.

Carlson, M. (2010, March). At last—The full story of how Facebook was founded. *Business Insider, 5.* Retrieved from http://www.businessinsider.com/how-facebook-was-founded-2010-3

Dawley, L. (2009). Social network knowledge construction: Emerging virtual world pedagogy. *On the Horizon, 17*(2), 109–121. Retrieved from http://edtech.boisestate.edu/ldawley/SNKC_pdf.pdf

Fleming, N. D. (1992). Not another inventory, rather a catalyst for reflection. *To Improve the Academy, 11,* 137–155. Retrieved from http://www.vark-learn.com/documents/not_another_inventory.pdf

Fleming, N. D. (2009). Research and statistics. *VARK: A guide to learning styles.* Retrieved from http://www.vark-learn.com/english/page.asp?p=research

Intel Corp. (2009, October 19). *Intel study reveals importance of keeping tech tasteful during the holidays.* News Release. Retrieved from http://www.intel.com/pressroom/archive/releases/2009/20091019corp.htm

Jones, B. F., Valdez, G., Nowakowski, J., & Rasmussen, C. (1994). *Designing learning and technology for educational reform.* Oak Brook, IL: North Central Regional Educational Laboratory. ERIC Document Reproduction Service No. ED 378940. Retrieved from http://www.eric.ed.gov/ERICWebPortal/custom/portlets/recordDetails/detailmini.jsp?_nfpb=true&_&ERICExtSearch_SearchValue_0=ED378940&ERICExtSearch_SearchType_0=no&accno=ED378940

Jones, M. H., Harmon, S. W., & O'Grady-Jones, M. (2004–2005) Developing the digital mind: Challenges and solutions in teaching and learning. *Teaching and Education Journal of South Carolina,* 17–24. Retrieved from http://coe.winthrop.edu/educ275/00_New_FALL_05/developing_digital_minds.pdf

King, D. (2009, August/September). Building the digital branch: Guidelines for transforming your library Website. *Library Technology Reports.* Retrieved from http://www.alatechsource.org/ltr/building-the-digital-branch-guidelines-for-transforming-your-library-website

Lampe, C., Ellison, N. B., & Steinfield, C. (2008). Changes in use and perception of Facebook. *Proceedings of the 2008 ACM Conference on Computer Supported Cooperative Work* (pp. 721–730). New York: ACM. Retrieved from http://delivery.acm.org/10.1145/1470000/1460675/p721-lampe.pdf?key1=1460675&key2=1936431721&coll=GUIDE&dl=GUIDE&CFID=86287197&CFTOKEN=19886229

Miller, M. H. (2010, April 2). East Stroudsburg U. professor returns after suspension for Facebook Posts. *Chronicle of Higher Education.* Retrieved from http://chronicle.com/blogPost/East-Stroudsburg-U-Professor/22244/

Peddycord, R. (2008, October 15). How Obama raised 87 percent of his funds through social networking. *Resource Nation.* Retrieved from http://www.resourcenation.com/blog/how-obama-used-social-networking-to-set-fundraising-records

Pew Research Center. (2010, February 24). *The millennials: Confident. Connected. Open to change.* Retrieved from http://pewsocialtrends.org/assets/pdf/millennials-confident-connected-open-to-change.pdf

Piaget, J. (1990). *The child's conception of the world.* New York: Littlefield Adams.

Prensky, M. (2001, October). Digital natives, digital immigrants. *On the Horizon, 9*(5). Retrieved from http://www.marcprensky.com/writing/Prensky percent20- percent20Digital percent20Natives, percent20Digital percent20Immigrants percent20- percent20Part1.pdf

Sousa, D. A. (2005). *How the brain learns.* Reston, VA: NASSP.

Wilcox, E. (2009, September 1). Decisions for dummies. *Canadian Medical Association Journal, 181*(5). Retrieved from http://www.ncbi.nlm.nih.gov/pmc/articles/PMC2734226/

Zaslow, J. (2009, November 4). The greatest generation of networkers. *Wall Street Journal Online.* Retrieved from http://online.wsj.com/article/SB10001424052748704746304574505643153518708.html

ABOUT THE AUTHORS

Keith J. Benson is associate professor of Management at Winthrop University, where he teaches courses in Health Care Management, Management, and Leadership. He is a member of the Knowledge Network Advisory Board for the Associations of University Programs in Health Administration (AUPHA). He has presented at various conference on using Web 2.0 in the classroom.

Josephine A. Koster is professor of English at Winthrop University, where she serves as Coordinator of the Medieval Studies Program and as Coordinator of XXITE, Winthrop's faculty initiative for XXIst Century Teaching Excellence. She has previously published on the uses of social media in the college literature classroom and made numerous presentations on the uses of social networking in college classrooms.

CHAPTER 8

IS THE iPHONE A UBIQUITOUS LEARNING DEVICE?

First Step Toward Digital Lecture Notes

Martin Ebner and Thomas Billicsich

ABSTRACT

Mobile devices are becoming more and more our daily used computers. Students are among the first to adapt to and even accelerate this progress. This opens new possibilities for teachers to reach and interact with their students and also increases the amount of information a learner has to cope with. This chapter describes the idea and prototypical implementation of a method to use the Web and digital devices to ease the digitalization of lecture notes and thus the accessibility of information gathered in the course of learning.

INTRODUCTION

Recent years have seen a dramatic increase in the number of mobile devices as well as mobile Internet connections. Platforms for so-called smartphones such as MeeGo, the iPhone OS, or Android offer new possibilities to deal with the Internet on the move. The latest AdMob Mobile Metrics[1] reports that "the

Ubiquitous Learning, pages 137–151

mobile Internet device category experienced the strongest growth of the three (Feature Phone, Smartphone, Mobile Internet Devices), increasing to account for 17% of traffic in AdMob's network in February 2010" (AdMob, 2010).

According to Gartner's Hype Cycle,[2] touch screen technology, augmented reality, and real-time collaboration (the "live Web") are the next steps toward the future Internet. Therefore it seems obvious that these new interaction paradigms (e.g., the iPhone and the iPad), new mobile system platforms (e.g., the Android), and the increased availability of free wireless network access points, affect the way how end-users interact with their devices in a pervasive and ubiquitous way. As Mark Weiser (1991) announced, "the most profound technologies are those that disappear. They weave themselves into the fabric of everyday life until they are indistinguishable from it." When we take a look at the availability of mobile phones among the youth, total saturation is reached by the age of about 15 (Hoedl, 2009). Furthermore, in Germany and Austria, there are more mobile phones than inhabitants (Springer, 2006), and according to the Austrian Central Bureau of Statistics[3] 2007, mobile phones are available in more than 90 percent of all private households. Ellis (2003) pointed out that in 2005, PDA/mobile phone device sales will outstrip PC sales, with the majority switching to wireless networks by 2008. The situation right now confirm that for example all beginners at the university own a mobile phone and using daily wireless networks.

So the interaction with these ubiquitous devices and their use for learning purposes extend the traditional e-learning paradigm into a new phenomenon called mobile learning (m-learning), or in consequence, ubiquitous learning (u-learning). Motiwalla (2007) mentioned an influence on the daily learning behavior in higher education because of the ubiquitous availability of mobile devices.

Zhan and Jin (2005) defined u-learning as a function of five parameters:

u-Learning = {u-Environment, u-Contents, u-Behavior, u-Interface, u-Service}

This simple function expresses that the application of u-learning requires different usability aspects (Kjeldskov & Stage, 2004; Venkatesh, Ramesh, & Massey, 2003; Zhang & Adipat, 2005) as well as different aspects of education (Ebner & Schiefner, 2008; Holzinger, Nischelwitzer, & Meisenberger, 2005; Tretiakov & Kinshuk, 2008). The dependence of learning and the high complexity of teaching processes on these different aspects is a big challenge for future work. Furthermore, learning must be seen as a highly social process (Holzinger, 2002), which will not happen by simply providing applications and tools. On the other hand, u-learning activities without technical preconditions will not allow innovative teaching. So research on u-learning has to focus on the interaction between human and computer, including all didactical as well as technological aspects.

Because information becomes more and more digital and therefore available on different devices, information can be analyzed by semantic technologies and might be personalized in the near future. Digital text, images or videos of events, meetings, or daily life situations will be available, at least on personal devices.

Bearing this in mind, the Department of Social Learning (DSL) at Graz University of Technology[4] (TU Graz) is thinking about how mobile devices can improve learning and teaching behavior. We will present examples of how DSL assists the u-learning approach and give a short overview in this chapter about how the learner can deal with digital lecture notes as well as offering a working prototype.

RESEARCH STUDY

According to the Introduction, it can be assumed that every student owns a mobile phone and, furthermore, is carrying it when attending a lecture. So our research idea is quite simple: when a student attends a face-to-face lecture, he/she normally writes down his/her notes. Sometimes he/she also gets the lecture slides from the teacher, but will lose all additional information. So there is no possibility to save audios, additional pictures, or video sequences. As a first consequence, we decided to create an iPhone application called Logbook, which will allow the digitalization of all lecture notes, quick and easy, without constraints on digitalization on demand. Afterwards, the student must be able to browse through the stored material and get a collection of his/her documentation on different devices.

From a u-learning perspective, a learning environment should be offered that allows the student to document, share, and discuss learning materials as well as provide access on demand from anywhere through a mobile device. As mentioned above, in the first step, the iPhone will be supported, due to the fact that the usability aspects can be taken into account easily using the appropriate Human Interface Guidelines (Apple, 2009).

Following, the implementation process is described as well as the first working prototype.

TECHNICAL IMPLEMENTATION

The Overall Idea

The core task of Logbook is to be a hub where various forms of data are uploaded to all kind of devices, and then bundled by information contained in almost all forms of digital data: time, mostly creation time.

A lifelike example for the usage of such a central information hub is a learner/student semester at university. Within these 4 to 5 months, the average student has to handle several courses and projects with fast and changing pace. Time is split in terms of hours, not days or weeks. In the morning, one could have the first lecture about, for example, design patterns, followed by a meeting with colleagues to discuss details about a project. After lunch break, the day continues with a lecture about mathematics and finishes after a laboratory course about software design notations. For each task, the learner is confronted with different kinds of digital data that should be stored and saved on his/her device. In other words, each learning activity can be seen as one (learning) event at a certain time. So the crucial attribute shared by all described events is that the learner is occupied at a certain time. This makes time the perfect variable to differentiate between different affiliations.

With smartphones and net-/notebooks being ubiquitous, portions of probably important data are recorded constantly. The usual approach of tagging urges users to make a decision about the importance of items at the time, when they are concerned with filtering the flow by deciding whether to keep a piece of information or throw it away.

Concept

Logbook is designed around events and resources. Events give a name to one or more frames of time associated with a specific occasion, like a seminar or a lecture. These time frames are called "active times" and can also be grouped together to, for example, represent a course. Resources stand for every type of content that can be bound to one point in time or directly to an event, extending to text, photos, video, audio, and location. Associated events that are manually linked to an event are called "external events," referring to their point in time being external to their events' active times.

The concept of bundling information by time allows the constant and instant gathering of all types of interesting data from different devices, without having to worry about their association in the course of action. Nearly all digital devices track the time of a recording, and it is very unlikely to be engaged in more than one important duty at a specific point within the timeline.

Figure 8.1 shows different events (Course 1, Course 2, Meeting, Laboratory) during the time line (April 4–5). The user stores different kinds of resources (URL, image, note, video) for each event. So if any kind of resource is taken, it is automatically assigned to the appropriate recent event.

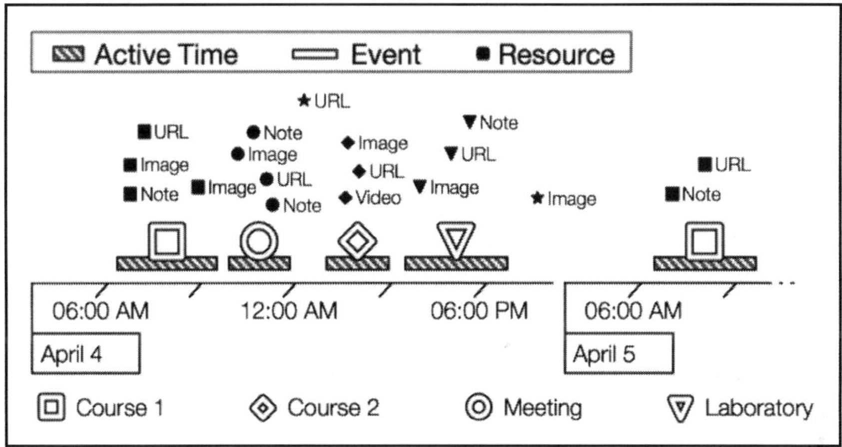

Figure 8.1 Overall concept.

Architectural Design

The near omnipresent access to the Internet makes a Web server the perfect way to realize the idea of Logbook. To be able to upload data, the perfect companion for a Web service is a mobile app. This combination is the approach the TU Graz team took to test the idea. The mobile app is built for the emerging platform of Apple's iPhone. Its purpose is mainly to view the contents of an event and to manage the metadata of events as well as to record all the necessary data. To enforce the demand on flexibility regarding content sources, the gathering of information is left to another service called Evernote. It provides applications for all popular mobile and desktop platforms and stands as an example for a variety of external services able to provide data.

Figure 8.2 describes a typical use case for Logbook. The digital camera and an iPhone are used as mobile sources for pictures that are automatically marked with the creation date and seamlessly uploaded to the Evernote server using the Internet (left side, "image upload"). This is possible since every iPhone already has a data connection available, and the camera is equipped with a Eye-Fi card that logs itself into a WiFi network. In addition, pictures can also be uploaded manually via a Web browser, in case there is no Eye-Fi card with the camera.

Events and their active times are managed via the Logbook iPhone client or the Web site. Once events are set up, Logbook automatically collects items for the relevant times from Evernote and associates them with the

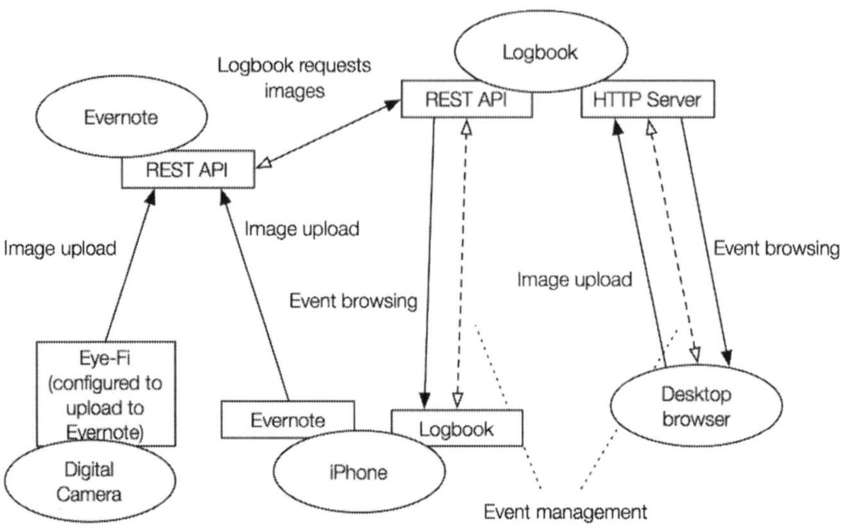

Figure 8.2 Architectural design of the prototype.

corresponding event. These events can then be examined again via desktop Web browser or iPhone client. The bundled information can also be downloaded to the local hard drive.

IPHONE USER INTERFACE

Building an iPhone Application

When thinking about implementing an iPhone application, one has to adhere to principles that contrast traditional desktop development (Apple Inc., 2009). On the technical side, memory and processing power are limited. Although the hardware is moderate, the user expects a responsive application. A program must "feel" fast. Apple gives some help by providing animations and transitions that make changes seem to happen instantly, but avoiding heavyweight operations while leaving the user in doubt of the current state is a constant challenge. On the interaction side, the usage pattern is a different one than the ones most of the paradigms in software development are made for: short application life, shallow usage, and people of all levels of technological knowledge have to understand and use it.

Most importantly, the only input device is the user's fingers. The touch screen itself puts force on the developer to spend the biggest amount of time and energy designing the interface. Users want to start an application; do one specific thing, like taking a note, sending an e-mail or taking a picture; and then shut it down again. The developer has to do his best to help the user achieve this goal.

The classic approach to designing software is to start with splitting up the big problem that one wants to solve into smaller portions. Apple argued that this was not the most important thing when developing the iPhone OS (Apple Inc., 2009). The limited size and the fingers as input device usually do not allow all the things initially planned. So by starting with designing the screens, the programmer quickly reaches the point of reconsidering the strategy, usually dropping features—a good thing on such a tiny device—and focusing on the actual problem at hand.

Design of User Interface

Programming of touch sensitive applications is a very young and academic research area, being sparse in this field. Furthermore, usability engineering on mobile devices differs arbitrarily from desktop computers. There are few research results (Ebner, Stickel, Scerbakov, & Holzinger, 2009; Kaikonnen, Kallio, Kekalainen, Kankainen, & Cankar, 2005; Roto, 2006) as well as advice that derives from experience (Holzinger & Errath, 2007; Holzinger, Searle, & Nischelwitzer, 2007; Nischelwitzer, Pintoffl, Loss, & Holzinger, 2007). A good way of starting to realize one's own ideas is by drafting them on paper by building an appropriate mockup. It is a fast method, imposes no restrictions when it comes to applying notes and comments, and there is no need or urge to be pixel-precise. It also offers a quick possibility to discuss the visual concept with others.

Figure 8.3 shows the paper mockup of the iPhone application Logbook. Logbook on iPhone is a native Cocoa (Apple Inc.'s native object-oriented application program environment) application that is used to manage event time slots and resources and to browse events. The user interface is divided into four parts (see Figure 8.4):

- display of current status
- navigation hierarchy
- event content list view
- timeline view

Display of Current Status

This display of the currently active events along with other quick actions allows the learner to quickly take action on the event at hand.

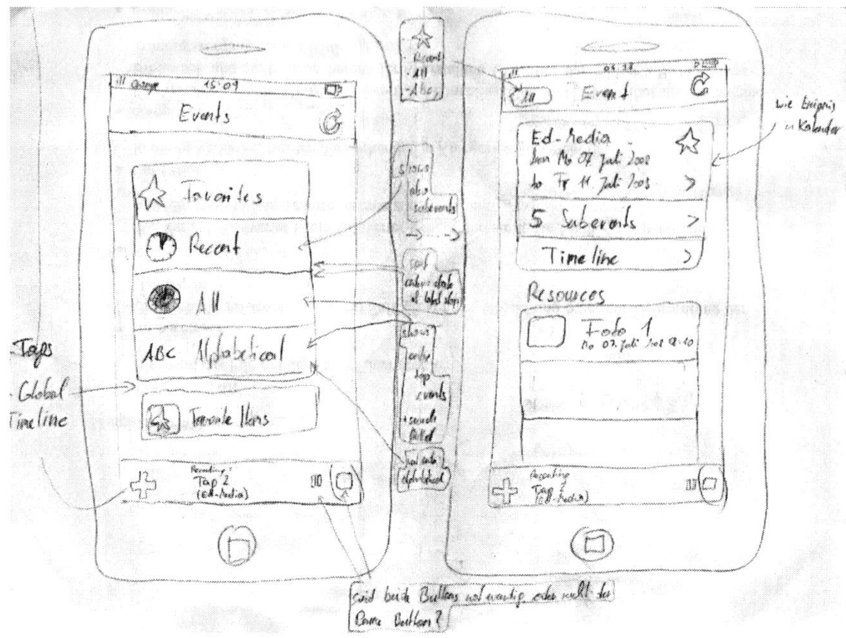

Figure 8.3 Paper mockup of the iPhone application.

Figure 8.4 Screensthots of the iPhone application Logbook.

Navigation Hierarchy

The navigation hierarchy is an iPhone-typical table view drill-down hierarchy with three levels. In its topmost level, which also works as the entry point of the application, it allows access to lists of events sorted by time or event name and to all resources. It further displays the name of the currently active event. Through the second level, the sorted listing of events represented by their name and last activity date, the user selects an event to be displayed and edited.

Event Content List View

This is the main view for editing an event. Event details and all associated resources in chronological order are displayed. Particular resources can be removed from the event and external resources can be added. Active times can be edited, removed, or added as well.

Timeline View

The timeline view is the key component of Logbook. It allows the learner to quickly scroll through all information gathered and get an overview of a certain event. The item of interest can be selected and more information about it can be being displayed. By combining text and image views, the timeline connects photos with notes just by their proximity in time.

WEB SERVER MODULES

The Web server is programmed in Ruby[5] with help of Ruby on Rails.[6] It's tasks are seen in Figure 8.5:

- user account management
- session handling
- storage of image data
- providing Web pages
- serving API requests

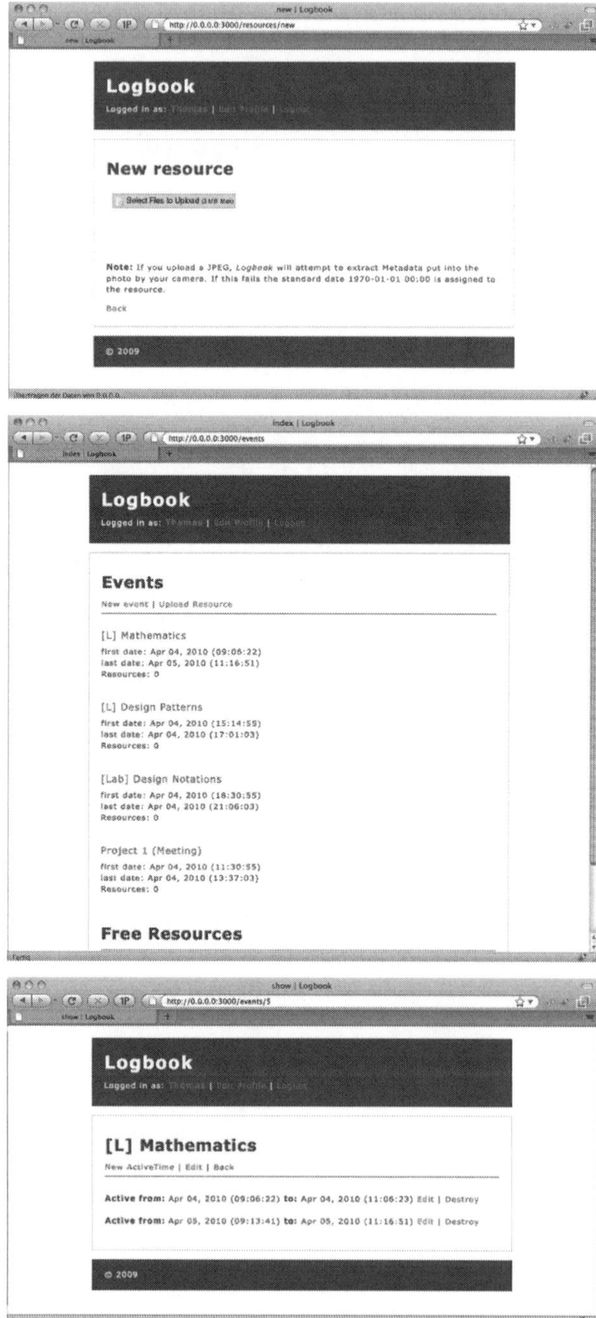

Figure 8.5 Screenshots of the Web server modules.

User Account Management

A user creates an account by providing a username and password. After that, the user can immediately start to define and name events, add active times, and upload photos. Username and password have to be typed in on the iPhone to connect the Web service and mobile application.

Session Handling

HTTP, a standard Internet protocol, requires only a browser and server to share a session ID; both can confer to authenticate and identify a person or device allowed to access certain resources.

Storage of Image Data

Images get a unique identifier and are stored in their original format on the server's file system. Supported file types are JPEG and PNG. JPEGs usually contain EXIF data, a metadata format that stores lots of information about camera and lens, the most valuable purpose being storage of the creation date. When uploading PNGs, Logbook relies on their creation date as stored in the desktop computers file system.

Providing Web Pages

Web pages give easy access to any user with a Web browser. This includes desktop and mobile browsers.

Serving API Requests

Web pages are an inefficient way of communication between devices. They are only suited for representation of data to users. Therefore an API has been defined, which provides data and can also alter data upon request. Through these REST requests, the iPhone application communicates with the Web part of Logbook.

Design of User Interface

The main part of the Logbook Web site is the overview as mentioned previously. It is the entry point after logging in, lists all events in alphabetical order, and shows their time span and resources. Links refer to details of specific events and to resource uploading. Although browsers do not allow the uploading of more than one file at a time, it is still possible to do this in Evernote by a small Flash-driven widget that only serves to display a window where files can be selected and then uploads one file after another to the Web server.

DISCUSSION

After implementing the first prototype, several end-users ($n = 9$) began a test run by installing the iPhone application on their own devices and registering on the Web application. We asked them to test the overall functionality as well as the usage for learning and teaching purposes. The feedback gives an insight as to whether the iPhone fits requirements of a u-learning device:

- Logbook is used for event documentation: The main purpose of this u-learning supporting application is the documentation of events (e.g., lectures). The first test run shows that the application is used exactly for this purpose. The main usage was taking pictures of additional temporary learning materials such as additional notes of teachers on blackboards or projections that are not part of the digital lecture notes. Notes as well as Internet links were stored comparatively rarely.
- iPhone is still a barrier in handling all tasks: It seems that for end-users, daily taking digital notes with their iPhone, as mentioned by one user, is not a common task. He needed some time to realize that he can simply take a picture instead of copying teacher's notes from the blackboard. Another user mentioned that he felt distracted from the lecture when he was busily handling his/her mobile device. Finally, some statements pointed out that, though typing on iPhone is quite easy, handwriting still seems to be faster and more common.
- Technical restrictions: In the end, there are also some technical restrictions, mainly according the use of the additional iPhone application Evernote. From an end-user perspective, it is not understandable why a third-party application is necessary to take pictures and afterwards to synchronize with the current event. Furthermore, the Web application lacks some additional features for filtering, searching, and sorting the collected data.
- The mobile and Web application landscape advance at an extraordinary pace: When this project was started, the iPhone SDK (Software Development Kit) had been released for only about 6 months. By

April 2010, the second major revision of its operating system had been revealed. In a similar manner, dynamical scripting of Web pages became a normal part of Web sites. That means 1 year into its life, the whole application suite needed a complete overhaul and extension.{/BL}

CONCLUSION

It is easy to see that u-learning is a task of the future when a look at the increasing number of mobile devices with Internet access is taken. It is readily imaginable that in a few years, each student will be able to get any available information on the Internet just in time, so dealing with digital resources will become a daily routine. Accordingly, this publication introduces the first consideration of, as well as a first working prototype for the digital documentation of learning events.

It can be shown that in principal, the concept is working, but there are restrictions on the user side (distraction, not a common task) as well as on the hardware (complicated input) and software sides.

Bearing in mind that in the future, completely new mobile devices will enter the classroom, surpassing the iPad and iPhone, we conclude that u-learning is one of the most important movements in technology-enhanced learning, also in terms of the personalization and individualization of the learning processes.

NOTES

1. http://metrics.admob.com/ (last visited April 2010)
2. http://www.gartner.com/it/page.jsp?id=1124212 (last visited April 2010)
3. http://www.statistik.at/ (last visited April 2010)
4. http://elearning.tugraz.at (last visited April 2010)
5. http://www.ruby-lang.org (last visited April 2010)
6. http://rubyonrails.org/ (last visited April 2010)

REFERENCES

AdMob. (2010, February). *AdMob mobile metrics report, 2010.* Retrieved from http://metrics.admob.com/wp-content/uploads/2010/03/AdMob-Mobile-Metrics-Feb-10.pdf

Apple Inc. (2009). *iPhone human interface guidlines.* Cupertino, CA.

Ebner, M., & Schiefner, M. (2008). Will e-learning die? In A. R. Lipshitz & S. P. Parsons (Eds.), *E-learning: 21st century issues and challenges* (pp. 69–82). Nova Publishers.

Ebner, M., Stickel, C., Scerbakov, N., & Holzinger, A. (2009). A study on the compatibility of ubiquitous learning (u-learning) systems at university level. *In Springer lecture notes in computer science* (pp. 34–43).

Ellis, K. (2003). Moving into m-learning. *Training, 40*(10), 12–15.

Hoedl, S. (2009). *m-learning in schools: A survey on existence of mobile phones.* Thesis, Graz University of Technology, Austria.

Holzinger, A. (2002). *Multimedia basics. Volume 2: Cognitive fundamentals of multimedial Information Systems.* New Delhi: Laxmi-Publications. Retrieved from http://www.basiswissen-multimedia.at

Holzinger, A., Nischelwitzer, A., & Meisenberger, M. (2005, March 8–12). Mobile phones as a challenge for m-learning: Examples of mobile interactive learning objects (MILOs). In D. Tavangarian, (Ed.), *Third Annual IEEE International Conference on Pervasive Computing and Communications IEEE* (pp. 307–311), Kauai, HI.

Holzinger, A., & Errath, M. (2007). Mobile computer Web-application design in medicine: Some research based guidelines. *Universal Access in the Information Society International Journal, 6*(1), 31–41.

Holzinger, A., Searle, G., & Nischelwitzer, A. (2007). On some aspects of improving mobile applications for the elderly. In C. Stephanidis (Ed.), *Coping with diversity in universal access, research and development methods in universal access: Lecture notes in computer science* (LNCS 4554), p. 923–932.

Kaikkonen, A., Kallio, T., Kekalainen, A., Kankainen, A., & Cankar, M. (2005). Usability testing of mobile applications: A comparison between laboratory and field testing. *Journal of Usability Studies, 1*(1), 4–46.

Kjeldskov, J., & Stage, J. (2004). New techniques for usability evaluation of mobile systems. *International Journal of Human-Computer Studies, 60*(5–6), 599–620.

Motiwalla. L. F. (2007). Mobile learning: A framework and evaluation. *Computers & Education, 49*(2007), 581–596.

Nischelwitzer, A., Pintoffl, K., Loss, C., & Holzinger, A. (2007). Design and development of a mobile medical application for the management of chronic diseases: Methods of improved data input for older people. In A. Holzinger (Ed.), *USAB 2007, Lecture notes in computer science* (LNCS 4799) (pp. 119–132). Springer.

Roto, V. (2006). *Web browsing on mobile phones—Characteristics of user experience.* Retrieved from http://lib.tkk.fi/Diss/2006/isbn9512284707/

Springer, A., (2006). *Marketing announcement: Market analyses telecommunication 2006,* Portal für den deutschen Telekommunikationsmarkt, study.

Tretiakov, A., & Kinshuk (2008). Toward designing m-learning systems for maximal likelihood of acceptance. *International Journal of Engineering Education, 24*(1), 79–83.

Venkatesh, V., Ramesh, V., & Massey, A. P. (2003). Understanding usability in mobile commerce—Ramifications for wireless design: "E" not equal "M." *Communications of the ACM, 46*(12), 53–56.

Weiser, M. (1991). The computer for the twenty-first century. *Scientific American, 265*(3), 94–104.

Zhang, D. S., & Adipat, B. (2005). Challenges, methodologies, and issues in the usability testing of mobile applications. *International Journal of Human-Computer Interaction, 18*(3), 293–308.

Zhan, G., & Jin, Q. (2005, December 5–8). Research on collaborative service solution in ubiquitous learning. *Environment 6th International Conference on Parallel and Distributed Computing, Applications and Technologies* (PDCAT'05) (pp. 804–806) Dalian, China.

ABOUT THE AUTHORS

Martin Ebner is currently head of the Social Learning team at Graz University of Technology. He is responsible for all e-learning activities of this university. His research focuses strongly on the use of Web 2.0 technologies for teaching and learning purposes. Martin has taught a number of lectures and seminars around the topic of e-learning and the use of computers in educational settings. He studied civil engineering from 1995 to 2000 and got his master's at the Institute of Structural Concrete. Afterwards, Martin worked as scientific assistant at the Institute of structural concrete and wrote his PhD thesis about "e-Learning in Structural Engineering." Since 2005, he's held a PhD in Technical Sciences from Graz University of Technology. From 2005 to 2006, he worked at the Institute for Building Informatics as assistant professor. Since September 2006, Martin has been senior researcher at the Institute of Information Systems and Computer Media. Find more details at http://www.martinebner.at

Thomas Billicsich is a student of telematics with a master's degree from the Graz University of Technology. While a member of the Social Learning team under the direction of Martin Ebner, he implemented the draft version of the Logbook iPhone application and an accompanying Web service. After spending a year as a foreign student at the Czech Technical University in Prague, he completed his Bachelor of Science degree in 2008, writing a thesis about automatic tagging of textual content in e-Learning systems. His research and work activities now comprise the development of native mobile applications and highly interactive Web applications in JavaScript and their usability for computer-unacquainted people.

CHAPTER 9

REMOTE LABORATORIES AND MOBILE DEVICES

Javier Garcia-Zubia, Jaime Irurzun, Pablo Orduña, and Diego López-de-Ipiña

ABSTRACT

Remote laboratories were born around 2000 as a learning tool that allows students to perform laboratory practices through the Internet, avoiding the timing and availability constraints involved by physical labs. The University of Deusto was one of the first centers involved in the research of this type of computer systems, having, since 2003, developed one of the first remote labs based on Web 2.0 technologies. Nowadays, remote labs are in the process of expansion and integration with heterogeneous systems and devices that can extend their didactic value. This chapter discusses, from a software point of view, the possibilities of using remote laboratories from mobile devices, one of the most suitable tools for ubiquitous learning.

INTRODUCTION

Remote labs are a tool that by themselves have much to do with ubiquity. A simple and clear definition can be the following: a remote lab is a computer system that enables the use of laboratory equipment in a remote way, i.e.,

Ubiquitous Learning, pages 153–175

from a distance. Of course, after reading this definition, we all dream about a person clad in a virtual reality helmet and two haptic gloves that let him manipulate dozens of test tubes from a last-generation chemical laboratory. No doubt the ideal goal of a remote lab is this: that the experience of anyone using it is exactly equal to that which would be physically there. The reality is that time and money are finite, and therefore only strict environments (such as telemedicine) are able to offer a similar user experience.

Here we will talk about common remote labs. In particular, remote laboratories applied to education. In this setting, the scene we will have to imagine is very different, but equally practical. Consider a student of electronic engineering who has to write a computer program to make a microcontroller work a certain way. In the traditional lab, the student would have to write the program in a computer lab and then connect the microcontroller to the PC to flush the chip with the program. Once flushed, he would have to check that the microcontroller actually behaves as he hopes, perhaps triggering some inputs (switches or buttons, for example) and watching the output (an LED that turns on or a motor that is activated at a certain speed). If not, he will need to fix his code with the text editor and reflush the memory.

In this scenario, we see that the student is making use of two physical resources (computer and microcontroller), but if we think about the value of both, we will realize that the truly valuable resource is the microcontroller, since the PC is only working as a simple common-software platform (a text editor and a compiler) to write the program. If we decided to convert this live experiment into a remotely accessible experiment used by a broad group of people, we would probably end up deciding that the most convenient strategy is to minimize the time using the physical resource (the microcontroller) so that more people can work with it without affecting the rest. Figure 9.1 shows an electronic experiment, similar to what we imagine, being used through WebLab-Deusto and the remote lab of the University of Deusto.

The students make use of this laboratory as follows: first, they have to write and compile the program on any PC with the appropriate software; second, they enter the lab with any Web browser, and they reserve the experiment; third, they need to submit the program file and watch through the Webcam how the microcontroller is flushed; after that, they are given a short period of time (around 150–200 seconds) to test the inputs and observe if the experiment behaves as they expected. While a student is using the resource, those who arrive are left waiting in a queue that shows them how many people are ahead. Later we will detail the features of this remote lab, since the needs of any educational institution are more complex than managing the queue of users. The important thing so far is to understand the usage scenario of a remote lab in the field of education.

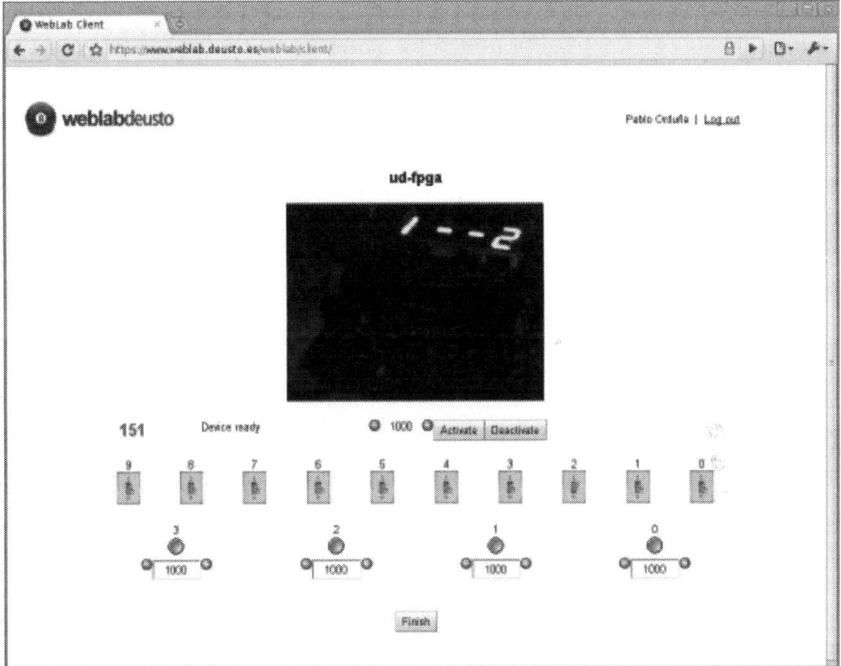

Figure 9.1 An electronic experiment used in WebLab-Deusto.

The next section presents remote labs as an educational resource, offering as an example of its implementation the experience at the University of Deusto. Folllowing is a more technical description of the architecture of a remote lab, which is necessary to finally discuss the application of mobile devices to this field. The chapter ends with conclusions and future trends.

REMOTE LABS IN EDUCATION

Before continuing, it is worth clarifying a question of names. So far we have talked about remote laboratories, precisely because this chapter addresses them specifically. However, remote laboratories belong to a broader set of tools: online laboratories. Online labs can be virtual, remote, or hybrids. The difference is that the user of a virtual laboratory does not control an actual device, but works with software that simulates the behavior. Remote laboratories, however, allow experimentation with a physical device, it being unnecessary to program an overall simulator, which makes it possible to offer such complex devices as may exist with fully reliable results. Finally, hybrid laboratories are a combination of the two.

Another name to which some online labs are commonly referred is "WebLabs." A WebLab is an online Web-based laboratory, that is, accessible from a Web browser with an Internet connection. The advantage of such laboratories is that, in principle, they facilitate their use in terms of software requirements as any Web application does in contrast to desktop applications.

Since 2000, a growing number of remote laboratories have been designed, implemented, and put into practice worldwide. Many papers and books have also been published, which focus on their advantages and disadvantages (Gomes & Garcia-Zubía, 2007), architectures (Gobbo & Vaccari, 2005), technologies (Indrusiak, Glesner, & Reis, 2007), educational value (Ma & Nickerson, 2006), and so on, demonstrating the interdisciplinary nature of this research field.

If we examine the consequences of tools like these, we see that the technical effort involved in building them is almost always rewarded. These are the main advantages offered by the use of a remote lab for the student, the teacher, and the center:

- Use of equipment. The laboratory equipment is available to students 24 hours a day, 365 days a year.
- Efficiency of laboratories: No need to keep the labs open all the time, you only need to keep operating the remote laboratory.
- Organization of student work: Both the student and the teacher can better organize their time, including class time.
- Autonomous learning: It promotes self-learning, important in the European Space for Higher Education (ESHE).
- Distance education: It facilitates the organization of engineering courses at a distance, making it the perfect complement to the LMS (Learning Management Systems) as a tool for e-learning.
- Accessibility: Since the devices are controlled by computers, physically handicapped people can use them using software designed for their particular needs.
- Cost savings: Maximizing the use, avoiding downtime, sharing resources, and reducing the necessary maintenance directly affects the performance of the investment made by purchasing the equipment.

The WebLab-Deusto Experience

WebLab-Deusto is the remote lab created and developed by the WebLab-Deusto Research Group at the University of Deusto in Bilbao, Spain. It was first used by the students of the faculty in 2004, focusing on experiments in electronics engineering. In particular, the laboratory currently offers the following:

1. **FPGA:** This is an electronic board managed by a Xilinx Spartan FPGA. The student submits his program file, the chip memory is flushed with its content, and then the student is given a short period of time to test the board's behavior by activating the inputs with the Web components and by watching the outputs through a Webcam. This is the experiment that we showed in Figure 9.1.
2. **CPLD:** Its use is exactly the same as that of the FPGA, but in this case, the set of components on the board are different, and the chip is a Xilinx XC9572 CPLD.
3. **GPIB:** This experiment is most peculiar. The shared resource is a PC connected to a spectrum analyzer and a function generator through a GPIB bus. The student submits his program in a file, and it is compiled and executed on the PC. Finally the student receives the output generated by the program, as well as the two standard outputs: messages and errors.
4. **LOGIC:** The LOGIC experiment is the simplest of all but has a didactic and demonstrative function. It offers the student a randomly generated logic gate circuit with certain input values. The resulting value of the circuit is connected to a set of 8 LEDs. Every door is of a particular type (AND, OR, XOR, NAND, or NOR) except for one, the one that the student will have to guess to make the resulting value of the circuit turn on the LEDs. When the student guesses the type of door, he scores a point, and he is presented a new random circuit. Finally, when he first fails solving a circuit, he can check his position in the overall points ranking.

To test the educational value of remote labs, the University of Deusto has carried out a satisfaction survey to their students each year. The survey consists of 12 questions, and it is filled out by the students at the end of each semester. Table 9.1 shows the results of the survey from 2004 to 2009 for the Programmable Logic (PL) and Electronics Design (ED) subjects. The minimum value is 1 ("I totally disagree") and 5 is the maximum value ("I totally agree"). The answers are grouped in three sections: Acceptance and Usefulness of the WebLab (1–4), Usability of the WebLab (5–10) and Problems in the WebLab (11–12). Question 12 asks the student about the experiments queues.

Table 9.2 describes the survey in the different years. It describes how many students were in each course, how many students completed the survey, and how many times the WebLab was accessed by the students.

The following figures integrate the results obtained from both subjects. The objective is to establish the differences and similarities between them. In Figures 2 through 4, odd elements are related to the PL subject and even elements to the ED one. This way, the elements are arranged in the

TABLE 9.1 Results of the Surveys Proposed to the Students (2004–2009)

	PL 04/05	DE 04/05	PL 05/06	DE 06/07	PL 06/07	DE 07/08	PL 07/08	DE 08/09	PL 08/09
Acceptance and Usefulness of the WebLab									
1. Has WebLab helped you with the subject?	4.60	4.10	3.80	3.84	3.75	3.50	4.20	4.10	4.50
2. What is your global satisfaction with WebLab?	4.70	3.90	3.70	3.72	4.00	3.70	4.10	4.40	4.40
3. Do you think it is a good idea if this WebLab experiment is extended to all the students?	4.70	4.60	4.20	4.13	4.10	4.20	4.20	4.50	4.40
4. Would you like to use WebLab in other subjects?	4.30	4.00	3.90	3.80	4.10	3.70	3.90	4.20	4.10
Usability of the WebLab									
5. Is it easy to use?	4.40	4.40	3.90	3.67	3.90	4.10	4.40	4.30	4.30
6. How is the quality of the Webcam?	3.20	2.40	2.70	2.95	2.50	3.20	2.80	2.40	3.40
7. Did you feel at ease managing the inputs?	3.70	3.10	3.00	3.51	3.10	3.40	3.60	4.10	4.00
8. What do you think about the inputs/outputs implemented?	3.80	3.20	3.40	3.41	3.50	3.70	4.00	4.10	4.30
9. What do you think about the time assigned to each connection?	3.70	2.70	3.10	3.23	2.40	3.80	3.70	3.10	3.60
10. Being far from the prototype, have you felt yourself to be in control?	4.10	3.70	3.60	3.64	3.70	3.70	3.90	4.30	4.30
Problems in the WebLab									
11. How many times was the server down?		3.10	2.20	2.46	2.10	2.70	3.30	2.50	2.60
12. How many times did you wait to use it?		2.50	2.10	2.49	2.00	2.60	3.90	2.70	3.60

Note: PL = Programmable Logic; ED = Electronics Design
Scale: 1 ("I totally disagree) to 5 ("I totally agree")

TABLE 9.2 Description of the Surveys

	Students	Surveys	Accesses
ED 05/06	31	17	495
ED 06/07	42	39	1,985
ED 07/08	33	28	1,147
ED 08/09	23	23	1,443
PL 04/05	90	10	1,706
PL 05/06	58	40	632
PL 06/07	37	33	1,012
PL 07/08	36	33	3,180
PL 08/09	65	48	3,453

time: 1. PL 2004/05; 2. ED 2005/06; 3. PL 2005/06; 4. ED 2006/07; 5. PL 2006/07; 6. ED 2007/08; 7. PL 2007/08; 8. ED 2008/09; 9. PL 2008/09. Figure 9.2 shows clearly that the usefulness of the WebLab has a very good mark. It is 4 points on average. This score is constant during the years in both subjects, except for year 2004/05 in PL.

Figure 9.3 reflects that the students, in different years and/or subjects, do not agree in their evaluation of the quality of the WebLab. The lines are very different among students, especially when asked for their reviews about connection time and the quality of the Webcam.

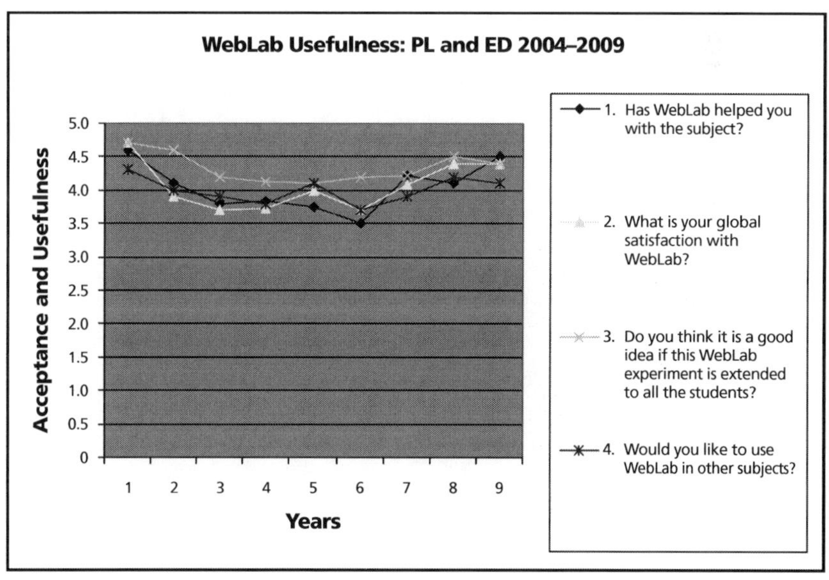

Figure 9.2 Comparison with respect to WebLab usefulness.

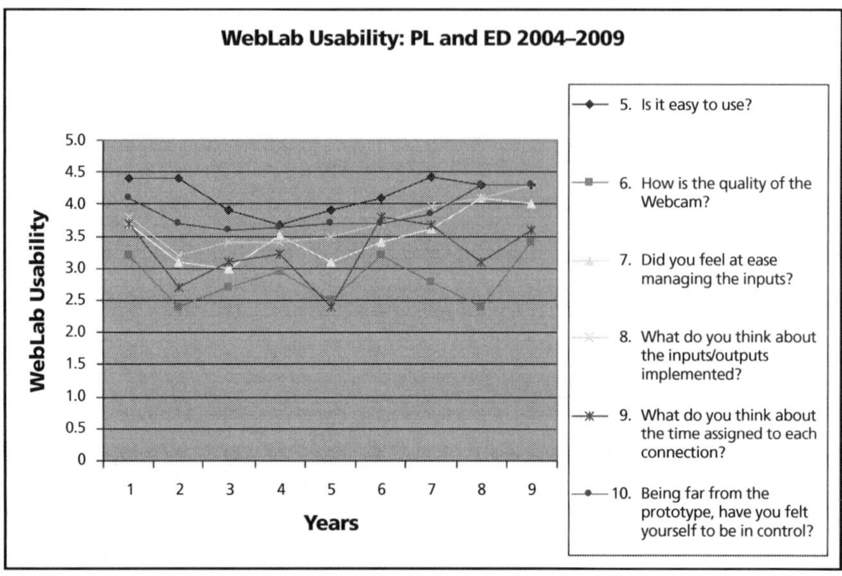

Figure 9.3 Comparison with respect to WebLab usability.

Anyway, the most important question of this group is related to the feeling of control. In both subjects, the students felt that they controlled the experiment. Figure 9.4 shows the questions related to the times the server was down and the waiting queue, which are around 2 points every year.

Other universities in the world are also very involved in research and application of remote labs in education. The Massachusetts Institute of Tech-

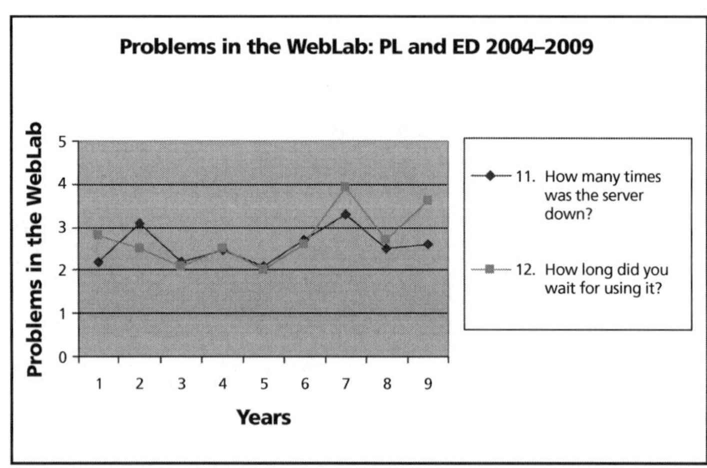

Figure 9.4 Comparison with respect to WebLab problems.

nology (MIT) was one of the pioneers in this field, developing the first version of the iLab (Harward et al., 2008), probably the most widely used remote laboratory in the world. The LabShare project (Lowe et al., 2009), which brings together five universities in Australia, is another representative example, as well as the work from the Carinthia University of Applied Sciences (Maier & Niederstätter, 2010), among others.

Remote Labs Inside

To understand the implications of the development of remote labs accessible from mobile devices, it is important first to understand the infrastructure behind a remote laboratory. To discover it, we will do a little tour through the architecture of WebLab-Deusto, with special *incapié* (emphasis) in the elements relating to those who want to integrate a new experiment in the lab.

But first, let's take a moment to look back at the evolution of remote labs research (Gravier, Fayolle, Bayard, Ates, & Lardon, 2008). The short history could be divided into three phases:

1. **Birth** (1995–2000). The initial objective of the laboratories was to overcome the technical barrier: that the shared resource could be used remotely, even under limited conditions and without much stability. The achievement was to make it work. Some examples of this first phase are PEARL, MARVEL, or the first experiments in iLab.
2. **Professionalization** (2001–2007). Having achieved the basic goal, the second phase was to professionalize those initially rudimentary laboratories. Most especially software architectures, ease of access, security concerns, new features required by the educational context. Some examples are the iLab (iLab Shared Architecture), LabShare (Sahara), WebLab-Deusto, eMERSION or VISIR.
3. **Globalization** (2008–). Current efforts are on the interoperability of remote labs, with the ultimate goal of extending their use and establishing them as an essential didactic tool. There are very different active initiatives: sharing experiments among different remote labs in a standard way (GOLC consortium), integration with the LMS (Moodle, .LRN, Sakai), access from immersive MMORPG environments (Second Life, OpenSim, Wonderland), access from unconventional devices (mobile phones, smartphones, game platforms), etc.

As might be expected, current conditions are very demanding for any remote laboratory that seeks to become the final solution. Access from mobile devices is just one of many technical requirements to which any modern platform is exposed.

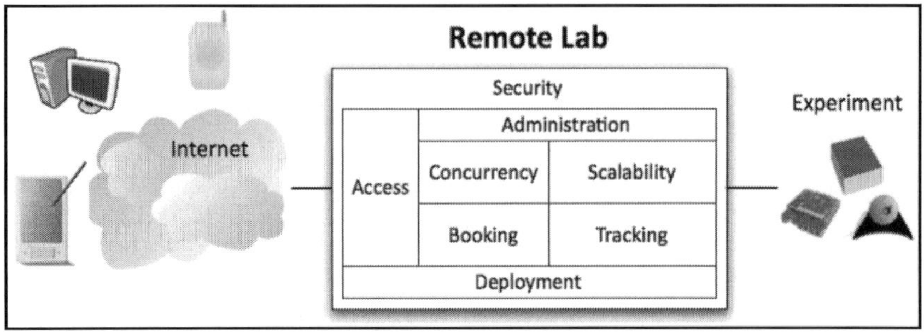

Figure 9.5 Overview of the architecture of a remote laboratory.

If we think of a remote laboratory as a closed box, the only thing that matters is whether it is able to communicate with everything around it. But if we look inside, we will understand exactly what points define the limits that make the laboratory an interoperable and extensible platform, capable of living in an ecosystem so populous and changing with the present one. Figure 9.5 shows, at a general level, the role of the remote laboratory platform as a mediator between those who want to use the remote experiments and the resources themselves.

We can see that, as mentioned above, the remote laboratory responsibilities go beyond managing the queue of requests for use. If we want a platform for experiments, a real laboratory, what makes sense is to delegate to it all the responsibilities that are common to the experiments to be offered, or potentially can offer. In Figure 9.5, we indicated the following:

- Access: The use of experiments must be controlled in terms of authentication (who can access the lab) and authorization (what each user can do once inside). Not only is it important that the system is secure, but also that it is flexible. For instance, a common need of schools and universities is to integrate all the authentication systems with a centralized service, such as Active Directory or any LDAP server.
- Concurrency: As we saw above, managing the queue of requests for use is one of the first requirements we can think about. The laboratory should manage concurrent access to multiple users, queueing the requests based on various criteria: first come, origin of the request, availability of the experiment, and so on.
- Booking: Laboratory experiments can provide two modes of operation: immediate (a student requests the experiment to be used immediately during a very short period of time) and booking (a student reserves the experiment for a specific date and time, usually

for a longer period of time). The laboratory should provide both methods and manage queues of requests accordingly.

- Scalability: Far from the ad hoc solutions for the first time, a modern remote laboratory should be allowed to escalate horizontally, that is, the more of the same type of physical devices we employ, the greater number of users we can serve concurrently.
- Deployment: The infrastructure of schools is often complex and may be composed of several geographically dispersed faculties. Even within the same faculty, the experiments offered by the laboratory may be in separate rooms and under very different conditions in terms of security and maintenance. The remote laboratory should make transparent the whole network.
- Security: In addition to providing secure access control, the laboratory must ensure that communications between the various servers that will collaborate on the system (from the client terminal to the resources offered by the experiments) are safe.
- Tracking: In an educational environment, it is important to record the use made by the students for each experiment. Returning to the examples shown before, a teacher should be able to review exactly what each student has activated in a board, as well as the program he has sent to flush the microcontroller.
- Administration: Finally, the laboratory shall provide facilities to its managers to perform routine tasks: manage users and permissions, configuration, monitoring access, usage reports, backups, etc.

The great value of a remote laboratory is to provide all these features immediately to any experiment that is integrated into it (Garcia-Zubia, Orduña, López-de-Ipiña, & Alves, 2009). WebLab-Deusto is one example that follows this approach. Let's see how it is built.

A Practical Example: The WebLab-Deusto Architecture

WebLab-Deusto is intended as a framework that abstracts the developers' experiments from the complexity of providing the common functionality (Orduña et al., 2009). Figure 9.6 gives an overview of its architecture, which, when taken to its extreme, could resemble an enormous tree of experiments physically located in different laboratories.

Looking at Figure 9.7, we see in detail the distribution of internal servers and the implemented communication protocols for exchanging messages.

What is interesting here is that at both ends of the architecture (the facade and the laboratory-experiment connection), we find a Web service implemented in a variety of communication protocols (SOAP, XML-RPC,

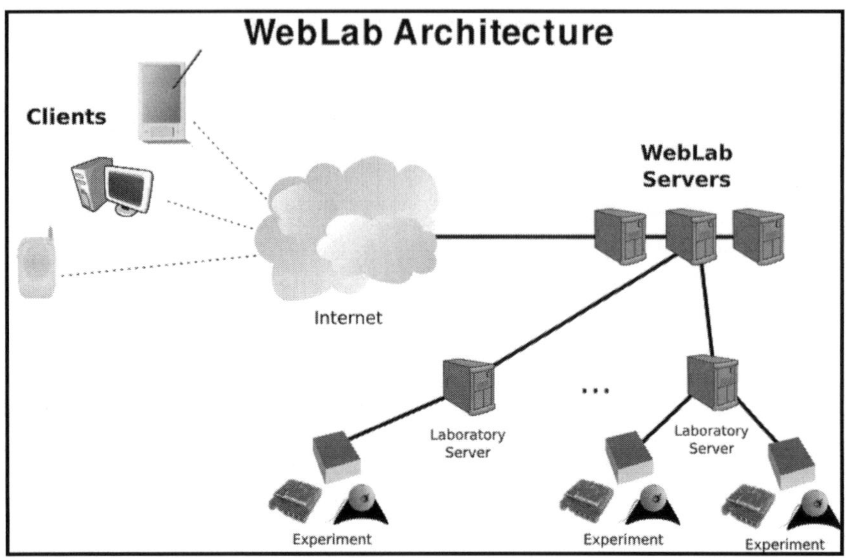

Figure 9.6 Overview of the architecture of WebLab-Deusto.

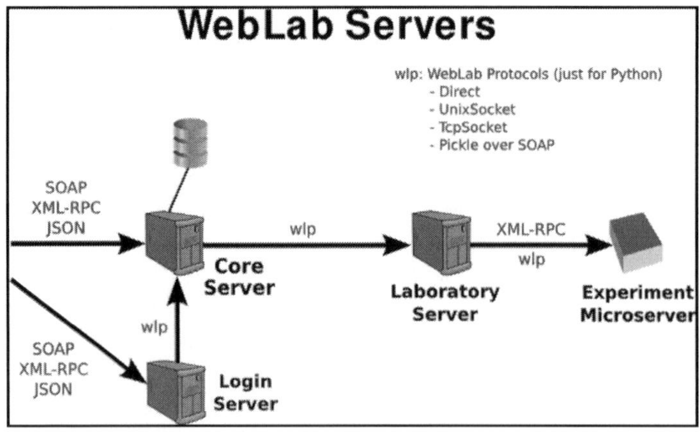

Figure 9.7 A closer look at the architecture of WebLab-Deusto.

and JSON). The reason is interoperability. The three protocols available on the facade of servers allow any client able to speak any of these three protocols to be a valid client to access the remote laboratory. Figure 9.8 is a clear example of this advantage; we can see a user programming a microbot remotely from Second Life, that is, a WebLab-Deusto client implemented in Second Life.

Figure 9.8 Accessing WebLab-Deusto from Second Life.

The only thing any client should be aware of is the interface that the Web service provides:

```
public interface WebLabDeustoFacade
 {
 SessionID login(String username, String password);
 UserInformation get_user_information(Session session);
 ExperimentAllowed[] list_experiments(Session session);
 Reservation reserve_experiment(Session session, Experiment
      experiment);
 Reservation get_reservation_status(Session session);
 Command send_file(Session session, String content, String
      file_info)
 Command send_command(Session session, Command command);
 void poll(Session session);
 void finished_experiment(Session session);
 void logout(Session session);
 }
```

We can see that this decoupling between the client and the server is also a great advantage for laboratory access from mobile devices. In addition to allowing the implementation of completely different clients, WebLab-Deusto also facilitates what is expected to be the most common task: to integrate any experiment into the WebLab-Deusto Web client. This method is much simpler, as the software layer common to every experiment (common user interface, communications, themes system) is also uncoupled from the experiment-dependent code. In this case, the task is almost as simple as defining the user interface needed for the experiment from a palette of prebuilt components: switches, buttons, potentiometers, Webcams, etc. The WebLab-Deusto Web client is written in Google Web Toolkit (GWT), the popular framework to develop Web 2.0 applications by Google. This technology itself has advantages and disadvantages that we will see later, but the client is also prepared to reuse user interfaces written in Javascript, Java applets, or Adobe Flash.

The other key point of the architecture is the communication between the Laboratory server and the Experiment server (see Figure 9.7). The Experiment server is the only other module that must develop those who want to integrate an experiment in WebLab-Deusto. Its mission is to process the messages sent by the user from the client (a click on a button or submitting a file to flush the memory of a microcontroller) and physically contact with the device to be controlled. In this case, the relationship between this small server and other remote laboratory architecture is also defined by an interface that both must meet:

```
public interface WebLabDeustoExperimentServer
 (
 void start_experiment();
 String send_file_to_device(String file_content, String file_info)
 String send_command_to_device(String command);
 void dispose();
 )
```

The simplicity of this interface is due to the following: If we think of any experiment, we realize that all can be simplified to an exchange of messages, simpler or more complex, between the user and the remote resource. This message dialog is completely linked to the experiment in question, and therefore WebLab-Deusto only provides the infrastructure necessary to deliver those messages (text commands or files) from the client to the server of the experiment. It is this server that must understand the meaning of each message and send the orders pertaining to the device being controlled.

As we saw in Figure 9.7, in this end of the architecture we find again a variety of protocols, featuring XML-RPC as the most flexible alternative, allowing the Experiment server to be implemented in any programming language with HTTP connectivity and at least some facility for processing data in XML format. The task is especially easy when using Java, .NET, C, C++, LabVIEW or Python as languages, as WebLab-Deusto offers libraries that simplify the writing of Experiment servers to the point that all work is to inherit from a parent class and implement the four methods mentioned above.

We have seen in detail what remote labs are and how they can be built. Now let's see how we can use mobile devices in a remote laboratory.

Using Remote Labs from Mobile Devices

Mobile devices began as small computers tailored to the needs imposed by the environment of mobility of his age (90s), mainly:

- GSM connectivity
- Small size
- Battery life

In recent years, people's needs have grown exponentially, but fortunately so has the evolution of technology. Therefore, today we find that the list of needs for mobility environments are almost comparable to that of a PC:

- GSM/GPRS/3G/WiFi/Bluetooth connectivity
- Recording and playback of audio and video
- Touch screen
- Small size
- Battery life

But software development on mobile devices remains very limited in these special conditions. PC software not only cannot be reused for reasons of architecture, but often must be redesigned taking into account two parameters that become unsolvable: computational performance (which affects consumption) and usability (radically different from the smaller size of the screen).

The operating system software that governs the main device is the first affected by such restrictions. Operating systems that govern these terminals are in turn limited versions of their older siblings. To compare only some of the most powerful: Windows Mobile is not Windows, Android is not Linux, and iPhone OS is not Mac OS X.

As we have seen, remote laboratories are a complex system as long as they are open to the complexity that wants to impose each experiment. Therefore, the possibility to adapt to different mobile devices will always depend on the experiments that provide the laboratory (López-de-Ipiña, García-Zubia, & Orduña, 2006). An example of this is the FPGA and CPLD experiments at the University of Deusto, mentioned above. These experiments will never be used from mobile devices while the mobile platform will not allow the user to perform the two tasks required by the experiment: first to use the Xilinx IDE to compile the program to be sent (the Xilinx IDE is not available on any mobile platform) and second, to select the file from the file system of the terminal (devices like iPhone and Android do not allow access to the file system). Despite this, the design of the remote lab is important to make easier or more complex the work on porting the experiments to these platforms.

Thinking about the architecture seen in Figure 9.6, if we want to access a remote laboratory from a mobile device, the situation will be that the terminal is acting as an additional client. Therefore, the problems we face are the same as those faced by any application you want to adapt to a mobile platform.

There are two ways to develop a mobile version of any application: as a native application to the operating system that governs the mobile device (smart client apps) or as a Web application accessible from a browser (browsing apps). Both have advantages and disadvantages, as discussed below.

Smart Client Apps

If we develop the client as a native application, the main advantage is that we can use all the resources of the mobile terminal, since we will be using the platform development framework (SDK). Depending on the features of the terminal, we could make use of 3D graphics, take advantage of geolocation, control the camera, connect to another Bluetooth device, play music and videos, access the file system, or consult a list of contacts. All these features are beyond the reach of Web applications.

The price to pay, however, is not negligible. If we do it this way, we will face a recurring problem in the history of software: each architecture is different, and therefore a software developed for a specific platform will work only on that platform. The direct consequence is that the application development and maintenance efforts are multiplied, which is now a special handicap in the world of mobility, since in recent years the number of mobile operating systems has not stopped growing: Symbian, Android, iPhone, Windows Mobile, LiMo, BlackBerry, and Maemo (now Meego), to name the most popular. There are two ways to avoid this problem, although both ways are partial solutions, as we shall see.

The first solution is to develop the application on an intermediate platform, as Java ME. Using the Java micro-edition, end applications run on the Java Virtual Machine (JVM), so that any software developed on them will work on any architecture for which there is a JVM. The problem here again is that not all existing mobile platforms support Java ME today. In particular, from the above list, only Symbian, BlackBerry and LiMo officially support it. Android and iPhone do not support it directly (although there are attempts to develop a JVM for Android), while the existing one for Windows Mobile is not officially supported by Microsoft and is not considered by the industry as reliable as Compact Framework, the .NET virtual machine for mobile devices. Finally, although there is a functional JVM for

TABLE 9.3 Compatibility of Languages and JVM Availability on Mobile Platforms

Mobile OS	Supported languages	JVM available?
Symbian	C, C++, Python	Yes
Android	C, C++, Java	Not
iPhone	C, C++, Objective-C	Not
Windows Mobile	C, C++,. NET	Partial
LiMo	C, C++	Yes
BlackBerry	Java	Yes
Maemo	C, C++, Python	Yes (manual)

Maemo, the impediment is that the user needs to install it manually, since it is not included in the default software repository.

The second possibility is to develop the application in a language supported by multiple platforms (such as C or C++) and decouple the device-dependent code (graphics, sound, geolocation, connectivity, etc.) from the business logic specific to the application. This solution will allow us to reuse common code between different versions of the application, significantly reducing both development and maintenance time. Table 9.3 shows a summary of both the programming languages supported by each of the platforms mentioned as the availability of Java ME virtual machines.

As we can see, both solutions are a partial approach to the ideal situation (see Figure 9.9).

Browsing Apps

The other approach we talked about is to implement the client as a Web application. In this case, the advantages and disadvantages are reversed, and the reasons are in the very nature of Web applications.

Web applications were born with the World Wide Web as a metaphor for dumb terminals, used for many years to access conventional computers in client/server architectures. The objective in creating Web browsers was to delegate all the intelligence to servers and let the browsers be simple displays of static documents (HTML). Over time, more power was required for them, and in the middle of the 1990s, leading brands of Web browsers (Netscape and Microsoft) included support for JavaScript in Netscape and Internet Explorer. Then, Web browsers started to become less light clients, but they would never achieve their full potential until the explosion of Web 2.0 around 2004. The widespread implementation of JavaScript in the most popular browsers led to taking advantage of the potential of asynchronous

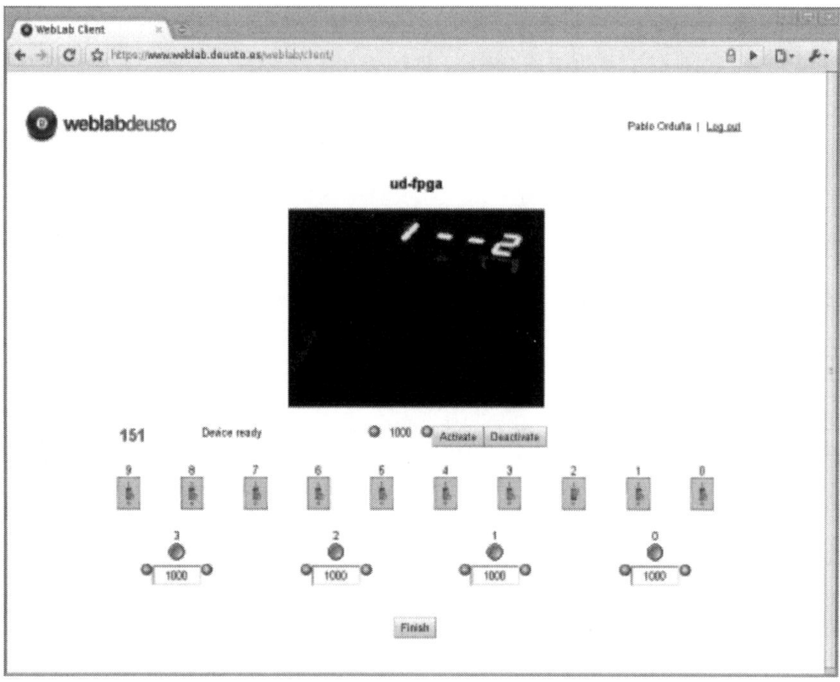

Figure 9.9 Web-Lab-Deusto user interface.

client/server requests via the XmlHttpRequest interface. Since then, the industry started talking about AJAX (Asynchronous JavaScript and XML) as a technology, but actually did not involve more than the combination of other previously existing technologies, such as JavaScript, DOM and XML (Garrett, 2005). The impetus provided by the Web site after the change was dramatic, to the point that since then we can talk about real Web applications and not just Web pages.

This evolution has made it necessary to consider that nowadays Web applications are an alternative to native applications. Asynchronous communication between Web browsers and servers has made it possible for both models to compete in terms of usability, since with synchronous communication it was impossible to alter the content of an HTML document with information from the server without fully refreshing the Web page that the user was viewing.

We said that the advantages and disadvantages of developing a Web application against a native were in their very nature. As we have seen, a Web site by itself is limited to a scripting language (JavaScript) designed to provide dynamism to the Web, but not to cross the barrier of the browser and access the rest of the operating system. Therefore, the main limitation of a Web application is the advantage of a native: we cannot access the advanced capabilities of the device (3D graphics, geolocation, camera, Bluetooth, etc.).

The only way to overcome this restriction is to rely on plug-ins for the Web browser programmed by third parties. The most popular are Java, Adobe Flash, and Microsoft Silverlight. These plug-ins allow you to run HTML objects in the browser more powerful than conventional Web (applets), facilitating the programming of complex Web applications and providing, among other things, interfaces with a user experience closer to native applications. The counterpart of these advantages is not trivial: on the one hand, we are limiting its use to environments in which the corresponding plug-in is available (again, a problem on mobile devices); on the other hand, we are compromising the safety of the user terminal to issue advanced permissions to a software (the plug-in) that might contain security flaws. Although today's Web is set on the standards already mentioned and this type of plug-in, fortunately things are changing, and the new version of HTML, HTML5, has been designed with the needs of today. So with HTML5, you can play audio and video, paint geometric graphics on the Web, geolocate the user (if expressly authorized), or store information in light databases, among other things; all this, within standards, without depending on any external plug-in. Although today it is in the process of adaptation, several popular Web sites (such as YouTube or Google Maps) already use these HTML vitamins if the user is using a browser that supports them. The interesting thing is that this approach is based on standards, so that sooner or later, all browsers will support it.

In contrast to the disadvantages of today's Web applications, there is also their greatest value: their requirement to run on a platform is just that this platform has to have a Web browser (if no plugins are used). Fortunately, this is not an impediment in any modern mobile platform, so developing a Web application today means reaching the full spectrum of mobile platforms.

WebLab-Deusto was thus conceived, and its Google-Web-Toolkit client separates the presentation layer through a system of interchangeable themes. Figure 9.10 shows as an example the LOGIC experiment at the University of Deusto, being used both in a PC Web browser as in a mobile phone with Android.

CONCLUSIONS AND FUTURE TRENDS

We have analyzed the two available ways to develop remote laboratories accessible from mobile devices. The conclusion is that a remote laboratory is a very open system for which the two strategies of development are always appropriate. The experiments offered by the laboratory are what really determine the need to opt for a native or a Web application.

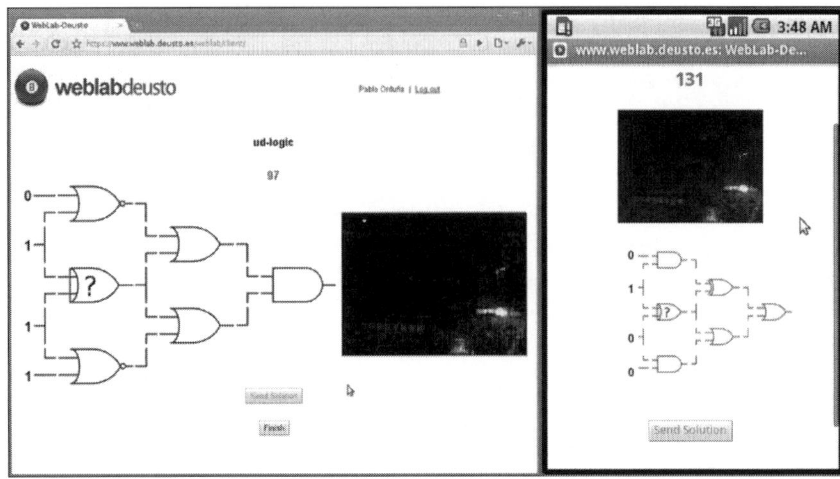

Figure 9.10 WebLab-Deusto from a PC (left) and a mobile phone (right).

The question we must ask ourselves is: Are the advanced resources of a mobile device meaningless to our remote laboratory? *A priori* one might think that some are very interesting:

- 3D graphics can be exploited to achieve a more immersive environment for the student. Off the field of mobility, that has already been done with different 3D worlds, such as Wonderland (Scheucher, Bailey, Gütl, & Harward, 2009) or Second Life (Garcia-Zubia et al., 2010).
- The accelerometers that provide some mobile terminals can be very interesting in improving the user experience in experiments that require movement of some kind.
- Access to the file systems might be useful to both sending and receiving results or scripts required by the experiment. FPGA and CPLD experiments at the University of Deusto, mentioned above, are clear examples of this.
- The calendar of the system could be used to integrate the booking system of the laboratory in a student's personal agenda.
- Foreground notifying systems could be very useful to alert the student that his turn has come, avoiding having to manually check while he is waiting in the queue.

Other resources, however, such as the user's geolocation, the Bluetooth connectivity, or the camera might be interesting only in very specific experiments.

What is certain is the benefit given by the Web-standards-based alternative when covering our needs. The adaptation of a general Web client to the mobile environment involves only the effort of redesigning the presentation layer, taking into account the special usability conditions that occur in a small device. If the client has also been designed anticipating this need, the effort required may be minimal (around 5% of the total code, according to Google) (Rasmussen, 2009).

Definitely there is no universal answer. It depends on the needs of each individual experiment, on the level of integration to be achieved with the advanced capabilities of the terminal, and, above all, on the real possibilities of the team responsible for the remote lab to undertake the work of developing and maintaining a set of native applications.

As for future directions in this area, everything points to two of the strongest applications to combine mobility and remote laboratories: 3D virtual environments and collaborative environments.

The interest in MMORPG environments is increasing, and it is expected that by the end of 2011, 80 percent of active Internet users will have a second life in a Virtual World (Gartner, 2009). In the specific area of remote experimentation, as previously mentioned, several studies have already combined both areas in a first approach (Garcia-Zubia et al., 2010; Scheucher et al., 2009). Since modern mobile devices offer hardware-based 3D graphics, it does not seem unrealistic to significantly advance in this direction looking for more immersive experiences for younger students.

Regarding collaborative environments, it makes sense that several students can interact together with the same experiment, either following a master/slave model or a totally collaborative one. This could be, in fact, the best weapon to combat the technical limitations we have seen in this chapter: if one partner is working collaboratively from another device without limitations (such as a laptop), the role of our mobile device may be secondary, and therefore it may not require all the functions that now pose a problem for the technical limitations of mobile platforms.

REFERENCES

García-Zubia, J., Irurzun, J., Angulo, I., Orduña, P., Ruiz-de-Garibay, J., Hernández, U. et al. (2010, April 14–16). SecondLab: A remote laboratory under second life. *IEEE Engineering Education.* EDUCON 2010, Madrid, Spain.

García-Zubia, J., Orduña, P., López de Ipiña, D., & Alves, G. (2009). Addressing software impact in the design of remote labs. *IEEE Transactions on Industrial Electronics, 56*(12), 4757–4767.

Garrett, J. J. (2005). *Ajax: A new approach to Web applications.* Retrieved April 29, 2010, from http://www.adaptivepath.com/ideas/e000385

Gartner. (2009). *Gartner says 80 percent of active Internet users will have a "second life" in the virtual world by the end of 2011.* Retrieved May 4, 2010, from http://www.gartner.com/it/page.jsp?id=503861

Gobbo, F., & Vaccari, M. (2005). Open standards for higher education in robotics by immersive telelaboratories. *Learning Technology Newsletter (IEEE Computer Society), 7*(3), 30–32.

Gomes, L., & Garcia-Zubía, J. (Eds.). (2007). *Advances on remote laboratories and e-learning experiences.* Bilbao, Spain: University of Deusto.

Gravier, C., Fayolle, J., Bayard, B., Ates, M., & Lardon, J. (2008). State of the art about remote laboratories paradigms—Foundations of ongoing mutations. *International Journal of Online Engineering, 4*(1), 19–25.

Harward, V. J., del Alamo, J. A., Lerman, S. R., Bailey, P. H., Carpenter, J., DeLong, K. et al. (2008, June 23–25). The iLab shared architecture: A Web services infrastructure to build communities of Internet accessible laboratories. *Proceedings of the IEEE Symposium. 96(*6), 931–950.

Indrusiak, L. S., Glesner, M., & Reis, R. (2007). On the evolution of remote laboratories for prototyping digital electronic systems. *IEEE Trans. on Industrial Electronics, 54*(6), 3069–3077.

López-de-Ipiña, D., García-Zubia J., & Orduña P. (2006, December). Remote control of Web 2.0-enabled laboratories from mobile devices. *2nd IEEE International Conference on e-Science and Grid Computing, eScience 2006,* Amsterdam, Netherlands.

Lowe, D., Murray, S., Weber, L., de la Villefromoy, M., Johnston, A., Lindsay, E. et al. (2009, December 6–9). LabShare: Towards a national approach to laboratory sharing. *Proceedings of the 20th Australasian Association for Engineering Education Conference (AAEE 2009),* Adelaide, Australia.

Ma, J., & Nickerson, J. V., (2006). Hands-on, simulated, and remote laboratories: A comparative literature review. *ACM Computing Surveys, 38*(3), 1–24.

Maier, C., & Niederstätter, M. (2010). Lab2go: A repository to locate online laboratories. *International Journal of Online Engineering, 6*(1), 12–17.

Orduña, P., García-Zubia, J., Irurzun, J., Sancristobal, E., Martín, S., Castro, M. et al. (2009, June 22–25). Designing experiment agnostic remote laboratories. *Proceedings of the International Conference of Remote Engineering and Virtual Instrumentation,* Bridgeport, CT.

Rasmussen, L. (2009). *Google wave developer preview at google i/o 2009.* Retrieved April 30th, 2010, from http://wave.google.com/about.html

Scheucher, T., Bailey, P. H., Gütl, C., & Harward, V. J. (2009, June 22–25). Collaborative virtual 3D environment for Internet-accessible physics experiments. *Proceedings of the International Conference of Remote Engineering and Virtual Instrumentation,* Bridgeport, CT.

ABOUT THE AUTHORS

Dr. Javier García-Zubia is head of the Industrial Technologies Department, Faculty of Engineering of the University of Deusto in Bilbao, Spain. He is also project manager and head of the WebLab-Deusto Research Group, whose main achievement is WebLab-Deusto, an open-source experiment-agnostic remote lab based on Web 2.0 technologies. (e-mail: zubia@deusto.es).

Jaime Irurzun is a computer engineer (2009) and MSc in Development and Integration of Software Solutions (2010) at the University of Deusto in Bilbao, Spain. He worked as research intern at the WebLab-Deusto Research Group sonce 2007 to 2010, mainly involved in the development and administration of the WebLab-Deusto Remote Lab. (e-mail: jirurzun@deusto.es).

Pablo Orduña has been a computer engineer at the University of Deusto in Bilbao, Spain, since 2007. Nowadays he is a research associate at the Ambient Intelligence Department of DeustoTech Deusto Institute of Technology, and PhD student at the University of Deusto. His research is focused on Remote Laboratories. He is the lead software designer and developer of WebLab-Deusto. (e-mail: pablo .orduna@deusto.es).

Dr. Diego López-de-Ipiña is research leader in the MORElab. He received his PhD from the University of Cambridge, UK on the topic of Sentient Computing. His main research areas are semantic service middleware, mobile-mediated user-environment interaction, and embedded reasoning techniques for system proactivity and reactivity. He is taking part in the MUGGES FP7 project and the uService ITEA2 project. He is the technical coordinator of the CBDP CELTIC project, which deals with mobile mediated user-environment service negotiation and recommendation. (e-mail: dipina@deusto.es).

PART III

A NEW DIRECTION TOWARD TEACHING AND LEARNING: UBIQUITOUS LEARNING

CHAPTER 10

A NEW LEARNING ENVIRONMENT BASED ON REPRODUCIBLE UBIQUITOUS COMPUTING

Experiences and Prospects

Patrick Wessa, Ian E. Holliday, and Peter Reddy

ABSTRACT

In this chapter, we explain why Reproducible Computing is important and how it can be used as a socially constructivist learning technology with characteristics of ubiquitous computing. Based on reported experiences and objective measurements from two different statistics courses, we present strong evidence that student perceptions and experiences are very positive toward this new type of technology and educational approach. The most remarkable observation is that the approach was well-received, notwithstanding the fact that students initially perceived the workload to be very heavy. The few criticisms that were formulated by students have no solid ground and may be solved through better and more extensive communication.

Ubiquitous Learning, pages 179–195

INTRODUCTION

Within the context of our newly developed technology for Reproducible Computing (henceforth RC) we developed a learning environment that supports a socially constructivist and (potentially) ubiquitous approach to statistics education. The implementation of this learning environment has been, without a doubt, an interesting and challenging experience for developers, instructors, and students alike. Our reflections about these experiences and the underlying design principles of the RC-based courses might therefore provide useful information for anyone with an interest in ubiquitous learning environments, which are based on computer-assisted learning and which have been embedded in the pedagogical paradigm of social constructivism.

In this chapter, we outline some of the ubiquitous characteristics of RC technology and explain why they are important within the context of socially constructivist learning. The main focus however, is on the learning activities and experiences of students that have been collected through a series of surveys, several focus panels, and objective measurements as derived from log files or databases. In spite of the fact the learning process is perceived to involve a heavy workload, it is clearly demonstrated that the overall learning experiences are very positive.

Our final thoughts focus on some of the future directions of RC technology that allow us to integrate reproducibility in applications that are not exclusively focused on statistics education. For instance, it is described how this novel technological innovation can be used to obtain an increase in productivity when supervising master/PhD dissertations or when RC is used within the context of educational games.

BACKGROUND

Within the context of computer-assisted and mathematical education, the pedagogical community has shown great interest in the role and importance of social and individual constructivism (Eggen & Kauchak, 2001; Smith, 1999; Von Glasersfeld, 1987) and its implementation in statistics education in particular (Mvududu, 2003).

While the relevance of the constructivist pedagogical paradigm is well documented, there seems to be no direct or obvious relationship with the problem of irreproducible research. Nevertheless, the problem of our inability to reproduce statistical computations that are presented in papers has received quite a bit of attention within the statistical computing community. The most prominent citation about the problem of irreproducible research is Claerbout's principle: "An article about computational science in a scientific publication is *not* the scholarship itself, it is merely *advertising* of the scholarship. The actual scholarship is the complete software development environment and the complete set of instructions that generated the figures" (de Leeuw, 2001, p. 1).

Statistics education is often based on course materials and articles that suffer from the same irreproducibility problems. From a pedagogical point of view, we simply cannot expect students to learn from (statistical) results in course texts if they are barely able to reproduce, let alone verify, the results from peers, educators, or researchers. Even though the pedagogical paradigm of social constructivism has often been propagated as a promising approach to achieve true learning, it is unclear how students should be empowered to engage in non-rote learning through interaction (with the subject under study), experimentation, critical thinking/reflection (through peer review), and other social activities that help them to construct knowledge. All of these aspects are impossible to achieve in a traditional course environment because the data, the software, the parameters, and the meta-information about the assumptions that underlie the statistical analysis cannot be communicated in a printed course text or in a traditional e-learning environment.

As one can imagine, the problem of irreproducible empirical research has caused a lot of concern within the statistical computing community. The fact that scientific findings (based on empirical analysis) are difficult, if not impossible, to reproduce and verify, has raised many questions about the status of science. Some of the leading arguments can be found in Peng, Dominici, and Zeger (2006); Schwab, Karrenbach, and Claerbout (2000); Green (2003); Gentleman (2005); Koenker and Zeileis (2007); and Donoho and Huo (2004). Several approaches to solving the problem have been suggested and implemented. Some of the more promising attempts are based on the concept of an electronic "Compendium" and have been described in Buckheit and Donoho (1995); Donoho and Huo (2004); and Leisch (2003). The proposed solutions are elegant (from a technological point of view) but very hard to implement in an educational setting due to a variety of reasons (Wessa, 2008).

More importantly, mentioned solutions do not have the ability to support ubiquitous computing or learning because they assume that all components that are required to make the statistical computation "reproducible" are bundled into one object (a so-called Compendium). More precisely, the Compendium is defined as *a collection of Text, Data, and Software that allows the reader to reproduce the research that is presented in the document* (Wessa, 2008). According to this definition, however, it is impossible to invoke the functions to reproduce a statistical computation from within small (or "ubiquitous") devices because they are often not capable of storing all the meta-data about a computation, let alone that the device would be able to perform the actual computing. For instance, it is unclear how a traditional

Compendium would be used on a cell/smartphone if it is required to have a working LaTeX compiler and R interpreter.

Ubiquitous learning does not only involve (mobile) devices, it is primarily related to the fact that the student is able to perform learning activities within various situations or contexts. In one context, the student may use a netbook computer or a smartphone on campus and during the lectures to verify the statistical computations that are demonstrated by the instructor. In another context, the student might do some homework at a home-based desktop computer while using VLE forums, instant messengers, and e-mail in order to collaborate with multiple friends at the same time. The use of Compendiums can support learning in this type of environment but are limited in application if their design requires local resources that mobile devices cannot support. If the Compendium would only contain references to remotely stored computational objects, and if these could be recomputed on remote machines, then there would be (almost) no limitation to the environment or situation in which it could be used or communicated.

Because of the above reasons, it was necessary to design a new and innovative technology, the so-called Compendium Platform (henceforth CP), which was based on a new (revised) definition of the Compendium: *a document with (open-access) references to (remotely) archived computations (including Data, Meta-data, and Software) that allows the reader to reproduce, and reuse the underlying analysis.* Unlike the old one, this definition allows us to specify new (and ubiquitous) environments in which reproducibility of research results is guaranteed to work because there is no requirement to store or compute anything locally; the only requirement is to have an active Internet connection (Wessa, 2008).

The CP solves the aforementioned problems because it allows any user (the educator or student) to quickly create electronic documents that contain statistical research results that are fully reproducible and reusable. The reader of a Compendium can simply click on a table's or graph's caption, which contains a hyperlink, to view and use the meta information that is connected to the research results in a remote and freely accessible repository, which is hosted at http://www.freestatistics.org. The reader can recompute the analysis in real-time (at http://www.wessa.net) and change any aspect of the underlying analysis—the data, the parameters, and even the underlying source code—at any time (Wessa, 2009a).

UBIQUITOUS LEARNING

Peer Review and Social Constructivism

Even though our RC learning environment has been tested and implemented in more than a dozen courses, we limit the description in the remainder of this chapter exclusively to two cases of particular interest. The first case is an advanced statistics course for undergraduate psychology students (+130) at Aston University, UK. The second case is a statistics course for undergraduate business students (131) and graduate students (154) who are required to complete a preparatory year before they are allowed to enter the master's program at one of the Business Schools of the K. U. Leuven Association.

Both courses covered a variety of statistical techniques and had a strong emphasis on social constructivism. For each type of analysis, students had one or several Web-based software modules available.

In order to implement these courses within the setting of social constructivism for large student populations, it was necessary to impose a strict assignment-review mechanism. This is illustrated in Figure 10.1, which shows a series of weekly events (lectures, assignments, and reviews) during the course period (at least one semester). The course ended with a final examination about a series of objective multiple-choice questions in an attempt to test the understanding of statistical concepts rather than rote memorization.

The main sections of the statistics course were built around a series of research-based workshops that require students to reflect and communicate about a variety of statistical problems at various levels of difficulty. Each workshop contained questions about datasets that are of interest to the student population. The business students were also required to perform various types of analyses about individual data series. In both cases, the workshops involved social interaction in the form of peer review and a substantial amount of individual work.

Each week there was a lecture that was held in a large lecture hall equipped with projection and Internet facilities. During the week, students were required to work on their workshop assignment and, at the same time, perform peer reviews about a prespecified number of randomly assigned submissions from peers. Each review was based on a rubric of a minimum of four criteria and required students to submit rubric scores and feedback messages.

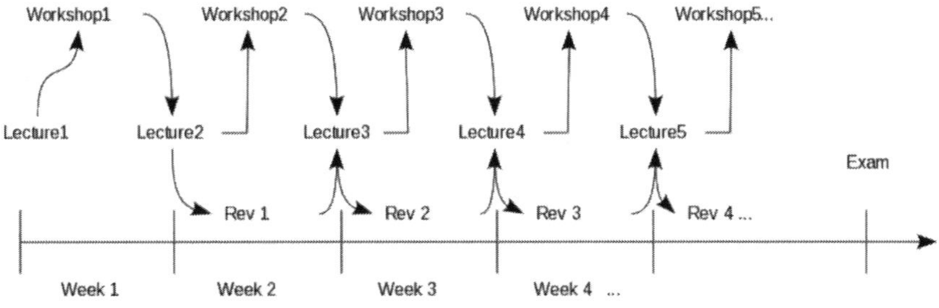

Figure 10.1 Peer reviews about weekly workshops.

The scores that were generated by the peer review process did not count toward the final grade of students whose work was peer reviewed because there should be no penalty for experimentation and creativity (Wessa, 2009b). Instead, the educator graded the quality of the written feedback messages that were submitted to other students. The grading was performed based on a sampling technique that allowed the educator to grade the quality of a relatively small, but fairly representative number of submitted feedback messages from each student (Wessa & De Rycker, 2010).

This feedback-oriented process is similar to the peer review procedure of an article that is submitted to a scientific journal. The key idea behind this constructivist environment is that students play the role of an active scientist who investigates problems, presents solutions, and reviews the work of peers. For obvious reasons, RC is a *conditio sine qua non* that allows students to engage in such peer review activities.

From the above description, it can be concluded that students are required to use RC in various situations and contexts. As pointed out before, this is possible only if the underlying technology supports ubiquitous computing by design; this is briefly explained in the next section.

Ubiquitous Technology for Reproducible Computing

The R Framework is a key component of the RC learning environment (see Figure 10.2). It allows educators and scientists to develop new, tailor-made statistical software called "R modules" based on the R language (R De-

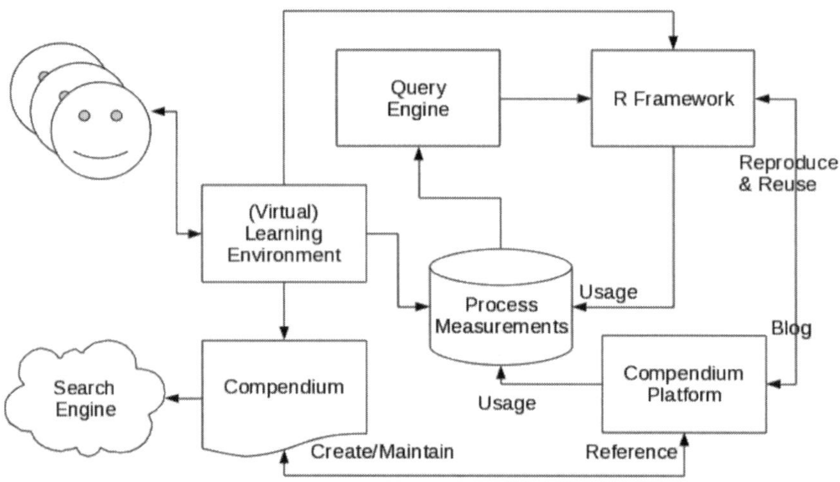

Figure 10.2 Reproducible computing and the Compendium.

velopment Core Team, 2010). Educators may browse the collection of available R modules at the R Framework's Web site (http://www.wessa.net) and use them for the purpose of generating research output that can be used to explain statistical techniques and concepts in their courses. If the educator has a working knowledge of the R language, then new R modules can be created and published.

There are some unique features of the Compendium Platform that are of particular importance:

- Any computation that is created within the R Framework can be easily "blogged" (i.e., archived) in the repository of the CP; there is no need for students to keep track of the data, the model parameters, or the underlying statistical software code.
- Any user who visits the unique URL of an archived computation is able to instantly reproduce the computation or reuse it for further analysis; only an Internet connection is required to use the repository.
- Educators and researchers are able to retrieve data for research purposes.

A detailed description of the components in Figure 10.2 is available in Wessa (2008).

RC has many ubiquitous characteristics, but some of the more important ones (from an educational point of view) are the following:

- No downloads are required, and all computations are performed on a distributed network of remote servers.
- Metadata are stored and maintained in an remote online repository.
- Interactions between computations are preserved/stored and can be used to offer customized information about similar or related computations.
- The user interface is based on html/xml and can be used on small-screen devices with low bandwidth; however, a minimum screen resolution may be required if one wishes to display charts.
- All usage data (creating, editing, reproducing, or viewing computations) are available for the purpose of customization of service and academic analysis.
- Social interactions (social networks) can be traced and visualized in so-called sociograms (Wessa, 2009c). In theory, this allows us to build new applications that take into account the social relationships between users in order to offer customized services.
- Peer review messages are linked to the computational repository, which allows us to support, monitor, and measure peer review activity based on objective measurements.

The bottom line is that there is a complete separation between presentation, storage, and computing. This is a fundamental requirement for ubiquitous computing and learning.

Reported Student Experiences

The survey data were obtained from the business students in Belgium because they were required to submit the surveys before the end of the semester. The questions were taken from three well-known questionnaires (ATTLES, COLLES, and CSUQ). The first survey (ATTLES) was available from the start of course and aims to measure students' attitudes toward thinking and learning (Galotti, Clinchy, Ainsworth, Lavin, & Mansfield, 1999). The first 10 questions relate to "connected" (empathic) ways of learning, whereas the last 10 questions are associated with "separate" (critical, detached) ways of knowing.

Students' perception of their online learning experience during the course was measured with the Constructivist On-Line Learning Environment Survey (COLLES), which focuses on a spectrum of important aspects of the learning experiences: relevance of the subject, reflective/critical thinking, interactivity, educator support, peer support, and interpretation of peer/educator messages. For every aspect, there were eight questions, four of which were related to the actually perceived experience. The remaining four questions have identical phrases but were related to the degree of what students prefer.

The third survey is based on IBM's Computer System Usability Survey (CSUQ) as originally developed by Lewis (1993), with additional questions as proposed by Poelmans et al. (2008), which are specifically focused on the relationship between software usability and statistics learning.

The analysis of the survey responses was performed in such a way that anyone is able to interpret the results. Each question was based on a 5-point Likert scale (5 is excellent, 3 is neutral, and 1 is poor). By subtracting a fixed constant (= 3), we obtained scores that are contained in the interval [−2, 2], where the neutral score is zero valued. This score $S_{i,j}$ represents the transformed reply (for all questions $i = 1, \ldots, Q$ and for all students $j = 1, \ldots, N$), for which the following definitions can be formulated:

- $D_{i,j}^{+} = 1$ if $S_{i,j} > 0$, $D_{i,j}^{+} = 0$ if $S_{i,j} \leq 0$
- $D_{i,j}^{-} = 1$ if $S_{i,j} < 0$, $D_{i,j}^{-} = 0$ if $S_{i,j} \geq 0$
- P_i^s is the sum of all positive scores: $P_i^s = \Sigma_{j=1}^{N} D_{i,j}^{+} S_{i,j}$ for $i = 1, \ldots, Q$
- N_i^s is the sum of all absolute values of negative scores: $N_i^s = \Sigma_{j=1}^{N} D_{i,j}^{-} |S_{i,j}|$ for $i = 1, \ldots, Q$
- P_i^c is the number of positive scores: $P_i^c = \Sigma_{j=1}^{N} D_{i,j}^{+}$ for $i = 1, \ldots, Q$
- N_i^c is the number of negative scores: $N_i^c = \Sigma_{j=1}^{N} D_{i,j}^{-}$ for $i = 1, \ldots, Q$

It is now possible to define three summary scores for each question:

1. the arithmetic mean: $(1/N)\Sigma_{j=1}^{N} S_{i,j}$ for $i = 1, \ldots, Q$
2. the difference between positive and (absolute) negative scores, divided by the absolute sum of all scores: $(P_i^s - N_i^s)/(P_i^s + N_i^s)$ for $i = 1, \ldots, Q$
3. the difference between the number of positive and negative scores, divided by the number of nonzero scores: $(P_i^c - N_i^c)/(P_i^c + N_i^c)$ for $i = 1, \ldots, Q$

The first two measures can be used only if a quasi-interval scale is assumed. The third measure does not make the assumption of a quasi-interval scale because the scores are substituted by frequencies (counts). The drawback of the third measure is that is does not differentiate between extreme answers (±2) and moderate answers (±1). In other words, the third measure has the advantages that are associated with ordinal (rank-based) measures but at a cost of loss of information. The first measure is contained in the interval [–2, 2] and the last two measures lie in the interval [–1, 1].

In each survey, and for all questions, a high summary score is associated with a "favorable" situation. A negative score indicates a weak point, which may be considered for improvement. Instead of displaying the computed statistics in this chapter, we include the links to the remotely stored computational objects. Any reader who wishes to examine, reproduce, or verify our findings is encouraged to visit the repository and, if so desired, to recompute or reuse the analysis on our remote network of computational servers.

The ATTLES survey scores are available online (Wessa, Holliday, & Reddy, 2010a; http://www.freestatistics.org/blog/date/2010/Apr/05/t1270471667mb02yn344mzcneh.htm/). The conclusion from the analysis is positive for most aspects of the ATTLES survey. Negative summary scores are found for the following two questions:

- Q2: I like playing devil's advocate—arguing the opposite of what someone is saying.
- Q9: I often find myself arguing with the authors of books that I read, trying to logically figure out why they're wrong.

The negative summary scores for these questions might indicate that our students dislike challenging others and don't have a critical attitude toward claims made by (book) authors. Hence, the introduction of new learning technologies that allow students to reproduce or challenge computations from peers is expected to be difficult and lead to negative learning experiences. As a consequence, it is rather unlikely that students enjoy assignments that are related to RC and peer assessment.

Fortunately, the analysis about COLLES (Wessa, Holliday, & Reddy, 2010b; http://www.freestatistics.org/blog/date/2010/Apr/05/t1270472835g8j33hyexeibe23.htm/) shows an overwhelming amount of evidence that, at the end of the semester, students perceive their learning experience as very positive. This comes as a surprise because of the fact that the workload is perceived to be high, and the observation that RC goes against students' attitudes toward learning and thinking, as measured in the initial ATTLES survey. All COLLES questions have a positive summary score; some are even close to the maximum value.

Another interesting result can be observed in the CSUQ analysis (Wessa, Holliday, & Reddy, 2010c; http://www.freestatistics.org/blog/date/2010/Apr/05/t1270473420yuhs2t83pn49hzj.htm/), which clearly shows that the Web-based software was highly rated by students. The only exception is related to question 10: "The Web site gives error messages that clearly tell me how to fix problems." This negative summary score is due to the fact that error messages (produced by the R language) are of a technical or purely statistical nature. For this reason, students were instructed to archive computational results with error messages and send the link to the instructor by e-mail or post it in the VLE forum. The Compendium Platform allowed the instructor to quickly reproduce the errors, detect problems, and solve any computational or software-related issue and report back to the student. This method of error handling is not only very efficient, it also provides a lot of valuable insight into the nature of problems that are commonly encountered.

Some results in the CSUQ analysis are of particular interest:

- Q21: Learning statistics with this Web site is more effective than with a traditional handbook.
- Q22: Overall, the Web site was helpful in learning statistics.
- Q23: I intend to use this Web site when I need to apply statistics in the future.
- Q28: To learn statistics, this Web site is better than the statistical courses I have had so far.
- Q29: Next year, I will probably use the Web site/software again if I have to do statistical assignments.
- Q35: The fact that I can reproduce computations of others is beneficial for my learning.
- Q40: My learning improves because the Web site allows me to reproduce and reuse the computations of others.
- Q41: I have a deeper understanding of statistics because the Web site's technology allows me to evaluate the work of other students.

The scores for these questions are quite large and imply that students believe that the Web-based CP helps them to learn statistics. The overall appreciation is very strong and might compensate for the fact that the learning process involves a lot of work, and that RC does not agree with their initial attitudes toward thinking and learning.

The survey results were confirmed by several focus group discussions in Belgium, which were conducted by independent and experienced people. Most students reported that they initially felt rather anxious due to the uncertainty that is associated when the new technology and pedagogical approach is introduced. However, almost all students became used to the new situation quickly (after about 2 weeks), and most of them began to appreciate the benefits of RC for the purpose of learning in a socially constructive setting.

Based on the focus groups and individual interviews, the following "most important problems" were identified:

1. A workload which is too high.
2. Uncertainty about the correctness of solutions and/or peer reviews.
3. No grades are received for the submitted workshops.
4. Everyone else is using traditional statistical software.

The first problem turns out to be a false one. There is a learning curve involved in acquiring the skills to do peer reviews of high quality. If there is proper guidance and support from the educator, this problem should disappear after a few weeks. The second problem can be solved during the lectures by introducing real examples of good and bad types of analysis, which can be found in the submitted workshops. In addition, the educator can provide students with an illustrated solution about the previous week's workshop assignment. The third problem is actually not a real problem but rather a matter of perception. Students should understand that the effort invested in their workshops ultimately leads to better understanding and a higher quality of peer reviews, which in turn are subject to grading by the instructor. In addition, it is possible to grade the quality of the peer reviews in an efficient and "fair" manner, as is demonstrated by Wessa and De Rycker (2010). The fourth problem is a rather poor argument in favor of traditional software. Almost all students agree that RC provides better support for learning, while traditional software involves many problems that are counterproductive due to a variety of issues, such as installing software, importing/converting data, emphasis on the user interface instead of the subject under study, old or outdated methods, etc. Most commercial software products for statistical computing are easy to learn (most of them come with a rich Graphical User Interface) once the user truly understands the statistical method to be applied and its underlying assumptions. The RC solution allows the educator to create tailor-made statistical software with the freedom to offer the features and choices in its implementation that are of importance and to take away the pain of data import and manipulation. The bottom line is that students can always (and easily) learn to use commercial software after they have acquired a true understanding of the underlying statistical concepts.

It is interesting to point out that many students reported that they particularly liked the ubiquitous nature of the learning environment. The fact that they were able to use RC in various contexts (whenever and wherever they liked) was one of the main aspects that contributed to their satisfaction.

Objective Measurements

Another way to assess the impact of RC on learning is to look at objectively measured statistics about the actual learning activities. Based on Web server statistics from the last three months of 2009, we were able to observe that our students

- viewed more than 143,000 pages, during a total of 26,107 visits, about blogged computations on the freestatistics.org Web site. Most of these pageviews can be associated with the weekly peer review activities. The average time on site per visit was 17 minutes and 33 seconds;
- generated more than 131,000 statistical computations during a total of 14,064 sessions on the wessa.net Web site. The average time on site per visit was 15 minutes and 16 seconds.

Based on the measurements of the peer review software, we found that the students spent an average of 12–15 minutes (depending on the course) between successive reviews. The number of feedback messages per review was 118–139 (depending on the course), and the average length of each message was 259–336 characters (depending on the course and the language). Each student reviewed, on average, 37–43 Compendia during an average of 11–13 unique days. The number of unique full hours in which reviews took place was 20–21.

Based on these statistics and making some mild assumptions, we estimate that students had an average workload of about 6–8 hours during each week, regular classes not included. An important aspect about this is the fact that the workload occurs in a regular (weekly) pattern throughout the course period. Figure 10.3 shows the number of daily visits of the freestatistics.org Web site by our students and clearly illustrates the weekly pattern.

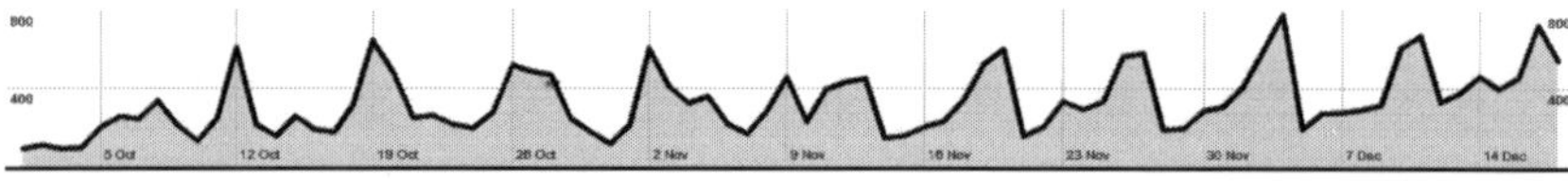

Figure 10.3 Daily visits of freestatistics.org by our students.

The ubiquitous nature of the learning environment is clearly illustrated by Figure 10.3, because there are still many visits during the off-peak days (even during the 1-week break in November). If the Web server statistics are investigated in more detail, we find that the off-peak period traffic is associated with IP addresses that are different from those that occur during the peaks. Also, the types of computers and devices that are used are different. For instance, in the business studies course, we see a lot more netbook and mobile devices during the weekdays and lecture hours. Another point of interest is the fact that many computations were viewed or reproduced through links that were transmitted by e-mail, forums, and various types of instant messengers. This confirms the information that was reported during focus group discussions.

FUTURE TRENDS

The future of RC promises to be challenging and exciting. The foundations of RC provide us with plenty of opportunities to pursue new roads of research and to build new applications. Within the educational context, there are three new projects that might be of particular interest.

The first project extends the CP to the field of collaborative, academic writing. Even though it may seem strange at first sight, statistical computations have a lot in common with snippets of text that are written by students. Most of the finished documents or papers that we observe are the product of multiple attempts to write and revise text snippets over a longer period of time. Toward the completion of the text, the snippets are glued together in order to obtain a text that makes sense to the reader. Similarly, in a statistical paper, we typically have several computations that have some kind of relationship to each other or relate to the same dataset. Moreover, a text snippet can be written/revised by an individual or through collaboration; it is also possible to review texts or text snippets. In this sense, it is possible to extend the database of the online repository of the CP to allow us to store, track, and reproduce entire texts that are produced by students. This is not limited to the snapshots (or versions) of texts (such as in a traditional wiki) but comprises the dynamic interactions between users and their respective contributions.

The second project focuses on scientific publishing and dissertations at the master's or PhD level. The underlying idea is that students should be allowed (or even encouraged) to publish their research in a student journal in which the primary requirement is not the novelty or relevance of the contribution but instead the scientific rigor and reproducibility. Just imagine how such an international journal would improve the productivity for supervisors and students alike. Instead of going through the lengthy effort of training each generation of students to become proficient in writing a dissertation in a particular field of interest, we could provide them with a head start if we could guarantee that the published dissertations from the previous generations are fully reproducible.

A third application emphasizes the embedding of RC into new or existing games with an educational purpose. One particular example is an online stock market game in which the students participate and play the role of a professional trader. The stock prices are influenced by the participants (the law of supply and demand) and a computer player that represents the rest of the market and acts according to research-based artificial intelligence rules. By introducing RC into the game, we empower students to learn about statistical-analysis techniques and financial models in an exciting, real-time environment, which can be partially controlled through the constraining parameters of the computer player. In addition, every important decision of the participant (which is based on analysis) can be monitored in real time and reproduced for the purpose of postgame analysis. By seamlessly integrating RC into the game, we provide valuable feedback to the learner and the educator, which was never available before. Educational games have the potential of becoming much more interesting (as an educational tool) because of the reproducibility of analysis-based decisions.

Best of all is the fact that RC and the CP are made available free of charge for the purpose of noncommercial research and education. Anyone can build new applications based on RC or contact the authors to discuss opportunities for scientific or educational collaboration.

CONCLUSION

We have described and discussed RC (and associated CP) as a socially constructivist learning technology with characteristics of ubiquitous computing. The technology builds a bridge between two seemingly unrelated worlds of statistical computing and educational science. At the same time, it solves some important problems in a manner that is flexible (tailor-made solutions) and easily accessible at the same time (no technical knowledge is required by the students).

Without the need to employ sophisticated analysis, we provided strong evidence that student perceptions and experiences are very positive toward this new type of technology and educational approach. The most remarkable observation is that the approach was well-received, notwithstanding the fact that students complained about a heavy workload in the beginning of the course. The few criticisms that were formulated have no solid ground and may be solved through better and more extensive communication.

REFERENCES

Buckheit, J., & Donoho, D. L. (1995). Wavelets and statistics. In A. Antoniadis (Ed.), *Wavelab and reproducible research.* New York: Springer-Verlag.

de Leeuw, J. (2001). *Reproducible research: The bottom line.* Department of Statistics Papers, 2001031101. UCLA Department of Statistics.

Donoho, D. L., & Huo, X. (2004, December). Beamlab and reproducible research. *International Journal of Wavelets, Multiresolution and Information Processing, 2*(4), 391–414.

Eggen, P., & Kauchak, D. (2001). *Educational psychology: Windows on classrooms* (5th ed.). Upper Saddle River, NJ: Prentice Hall,.

Galotti, K. M., Clinchy, B. M., Ainsworth, K., Lavin, B., & Mansfield, A. F. (1999). A new way of assessing ways of knowing: The attitudes toward thinking and learning survey (ATTLS). *Sex Roles, 44*(9/10), 745–766.

Gentleman, R. (2005). Applying reproducible research in scientific discovery. *Bio-Silico.* Retrieved from http://replay.waybackmachine.org/20090522191157/http://gentleman.fhcrc.org/Fld-talks/RGRepRes.pdf

Green, P. J. (2003). Diversities of gifts, but the same spirit. *The Statistician, 52*(4), 423–438.

Koenker, R. & Zeileis, A. (2007). *Reproducible econometric research (A critical review of the state of the art).* (Research Report Series, No. 60). Wirtschaftsuniversität Wien, Austria: Department of Statistics and Mathematics.

Leisch, F. (2003, March 20–22). Sweave and beyond: Computations on text documents. In *Proceedings of the 3rd International Workshop on Distributed Statistical Computing,* Vienna, Austria.

Lewis, J. R. (1993). *IBM computer usability satisfaction questionnaires: Psychometric evaluation and instructions for use.* (Technical Report No. 54.786). IBM Corporation.

Mvududu, N. (2003). A cross-cultural study of the connection between students' attitudes toward statistics and the use of constructivist strategies in the course. Retrieved from http://www.amstat.org/publications/jse/v11n3/mvududu.html.

Peng, R. D., Dominici, F., & Zeger, S. L. (2006). Reproducible epidemiologic research. *American Journal of Epidemiology, 163*(9), 783–789.

Poelmans, S., Wessa, P., Milis, K., Bloemen, E., & Doom, C. (2008). Usability and acceptance of e-learning in statistics education, based on the compendium platform. In *Proceedings of the International Conference of Education, Research and Innovation;* International Association of Technology, Education and Development.

R Development Core Team. (2010). *R: A language and environment for statistical computing* ISBN 3-900051-07-0. Vienna, Austria: R Foundation for Statistical Computing.

Schwab, M., Karrenbach, N., & Claerbout, J. (2000). Making scientific computations reproducible. *Computing in Science & Engineering, 2*(6), 61–67.

Smith, E. (1999). Social constructivism, individual constructivism and the role of computers in mathematics education. *Journal of Mathematical Behaviour, 17*(4), 411–425

Von Glasersfeld, E. (1987). Learning as a constructive activity. In C. Janvier (Ed.), *Problems of representation in the teaching and learning of mathematics* (pp. 3–17). Hillsdale, NJ: Lawrence Erlbaum Associates.

Wessa, P. (2008, October 22–24). Learning statistics based on the compendium and reproducible computing. In *Proceedings of the International Conference on Education and Information Technology*, San Francisco.

Wessa, P. (2009a). A framework for statistical software development, maintenance, and publishing within an open-access business model. *Computational Statistics, 24*(2), 183–193.

Wessa, P. (2009b). How reproducible research leads to non-rote learning within a socially constructivist statistics education. *Electronic Journal of E-Learning, 7*(2), 173–182.

Wessa, P. (2009c, December 1–2). Exploring social networks in reproducible computing and collaborative assignments. In *Proceedings of the International Conference on E-Learning 2009*, University of Toronto, Canada.

Wessa, P., & De Rycker A. (2010, July 12–13), Reviewing peer reviews—A rule based approach, In *Proceedings of the 5th International Conference on E-Learning 2010*, Penang, Malaysia.

Wessa, P., Holliday, I., & Reddy, P. (2010a). *Statistical computations at freestatistics.org.* Office for Research Development and Education. Retrieved from http://www.freestatistics.org/blog/date/2010/Apr/05/t1270471667mb02yn344mzcneh.htm/

Wessa, P., Holliday, I., Reddy, P. (2010b). Statistical computations at freestatistics.org. *Office for Research Development and Education.* Retrieved from http://www.freestatistics.org/blog/date/2010/Apr/05/t1270472835g8j33hyexeibe23.htm/

Wessa, P., Holliday, I., Reddy, P. (2010c). Statistical Computations at FreeStatistics.org, *Office for Research Development and Education.* Retrieved from http://www.freestatistics.org/blog/date/2010/Apr/05/t1270473420yuhs2t83pn49hzj.htm/

ABOUT THE AUTHORS

Patrick Wessa, PhD, studied Quantitative Economics in Belgium and obtained his PhD at the Institute for Econometrics and Statistics (University of Basel, CH). He leads the Reproducible Computing project at the Leuven Institute for Research on Information Systems (Belgium). His research interests are primarily focused on the intersection between information technology, statistics, and education. In past years, he designed several innovative and successful Web applications for private companies, universities, and the European Commission.

Ian Holliday, PhD, graduated in physics from Imperial College, University of London, from where he also obtained his PhD. His main research work has focused on human vision, both normal and abnormal, using psychophysical methods, MEG, and fMRI. Some of his research interests include MEG investigations of pattern processing, motion perception, computer simulation about MEG signals, and the application of MEG to clinical conditions. Having become aware of the general problem of reproducibility in science and its implications for his research, his interest in Reproducible Computing was spurred when he took up teaching responsibilities about advanced statistics at Aston University.

Peter Reddy, BSc, MSc, PGCE, joined Aston University in 1999 after working in social work, counseling, and further education. His time is split between research at the Centre for Learning Innovation and Professional Practice, and teaching and research in psychology with the Health and Human Development research group. He is a member of the Higher Education Academy Psychology Network Advisory Board, the British Psychological Society Division of Teachers and Researchers in Psychology committee, and the EUROPLAT working group. He is interested in research to improve student learning, including e-learning, undergraduate development, transition to university, educational relationships, and graduate employability. His research is in the Centre for Learning Innovation and Professional Practice and the Health and Human Development research group in Psychology in the School of Life and Health Sciences.

CHAPTER 11

THE GOOD TEACHER

Effective Teaching Strategies for a Ubiquitous Learning Environment

Torria Bond

ABSTRACT

This chapter applies the attributes of good teachers and the elements of good teaching to ubiquitous environments. Among learners, Web 2.0 tools are harnessed to foster community, facilitate collaboration, accommodate varying learning styles, and encourage professional discourse. The premise is that learner satisfaction and performance in the online course environment is enhanced by good course management, rapport building, and instructional methodology. Suggestions for Web 2.0 technologies that can integrate the best attributes of traditional instruction into the ubiquitous environment are the focus of this chapter.

INTRODUCTION

There is very little disagreement in the field of education about what constitutes good teaching (Bain, 2004; Corbett & Wilson, 2002; Haberman, 1995;

Ubiquitous Learning, pages 197–207

Thompson, 2003). Whether the instruction takes place face-to-face or online, good teaching involves gaining the learners attention, inspiring independent study and original thoughts, developing problem-solving skills within the learner's unique context, and using a variety of teaching methodologies. Consequently, good teachers are good teachers regardless of the instructional medium. Good teachers have high expectations for learners, provide the support necessary to reach learning outcomes, differentiate instruction according to individual student needs, and make every effort to get to know their students (Corbett & Wilson, 2002).

In addition, some of the best teachers make it a practice to design course environments that support these elements (Bain, 2004). An online course should not be a place to simply house a list of assignments. It should be a communal place conducive to scholarly inquiry, which respects the exchange of ideas between colleagues or peers. Just as with face-to-face classes, a ubiquitous learning environment, conducive to collaboration and study, must be purposefully created. The online environment should foster curiosity, academic and professional discourse, networking, respect for human differences, and an atmosphere of support and problem solving. Such a communal environment can be fostered through attention to course management, rapport building, and instructional delivery systems. Can the face-to-face attributes of good teachers be showcased in the ubiquitous environment? How can the elements of good teaching be embedded in various course platforms? The integration of the attributes of good teachers with the elements of good teaching within the online course environment will be the focus of this chapter.

COURSE MANAGEMENT

Course management is the equivalent of "classroom management" in traditional classrooms. In the online environment, course management refers to the organizational tools used to create a positive and productive learning experience. Elements of course management include, but are not limited to, communication methods, lesson submission formats, platform format, norms for posting and responding to discussion prompts, and general course information. Effective course management will enhance the learners' ability to navigate the features of the course with ease, access resources within and outside the course platform, comply with assignment submission expectations, and ultimately meet the learning outcomes of the course.

Ubiquitous environments can potentially isolate learners from the valuable exchange of ideas among their peers or colleagues. Collaboration and feedback are salient features of any learning experience. In the absence of collaboration and feedback, learners have no context or frame of reference outside their own. Opportunities are missed to engage and challenge the ideas of others while developing an informed opinion. Furthermore, critical thinking and analysis of complex ideas cannot take place. In the online classroom, e-mail is the most basic and expected form of communication between K–12 schools, universities, and their students. Internal message systems within the institution can facilitate communication between learners. However, other forms of communication can supplement this method. Later in this chapter, video conferencing, chats, social media, threaded discussions, and providing assignment feedback will be discussed. Used together, these communication methods foster a sense of collegiality and connectedness.

Many online professors facilitate multiple courses. Therefore it is beneficial to have assignments formatted in a standard manner and uploaded to a particular folder or portal within the course. The assignment format can be as simple as using the header and/or footer within a wording processing document that includes the identifying information required for your course, right justified. Requiring an assignment cover page in a standard publication format such as APA, MLA, or Chicago is a more formal format that can be used. An instructor feedback form that contains a text box for qualitative remarks, in addition to the use of track changes or comment inserts may also be beneficial to both the professor and the learner. An assignment format allows instructors and students to conveniently organize and save completed or evaluated assignments.

Online instructors will also need to carefully plan the course layout design. Free learning management systems such as CourseSites by Blackboard, as well as licensed course platforms such as Blackboard Learn, Moodle, and a plethora of other learning management systems allow the instructor to create tabs. Tabs can be created by weeks in the course, learning modules/units of study, or by course components. Formatting your course by weeks or session numbers has the benefit of providing time-management assistance for your learners. Each week/session contains all the information and resources needed to complete the reading assignments, view instructional media, identify learning activities, and upcoming assignment due dates. Formatting your course by learning modules provides learners with a visual of the major learning outcomes, topics, or units of study. Inside each tab, an instructor may want to include a suggested timeline for completion as this won't be apparent in this particular format. Another formatting option to consider is course components. Formatting your course-by-course components is also an option. Course components might include course policies, activities, instructional media, and course resources. The course resource section is an area that might house supplemental readings or links to related sites on the Web. The format you choose should enhance the continuity of the course.

Scholarly discourse is enhanced when there is an exchange of ideas representing differing ideological perspectives on a given topic. Learners have to be able to demonstrate respect for the opinions of others in their writing to stimulate critical thinking among the group. Establishing discussion norms is one way to foster mutual respect in writing. For example, a discussion post should demonstrate that the author takes responsibility for the view posted and that views are related to the readings or other course resources. Using writing prompts with appropriate citations helps to ensure that discussions stay on the topic without attacking their peer. Requiring that learners respond to posts made by their peers facilitates exposure to the views of others. Discussion norms help to create an atmosphere of collegiality and support for the professional exchange of ideas.

An area within your course where learners can access general information is also helpful. In this area, an instructor might add information on how to navigate the course platform, post teacher announcements, provide a "student lounge" where informal chats can be held, and synchronous collaboration activities or learner message board for student announcements or concerns. The general information section might also contain documents or links to all information pertinent to the successful completion of the course.

BUILDING COMMUNITY

Good teachers make every effort to learn as much about their students as they expect the students to learn about the course topic. The rapport between the learners and the professor is as important as developing the rapport between learners. A good online course community invites students to freely engage in the course content, challenge opposing views, and develop their own perspectives. There are a growing number of Web 2.0 tools that can enrich online course communication. Let's explore potential uses of Web 2.0 tools for building community in the online course.

Web 2.0 is, not by consensus, jargon that refers to second-generation Internet technologies. It attempts to be all-inclusive of the totality of various interactive and collaborative Web-based technology applications, which includes, but is not limited to video conferencing, social media, and cloud computing. All of these applications are accessible to users without cost, making them excellent resources for academia online. Skype, for example, is a free voice over Internet protocol (VoIP) video conferencing application that allows calls over the Internet. Currently, Skype shares the video stage with ooVoo, SightSpeed, and others. Social networks help learners stay-in-touch with one another, share electronic resources, and can potentially facilitate professional networking. For example, if an online course has a fieldwork component, a Twitter app can be downloaded to a learner's mobile phone and used to tweet highlights of the fieldwork experience as they occur. In addition, learners and instructors can use Twitter to follow professional organizations within any discipline. Furthermore, students can create or modify wikis, start blogs, and participate in voicethread discussions, versus just text based discussions related to course content. Providing meaningful opportunities for learners to interact with one another within the context of course assignments and discussions helps create a climate of collegiality and is useful to blended or fully ubiquitous environments.

INSTRUCTIONAL METHODOLOGY

Good teachers make every effort to meet the needs of their learners through strategies reflective of all philosophical orientations to education. This attribute of good teachers involves anticipating the needs of their learners and planning a delivery system that addresses challenges before they arise. In the absence of the interactional cues that help instructors determine student needs in face-to-face courses, online instructors will need to consider delivery systems that address learning styles, as well as academic and practical experience levels of students in a course. Given this necessity, differentiated instruction in the online environment requires the instructor to provide content knowledge, lesson delivery, and course assignments that precede knowing your students. Its purpose is to ensure that all learners at all levels of course experience are given the opportunity to achieve the same learning outcomes while insuring that learners with more experience are challenged and those with the least experience are not overwhelmed. Differentiated instruction is at the core of academic rigor, curriculum access, and equity in the evaluation process. Therefore it is salient that instruction takes advantage of all available media in order to reach all types of learners. In addition to textbook and journal article readings, online instructors should also consider video, podcasts, experiential learning exercises, service learning activities, and partner or group collaboration opportunities.

Video: There are several sources for academic videos that can be uploaded or linked to your course platform. Commercial videos are the easiest to locate from professional catalogs, the school, or university's library holdings. However, due to copyright laws, the technology media representative for the school or university may want to upload the course in such a way that only course learners have access to the copyrighted media (The Teach Act, 2002). This process can take time and must be factored into the time available for preparing your course. Google and YouTube videos are readily accessible as are videos from Ted.com, and OpenCourseWare sources. You can search by topic or by video name and preview the available options. This is the simplest way to add media to your course. However, the selection of applicable course content may be minimal. By adding a link to the video or embedding the video within your course platform, the availability of the resource is instantaneous. The drawback is that author's have the ability to remove a link without notice, making it essential that you verify the links prior to each use. Instructor-created videos are also an option. With a Webcam, instructors can videotape minilectures, guest speakers, panel interviews, demonstrations, simulations, and other helpful learning aids.

Weblog: Reflection is a skill required of professionals and students of every discipline. Sometimes professionals discuss the outcomes of a particular course of action, and individuals reflect on the advantages and disadvantages of choices made. While some of these reflections take place verbally or in written diaries, blogging is the digital equivalent to handwritten journals. Through free Weblog hosting, instructors can post their own blogs and encourage students to respond to them. As a variation to the traditional research assignment, students can create blogs focused on course topics, upload podcasts, subscribe to RSS feeds, view videos, and access Weblinks. Peers can be asked to review or respond to the blogs of their classmates. It's an excellent way to encourage learners to engage politically in issues of importance to them individually or professionally.

RSS feeds: Many students are unable to distinguish between credible and questionable Web sources. Because many academic journals now offer free RSS feeds, peer reviewed articles can automatically be downloaded to an instructor's Weblog or course management system and made available to students. While students can also create Weblogs and subscribe to RSS feeds free of charge, instructors can provide guidance to credible, peer reviewed content that helps students stay current on the latest research in their discipline. RSS stands for Real Simple Syndication and allows an instructor's Weblog to receive feeds from electronic sources without visiting each one individually. Because there are so many electronic sources with news feeds, instructor guidance is helpful until students learn to distinguish between credible and questionable sources of Web content (see Table 11.1).

Podcasts: Podcasts are audio or video files that are created regularly and can be downloaded to an mp3 player, mobile phone, or computer. Podcasts can be created by an instructor, uploaded to an instructor's Weblog, and downloaded by students. Instructors can create podcasts of speeches, interviews, or course lectures. Podcasts are relatively easy to create, as most computers allow you to connect a microphone to the system and record voice or music. Once an audio file is created, the podcast can be uploaded to your blog or course management system, and downloaded by students. Instructors can create podcasts of speeches, interviews, or course lectures. Thanks to many free podcasting sites, podcasts are easy to create, as most computers allow you to connect a microphone to the system and record voice or music. As a source of content within a discipline, students can use podcasts within assignment presentations. As a class, students can contribute one episode toward a series of podcasts on a controversial topic within a discipline and make it available to a wider audience than just the instructor and their peers..

Experiential learning exercises: Part of any good course is developing attitudes, values, and beliefs appropriate for interacting with clients, colleagues, or the target audience for your profession. Experiential learning exercises help create genuine empathy for the plight of others within the context of learning about a particular professional environment. For example, if you want to help a new teacher understand what it is like to be a non-English speaker in a classroom where a teacher lectures for an extended period of time, you could upload a video or podcast of a lecture in a foreign language and require that a 100-point exam be taken on the content. You could create discussion or journal items on the learners thoughts while listening to the lecture and taking the exam. You could pose questions as to what might make it easier for a non-English speaking student to understand the content of a lecture. Addressing the intangible dispositions of learners is equally important in the ubiquitous environment as it is in the face-to-face format.

Service learning: Online learners can still provide a valuable service to their community while participating in courses ubiquitously. It is essential for academic disciplines that require fieldwork of learners integrate service learning tasks in order to give learners the experience needed to be successful in fieldwork experiences. For example, teachers pursuing licensure or credentials typically have to serve a number of hours at schools interacting with students, teachers, parents, and colleagues. A service learning project might include partnering with a teacher to create lesson plans, helping a teacher evaluate papers or projects, or perhaps a learner could serve as an online tutor using an online interactive whiteboard. With the increasing number of working adults and career changers seeking online degree programs, service learning activities can be an effective way to provide learners with preparatory experiences.

Collaboration opportunities: In all facets of our lives, we will be working with others in some capacity. It is not acceptable to allow students to go through elementary, secondary, and postsecondary degree programs without having to work collaboratively. Synchronous and asynchronous opportunities for collaboration exist through a growing number of Web 2.0 sites. Because the sources of collaboration are free, instructors can harness their popularity for educational purposes. For example, Google Docs allows learners to write collaboratively, Voicethread.com allows for verbal discussions and narrated presentatons, Animoto.com allows for the creation of video presentations set to music, and Glogster.com allows for the creation of digital posters. Learners can create Web sites free accounts and publish their work for a larger audience. With the variety of synchronous and asynchronous options available, the ubiquitous environment can provide rich opportunities for collaboration.

Incorporating technology tools into instructional units for learners is the most creative aspect of online instruction. Decisions about online teaching methodology will still be centered around the learning goals, objectives, and outcomes. Unlike face-to-face courses, many ubiquitous environments rely heavily on text for conveying instructional information and assignment requirements. This does not have to be the case. A willingness to use a variety of technological tools can ensure academic success and increase learner satisfaction with online course delivery. Engaging students through authentic means is essential to learning. Each of the strategies mentioned has the potential to create an authentic audience and purpose to coursework. Students write and speak to audiences larger than the instructor and their classmates. Having a broader audience can provoke conscientious completion of learning tasks and increase motivation.

SUMMARY

The elements of good teaching remain the same regardless of the course format. Good instruction requires the use of methods that capture learners' attention, provoke further study, elicit original thoughts, and facilitate problem solving within a particular context. Communicating high academic expectation within a supportive environment, differentiating instruction based on learner needs, and building a rapport with students are elements of good teaching that remain the same regardless of the learning environment. The integration of Web 2.0 technologies can facilitate the best attributes of traditional instruction into the ubiquitous environment.

Strategy Highlight 1: Building Community between learners in a course

- Create a social networking site for students within the same course: Edmodo.com and Facebook allow the creation of private groups whose members must be invited in order to gain access. Ning.com is a networking site that can be created for the same purpose. Within these groups instructors can create ice-breaker activities, post discipline related events, or even present virtual fieldtrips.
- Create a Twitter hashtag for your course: Once a twitter account is created by the instructor, a hashtag such as #cbu101 would allow course related tweets to appear together. If learners are participating in a fieldwork activity, for example, learners can register their

mobile numbers to their twitter account and send tweet from their mobile phone when interesting learning moments occur.

- Encourage peer editing or feedback: Using Google Docs, learners can edit an assignment together in real time before submitting it to the instructor. Students can also use the "comments" insert or "track changes" in Microsoft Word to provide feedback.
- Create a Skype account: Instructors can use video conferencing to hold regular office hours and students can use video conferencing for collaboration purposes.
- Create a "community lounge" folder within the course management system: Encourage students to submit a 100-word biography and picture of themselves, along with a collage of illustrations that reflect their interests or hobbies. Learners can respond to these introductions and use the community lounge for social announcements like new births, birthdays, anniversary, and other conversations.

Strategy Highlight 2: Share peer reviewed and other credible web resources

- Subscribe to RSS feeds: Create a free subscription on a weblog such as blogger.com or other website host that accommodates blogging. Go the websites of your most trusted academic journals and click the RSS feed icon or paste the URL into your blog according to the service providers directions. When students or colleagues subscribe to your blog, they will be able to access the RSS feeds to which you have subscribed. In this way, instructors make peer reviewed, credible web sources available to learners.
- Share "bookmarks" with learners: Delicious.com is a social bookmarking site that instructors can create, make public, and thereby share with learners. This particular bookmarking site allows you to create tags and annotate your bookmarks so that learners can easily access resources needed.

Strategy Highlight 3: Integrate Web 2.0 tools into collaborative assignments

- Use Voicethread for learner led discussions: Pairs of small groups of students can make presentations and plan for a Socratic Dialogue around the topic of the presentation. Hearing learner voices expands learner presence in the course.
- Encourage the use of a variety of media within a collaborative presentation: Web 2.0 tools allow for the easy integration of audio, video, and images. When presentations are not dominated by text, learner engagement is enhanced.

- Synchronous group planning: Students can collaborate on group assignments by using Skype or other video conferencing tools, chat features available in course management systems, and Google Docs for collaborative editing.

REFERENCES

American Library Association (n.d). *Distance education and the teach act.* Retrieved from http://www.ala.org/Template.cfm?Section=Distance_Education_and_the_TEACH_Act&Template=/ContentManagement/ContentDisplay.cfm&ContentID=25939

Animoto. (n.d.). Retrieved from http://animoto.com/

Bain, K. (2004). *What the best college teachers do.* Cambridge, MA: Harvard University Press.

Blogger. (n.d.). Retrieved from http://www.blogger.com

Bonk, C. & Zhang, K. (2008). *Empowering online learning: 100+ activities for reading, reflecting, displaying and doing.* San Francisco, CA: Jossey-Bass

Corbett, D., & Wilson, B. (2002). What urban students say about good teaching. *Educational Leadership, 60*(1), 18–22.

Blackboard. (n.d.). *CourseSites.* Retrieved from http://www.coursesites.com

Blackboard. (n.d.). *Blackboard Learn.* Retrieved from http://www.blackboard.com/Platforms/Learn/Overview.aspx

Edmodo. (n.d.). Retrieved from http://www.edmodo.com

Facebook. (n.d.). Retrieved from http://www.facebook.com

Glogster. (n.d.). Retrieved from http://www.glogster.com

GoogleDocs. (n.d.). Retrieved from http://www.docs.google.com

Haberman, M. (1995). *Star teachers of children of poverty.* Indianapolis, IN: Kappa Delta Pi.

Moodle. (n.d.). Retrieved from http://www.moodle.com

Ning. (n.d.). Retrieved from http://www.ning.com

ooVoo. (n.d.). Retrieved from http://www.oovoo.com

OpenOffice. (n.d.). Retrieved from http://www.openoffice.org

Palloff, R & Pratt, K. (2007). *Building online learning communities: Effective strategies for the virtual classroom.* San Francisco, CA: Jossey-Bass

Podbean. (n.d.). Retrieved from http://podbean.com/

Richardson, W. (2010). *Blogs, wikis, podcasts, and other powerful Web tools for classrooms.* Thousand Oaks, CA: Corwin

Shank, P. (2007). *The online learning idea book: 95 proven ways to enhance technology-based and blended learning.* San Francisco, CA: Pfeiffer

SightSpeed. (n.d.). Retrieved from http://www.sightspeed.com

Skype. (n.d.). Retrieved from http://www.skype.com

Solomon, G. & Schrum, L. (2010). *Web 2.0: How-to for educators.* Washington, DC: International Society for Technology Education.

TED. (n.d.). Retrieved from http://www.ted.com

Thompson, G. (2003). *What African American parents want educators to know.* Westport, CT: Praeger Publishers.
Twitter. (n.d.). Retrieved from http://www.twitter.com
VoiceThread. (n.d.) Retrieved from http://voicethread.com/

ABOUT THE AUTHOR

Dr. Torria Davis Bond is currently an Instructional Designer and Adjunct Professor for the Online and Professional Studies Division of California Baptist University in Riverside, CA. Her research interests include issues of diversity in schools, African American student success, and teaching methodology, particularly the infusion of new technologies in the teaching and learning process. She lives in Rancho Cucamonga, California, with her husband of 18 years and has three children.

CHAPTER 12

HELPING YOUR LECTURERS TO CREATIVELY INTRODUCE UBIQUITOUS COMPUTING TECHNOLOGIES INTO THEIR TEACHING

What Every Lecturer Should Know

Lisa-Dionne Morris

ABSTRACT

While many lecturers acknowledge the drive in higher education to improve their teaching practice through educational technologies, they will struggle to do this in practice. A frequent reason for this is that many lecturers will have limited training in the use of educational learning technologies. As a result, they might experience frustration and may also struggle to embed educational technologies, such as mobile or ubiquitous computing technology into their teaching. The purpose of this chapter is to support institutions through equipping lecturers with the attitudes, principles, and skills they need to enjoy creatively introducing ubiquitous computing technologies into their teaching. This chapter looks at creativity with ubiquitous technology

Ubiquitous Learning, pages 209–228

in the context of education, and seeks answers to the following questions: How can ubiquitous computing technology help educators produce better pedagogical solutions for teaching and learning? *Why is* ubiquitous computing technology *important? How does* ubiquitous computing technology *work? How do we foster creativity when using ubiquitous computing?* The chapter argues that with the digital age of computer support for teaching and learning in informal learning environments, individuals and organizations need, if they are to flourish, creative minds when it comes to helping lecturers creatively integrate ubiquitous computing technologies into their teaching practice. The premise is that training in the use of ubiquitous computing technologies can provide new opportunities for learning in the context of activity. Learning in the context of activity provides unique opportunities for learning scenarios, such as ubiquitous learning, to bridge the gap between UK Higher Education Institutes (HEIs) learning requirements and technological drivers. The chapter seeks to identify what creativity is when using ubiquitous computing technology in their teaching practice and why it is essential for educational succes. It puts forward a number of ways to enhance an individual's creativity and build communities of creative ubiquitous learning.

INTRODUCTION

There is a strong technological and economic push for higher education providers to adopt educational technologies. This is driven, in part, by the requirement of industry for lifelong learning on a flexible, just-in-time basis (Radcliffe, 2002). Many HEIs would like to embrace enhanced learning technologies in their teaching practice. There is concern however, particularly among lecturers, that educational technology should be discipline-specific. Many lecturers suffer significant frustration with technologies because they do not have expertise in learning technologies. Much of the anguish stems from not knowing how to use education technologies in their teaching practice. HEIs in the UK have within their power the ability to alleviate such anguish, but to do so, they must teach lecturers the attitudes, principles, and skills necessary for introducing advanced and enhanced computing technologies into teaching and learning activities. Training in the use of ubiquitous computing technologies can provide new opportunities for learning within the context of activity. Learning within the context of activity provides unique opportunities for learning scenarios, such as ubiquitous learning, to bridge the gap between HEI's learning requirements and technological drivers.

BACKGROUND

Lefoe, Olney, Wright, and Herrington (2009) explain that ubiquitous computing technologies provide development opportunities for a fundamental change in *HEI's teaching and learning.* Hennessy (1999) asserts that despite significant infrastructure barriers, such as a lack of appropriate training and guidance on integration and learning design, this has not limited the widespread adoption of ubiquitous computing technologies in HEIs. At present, models for developing ubiquitous learning applications are lacking (Herrington, Herrington, Mantei, Olney, & Ferry, 2009), and training strategies for the use of ubiquitous computing technology are ill-defined and inconsistent (Sharples, 2009).

Early adoption of ubiquitous computing technology tended to focus on the capacity of technology rather than its effectiveness as a teaching or learning tool. The current challenge for *HEIs* is how best to utilize the available ubiquitous computing technologies and how to develop subject-appropriate pedagogies that have cross-subject applicability. From an educational perspective, creativity introducing ubiquitous computing into teaching is seen as a continuous conversation between learners, lecturers, and the learning environment. In this way, ubiquitous computing technology provides new and unique opportunities for helping lecturers creatively introduce ubiquitous computing into their teaching to bridge the gap between HEIs and technological drivers.

Ubiquitous Computing Technology

After the initial impact of computers in education, the introduction of e-learning, m-learning, and blended learning epitomized the constant transformation and evolution of educational technologies (Jones & Jo, 2004). The absorption of ubiquitous computing technologies in HEIs marks another step forward, with ubiquitous learning emerging through the concept of ubiquitous computing. Ubiquitous computing technologies now have the potential to revolutionize education, removing many of the physical constraints of traditional learning that did not support learning in the context of activity. Ubiquitous computing technology is constantly evolving and growing. The development of ubiquitous media for the delivery of education is another emerging approach to support learning in the context of activity, where such technologies weave themselves into the fabric of environments until they are indistinguishable from them (Weiser, 1991). Ubiquitous computing technology is seen as the next stage in how learners interact with computing systems embeded in learning environments, affording learners the chance to use real-time data and feedback to support their learning.

The basic assumption is that ubiquitous computing technologies are types of ubiquitous systems interfaced via a ubiquitous computing device. Figure 12.1 outlines some of the benefits and how they can support learning.

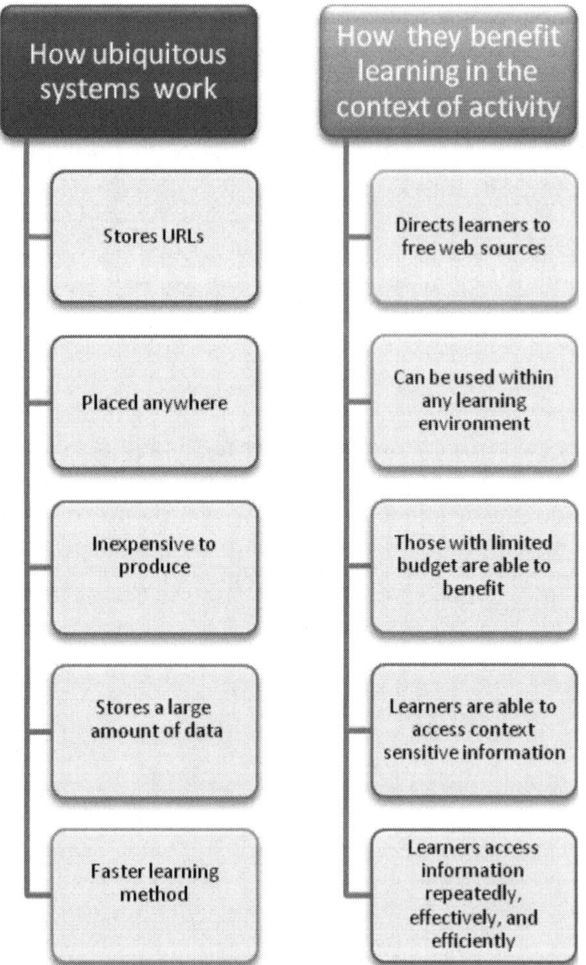

Figure 12.1 Ubiquitous systems benefits framework.

Learning Within the Context of Activity

Learning in the context of activity is a process in which learners can become totally immersed in the learning process. Cooke, Pachler, and Bradley (2008) describe this as learning-conscious learning or task-conscious learning, where learners are aware of their knowledge expanding, and learning takes place while engaged in activity. The benefit of learning within the context of activity is that a high level of competency is reached due to a more enriched learning experience. It is widely used in HEIs today and increasingly so, with emphasis on the sector's role in supporting and developing both local and national economic infrastructures and developing the employability and skills for graduates (Brodie et al., 2007). Learning from study or experience is usually where students are encouraged to reflect and report on the work carried out or relevant skills they have developed.

Learning within the context of activity is the amalgamation of formal knowledge, reflection, and expertise of work. It is the structured learner-controlled method of improving and developing skills and knowledge related to specific work activities by providing an alternative mode for learners and lecturers who prefer a more contextually specific learning environment. Learning within the context of activity challenges traditional views of formal knowledge and learning, and requires a different level of participation and responsibility by learners, lecturers, and HEIs, compared with more traditional educational practice, and as such, can offer richer experiential opportunities.

Dorn (2005) describes these types of learning as experiences that connect knowledge and skills obtained in the classroom to those needed outside the classroom, often comprising a range of diverse activities and instructional strategies designed to assist students in fulfilling their education plans. Learning within the context of activity can improve UK HEIs learning requirements to develop the employability and skills for graduates by giving learners the opportunity to develop practical skills that will give them a valuable competitive advantage when it comes to further employment.

Ubiquitous Computing Technologies are Good for Learning Within the Context of Activity

Learners have the opportunity to conduct investigations and develop analytical and critical thinking skills during work activities done in diverse locations in class or off-campus. Ubiquitous computing technologies can provide relevant information in context in the time and place needed. In such cases, learning activities would be able to adapt to a range of unique learning characteristics. This is important for learning, as it allows lecturers to customize and personalize information. Bomsdorf (2005) explains that ubiquitous computing technologies enable a seamless combination between virtual environments and physical spaces that supports the learning process. Bomsdoft remarks that it is inevitable that professional off-campus learning activities will become a part of modern education, and interactive learning will become commonplace in education. He argues that the integration of ubiquitous computing technologies will be successful only if the technology is fully developed before its implementation into learning and teaching scenarios. Morris (2008) supports Bomsdorf's argument, suggesting that the educational challenge is the implementation and iteration of the ubiquitous computing technologies in an effective process, whereby computers are used to provide relevant information in the correct place, providing students with a multifaceted experience.

Ubiquitous computing technology can provide relevant information as and when it is needed for learning in context with minimal interruption to working tasks. Learning in context allows skill and knowledge to be obtained through computerized instruction, delivering real-time contextual data, and supporting experiential learning (Ley, 2007).

The Process for Integrating Ubiquitous Computing Technology into Learning Within the Context of Activity: Three Principles Your Lecturers Must Learn

There are three principles of creative technology management for introducing ubiquitous computing technology into learning within the context of activity, and they are quite simple. The first concerns the need to collaborate with students, lecturers, and faculty representatives to develop and evaluate ubiquitous teaching tools. This represents the "Dream." The second seeks to elicit underlying pedagogical expertise to make teaching material more creative. This represents the "Enabler." The third focuses on context-driven and performance-supportive models for teaching that focuses on the developmental process of how to integrate ubiquitous computing technology into their teaching practice by interfacing with others. This represents the "Interface."

These three principles underpin innovation and creativity in education using ubiquitous computing technology. Inherited characteristics persist in each principle. The basic process is illustrated in Figure 12.2 and comprises the knowledge, skills, and attitudes needed for creatively introducing ubiquitous computing technologies into teaching practice.

In Figure 12.2, the Dream is constrained by the learning experience or pedagogy design and originates from the HEI itself, from the lecturers, and from the learners. The Enabler allows you to produce a dream via the learning strategy, ubiquitous computing technology, and learning activity. The correct tool will allow experimentation and innovation, which is a necessary part of creative endeavor. The Interface utilizes the expertise of the educational and other digital infrastructure. The following explains the process of engaging the model.

DREAM (KNOWLEDGE)

The Dream is the essential component of the learning experience. This section presents ideas on setting up and managing project activities.

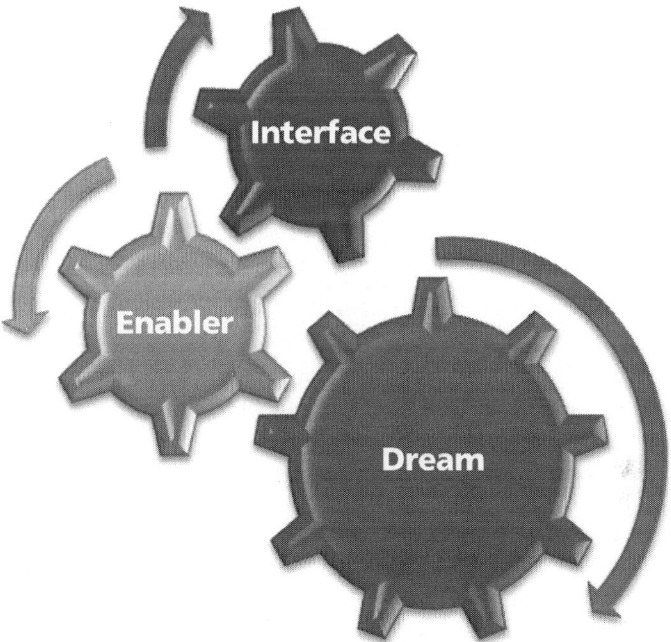

Figure 12.2 Ubiquitous creativity model.

Students Dream

Learners can easily generate a set of interesting ideas for design and development projects using ubiquitous computing technologies. Ask students to prepare a one-page written proposal and a 60-second presentation on how they would like to use technologies that allow learning within the context of activity. After listening to the presentation, ask the learner to fill-out a Ubiquitous Preference Card, stating the information they would like to know and the skills and background they have and would like to develop in this learning scenario. Warn students against expressing a preference for a project that is too complex.

Tutors and Industry Dream

In most cases, industry-supported projects, combined with the learner's conceived project, are most successful. This is relatively simple to manage by having representatives from the supporting company prepare a one-page proposal and make a 60-second presentation. Then students involved in the project will simply express a learning task on their Ubiquitous Preference Card.

HEIs Dream

On many occasions, proposed project ideas will come from faculty-specific projects. These ideas are often suggestions from colleagues or others affiliated with the school. These projects have some interesting characteristics. Be patient and diligent, because thrift might well be a discerning factor when developing these projects.

ENABLER (SKILLS)

In many HEIs, one significant obstacle to developing ubiquitous teaching scenarios may come in the form of a heavily prescribed curriculum, but this can be seen as an opportunity. The basic collaborative model around which ubiquitous teaching scenarios are developed focuses on timing, the learning strategy, and the out-of-class activity. These goals could be shared through existing assessment and learning channels. The design strategy for developing ubiquitous teaching scenarios is shown in Figure 12.3, which takes into account the importance off-campus activities, the importance of considering the ubiquitous learning activity, its impact on the context of learning, and the importance of assessment for learning. The session can follow this flow:

The enabling process model in Figure 12.3 shows timing, illustrates the learning strategy, and positions out-of-class activity. It will prove useful for

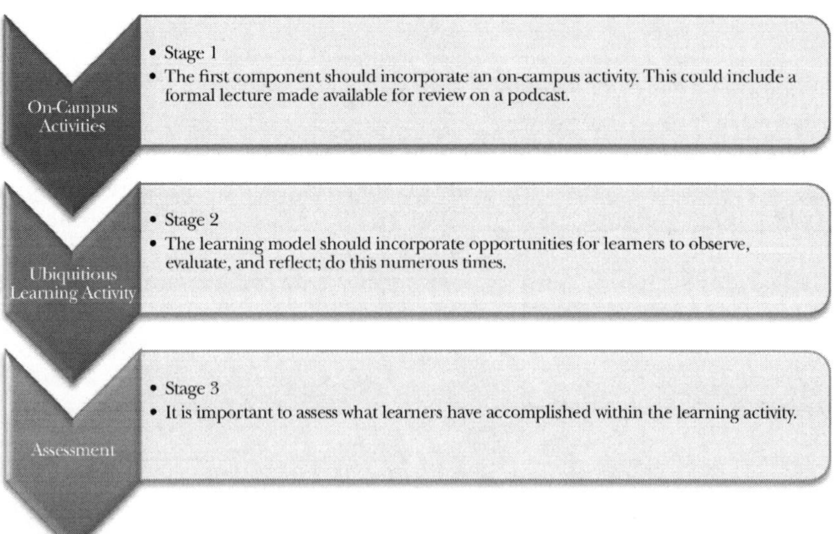

Figure 12.3 The design strategy for developing ubiquitous.

HEIs, lecturers, and learners to understand what is involved in the whole learning activity before they start the task. In general, ubiquitous learning sessions should be in the middle of the process, supported by an on-campus activity, finishing with an assessment. Sessions can be used to emphasize the fundamental metric of student learning. For many learners, this will be their first exposure to a structured methodology for using ubiquitous computing technologies for learning within the context of activity. In general, off-campus activity should take 30 to 40 minutes. It is useful to choose an environment learners understand well enough to engage in actions without prior research.

An additional obstacle is managing the teaching content. The style in which managing teaching content is undertaken is critical to the success of the ubiquitous computing tool. The role of the manager within a teaching context is crucial in providing inspiration, access to resources, and a safe environment where learning can take place. The best managers in the ubiquitous context will engage in collaborative conversations in which all are involved and all give their input. Managing the teaching content requires individual collaborative thinking time and space for experimentation. Figure 12.4 presents a structure developed to take into consideration three key aspects required for designing good ubiquitous teaching content: planning, preparation, and learning through reflection.

The multiple action stages, where information about the processed can be logged and recorded, allows lecturers to review progression in terms of task completion.

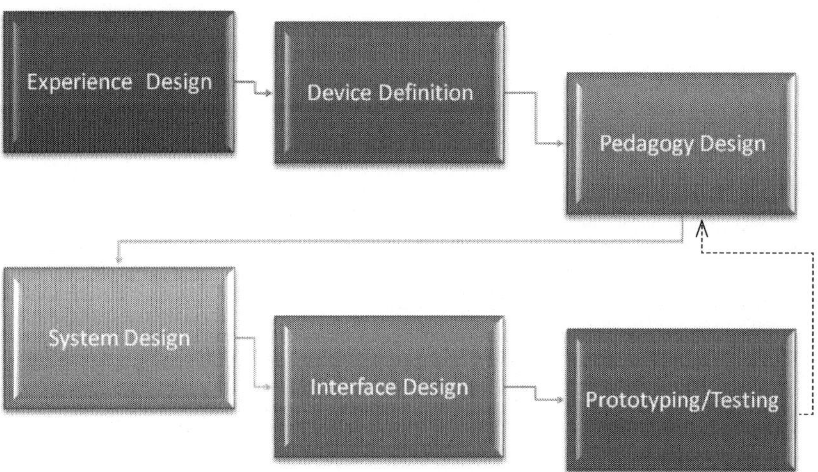

Figure 12.4 Six key aspects required for designing good teaching context.

INTERFACING WITH PEOPLE (ATTITUDES)

A basic understanding of issues surrounding ubiquitous computing technologies is essential for lecturers, whether they work in an established education technology environment or not. Assuming that the faculty do not have the technological expertise to lead this venture, there are still several viable alternatives including this topic in a professional development course, and experiment with the following:

- Invite an educational technologist from a local firm to speak about innovation, design, and utility using digital technology.
- Invite a suitably trained guest from the education, computing, or design faculty to speak, if one can be identified; speak on the above topic.
- Invite a corporate professional with expertise in ubiquitous computing technologies to speak.
- Include topics relating to the subject, such as e-learning and m-learning in the same manner, using an appropriate guest speaker.

Innovation succeeds when the successful adaptation of all aspects of the ubiquitous creativity model shown in Figure 12.5 is applied in specific disciplines and pedagogical underpinnings. It is discipline uniqueness that provides effective learning activities.

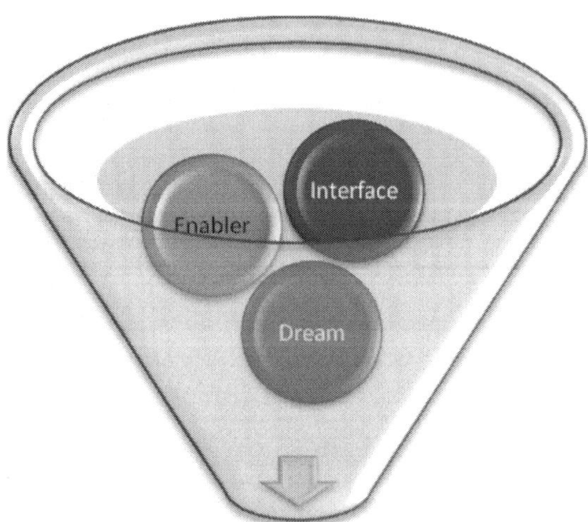

Figure 12.5 Ubiquitous learning model.

INVOLVING STUDENTS IN THE DEVELOPMENT AND EVALUATION OF A UBIQUITOUS LEARNING APPLICATION FOR A DESIGN PRACTICE SETTING

The following case study describes how lecturers on the Product Design program at the University of Leeds felt it important to introduce to the program the following elements: an authentic learning context and learning in a nonthreatening and informal setting. In addition to this, the lecturers wanted to develop skills of self-reflection on the design journey; a skill which is considered to be important for professional designers in the design-practice setting. Last but not least, lecturers wanted to find a meaningful way of introducing to their students an understanding of the principles of Sustainable Design, an area that is sometimes sadly neglected in formal design education.

The three principles of creative technology management are very simply employed in this case study. First, lecturers sought to elicit underlying pedagogical expertise and reflective models used in design practice settings, making teaching material more explicit. Second, lectures designed, developed, and evaluated the ubiquitous learning tool in use. Third, lectures focus on a context-driven, task-sensitive, and performance-supportive model of reflection for teaching specific Sustainable Design issues gained through engaging the expertise of other lecturers.

CASE STUDY 1

Involving Students in the Development and Evaluation of a Ubiquitous Learning Application for a Design Practice Setting (Morris & Connelly, 2010)

Context

This case study centers on the need to present new collaborative opportunities between students (users) and academics to bridge the gap between pedagogical and technological drivers.

Method

The project aimed to create a ubiquitous learning tool that would enhance students' understanding of Sustainable Design. The outcome was the production of a free Web-based ubiquitous learning application for Web-enabled mobile and ubiquitous devices (iPhone) to be used in museums and galleries, facilitating a more stimulating student exploration of the topic of Sustainable Design, through design obsolescence and physical artifacts. It was intended that the ubiquitous learning application would provide students with the necessary skills and knowledge in context to improve their critical and analytical skills during informal learning activities. On completion of the learning activities, it was anticipated that students would be able to use and develop frameworks; identify and describe emerging sociocultural trends, including sustainability; and understand the relevance of these to design. It was hoped that the ubiquitous learning application would engender in students the necessary skills and knowledge to learn independently and, through improving their critical and analytical skills, would enable them to find better ways of developing new consumer electronic products in the future.

The Learning Activity

The subject chosen was Obsolescence in Design. The external location, defined as the National Media Museum, Bradford, UK, was chosen for its association with consumer electronic design in the 20th century, specifically television and cameras. Thirty students, split into six groups, and each group asked to work together to complete the tasks. The session was as follows:

A. Technology Interaction
Learners were presented with information via QR Codes (see Figure 12.6) on a chosen product. The groups were asked to discuss a series of questions around why a museum artifact (a television) had become obsolete.

Figure 12.6 Use of QR codes in the learning activity.
Note: These codes, once scanned, link directly to a component of the iteration. Placing these codes in strategic positions around the learning environment (the museum) allowed for information on the application to be presented at the correct time and in the correct place, thus affording learning through the construction of knowledge, as described by Bouzeghoub and Garlatti (2009).

B. Observations

Learners were then presented with expert opinions from the different perspectives of design, business, ethics, and sustainability. An example of the interface presented to students is shown in Figure 12.7.

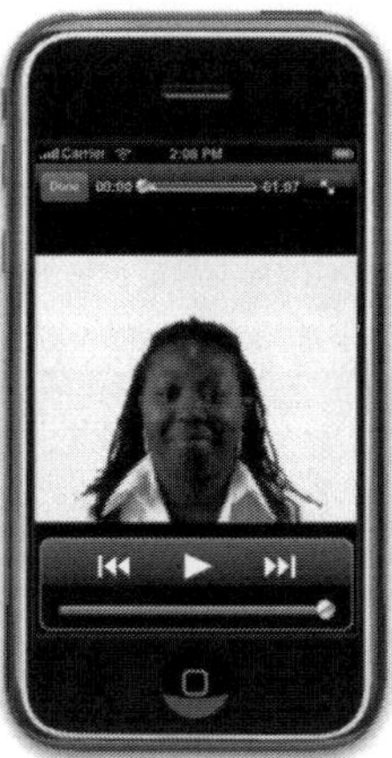

Figure 12.7 Expert opinions.

D. Evaluation

Learners were asked to reevaluate each others' answers in groups and to provide a new group answer in response to newly learned information. This is shown in Figure 12.8.

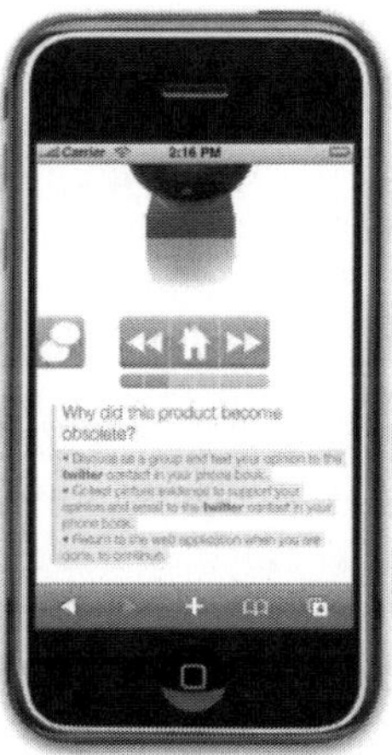

Figure 12.8 Interface for the Twitter upload.

E. The Process of Reflection
Consciously and subconsciously, the process prompted personal reflection on the subject matter.
Learners were finally asked to gather information on a product and to analyze it with respect to what had been learned. From this, knowledge was implemented in a design task.

What Insight Did This Method Provide?

- Ubiquitous computing was found to provide answers to many of the challenges presented by learning in informal environments. Furthermore, it enabled students to interact with physical products in situ, facilitating the interaction of students with each other and generating conversations that led to meaningful learning.
- The ubiquitous tool in this case study was based on a cycle of observation, evaluation, and reflection, and it is perceived that future development of ubiquitous computing tools could, if based around this cycle, greatly improve the potential for learning within the context of activity.

MAKING A DIFFERENCE TO THE ACCESSING OF INFORMATION IN CLINICAL WORK-BASED LEARNING ENVIRONMENTS

Case Study 2 responds to ubiquitous learning challenges, the appropriateness of ubiquitous computing technologies for providing answers to current issues, and the pedagogical problems associated with work-based learning. It is important to note that the pedagogical underpinning builds upon the ideas and actions associated with nurturing proper attitudes to work-based learning. This is presented in Figure 12.9.

It is easy to have a limited vision of ubiquitous computing and to claim ignorance about how to integrate ubiquitous computing systems into teaching practice. If HEIs and lecturers view ubiquitous computing technology as simply just another educational gadget, a great educational opportunity will be lost. Ubiquitous computing technology can be both personal and public, and it can be ever-present. It has the potential, therefore, to have a serious impact on the future of educational technology. Carefully thought-out, inspired, and innovative use of ubiquitous computing systems can change learning spaces in formal and informal learning environments, helping lecturers, learners, and HEIs in their endeavors to teach and be taught. Tables 12.1 and 12.2 help to explore some of the issues and problems associated with developing ubiquitous learning scenarios relating to Case Study 2.

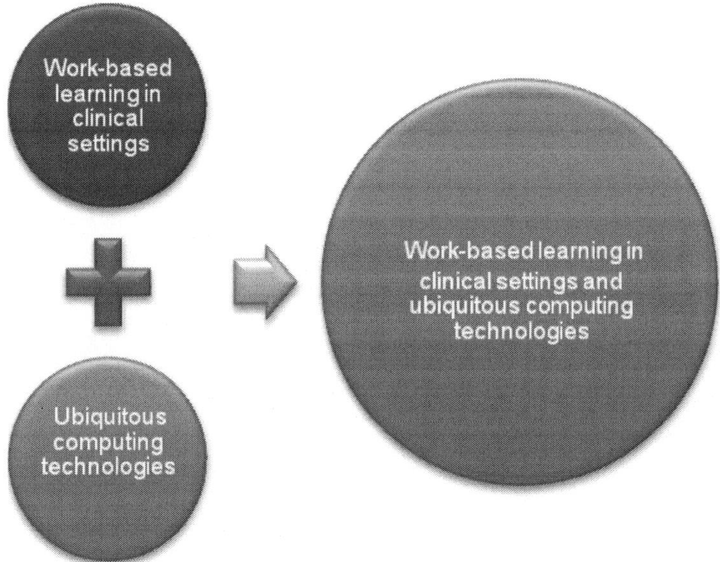

Figure 12.9 The Areas of Intersection of Case Study 2.

CASE STUDY 2

Making a Difference to the Accessing of Information in Clinical Work-Based Learning Environments

Context

The project focused on skills development and on the development and implementation of ubiquitous learning to enhance the student learning experience within the context of work-based learning in clinical environments. The project makes use of recent developments in ubiquitous computing technology and will take advantage of the fact that most students now possess a mobile or ubiquitous device that (a) has the capacity to capture still images and (b) is Web enabled. The involvement of students is essential.

Method

Quick response codes can store Internet addresses and enable information to be attached to physical objects by means of a two-dimensional bar code. In this project, the ubiquitous learning application contains context-sensitive information relating to pieces of clinical equipment, information on the ethics of using certain pieces of equipment, and carrying out certain activities related to patient care.

TABLE 12.1 Workshop Questions

There are two tasks to be completed:

Task 1: Analyzing the learning situation (15-minute group or individual task)

This activity focuses on one of the following thematic areas:

1. Internal learning environment strengths
2. Internal learning environment weaknesses
3. External learning environment strengths and weaknesses
4. External learning environments: collaborators, opportunities, and challenges
5. Aligning external learning opportunities, internal and external learning strengths
6. Future vision
7. Strategic learning priorities

Task 2: Actions to help introduce ubiquitous computing technologies into their teaching practice (15-minute group or individual task)

For this activity, focus on the following questions:

- What type of information is top priority, and what actions need to be taken to reach desired goals?
- How would current thinking change if the project title is changed to "Making a Difference to Health and Safety Information in the Laboratory?"

Source: Adapted from a Work-based Learning and Ubiquitous Computing workshop in 2010.

TABLE 12.2 Design Tips

- Develop a "ubiquitous attitude" to teaching situations. Identify a small number of coherent learning objectives to be delivered simply in a direct way.
- If the proposed learning activity does not contain at least two clear learning objectives that will allow learning to be carried out off campus, think again.
- Step back from the detail and look for general qualities learning within the context activity embodies. Name them and expand on how to develop these general qualities using ubiquitous computing technologies.

THREE ATTITUDES LECTURERS MUST ACQUIRE

If lecturers are to experience success in introducing ubiquitous computing technologies into their teaching practice, they must first acquire the proper attitudes. Three of these provide a solid foundation for fostering creativity with the use of ubiquitous computing technologies:

- Thrift
- Diligence
- Patience

Thrift

At an economic-level thrift is necessary to produce new and innovative ubiquitous learning experiences. In an increasingly competitive world of funding for learning and teaching investment in HEIs, ubiquitous computing systems and technologies can be successfully integrated without huge financial implications. In traditional pedagogical scenarios, thrift was a means of reserving raw material; in terms of ubiquitous computing technology, thrift refers to teaching time and money. It is not necessary to spend excessive amounts of money on the production, vast learning resources, and software. Ubiquitous computing technology, *although* intangible, should add value to the educational experience without large financial investment, whether internally or externally, in informal learning environments, such as the workplace.

Diligence

Diligence is central to improving the functioning and development of learning scenarios, collaborations, and relationships. This positive attribute is essential to ubiquitous learning and teaching practices in increasingly complex, frequently changing, and challenging learning environments. Diligence is also needed to manage conflicts of interest with competing stakeholders and attentively understand the needs of others.

Patience

It is normal to approach ubiquitous computing with a degree of uncertainty; however, as knowledge and skills expand, so do opportunities for teaching. To realize their opportunities, make up your mind to be persistent. You will be responsible for embedding ubiquitous computing into teaching practice, so try to be tolerant. Ultimately, it will not fulfill either your potential for growth or that of your HEI if you do not continue with your endeavors. Patience is important in relation to aspects of ubiquitous computing technology and ourselves.

What you need to know is that your teaching scenarios are not trapped by routine thinking; teaching practice can be innovative. Lecturers should allow learners to experience the unpredictability of technology and to work through it, and to experience the uncertainty of technology and not be fearful or reluctant to use it. We need learning activities that introduce an element of surprise. Learners need lectures that provide both order and adventure, and they need lecturers who are willing to do the unexpected and to take risks as they introduce ubiquitous technology into their teaching practice.

CONCLUSION

When attempting to discuss support technologies in HEIs, bear in mind that this is usually covered by e-learning and blended learning. In many lecturers' experience, this has historically been presented as a series of sessions in which basic technologies are explained and demonstrated; but there has been limited or even no training on how best to integrate technology into learning scenarios. Training on how to integrate such technologies into learning activities is important. Training in the use of ubiquitous computing technologies can provide new opportunities for learning within the context of activity, and provide unique opportunities for ubiquitous learning scenarios outside of the HEIs settings in order to bridge the gap between HEIs learning requirements and technological drivers. There are some substantial issues for the use of ubiquitous computing technologies in class concerning the effectiveness of these technologies in such situations. However, such technologies should be evaluated in terms of the benefits they bring to off-campus and out-of-class activities, where learning within the context of activity is essential for professional development. Ubiquitous computing technology support should be thought of in the same way as any technology: what are its benefits, how does it support what is already done, and what ubiquitous computing technologies would be enabled next time.

REFERENCES

Bomsdorf, B. (2005). *Adaptation of learning spaces: Supporting ubiquitous learning in higher distance education.* Paper presented at the meeting of Mobile Computing and Ambient Intelligence: The Challenge of Multimedia, Dagstuhl Seminar Proceedings No. 05181, Schloss Dagstuhl, Germany.

Bouzeghoub, A., & Garlatti, S. (2009). *Context modeling and adaptation. Technology enhanced learning summer school mobile learning.* Brest, France: Telecom Bretagne.

Brodie, P., & Irving, K. (2007). Assessment in work-based learning: investigating a pedeagogical approach to enhanced student learning. *Assessment & Evaluation in Higher Education, 32*(1), 11–19.

Cook, J., Pachler, N., & Bradley, C. (2008, Spring). Bridging the gap? Mobile phones at the interface between informal and formal learning. *Journal of the Research Centre for Educational Technology: Special Issue on Learning While Mobile,* 4(1), 3–18.

Dorn, R. (2005). *Program implementation guidelines for alternative learning experience.* (p. 4). Olympia, WA: Office of Superintendent of Public Instruction.

Hennessy, S. (1999). The potential of portable technologies for supporting graphing investigations. *British Journal of Educational Technology, 30*(1), 57–60.

Herrington, J., Herrington, A., Mantei, J., Olney, I., & Ferry, B. (2009). Using mobile technologies to develop new ways of learning and teaching (ch. 1). In J. Herrington, A. Herrington, J. Mantei, I. Olney, & B. Ferry (Eds.), *New technologies, new pedagogies: Mobile learning in higher education.* Wollongong, NSW, Australia: University of Wollongong.

Jones, V., & Jo, J. H. (2004). *Ubiquitous learning environment: An adaptive teaching system using ubiquitous technology. Ascilite.* Queensland, Australia: Griffith University Gold Coast.

Lefoe, G., Olney, I., Wright, R., & Herrington, A. (2009). Faculty development for new technologies: Putting mobile learning in the hands of the teachers (ch. 2). In J. Herrington, A. Herrington, J. Mantei, I. Olney, & B. Ferry (Eds.), *New technologies, new pedagogies: Mobile learning in higher education.* Wollongong, NSW, Australia: University of Wollongong.

Ley, D. (2007). *Emerging/technologies for Learning—Becta.* Retrieved Feb 4, 2010, from http://schools.becta.org.uk/upload-dir/downloads/page_documents/research/emerging_technologies07_chapter6.pdf

Morris, L. D. (2008). Design as a process of knowing. *5th University of Leeds Learning and Teaching Conference,* University of Leeds, UK.

Morris, L. D., & Connelly, A. (2010). Involving students in the development and evaluation of a ubiquitous learning application for a design practice setting. *Ubiquitous Learning: An International Journal, 2*(4), 21–38.

Prensky, M. (2007). How to teach with technology: Keeping both teachers and students comfortable in an era of exponential change. *Emerging Technologies for Learning, 2*(2007). Retrieved July 23, 2007, from http://partners.becta.org.uk/page_documents/research/emerging_technologies07_chapter4.pdf

Radcliffe, D. (2002). Technological and pedagogical convergence between work-based and campus-based learning. *Educational Technology & Society, 5*(2), 1–9.

Sharples, M. (2009). *A theory of learning for the mobile age. Technology enhanced learning summer school on mobile learning.* Brest, France: Telecom Bretagne.

Weiser, M. (1991). Some computer science issues in ubiquitous computing. *Communication of the ACM, 36*(7), 75–84.

Weiser, M. (1998). The future of ubiquitous computing on campus. *Communication of the ACM, 41*(1), 42–43.

ABOUT THE AUTHOR

Lisa-Dionne Morris is a Senior Teaching Fellow for the MDes in Product Design at the University of Leeds, England. She has a design career spanning 10 years, with experience in both the automotive and product design sector. She graduated from the Royal College of Art with an MA in Industrial Design and worked as an Industrial and Mobile Experience Designer with such companies as IBM Corporation in the United Kingdom. She has numerous designs that have been both nationally and internationally recognized and has dedicated much of her work to developing good operational interfaces. She is currently studying for her PhD in Operational Interface Design at the University of Leeds. This work continues her interest in operational interfaces.

Since graduating with distinction from the Royal College of Art, Lisa-Dionne has been involved in all aspects of engineering and design education. Her experience includes working as an in-house designer, an external designer for several mobile design consultancies and higher education institutes, and as an advisor to industry. Lisa-Dionne's varied background has allowed her to exercise and refine her learning and teaching skills as an accomplished mobile experience designer. She has a proven track record of delivering successful ubiquitous learning and teaching applications from the initial flash of creativity to the detail necessary for effective implementation.

Currently, Lisa-Dionne is leading an internal team at the University of Leeds looking at ubiquitous computing and work-based learning settings. Her leadership style ensures that the technology application is always well motivated while recognizing its responsibilities to add value within the current competitive educational climate. Within this, all aspects are covered from the next generation enhanced-learning scenarios to areas of student experience.

CHAPTER 13

PEDAGOGICAL USE OF VIDEO PODCAST IN ENGINEERING

Teaching, Learning, and Assessment

Ying Xiong and Imin Kao

ABSTRACT

Wider adoption of podcasts in higher education has made it possible to create a learning environment where students can access learning materials and participate in active learning activities anytime, anywhere. This chapter illustrates applications of instructor-produced and student-produced video podcasts in engineering courses at Stony Brook University, New York. The instructor-produced video podcasts have demonstrated their utility in providing effective lecturing and supplementary materials to classes. The use of student-produced video podcasts has empowered students to create and disseminate knowledge in creative ways. A podcast rubric, as an active learning tool for students and an assessment tool for the instructor, is also established for the purposes of guiding the podcast production, student self-reflection on learning, and assessment of student learning. Analysis of students' reflections on their podcast production and results of student surveys will be discussed to evaluate whether the use of instructor-produced and student-produced video podcasts can help facilitate learning, foster active learning, increase learning

Ubiquitous Learning, pages 229–247

motivation, and develop skills to enhance students' confidence in academic and career advancement.

INTRODUCTION

Communication skills are required for engineering students. Such skills are mandated by the Accreditation Board of Engineering and Technology (ABET) in outcome (g) "an ability to communicate effectively in written, oral, and visual form" (ABET, 2010). Employers also want to hire engineers who have strong oral and written communication skills, and often suggest that it is critical that this be part of the curriculum in engineering.

Traditionally, written and oral communication skills are taught and assessed through reports and in-class presentations. While these teaching and assessment methods have their own merit, there are issues of concern. In-class oral presentations can be time-consuming and are not suitable for medium or large classes. They often do not encourage self-reflection and assessment, and it is difficult for such work to provide later reference. Reports are perhaps the most commonly used; however, they do not provide an easy way to get feedback from peers and instructors. Furthermore, they do not fit the diverse learning styles of millennial students.

Awareness of learning styles leads a teacher to think about his/her way of teaching. Any application of educational technologies should be justified by a good understanding of different learning styles. A number of survey studies cited in Berk (2009) have revealed that students of the digital age share unique learning preferences. Generally, millennial students respond quickly and expect rapid responses in return. They favor learning materials that are accessible anytime and anywhere.

They are more engaged in active learning when their participation and their ownership of educational contents are greatly encouraged. Those characteristics promote the transition from e-learning to m-learning, and then to u-learning.

Reasons Behind the Use of Student-Generated Video Podcasts

First we consider the millennial students and modes of learning. The characteristics of millennial students include access and use of technology, as well as their specific learning preferences (Berk, 2009). It was reported in Berk (2009) that 90 percent and 94 percent of millennial students own a computer and cell phone, respectively. More than half of them own mp3 players and create media, such as blogs. The millennial students are technologically savvy and interested in multimedia. They also respond quickly and expect rapid responses in return.

The second consideration is the perceived value of a college education and active learning. In a recent Squeeze Play 2010 report, Immerwahr and Johnson (2010) and Kelderman (2010) pointed out an obvious dichotomy that "the public increasingly believes that a college degree is important, but the college education has become less affordable, with students having degraded education experience." While 31 percent, 50 percent, and 55 percent believe that a college education is necessary for a person to be successful in today's work world, in 2003, 2007, and 2010, respectively, they also think that the colleges' capacity to make sure students have a good educational experience has dropped from 43 percent in 2007 to 32 percent in 2010.

Finally, the experience of requiring students to produce video podcasts as a term project as well as the process of continuous improvement, has convinced the authors of the merits of such learning activities and tools. Engineering education, by its nature, requires students to be exposed to educational content that is typically presented in visual diagrams, problem schematics, mathematical equations, hands-on demonstrations, and case studies (Berger, 2007). The increasing popularity of portable video technologies propels teaching and learning out of the classrooms and makes ubiquitous learning a practical concept in engineering. The authors of this chapter have explored the idea of u-learning in engineering courses at both the undergraduate and graduate levels by adopting the technology of video podcasting.

BACKGROUND

A podcast is a series of digital media files (audio or video) that are released episodically and downloaded automatically through an automated feed with computer software like iTunes (Wikipedia, 2010). With featured characteristics like multimedia-richness, accessibility, and immediacy, video podcasting becomes a very attractive teaching and learning tool for both instructors and students. The omnipresence of portable digital media devices (e.g., smartphones, iPod touch, iPad, and Netbooks) in a college student's life also supports new ways of producing and disseminating learning materials to facilitate active learning on the podcasting platform. In this chapter, we focus only on video podcasting as a tool for teaching and active learning.

With all the possibilities offered by podcasting, teaching and learning is no longer confined to the classrooms. In recent years, the use of podcasts in higher education has gained popularity. Quite a few empirical studies in the literature describe academic experiences in podcasting (Abt & Barry, 2007;

Chan & Lee, 2005, 2007; Chan, Lee, & McLoughlin 2006; Frydenberg, 2006; Griffin, Mitchell, & Thompson, 2009; Lazzari, 2009; Parslow 2009).

There are two categories of video podcasts that the authors employed to enhance student learning experience. One is instructor-produced lecture podcasts and the other is student-generated podcasts, as illustrated in Figure 13.1.

Similar to the four types of instructor podcasts presented in O'bryan and Hegelheimer (2007) and Hew (2009), including backup, supplementary, preparatory, and student showcase for future stakeholders, three types of instructor podcasts are used by Kao, as seen in Figure 13.1. First, lecture podcasts are recorded lectures with presentation of course materials in class. Students can access the podcasts to review the materials covered in the lectures, when they wish to catch up on a missed class or clarify things that they did not understand in class. Second, supplementary podcasts are produced outside of the classroom, typically in response to questions raised by students in class, during office hours or through e-mails. This Q&A type of podcast provides equal learning opportunities for all students, especially for those who cannot afford to attend office hours due to time conflicts or those who are too shy to raise questions in class. Compared with the backup podcasts, they are often more topic-specific and question-focused. The third type of instructor podcast includes topical discussions and blogs on relevant subjects, such as a case studies or preparation and review of an upcoming discussion and presentation. They help students make a smooth transition from previous classes to an upcoming class. Regardless of the

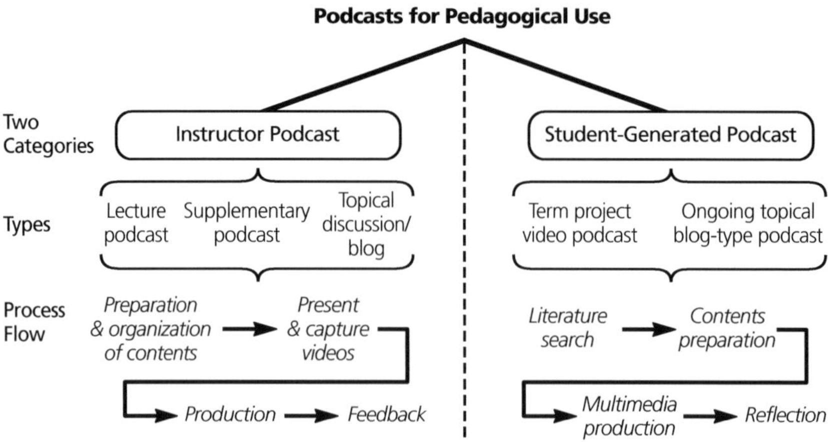

Figure 13.1 Illustration of the two categories of podcasts for pedagogical use. Each category consists of different types of podcasts, as well as process flow for the production of such video podcasts.

different uses of instructor podcasts, the process flow of production encompasses the following:

- Preparation and organization of contents
- Presentation and video capture
- Production and posting of video podcasts
- Feedback

Figure 13.2 illustrates the preparation and organization of an engineering topic for an instructor podcast, as well as presentation and video capture (with sample snapshots of video podcast).

Student-generated podcasts can be in the form of a term project assignment or an ongoing topical blog like a podcast. The former is a well-defined term project with required tasks in multimedia production. The latter is a more flexible and topic-based presentation intended for follow-

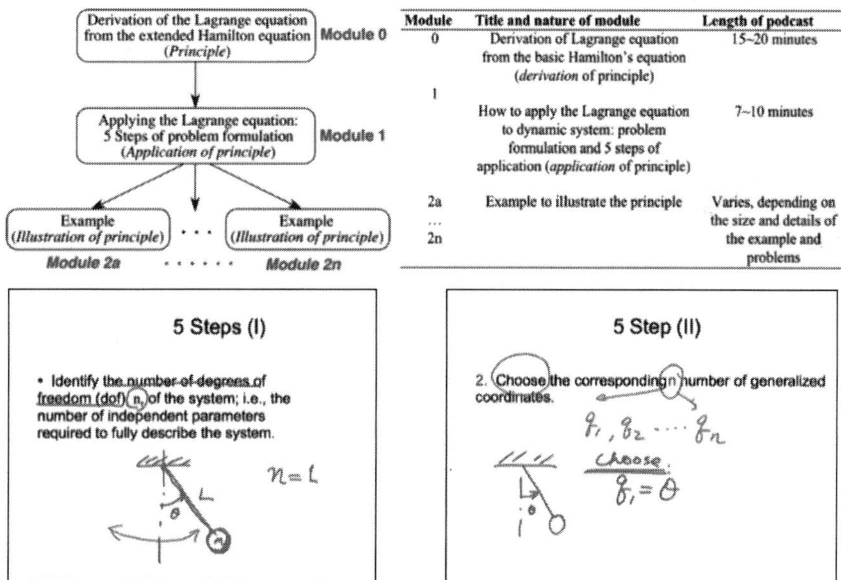

Figure 13.2 An example of instructor-produced lecture podcast (upper left). Flow chart for the preparation and planning of the presentation of an engineering topic and breaking it into podcast modules (upper right). The title and nature of the modules and planned length of each podcast module (lower right). Screenshot 1 of module 0: Step 1 of the five-step application of the Lagrange equation for dynamic systems. The handwritten notes are overlaid onto the prepared text and become part of the video podcast production (lower right). Screenshot 2: Step 2 of the presentation of the Lagrange equation for dynamic systems (Kao, 2008).

up discussions and interactions. The process of production encompasses the following:

- Literature search
- Content preparation
- Multimedia production and posting
- Reflection

In both undergraduate and graduate courses, video podcasts of lectures can facilitate and enhance students' learning experiences. When instructors produce video podcasts, lectures, or supplementary learning materials, students are able to learn in ways that fit their diverse learning styles anytime, anywhere. They can review learning materials at their own pace, repeat or skip materials of their choice, and self-initiate interaction with instructors and peers in the form of synchronous or asynchronous communication. Allowing students to produce their own podcasts enhances their active learning through participation. They are empowered to engage in literature searches, prepare and produce content, and demonstrate their ability to communicate academic topics in a technology-enhanced way.

In addition to teaching and learning, student-produced video podcasts have been used to gather information for assessing and improving student learning in higher education. This new assessment approach not only frees up enormous in-class assessment time for face-to-face courses, but also suggests a new way of assessing student performance for online courses.

In this chapter, we will focus on the pedagogical use of student-generated podcasts as a term project assignment and the assessment in learning.

VIDEO PODCAST AS A TOOL FOR ACTIVE AND U-LEARNING

This section describes how student-generated video podcasts are used in an engineering course at the State University of New York (SUNY) at Stony Brook. Readers will find information regarding the guidelines and production of video podcasts, grading of video podcasts using rubrics, peer review, student self-assessment through reflection statement, and student survey results.

Guidelines and Production of Video Podcast

The guidelines for the video podcast term-project assignment are designed to be as broad as possible so as not to limit students' creativity and freedom to choose the topics of their preference. The following guidelines are given as part of the assignment of the video podcast project.

Objective:

To create a video podcast to demonstrate your ability to communicate engineering topics relevant to this course effectively in a technology-enhanced way.

Requirements:

- The topic should be chosen from the topics/concepts related to the topics of the class. The topic should be chosen by the student and approved by the instructor.
- The podcast should NOT duplicate the instructor-created podcasts if a similar topic is chosen.
- Your podcast must not exceed 5 minutes in length. Video podcasts longer than 5 minutes require the prior written approval of the professor.
- Your podcast must include all of the following:
  - A title and a podcast name
  - An introduction
  - Content
  - Audio or visual enhancements (e.g., some background music, pictures, graphic images, and/or video clips).
  - Your own speech/narration
  - A conclusion
  - Sources/citations/bibliography

Reflection Statement:

In addition to the video podcast, each student is asked to write a reflection statement and submit it separately. The reflection should address the following:

- What have you learned from the production of video podcast?
- Which elements are the most effective in your podcast? Which parts need refinement?
- What barriers have you experienced during the production? How did you overcome them?
- How will you be able to take advantage of podcasting in the future for career advancement?

Students are provided with selected samples of video podcasts from the podcast library in order to establish a reference of the expectation of the quality of video podcast production. They are also provided with available resources at the university computer labs to produce the video podcast, including recording and editing of the video files. The following five steps are adopted to produce and make available the video podcasts.

1. Recording: The presentation typically is prepared using PowerPoint slides, including videos and other multimedia presentations.
2. Editing: After the presentation and video are captured or recorded, students can use software such as QuickTime and other programs to edit the video files, and output the podcast file in .m4v (iTunes) or .wmv or .avi or .mpg formats.
3. Submission: The video podcast file can be submitted via the blackboard digital dropbox options or other means such as FTP.
4. Posting videos on university podcast server: The video podcasts submitted by students were examined and posted by the instructors on the university podcast server.
5. Distribution and subscription: Once the video podcasts are posted, students can subscribe to the video podcasts and import all episodes using RSS under a playlist in iTunes. Students can also view the video podcasts directly on the university podcast server using a PC or Mac.

Steps 1–4 are performed by the students. Once the podcasts are received, the instructor will check the contents and the format of the video file for posting. The posting of video podcasts on the university podcast server is performed by the instructor or teaching assistant. Two examples of student-generated podcasts are illustrated in Figure 13.3.

Grading of Video Podcasts Using Rubrics

One issue about the student podcast project is the fairness of grading. The guidelines presented in the previous section and the availability of

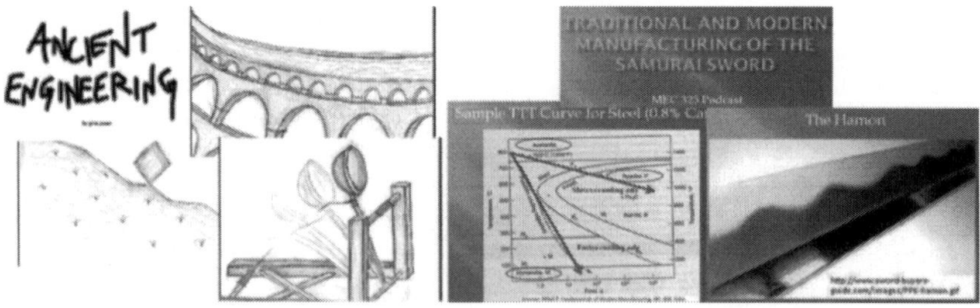

Figure 13.3 Two examples of student-produced podcasts with screenshots: (left) a podcast production consisting of animation of several ancient engineering technologies and innovations; (right) a podcast on the manufacturing technology of samurai swords, both traditional and modern manufacturing processes, with comparison.

sample podcasts can help students to understand what is expected. Because this podcast accounts for 8 percent to10 percent of the semester grades, students are naturally concerned with the grades on this project.

The grading rubric is created as a result of the consideration of fairness and consistency in grading. The goals of this rubric are twofold: to serve as a *learning tool* for students and an *assessment tool* for evaluating student podcast projects.

In order for the rubric to serve as a learning tool for students, it is discussed and made available to students early in the semester. By doing this, we ensure that students have access to the same standards by which grading is performed. This eliminates the apprehension of students and avoids any grading disputes. In addition, assistants and instructors can use the same rubric for consistent grading—a distinct advantage for large classes, since grading can be performed consistently by more than one person.

The development of the rubric follows the three steps, outlined in Figure 13.4, to establish the key dimensions of effective podcasts. The three steps include a literature survey to learn the state of the art, conducting student surveys to gather students' perspectives, and identifying themes and categories emerging from preliminary examination of existing student podcasts.

An extensive search of the literature reveals several critical aspects that should be considered and included in rubric design and grading. These have been organized into seven dimensions. They are Introduction, Content, Organization, Audio and Visual Enhancement, Text, Narration, and Length. The dimensions of Introduction and Multimedia Enhancement are critical because they establish navigability and engagement. These two components are critical to the success and efficacy of a podcast (Griffin, Mitchell, & Thompson, 2009), since a podcast that cannot be easily navigated or fails to engage its audience cannot promote and engage the

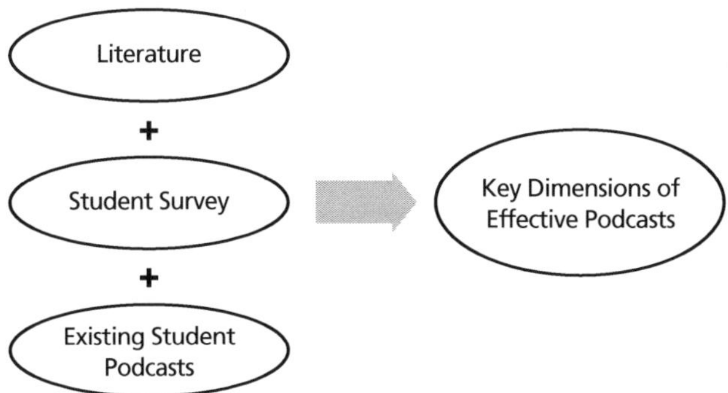

Figure 13.4 Development of the rubrics for the assessment and grading of students' video podcast.

student in learning. The second dimension is Content. The video podcast can promote learning of complex concepts and higher-order thinking skills (HOTs) (Stephenson, Brownand, & Griffin, 2008) by encouraging the student to research the current literature and organize intellectually stimulating and updated content. The dimension of Organization needs to be evaluated, because in a Podcast, the presenter controls the pace (Morgan & Whitener, 2006). This is in contrast to traditional lecture/classroom environments where there can be instantaneous real-time feedback and communication from presenter to audience and vice versa. Morgan and Whitener (2006) suggested that the interactions between the presenter and audience require a clear explanation on images, graphs, and video clips. This encompasses the dimensions of Text and Narration. Less intuitive is the dimension of Length. Frydenberg reports that the optimal length of a podcast is 5–10 minutes, similar to the length of a song (Frydenberg, 2006). The podcasts are meant to be short supplementary tools to enhance learning, address difficult questions, and engage students while being cognizant of attention span. The ideal length of a podcast is designed with this in mind. In this podcast assignment, the Length was prescribed at 5 minutes or less, unless a prior approval to exceed 5 minutes of length was given by the instructor. Categories and themes emerging from the student survey and the preliminary examination of the existing student podcasts also mirror the findings from the literature review.

The rubric is presented in Table 13.1. A total of seven dimensions are listed, each containing four levels of achievements and grades: (1) Exemplary, (2) Proficient, (3) Good, and (4) Improvement needed. More detailed descriptions and specific scenarios are also given for clarification. The seven dimensions are also presented in a graphical illustration in Figure 13.5, along with the recommended weights of each dimension according to importance. These constitute the overall podcast quality.

Peer Review and Self-Assessment

In addition to the grading using the rubric by the instructors and graders, students are also required to review the video podcast through a peer-review process. This process requires students to view all posted video podcasts and vote for the top three. The votes are tallied and the three students with the highest number of votes receive a gift from the instructor. However, the results of peer review and voting do not play a role in the grades of the assignment.

The peer review process promotes interaction among students and also calibrates the quality of the video podcasts. Students will be able to learn from one another and reflect on their own podcast production. This peer

TABLE 13.1 Rubric as a Learning Tool for Students and an Assessment Tool for the Instructors and Graders. The Rubric has 7 Dimensions, Each with 4 Levels of Grade

Dimensions	Exemplary 4 points	Proficient 3 points	Good 2 points	Improvement Needed 0–1 points
Introduction (5%)	• Includes a meaningful and logical title and podcast name. Audience is clearly provided with good information on • Who is the speaker • What is the topic • What is the take-home message for the audience	• The title and podcast name are logical and specific. Audience is provided with adequate information on • Who is the speaker • What is the topic • What is the take-home message for the audience	• The title and podcast name are very general. Audience is provided with some information on • Who is the speaker • What is the topic • What is the take-home message for the audience	• The title or podcast name is missing or unclear. Needs to tell the audience information on • Who is the speaker • What is the topic • What is the take-home message for the audience
Content (20%)	Covers topic in-depth with a variety of supporting materials. Subject knowledge is excellent. Accurate information and succinct concepts are presented. Some elements of the content are quoted and source information collected for all content and media used in the podcast. Majority of the content is original, providing new and creative ideas and insights.	Includes essential knowledge about the topic with supporting materials. Subject knowledge appears to be good. The content is appropriate or accurate. Product shows a large amount of original thought. Source information collected for most quoted content and media used in the podcast.	Includes some knowledge about the topic with some supporting materials. Some subject knowledge is evident. Some of the content is inappropriate or inaccurate. Quite a lot of content is directly copied. Some source information collected for content and media. Product shows some original thought and some creative ideas.	Includes little knowledge about the topic. Subject knowledge is not evident. The content is inappropriate or inaccurate. Most content is directly copied. Uses other people's ideas without giving them credit almost throughout the podcast. There is little or no original content.
Organization (15%)	Content is highly organized and flows smoothly to clearly enhance the understanding of the concepts. Includes components including title, introduction, content, conclusion/discussion, and citations. Transitions are smooth and spaced correctly without dead space.	Content is well organized and enhances the understanding of the concepts. Information is transitioned in a smooth way to cover most of the components.	Content is logically organized for the most part but is somewhat disorganized.	Lack of many components in the podcast. The structure of the podcast confuses audience and detracts from the understanding of the concept(s). Transitions are abrupt with dead space.

(continued)

TABLE 13.1 (continued) Rubric as a Learning Tool for Students and an Assessment Tool for the Instructors and Graders. The Rubric has 7 Dimensions, Each with 4 Levels of Grade

Dimensions	Exemplary 4 points	Proficient 3 points	Good 2 points	Improvement Needed 0–1 points
Audio & visual enhancements (20%)	Photos, video, and/or music used in the podcast always enhance the quality and understanding of the presentation. Uses various strategies to engage audience, including pleasant and background music.	Majority of the photos, video, and/or music in the podcast are relevant and enhance the quality and understanding of the presentation. Multiple strategies are used to engage audience.	Some of the photos, video, and/ or music in the podcast are irrelevant or inappropriate. Some audio and visual materials distract from understanding of the presentation. Few strategies are used to engage audience.	Uses irrelevant photos, video, and/ or music without clear purposes. No strategies are used to engage audience.
Text (15%)	Consistently uses correct grammar and spelling. Text in each slide is properly laid out with excellent design in terms of font size, color, and bullets.	Always uses correct grammar and spelling. Amount of text is appropriate and easy for audience to follow. Font size, color, and bullets are properly designed and used.	Some grammar errors and typos. Some slides are packed with too much text and difficult to follow. Some font sizes are too tiny; the text color is too light. Bullets are not used when needed.	Information crowded in one slide. Tiny fonts. Text overlapped with pictures or is illegible. Lots of grammatical errors or typos.
Narration (20%)	Well rehearsed. Elaborate on pictures and clips. Voice is audible and clear to enhance presentation. Appropriately paced. Speech is fluent and no dead spaces exist.	Evidence is present to indicate good rehearsal. Explanation is provided when graphic images or video clips are used. Speech quality is clear and properly paced. Period of silence occurs occasionally.	The podcast shows some rehearsal and preparation. Some explanation is provided when only images or clips are used. Sometimes the pace is too slow or too fast. Periods of silence occur occasionally.	Poorly rehearsed. No explanation is present when needed. Monologues—just reads the text. The volume of voice is too low and difficult to hear. Pace is too slow or rushed. Periods of silence occur often. Speech lacks fluency.
Length (5%)	Podcast length keeps the audience interested and engaged. The length of the podcast is appropriate for its content.	Podcast length is appropriate for its content. The information is presented adequately and clearly within the time frame.	Podcast is somewhat short or long. Conciseness is not evident in the podcast.	The podcast is designed too long or too short than necessary.

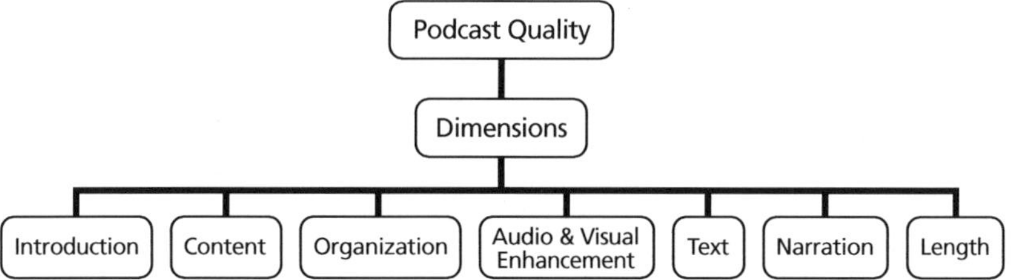

Figure 13.5 An illustration of the seven dimensions of the rubric, each carrying different weights according to their importance: Introduction: 5%, Content: 20%, Organization: 15%, Audio and Visual Enhancement: 20%, Text: 15%, Narration: 20%, Length: 5%.

review process motivates students to contribute to the class and feel accountable for each other. Students reported that "this is a good assignment, and we get to learn different things from the other podcasts."

In order to promote in-depth learning and document students' learning experience with this term project, students have a chance to write a personal reflection statement to capture aspects of their learning. At the end of the 2010 spring semester, 54 students (93% of enrolled students in the class) submitted their reflection statements along with their podcasts. As the guidelines suggested, each of the students reflected on their experience with the podcast project by addressing questions including (a) what has been learned, (b) what were the strengths and weaknesses of their podcasts, (c) what barriers have they encountered and overcome, and (d) what would be the impact of this project on their future career. For most students, it was the first time that they had ever created a video podcast. They enjoyed the new challenge and achieved a great sense of accomplishment when they conquered this new territory. They were "impressed with the result that they were able to create an effective podcast" and even "boosted their confidence in public speaking."

Several interesting findings surfaced from the analysis of students' reflection statements. Unlike in-class presentations, podcasts target a broader audience, and students are allowed to keep refining their podcasts as many times as they please. Knowing that their podcasts will be distributed online for many people to view, students usually would take their own initiative to revise their podcasts several times until they were satisfied with the final product. Students' ownership of their podcasts made them more engaged in active learning. One student said that he rehearsed multiple times in order to get the narration the way he liked it. We also believe that knowledge sharing is the best motivation for students to learn better and understand more. Taking the audience into consideration makes students more cautious about how they convey information in an effective way. This is suggested by students' statements like "using podcast, I learned how to communicate more effectively when I would like to share some knowledge," and "after choosing my topic, I had to think of an appropriate way to portray my ideas and the subject matter in a way as to entice an audience as well as educate them."

Due to the 5-minute time limit, students learned to organize their ideas and select presentation elements (i.e., movie clips, pictures, or graphics) purposefully. They no longer just threw nonedited videos into the presentation, but they carefully evaluated each segment of the video and selected those that fit their needs best. This evaluation and selection process promoted students' critical thinking skills. Students were amazed to find out that "a decent amount of information can be fit into a short presentation that can be viewed over and over."

Technical difficulty is still the number one barrier that students encountered, since podcast production is new to most of them. As challenging as it may sound, students were able to tackle the problems and teach themselves different movie-making software, including Windows Media Player, Windows Movie Maker, Camtasia, QuickTime, and GarageBand. This is consistent with observations that millennial students can pick up new technologies very easily and quickly. Many reported that the most difficult part of podcast production is how to combine audio and video files. They found various solutions to this problem, which provides evidence of students' problem-solving skills.

Most importantly, this podcast project reinforced student learning. From selecting an interesting topic, organizing ideas, evaluating visual aids, to presenting ideas within a 5-minute time frame, students were actively engaged in learning new topics in Mechanical Engineering. Very strong statements were found in students' reflections regarding how much they had learned about the subject matter through this project.

> At the start of the video podcast assignment, I did not think that it would be a better learning tool than a semester project or presentation. However, upon completing the podcast, I feel that it was more of an overall learning experience than previous projects... I also felt that since I was essentially teaching the viewer about my topic—synthetic diamonds—I learned more than I would have if I had just taken a test about the topic.

In addition to the benefits of helping students improve their communication skills, problem-solving skills, critical thinking skills, and knowledge of subject matters, this podcast project also provided students with skills that can be transferable to their future study and future career. One student was inspired to create an introductory video as part of her résumé, and many students expressed enthusiasm to continue to produce video podcasts in the future on other topics. After completing this assignment, students "have the knowledge necessary to effectively record, edit, and produce video with precision and ease. This ability will prove to be invaluable in their career."

CONTINUOUS IMPROVEMENT AND FUTURE WORK

A very critical and integral part of this video podcast application in engineering courses is the continuous improvement based on student feedback. A paper-and-pencil survey was conducted in fall 2009, with questions focused on how students use instructor-produced podcs (see Figure 13.1) in their learning. Highlights of the survey results based on 19 responses include:

- Students used podcasts for review of lectures, preparation of exams, or when they missed classes.
- The majority of the students (94%) viewed the podcasts when the podcasts are available.
- Preferred (or optimal) length of video podcasts is 5–15 minutes.
- Majority of the students (89%) were not engaged in other activities when they were viewing the video podcasts. This is somewhat interesting because the millennial students are known to multitask.

Figure 13.6 presents the results of the student survey. The left side indicates that 88 percent of students use a PC/Mac to view instructor podcasts. Only 12 percent indicated that they use a portable device. The right side shows that 50 percent of the students reported using Web streaming on the podcast server, and 33 percent used direct downloading. A total of 28 percent subscribed to the podcasts and imported them through RSS. Of that 28 percent, 12 percent also used portable devices.

When asked about barriers that limited students' use of video podcasts, 22 percent reported difficulty with technical problems, and 11 percent were unfamiliar with podcasts and felt the learning style was a mismatch. A total of 34 percent reported no barriers. The results are plotted in Figure 13.7.

In addition to the student survey, we plan to extend the scope of our assessment in the future to refine the use of podcasts in our classes, including (a) assessment of the rubric, to evaluate the validity and reliability of the rubric for the assessment of student podcasts; and (b) comparison of the quality of previous podcasts with the current ones to determine if the rubric helps improve podcast quality.

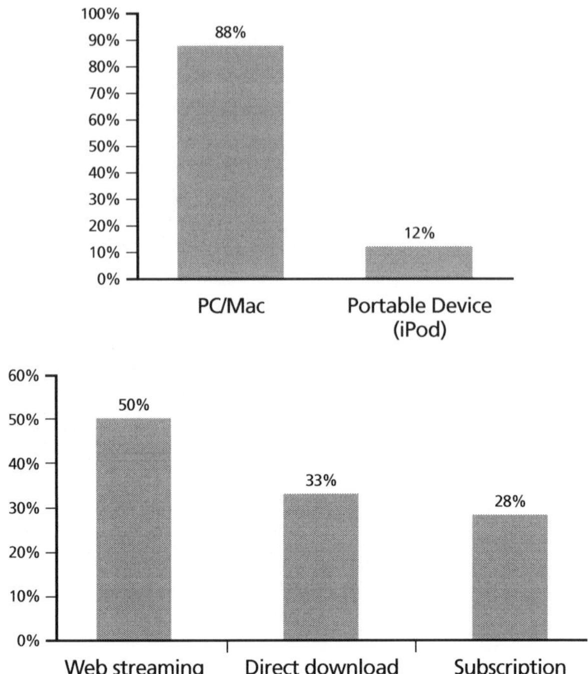

Figure 13.6 Survey results of instructor podcast: (top) response to the question of how the podcasts are viewed; (bottom) ways in which students access the podcasts. Students were asked to check all that applied.

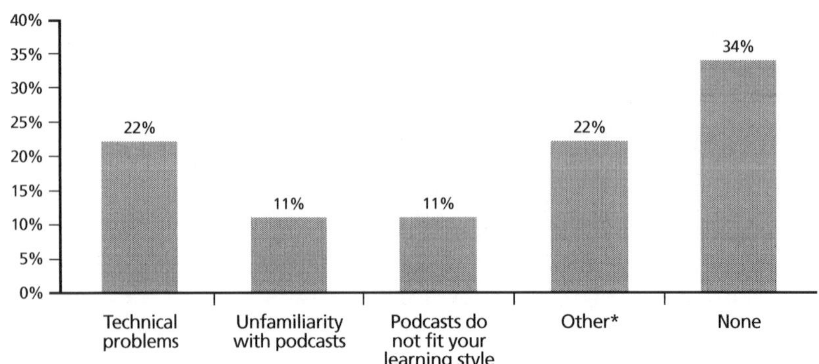

Figure 13.7 Survey results of instructor podcast regarding various barriers that limit the use of video podcast. The "Other*" category includes "Do not have time to view podcasts" or "No need for supplementary materials."

Finally, we would like to conclude this chapter by quoting one of our students' reflection statements:

> Podcasts are definitely a fun and interactive method for dispersing information through today's technology. Because current generations are adapted to the fast delivery of information through pictures and video due to televisions, communicating through podcasts is a proven, effective method for capturing one's attention. Podcasts should be used more frequently, given that it will be produced effectively and with an objective/goal that is met at the end of podcast production and presentation.

REFERENCES

ABET, (2010). EAC Program Criteria: Criterion 3. Student Outcomes. Retrieved from http://abet.org/Linked%20Documents-UPDATE/Program%20Docs/abet-eac-criteria-2011-2012.pdf

Abt, G., & Barry, T. (2007). The quantitative effect of students using podcasts in a first year undergraduate exercise physiology module. *Bioscience Education eJournal, 10*, 8–10.

Berger, E. (2007). Podcasting in engineering education: A preliminary study of content, student attitudes, and impact. *Journal of Online Education, 4*(Oct–Nov), 1–6.

Berk, R. A. (2009). Teaching strategies for the net generation: Transformative dialogues. *Teaching & Learning Journal, 3*(2), 1–23.

Chan, A., & Lee, M. J. W. (2005, September 5–7). *An mp3 a day keeps the worries away: Exploring the use of podcasting to address preconceptions and alleviate pre-class anxiety amongst undergraduate information technology students.* Paper presented at the Charles Sturt Student Experience Conference, Wagga Wagga, NSW, Australia.

Chan, A., & Lee, M. J. W. (2007). Reducing the effects of isolation and promoting inclusivity for distance learners through podcasting. *Turkish Online Journal of Distance Education, 8*(1), 85–104.

Chan A., Lee, M. J. W., & McLoughlin, C. (2006, December 3–6). Everyone's learning with podcasting: A Charles Sturt University experience. *Proceedings of the 23rd annual Ascilite Conference: Who's learning? Whose technology?* Sydney, Australia.

Frydenberg, M. (2006, November). Principles and pedagogy: The two P's of podcasting in the Information Technology classroom. *Proceedings of the Information Systems Education Conference,* ISECON 2006 (p. 23), Dallas, TX.

Griffin, D. K., Mitchell D., & Thompson, S. J. (2009). Podcasting by synchronizing PowerPoint and voice: What are the pedagogical benefits? *Computers & Education, 53,* 532–539.

Hew, K. F. (2009). Use of audio podcast in K–12 and higher education: A review of research topics and methodologies. *Education Technology Research and Development, 57,* 333–357.

Immerwahr, J., & Johnson J., (2010). *Squeeze Play 2010: Continued public anxiety on cost, harsher judgments on how colleges are run.* A Joint Project of The National Center for Public Policy and Higher Education and Public Agenda. Retrieved February 2010, from http://www.highereducation.org/reports/squeeze_play_10/squeeze_play_10.pdf

Kao, I (2008, March 28–29). Using video podcast to enhance students' learning experience in engineering. *Proceedings of ASEE Zone I Conference,* West Point, NY.

Kelderman, E., (2010). Public opinion of higher education continues downward slide. *The Chronicle of Higher Education.* http://chronicle.com/article/Public-Opinion-of-Higher/64217/

Lazzari, M. (2009). Creative use of podcasting in higher education and its effect on competitive agency. *Computers and Education, 52,* 27–34.

Morgan, S., & Whitener, B. (2006). *Speaking about science: A manual for creating clear presentations.* Cambridge, MA: Cambridge University Press

O'bryan, A., & Hegelheimer, V. (2007). Integrating CALL into the classroom: The role of podcasting in an ESL listening strategies course. *ReCALL, 19*(2), 162–280.

Parslow, G. R. (2009). Commentary: Downloaded lectures have been shown to produce better assessment outcomes. *Multimedia in Biochemistry and Molecular Biology Education, 37*(6), 375–376.

Stephenson, J. E., Brownand C., & Griffin, D. K. (2008). Electronic delivery of lectures in the university environment: An empirical comparison of three delivery styles. *Computers & Education, 31,* 640–651.

Wikipedia. (2010). *Podcast.* Retrieved February 1, 2010, from http://en.wikipedia.org/wiki/Podcast

ACKNOWLEDGEMENT

The authors would like to thank Ms. Jennifer Adams and Mr. Jag Yersson Gaona, who assisted the instructor in the administration of podcast servers and helped students in the access of university resources in video production. The facility of the College of Engineering and Applied Sciences (CEAS) is provided to the instructor for the capturing of lectures in video podcast format, assisted by Mr. Jag Yersson Gaona.

ABOUT THE AUTHORS

Ying Xiong received her Master's degree with a concentration on Measurement, Evaluation, Statistics and Assessment from University of Illinois at Chicago (UIC). Currently, Ying works for The Faculty Center at Stony Brook University as the Assessment Specialist, providing pedagogical support for faculty on assessing their courses and academic programs. Her work blends qualitative and quantitative approaches to assessing learning outcomes and teaching effectiveness. Prior to Stony Brook, she worked for the Office of Program Evaluation at University of South Carolina, and the Chicago School Initiative, focusing on arts assessment, survey design, and program evaluation.

Dr. Imin Kao is the Associate Dean of the College of Engineering and Applied Sciences (CEAS), and a Professor of the Department of Mechanical Engineering at Stony Brook University (SUNY). He is also the founding Faculty Director of the Information and Technology Studies Undergraduate College (ITS College)—one of the six thematic Undergraduate Colleges at Stony Brook University, established to transform the university life and learning experience for the undergraduate students at Stony Brook. Since becoming the Associate Dean of CEAS, he has been leading and/or participating in various curricular initiatives such as the new Civil Engineering, 5-year BE/MS, and Mechatronics programs. He is also responsible for College-wide ABET assessment and accreditation. Professor Kao has received Student Service Award and Center for Prevention and Outreach Partnership Award. Being the Director of the Manufacturing and Automation Laboratory (MAL) at Stony Brook, he conducts research in the areas of Microsystems and MEMS, intelligent fault detection and diagnosis, robotics, intelligent contact interface, stiffness control, wafer manufacturing, and wafer slicing using wiresaw. Dr. Kao served as an Associate Editor of the *IEEE Transaction of Robotics and Automation* as well as the *International Journal of Advanced Manufacturing Systems.*

CHAPTER 14

UBIQUITOUS MATHEMATICS FROM SOUTH AFRICA TO FINLAND

Does Reverse Transfer Work?

Teemu H. Laine, Eeva Nygren, Erkki Sutinen, Carolina Islas Sedano, Mike Joy, and Seugnet Blignaut

ABSTRACT

Ubiquitous learning spaces are inherently context adaptive: their context-aware features allow an educational system to be automatically configured to a set of aspects of a given context. UFractions is a ubiquitous mobile game that combines a story line with manipulatives for learning fractions, and in which context adaptation is limited to the set of manipulatives. UFractions was created for a South African context and then reverse transferred to a Finnish context. In reverse transfer, a technology designed in and for a technology-alien context is taken as such to a technology-familiar context. An evaluation of UFractions in the two countries indicates that the game needs to be adapted to the pedagogical and cultural contexts of its users. Hence, reverse transfer is not enough for a successful learning environment—context adaptation is required. For ubiquitous learning games such as UFractions, our findings indicate that learning content and activities need to be recontextualized.

Ubiquitous Learning, pages 249–282

INTRODUCTION

New technologies offer new educational opportunities, and the increasing availability of affordable mobile devices, in particular mobile phones, allows the educational benefits to be available in communities that have hitherto not had access to those new technologies. A particular approach that may be effective is game-based learning, not least because the engagement of students with playful activities in the learning process can be highly motivational.

In this chapter, we consider a technology developed to support mobile game-based educational software and present a case study of a game developed using the technology. This game—*UFractions*—was written to support learners in South Africa who are learning fractions as part of their mathematics curriculum and has been deployed in South African schools. The same game was subsequently delivered to a class of Finnish learners on the same grade level who were also learning about fractions. We call this delivery *reverse transfer*, in contrast to a typical technology transfer, which takes a technology created in a technology-familiar environment (like Finland) to a technology-alien environment (like many places in South Africa).

We hypothesized that the two groups of learners would react differently to the technology and to the educational content, and we wished to explore how those differences would manifest themselves and what underlying reasons might account for them.

The chapter proceeds as follows. We first outline the technical and the theoretical foundations for our approach. We then describe the contextualization and reverse transfer together with the UFractions game, including the game design, its implementation, and how we evaluated it when we tested it with learners. This is followed by a discussion of the evaluation results and, before concluding the paper, we outline how the results of this chapter inform the development of future ubiquitous learning spaces.

BACKGROUND

Research Contexts

The UFractions game was designed in and for the South African context, and then reverse transferred to the Finnish context. Specifically, the North West Province in South Africa, and the North Karelia Province in Finland were the geographical areas of this research (see Figure 14.1). In this section we describe the key aspects of these contexts, which are summarized in Table 14.1.

South Africa

South Africa is situated at the Southern-most tip of Africa and consists of nine provinces with huge differences in size, economical viability, and

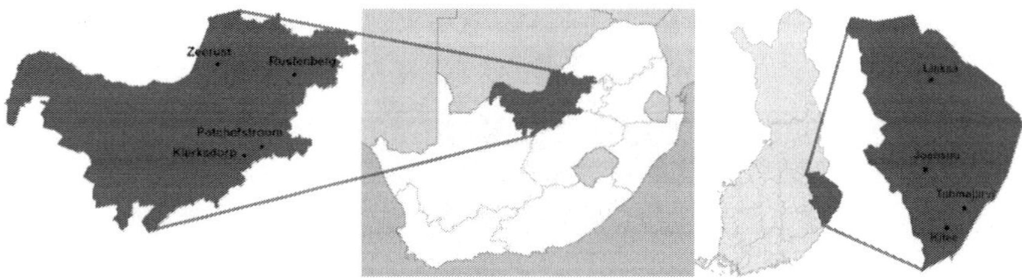

Figure 14.1 Locations of the North West Province in South Africa and the North Karelia Province in Finland.

TABLE 14.1 Comparison of Key Statistics of Finland and South Africa

Finland	South Africa
Population: 5,400,000 **Density:** 15.7 inhabitants/km^2	**Population:** 49,320,500[a] **Density:** 40.4 inhabitants/km^2
Area: 338,145 km^2	**Area:** 1,221,037 km^2
Official languages: Finnish and Swedish	**Official languages:** Afrikaans, English, isiNdebele, SeSotho, Sepedi, siSwati, Setswana, Xitsonga, Tshivenda, isiXhosa and isiZulu
Literacy rate: 99.0%[b]	**Literacy rate:** 82.4%[b]
Mobile cellular subscriptions per 100 inhabitants 2008: 128.76	Mobile cellular subscriptions per 100 inhabitants 2008: 90.60
Ratio of mobile cellular subscriptions to fixed telephone lines: 4.1:1	Ratio of mobile cellular subscriptions to fixed telephone lines: 10.2:1
Compound Annual Growth Rate (%) in mobile cellular subscriptions 2003–2008: 7.5[c]	Compound Annual Growth Rate (%) in mobile cellular subscriptions 2003–2008: 21.7[c]
The Second Information Technology in Education Study[d] • Level of access to computers: 100% • Level of access to Internet: 100% • The amount of computers per school is approximately 64, of which 72% were used by pupils, 13% by teachers, and 6% by administrative personnel. • The number of computers per school varied from 11 to 304. • Mobile devices were used for learning in 11% of schools • Ratio pupil/computer: over 70% of schools had fewer than 10 students per computer • Educational software in 66% of schools	The Second Information Technology in Education Study[d] • Level of access to computers: 38% • Level of access to Internet: 67% • Computer access at schools: 38% • Only 15% of mathematics and science teachers use ICTs for teaching and learning.
North Karelia	**North West Province**
Population: 166,000 **Density:** 9.34 inhabitants/km^2 **Area:** 21,584 km^2	**Population:** 3,450,400 **Density:** 32.39 inhabitants/km^2 **Area:** 106,512 km^2

[a] Statistics South Africa, 2009
[b] http://en.wikipedia.org/wiki/Literacy (accessed April 27, 2010)
[c] International Telecommunication Union, 2008
[d] Kankaanranta & Puhakka, 2008

population density. Each province has its own legislature, premier and executive council, distinctive landscape, population, and climate. They are the Eastern Cape, the Free State, Gauteng, KwaZulu-Natal, Limpopo, Mpumalanga, the Northern Cape, North West, and the Western Cape. South Africa can be described as a medium-sized country consisting of a total land area of slightly more than 1.2 million square kilometers. The North West province is one of the smaller and less affluent provinces. The over 49 million people have a wide variety of cultures, languages, and beliefs. Although KwaZulu-Natal has the most people, Gauteng is most densely populated province. Of the 11 official languages, English is the most spoken in commercial public life. IsiZulu is the mother tongue of 23.8 percent of South Africa's population, followed by isiXhosa at 17.6 percent, and Afrikaans at 13.3 percent. South Africa's first democratic election took place in April 1994, with victory to the African National Council (ANC) with Nelson Mandela as president (Southafrica.Info, 2010).

South Africa has 12.3 million learners, about 386,600 teachers, and 26,292 schools. About 6,000 are high schools (grade 7 to grade 12) and the rest are primary schools (grade 0 to grade 6). The national Department of Education is responsible for education across the country as a whole, while each of the nine provinces has its own education department. The central government provides a national framework for school policy, but administrative responsibility lies with the provinces. School life spans 13 grades from grade 0 through to grade 12. Under the South African Schools Act of 1996, education is compulsory, but not free in all cases for all South Africans from age 7 (grade 1) to age 15, or the completion of grade 9 (Southafrica.Info, 2010). Very poor schools are excluded from school fees and subsidized meals are provided.

South Africa is rich in diversity in terms of income, culture, languages, and technology. On the one hand, South Africa is renowned for its technological innovation and development, but on the other hand, the majority of South Africa's learners do not share in the expectations of the information age. These inequalities become obvious in educational delivery where only about 65 percent of learners who enter the final school examination pass it. South Africa performed less than adequately in the most recent International Mathematics and Science Study (TIMMS), where its learners were bottom ranked (Gonzales et al., 2004). The Progress in Reading Literacy Study (PIRLS) indicated that grade 3 and 4 learners' reading skills by far do not meet international standards (EDAC Wowe, 2008). The results of the most recent Second International Technology in Education Study (SITES, 2006)—a longitudinal large-scale international comparative survey on the use of Information and Communication Technologies (ICTs) in schools (Law, Pelgrum, & Plomp, 2008)—indicated that South Africa was the only country in the SITES 2006 study that could not provide students with full access to computers. South African schools' overall computer access (38%) remains low when compared with other education systems in developing countries such as Estonia (100%), Chile (96%), and Israel (96%) (Blignaut, Els, & Howie, 2010). Only about 15 percent of South Africa's mathematics and science teachers used ICTs in their teaching and learning (Blignaut & Els, 2010).

To consolidate and guide diverse initiatives toward the educational transformation, the Ministry of Education published the White Paper on e-Education, "Transforming Learning and Teaching Through Information and Communication Technologies" during August 2004 (Department of Education, 2004). This initial and, to date, only ICT policy for South African education, presents a framework for the strategic, political, pedagogical and developmental facets of implementing e-education in South Africa. The unobtainable strategic objective of this e-education policy states that "Every South African manager, teacher and student in the general and further education and training bands will be ICT capable, that is, use ICTs confidently and creatively to help develop the skills and knowledge they need as lifelong learners to achieve personal goals and to fully participate in the global community by 2013" (Department of Education, 2004, p. 17). The e-education policy framework supports four key elements of ICT use in teaching and learning: equity, access to ICT infrastructure, capacity building, and norms and standards.

Finnish Context

Finland is located in northern Europe between Russia and Sweden, and the majority of the 5,400,000 population reside in southern Finland (about 1,000,000 in the metropolitan area of Helsinki). The geographical area of Finland is 338,145 km^2, and is the most sparsely populated country in the European Union with 15.7 inhabitants per km^2. Official languages are Finnish and Swedish, although Finnish is the most common language spoken by 90 percent of inhabitants (Statistics Finland, 2010). Following 700 years of rule by Sweden, and later Russia, Finland became an independent parliamentary democracy in 1917 and is now a member of European Union (Finland Promotion Board, 2010).

Finnish students are highly placed in international comparisons of science skills, such as the OECD PISA (Programme for International Student Assessment) surveys that test the mathematics, science, reading literacy and problem-solving skills of 15-year-old students in over 40 countries. PISA tests address essential knowledge that is not specific to any curriculum (Ministry of Education, 2010), and Finnish students' scores have been among the best in all subjects in all four PISA surveys (OECD, 2007, 2010).

Finnish students' performances in PISA tests have been consistent and the differences between the strongest and weakest results in Finland are small, as are the differences among schools and regions. Socioeconomic background and language group have a lower impact on Finnish students' performance than in the other PISA countries. The Ministry of Education and Culture identifies reasons for success that include equal opportunities; comprehensiveness of education; competent teachers; the autonomy given to schools; student councelling and special needs education; encouraging evaluation; and a flexible system based on empowerment, cooperation, and a student-oriented, active conception of learning, rather than financial expenditure on education (which is the OECD average) (Ministry of Education and Culture, 2007).

The Finnish education system consists of a 1-year voluntary preprimary education, a 9-year compulsory basic education (comprehensive school) followed by an upper secondary education and higher education. Students start their compulsory schooling at the age of 7 years and continue until they have accomplished all nine grades or are aged 17. Almost all Finnish students (99.7%) complete the basic education syllabus (Finnish National Board of Education, 2010).

Basic education in Finland is free of charge, including books, school meals, and health care. Most comprehensive schools are public schools, and compulsory education is monitored by local authorities. Basic education providers construct their own curricula according to the instructions in the national core curriculum given by the Finnish National Board of Education. Generally, teachers are highly qualified, and a master's degree is required at all school levels (Finnish National Board of Education, 2010).

The Second Information Technology in Education Study (SITES) assessed the use of ICT in lower secondary schools in 2006 in different countries (Kankaanranta et al., 2008). Although the use of ICT in Finnish schools is quite high (see Table 14.1), not all Finnish students have equal possibilities to use ICT for learning and developing good ICT literacy skills. SITES research also showed that 61 percent of science teachers and less than 48 percent of mathematics teachers had used ICT during a specific period during the school year, and there are many teachers who have never used ICT in their lectures, suggesting that the pedagogical opportunities of ICT are still untapped (Kankaanranta & Puhakka, 2008).

MOBILE, UBIQUITOUS, AND PERVASIVE LEARNING

Mobile learning, or m-learning, is a form of informal learning where the learner traverses one or more physical contexts carrying a personal mobile device that provides learning materials and activities. Wireless networks can enable content sharing among learners as well as retrieval of learning materials from the server and support for collaborative activities. The key benefit of m-learning is that it enables learning experiences regardless of location and time. Affordable mobile technology is appealing for learning applications and is particularly useful in informal settings outside the classroom environment in addition to use in classrooms (Eschenbrenner & Nah, 2007; Naismith, Lonsdale, Vavoula, & Sharples, 2004; Trifonova, 2003).

The Merriam-Webster dictionary defines the word *ubiquitous* as "existing or being everywhere at the same time," i.e., being all around us. The term *ubiquitous computing* was coined by Marc Weiser with the popular phrase, "The most profound technologies are those that disappear. They weave themselves into the fabric of everyday life until they are indistinguishable from it" (Weiser, 1991, pp. 94–104).

Weiser also accurately predicted that ubiquitous computing would become the dominant mode of computer access 20 years following the article's publication. In particular, wearable computers (e.g., augmented reality visors, smart clothes, body sensors) and wireless sensor networks (e.g., environmental monitoring, vehicle monitoring, area surveillance) are increasingly being researched and deployed.

Ubiquitous learning, or *u-learning*, is a subcategory of mobile learning with an emphasis on embedded, ubiquitous computing and context-awareness. In addition to anywhere, anytime properties inherited from m-learning, the context-aware nature of ubiquitous learning takes into account aspects of the learner's context, such as who else is with the learner, what resources are nearby, what the learner is doing, and what the environmental parameters are. In other words, "context is all about the whole situation relevant to an application and its set of users" (Dey, 2001).

So, how can ubiquitous learning utilize available ubiquitous computing devices? Context-awareness enables the technologies to be used to provide the richest possible set of contextual information. The extent to which context-awareness can be supported depends largely on the available technical resources as well as on the requirements of the application. At its simplest, context-awareness can be mere location awareness (e.g., GPS). This might include the learner's direction (compass), nearby peers (interconnected client devices), weather (temperature, humidity, wind sensors), body awareness (heart rate, body temperature, stress level), information on the learner's preferences (user-profile management and background-data elicitation), and the possibilities to provide highly relevant learning content increase rapidly. In addition to context-awareness, ubiquitous technologies address the shortcomings of client mobile devices used in learning applications. A small screen can be complemented, for example, with a touch screen installed at a bus stop, interacting with the learner's mobile device. Poor input capabilities can be enhanced by moving from text-only input toward providing alternative ways of recording the learner's status via, for example, voice or facial expression recognition, or biosensors affixed to the learner's body. Finally, the restraint set by the low processing power can be tackled by using high-capacity servers to perform computationally complex operations.

Pervasive learning, or *p-learning*, is another subcategory of m-learning and closely related to ubiquitous learning. Although the phrases pervasive learning and ubiquitous learning are sometimes used interchangeably, we make a distinction between the two at the level of the learner's mobility (Lyytinen & Yoo, 2002). In ubiquitous learning, the learner is traversing different contexts, and the embedded technology supports this transition, whereas in pervasive learning the learning process and the learner are typically attached to a particular context such as a museum. Both ubiquitous learning and pervasive learning have a strong connection to context-awareness. A ubiquitous learning equivalent for a pervasive learning application in a specific museum could be a citywide learning environment where the learner would be able to traverse several museums, receiving context-sensitive learning activities at each location. However, in ubiquitous learning, context sensitiveness is more limited than in pervasive learning, where the learning technology is specifically designed for a particular context, and the more there are differences between the contexts, the harder it becomes for the ubiquitous learning environment to provide deep contextual information from each target context.

Context-aware learning environments that support ubiquitous and pervasive learning are referred to as a *ubiquitous learning space* (ULS) and a *pervasive learning space* (PLS) respectively.

Game-Based Learning

There exists considerable interest in the use of technology for gaming, due to the ubiquitous nature of technology in modern society and our natural human approach to play. Consequently, at the end of the 1990s, research in digital games commenced.

The use of play as exploratory learning is not new (Reilly, 1974). Alessi and Trollip (2001) note that educators consider games suitable for children, and also highlight the use of games for business school students. Game researchers have categorized as *serious games* those games that have a purpose beyond entertaining (Michael & Chen, 2006) and, in particular, game-based learning focuses on games with well-defined learning outcomes.

Kirriemuir and McFarlane (2004) identify a need for a better understanding of games as tools and the use of games within educational constraints (schools, teachers, parents, resources, curricula, student's time, etc.), and this study contributes to understanding requirements for educational games.

Despite the large number of different game genres and technologies, most current games are designed to be context-neutral; that is, they are played in any place by anyone. This applies particularly to mobile-based games, which are confined to the screen of a mobile device and thereby disregard the richness of the surrounding environment. In this chapter, we specifically focus on the ubiquitous side of game-based learning, where mobile devices are used as learning tools and on games designed to support context-awareness. In addition to mobile devices, game-based ULSs may use real-world objects as part of the game play. Therefore, context-awareness in ubiquitous (and pervasive) learning games opens new possibilities for rich interactions with the physical environment.

TECHNOLOGIES FOR MATHEMATICS EDUCATION

There exist various educational technologies to support the learning of abstract mathematical concepts. In this section, we present two of which are relevant to the UFractions game: concrete manipulatives and mobile applications for supporting mathematics learning.

The Use of Manipulatives in Mathematics

Mathematical *manipulatives* are concrete objects designed to support the learning of mathematical concepts. The importance of involving physical senses in the learning process of formal and abstract mathematical ideas is well understood (Piaget, 1969). Concrete manipulatives, like pattern blocks, fraction bars, tangrams, and geoboards, are widely used in today's classrooms, although recent research has not shown unambiguously their effectiveness.

Proponents of manipulatives suggest that the long-term use of concrete manipulatives improves students' mathematical achievements (Raphael & Wahlstrom, 1989; Sowell, 1989), encourages students thinking during mathematical problem solving (Kamii, Lewis, & Kirkland, 2001), and improves students' attitudes toward mathematics (Sowell, 1989). Critics of concreteness suggest that using manipulatives does not automatically guarantee better learning outcomes and meaningful learning (Clements, 1999; Scudder, Uttal, & Deloacher, 1997). Many studies agree that the critical factor for the effectiveness of manipulatives is the manner in which they are integrated into the learning process (Clements, 1999; Kamii et al., 2001). To use manipulatives successfully, teachers should take into account students' ideas and perceptions of what the manipulatives represent, manipulatives must be chosen

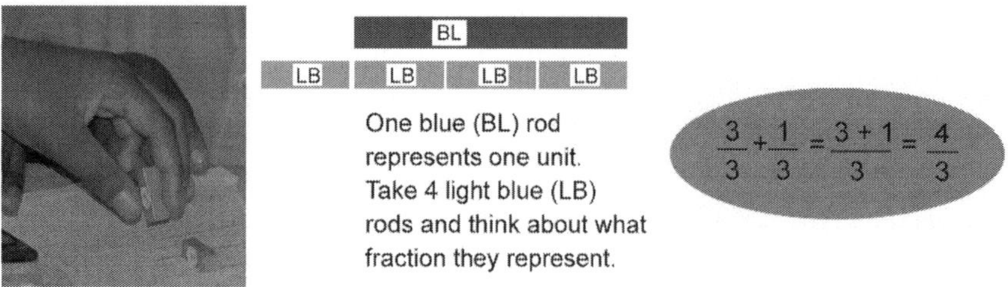

Figure 14.2 An example of the CRA instructional approach in learning fractions.

and used meaningfully (Scudder et al., 1997), and they should be used before the introduction of formal symbolic instruction (Sowell, 1989).

The use of concrete manipulatives especially helps the understanding and conceptualization process of students with learning disabilities (Brigham, Wilson, Jones, & Moisio, 1996; Cass, Cates, & Smith, 2003; Maccini & Gagnon, 2000). The Concrete-Representational-Abstract (CRA) instructional approach suggests that mathematical concept development happens through three stages: (a) concrete, (b) representational (pictorial or semiconcrete), and (c) abstract. During the concrete stage of CRA, learners manipulate real objects to demonstrate a mathematical idea. In the representational stage, a concrete model is transformed into the representational level by representing relational statements, for example, by drawing pictures or diagrams. Finally, during the abstract stage, a mathematical concept is modeled at the symbolic level, using only numbers, notations, and mathematical symbols (Maccini & Gagnon, 2000). Figure 14.2 presents how CRA strategy could be used for learning fractions with the help of fraction bars (also called Cuisenaire Rods[1]).

Mobile Technology in Mathematics

Much research has been done in the use of mobile devices for learning purposes; some applications having more game-like features than others. For mathematics education, there are several mobile-based tools of which a selection is presented in this section. While the tools we present here have emerged from the scientific community, there are also commercial mobile-based learning tools for mathematics.

Dr Math (Butgereit, 2007) is a South African mathematics tutoring environment built on the mobile-based MXit instant messaging service, which is highly popular among South African youngsters.[2] The key idea behind Dr Math is that teenagers using MXit can anonymously ask text-based questions related to mathematics from tutors behind the Dr Math avatar. The tutors in turn, from behind desktop computers, provide individual help to the teenagers. The service was set to run on certain days and times each week, and advertisements were posted at a local high school. According to evaluations (Butgereit, 2007), Dr Math was an enjoyable and encouraging experience for the participants, although a drawback was the inability to use drawing and illustration tools. At the time of writing, Dr Math is being adapted to the Mobicents telecommunications platform, making it more scalable and accessible to a wider audience (Butgereit & Botha, 2010).

Sudoku[3] is a popular pastime that is very suitable for mobile devices due to its simple layout and operation. Nestler, Echtler, Dollinger, and Klinker (2008) took the idea of mobile-based sudoku one step further, combining it with a multitouch table for collaborative game playing. Views on the table and on mobile devices are synchronized so an action performed by a player on a mobile device is immediately shown on the touch screen table, and vice versa. This research is an example of how the coupling of mobile devices and a tactile user interface could be used to support collaborative game play and learning.

Math4Mobile is a suite of Java-based graphical mathematics tools to support learning of mathematics at the high school level and above. Learning materials can be constructed and shared with other users. Botzer and Yerushalmy (2007) studied the use of Math4Mobile for modeling real-life scenarios and increasing collaboration between test participants. The study followed four students who were given a task to engage in mathematical modeling in their everyday life situations, using a camera to record the target situations. Created models and recordings were then shared among the participants and commented upon. This study shows that it is indeed possible to combine abstract mathematical concepts with concrete aspects of the real world.

The MOBI project is a South African initiative that aims to alleviate the South African science and mathematics education problem through the use of Java-based mobile applications (Matthee & Liebenberg, 2007). The project has yielded a mobile learning environment that includes live tutoring (similar to Dr Math), radio, chat, and mathematics training. Before using the environment, users are assessed by a multiple-choice test to determine their proficiency level in the subject so as to provide adapted content.

Skills Arena is a suite of mobile-based games for learning basic arithmetic skills. After creating an avatar, players choose a suitable game type and skill level for their ability and learning goals. There is a time limit for given tasks, and immediate feedback is provided after answering. The use of Skills Arena and the use of flash cards in learning basic arithmetic skills have been compared, and results suggest that a mobile game such as Skills Arena has a positive impact on students' learning in mathematics, especially those with low skill levels (Shin, Norris, & Soloway, 2006).

SUMMARY

While many mobile-based games for learning mathematics have been developed, to our knowledge, nobody has yet combined concrete manipulatives and a mobile-based game to form a ULS that can be used in different contexts. In this chapter, we introduce UFractions, a ULS which combines a story-based mobile game with fraction sticks. The game was designed for learning mathematics in the South African context. Our motivation to target South Africa stems from the fact that mobile devices are the primary computing and communication devices for many South Africans. Additionally, especially in developing regions of South Africa, the challenges in mathematics education are enormous. Finland, on the other hand, is a technologically advanced country with an excellent educational system. Technologies developed in countries like Finland are typically transferred to developing contexts. In this research, we take the unexplored road of reverse transfer by designing the UFractions game in and for technology-alien South African regions and then taking it to technology-familiar Finland. In the next section, we define related concepts and describe UFractions. We then evaluate how well reverse transfer works from the perspectives of the cultural, pedagogical and technological contexts.

CASE STUDY ON REVERSE TRANSFER: UFRACTIONS

Contextualization and Reverse Transfer

In the design process of technologies, including educational games, there is a need for a contextualized approach (Vesisenaho, 2007). In short, contextualization refers to a design principle that takes seriously the expectations, needs, and especially the strengths of the context that the proposed technology should serve.

Context has many aspects, such as cultural, pedagogical, physical, and political. *Technology-alien* describes a context that uses relatively little technology, whereas a *technology-familiar* context is known for its high exploitation level of technology.

Needs-based design is a conventional approach to creating contextually relevant technologies. However, when basing the design on existing lists of needs or demands, the needs-based approach does not take into account the resources of a particular context.

Strength-based design (Sutinen, 2010) starts the contextualization stage by exploring the strengths and resources of the intended user context of the technology. Compared with the deductive needs-based approach, the strength-based approach requires creativity and induction.

Whereas conventional needs-based design is quite straightforward, the strength-based approach to contextualization requires participatory design, which embeds the potential users of the technology into the design process. An example of strength-based design is the design process of HIV/AIDS educational learning materials in Tanzania, where youngsters used their own experiences to come up with meaningful educational content based on their real-life experiences and stories (Duveskog & Sutinen, 2009).

Recontextualization is a process that adapts a contextually designed technology into a new context (Bada, Duveskog, Suhonen, & Sutinen, 2009). The aim is to design viable technologies that can not only sustain but also modify and reproduce themselves in a new environment.

Recontextualization relates closely to context-awareness, which is an inherent property of both ubiquitous and pervasive learning. A future highly context-aware technology could, in principle, be used to automatically adapt an educational system and material to a new context, that is, to recontextualize it. Until such a powerful technology emerges, contextual design remains a key factor for successful recontextualization.

In this chapter, we explore the process of reverse transfer of a ULS and the relevance of its outcome to the users of a new context. Reverse transfer refers to a process wherein a technology, designed for and within a technology-alien context, is transferred as such to a technology-familiar environment. Thus, reverse transfer does not recontextualize the technology, and its outcome can be used to analyze the role of contextualization of technology.

Context Adaptation

Being aware of the context is one of the key features both in ubiquitous learning and in pervasive learning. Even though pervasive learning is tied more to a specific context than ubiquitous learning, both utilize embedded technologies to provide the system with context-sensitive information about the learner's current context. *Context adaptation* refers to the ability of a system to adapt automatically to diverse aspects of context (e.g., physical, cultural, political, technological, social) when the system is being transferred to a new context. Figure 14.3 illustrates the levels of context adaptation in plain mobile learning, pervasive learning and ubiquitous learning. For example, when a context adaptive learning game is being transferred from context A to context B, it is expected to automatically adapt to the culture, available technological infrastructure and pedagogical requirements of the target context B. In addition, the context-adaptive system may take into account other aspects such as the learner's identity, environmental conditions, financial constraints and political reality. In the case of reverse transfer, the importance of technological context adaptation is low because the

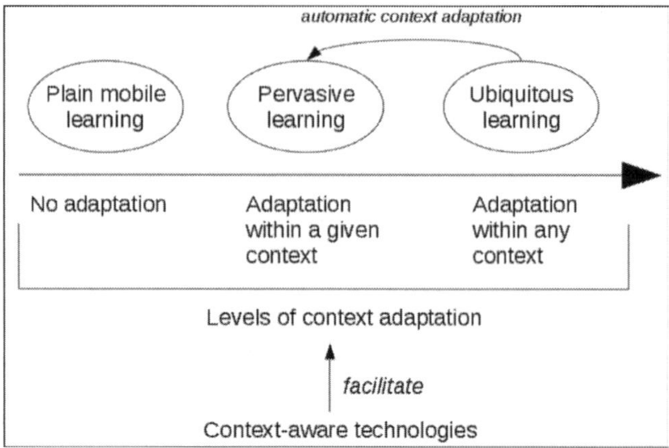

Figure 14.3 Levels of context adaptation in mobile-based learning approaches.

users in the target (technologically-familiar) context are unlikely to have problems operating the transferred technology.

Automatic context adaptation has a two-tier structure: a ULS is adapted into a PLS, which in turn is adaptive within its respective context.

Context adaptation is facilitated by context-aware technologies such as smart tags and wireless sensors. According to this view, a ULS is able to adapt automatically within any context that it is transferred to. For example, in the case of museums, a perfectly adaptive ULS would be able to transfer from one museum to another without requiring interventions from technical or design perspectives. To our knowledge, currently available technologies cannot yet perform completely automatic context adaptation, thus transferring the current ULSs across all possible contexts is not possible. In the case of pervasive learning, this transfer is not required, as a PLS is designed for a particular context. One could view a true ULS also as a set of context-specific adaptations of a generic system, and these adaptations could in turn be referred to as PLSs as they are automatically adapted, or designed, to a given context.

Context adaptation is evaluated through various aspects of context. In this chapter, we use cultural, pedagogical and technological aspects of the context in the evaluation of UFractions.

UFRACTIONS

UFractions is a ULS combining a story-based mobile game with fraction rods so as to motivate the pupils to learn fractions in a novel way. To our knowledge, no work has yet been done in combining concrete manipulatives with mobile gaming. The combination of the two different learning tools provided us with new opportunities not only to motivate the pupils but also to create new connections between a fictitious story, fraction theory, and physical objects (i.r., fraction rods).

The ubiquitous nature of UFractions is not so much technical as it is conceptual—the context comprises the mobile game and the concrete manipulatives, and the game can be transferred from one tabletop to another. In terms of cultural and pedagogical contexts, however, UFractions lacks context adaptation, as we will find out in a later section. Before that, the UFractions game is described from the perspectives of design and implementation.

Design Process

UFractions was designed within and for a technology-alien environment in rural South Africa. The design process started with an idea for a story-based game related to animals. The story for the game was made with the help of South African cultural experts, and a suitable level of mathematics for the game was defined with the help of secondary school teachers from North West province and the Revised National Curriculum Statement Grades R–9 (Department of Education, 2002; Turtiainen, Blignaut, Els, Laine, & Sutinen, 2009). We chose the game format to be similar to that of LieksaMyst (Laine, Islas Sedano, Vinni, & Sutinen, 2009), a story-based game for a living museum in Finland, so we had to adapt the content of UFractions to fit the same format.

The main characters in the UFractions game are Mother Leopard and her cub Senatla, whose appearances were drawn during the design process. While playing the game, the learners assist Mother Leopard to raise her

Figure 14.4 Mother Leopard and her cub Senatla; an example of mathematical problem and the use of fraction rods.

cub and fight against hunger and enemies living in the South African savannah. Players earn points by solving fraction challenges related to the lives of the two leopards with the help of fraction rods. Therefore, the players must gain an understanding of the problem and the concept of fractions in order to be able to find the correct solutions.

The chosen game format (LieksaMyst) requires the answers to the problems to be numbers or choices from a list. The limited set of question types complicated the planning of meaningful mathematical problems, and because of the restricted screen space, explanations had to be concise. Suitable hints for every problem were also created, so players are able to ask for advice after an incorrect answer. Hints do not provide the answer immediately, but lead players to the right path of solving the problem instead. Positive feedback was tailored for each problem and negative feedback was randomly picked from a pool of negative feedbacks assigned for each character.

The game starts with an introduction, where players are introduced to the leopards and challenged to solve four introductory problems that guide them to using the rods. After the introduction, the players can select a level: feeding the cub: 0–16 weeks; lessons to hunt: 4–6 months; pro hunting: 6–12 months or whole year. The story line involves different paths that the players can choose (see Figure 14.5).

In addition to the story-based game UFractions can record evidence of the players showing their knowledge of fractions and identifying mathematics from their everyday environment by taking pictures and adding comments to the pictures. The game Web site[4] displays a real-time status of the leopards' and the players' struggle against hunger and enemies—the two main threats to the leopards—and presents the scores of the teams, recorded evidence, and guestbook entries.

When UFractions was reverse transferred to the technology-familiar environment in Finland, the story line was not changed at all, but was translated into Finnish, although some sentences had to be shortened or split to fit to the mobile phone screen. Also, color codes used in the game were kept intact, so, for example, "Valkoinen" (white) remained coded with a letter "W."

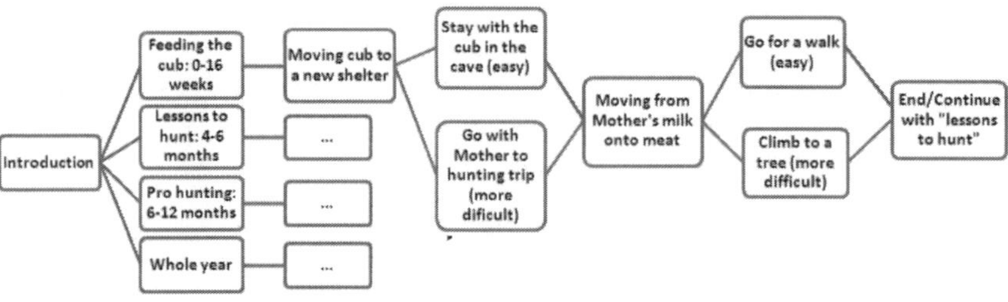

Figure 14.5 An example story line fragment, "Feeding the cub."

Implementation

The development process of UFractions was financially challenging and time constrained, so we decided to use an existing platform that would enable fast and easy game development. For this purpose, we analyzed two pervasive games that were previously constructed at University of Eastern Finland (University of Joensuu). SciMyst (Islas Sedano, Laine, Vinni, & Sutinen, 2007) is a quiz-based competitive, pervasive adventure game created for the annual SciFest science festival held in Joensuu, Finland, in which players use mobile devices to explore the festival arena by solving challenges related to the surrounding objects and phenomena, and answers to the challenges are found from the physical environment. LieksaMyst is a story-based game situated at the Pielinen museum, a large open-air living museum in Lieksa, Finland (Laine et al., 2009). In LieksaMyst, players use a mobile device to make a relaxed (noncompetitive) journey back in time to meet and interact with fictitious characters from the past. The characters tell the players how life was like in their respective periods of time and ask for assistance in performing various daily activities such as churning butter or warming up the house.

After analyzing the applicability of both game types for learning mathematics in the South African context, we chose LieksaMyst's story-based structure as a template for UFractions and added competitive features from the SciMyst games. Merging features of the two games was easy because both are based on the Myst pervasive learning platform (Laine, Vinni, Islas Sedano, & Joy, 2010). It is important to note that, in this process, a pervasive learning platform was used to create a ULS. This activity provided us valuable experience on how the same technological foundation can be used to support both pervasive and ubiquitous learning.

The Myst platform was developed on top of Nokia's MUPE (Multi-User Publishing Environment) software (Suomela, Räsänen, Koivisto, & Mattila, 2004). MUPE uses a client-server approach, where the Java-based server pushes game content to J2ME-based clients in a predefined XML format over a network connection. The advantage of this content-delivery model is that if changes are made to the content, the clients do not need to be upgraded. Furthermore, the same client can be used to access several MUPE-based games, and the player's status is stored on the server, that is, the game can be resumed after a period of absence.

UFractions does not use any context-awareness technology (e.g., 2D bar codes, NFC, location input) because it is location-agnostic. The context in the case of UFractions is the table on which the fraction rods and the game content on a mobile device interact. This interaction is managed by explicitly expressed color codes on the rods and in the story (e.g., W for a white rod).

Evaluation

The aim of the overall evaluation was to compare the differences between South African and Finnish school 8th-grade contexts in the use of UFractions, particularly focusing on the effects of reverse transfer. A multimethod approach comprising qualitative and quantitative strategies was employed to achieve the aim. In this chapter, we concentrate on results that measure how well the game is adapted to the cultural, pedagogical and technological contexts in the two countries. We do this to show the importance of recontextualization rather than just reverse transfer of a ULS such as UFractions. The results are primarily derived from quantitative questionnaire data, and the findings are supported by qualitative comments from the participants.

EVALUATION SETTING

Evaluations were conducted in five South African schools and four Finnish schools during March 2009 (South Africa) and March 2010 (Finland). Key figures of the target schools and test groups are presented in Table 14.2.

Students and teachers filled in a questionnaire that included open-ended and multiple choice questions, where they selected the most appropriate

TABLE 14.2 Key Figures of the Schools and Test Participants

North-West Province School (Grades)	Total Number of Students	Number of participants (males/ females)	Percentage of mobile phone owners in test group
Alabama Secondary (8–12)	1300	21 (8/13)	38%
Lebone II (1–12)	255	22 (11/11)	77%
Seiphemelo Secondary (8–12)	1063	16 (6/10)	25%
High School Zeerust (8–12)	573	27 (11/16)	78%
Zinniaville Secondary (8–12)	987	19 (8/11)	84%
North Karelia School (Grades)	**Total Number of Students**	**Number of participants (males/ females)**	**Percentage of mobile phone owners in test group**
Arppen koulu (7–9)	307	32 (14/18)	100%
Lieksan Keskuskoulu (7–9)	406	31 (16/15)	100%
Joensuun Normaalikoulu (7–9)	201	18 (9/9)	100%
Tietäväisen koulu (1–9)	201	23 (14/9)	100%

option from Strongly Agree (5), Agree (4), I don't have an opinion (3), Disagree (2), Strongly Disagree (1). Students also attempted a few fraction exercises to test their mathematical competency. The qualitative data consists of open-ended questions, observations, and interviews of students and teachers, and multiple-choice questions offer extensive quantitative data. We performed a descriptive analysis of the quantitative data, using mean and standard deviation calculations. The findings were then supported by qualitative data. A previous cluster analysis of the qualitative data showed that South African students immersed themselves in the story, and that the story induced ethical, physical, and cognitive rationales. The South African participants liked mathematics in the UFractions game for affective (intrinsic motivation to mathematics), functional and action-oriented reasons (Turtiainen et al., 2009).

Each school testing session started by filling in the first part of the questionnaire and dividing the students into groups—in South Africa the group sizes were 2–4 students and in Finland 1–3 students. The researchers presented a slide show of UFractions to the students and explained the game idea, as well as different functions of the game, the use of the mobile phones, and one problem example. Then the students played the UFractions game for 30–45 minutes (see Figure 14.6). During the game play, the researchers observed the players' reactions to the game. The researchers, as well as the teacher, helped students if they had problems in the mathematical content or the use of UFractions.

After playing the game, students and teachers completed questionnaires, and in each class, three to five students and the teacher were interviewed to collect data on the unique experiences and attitudes of the teachers and learners, as well as the technical aspects and usability of the game.

Figure 14.6 Pupils engaged in game play in South Africa (left: March 2009) and Finland (right: March 2010).

In the following sections, we present the evaluation results on cultural and pedagogical context adaptation, followed by the results of technological context adaptation.

CULTURAL CONTEXT ADAPTATION

To evaluate the adaptation of UFractions to a cultural context, we considered the elements of the language used (see Figure 14.7, statement 1), as well as the story and the player's immersion (concentration on the story) in it (statements 2–5). Immersion can lead to *flow*, which in turn can be interpreted as deep, intrinsically motivated, and therefore effective, learning experience (Csikszentmihalyi & Hermanson, 1995). Figure 14.7 illustrates the evaluation results on cultural context adaptation, and reveals several differences between the Finnish and the South African datasets. The South African pupils were very positive about all evaluated aspects, as only few pupils gave negative answers. Finnish pupils, on the other hand, were rather negative about most aspects, particularly in those that concerned the story and the players' immersion in it.

Language was considered to be easy to understand, resulting in the highest positive ranking of all results in the cultural context category in both datasets (Finland: 88%, South Africa: 97%). What makes this very interesting

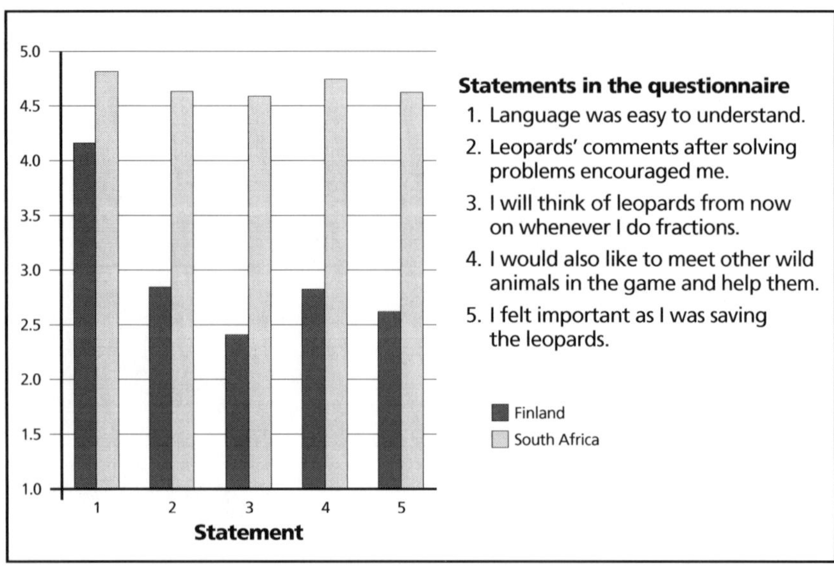

Figure 14.7 Evaluation of cultural context adaptation (1 = Strongly Disagree; 2 = Disagree; 3 = No opinion; 4 = Agree; 5 = Strongly Agree).

is that in South Africa the game was played in English while the majority of the pupils (77%) reported their native language to be other than English. On the other hand, the South African pupils were taught in English in most cases so they most likely had the necessary language skills to understand the story and the challenges in the game. In Finland, there were only two pupils who reported their native language to be something other than Finnish, and they disagreed with the first statement.

The second statement measured the motivational value of immediate comments after solving a challenge. South African pupils highly appreciated the comments (91% of positive answers), which was consistent with the other story-related statements, suggesting that the South African pupils were able to immerse themselves in the story. Finnish pupils reported more negative (42%) than positive (28%) answers for this statement, and 30 percent did not give their opinion. These results, together with the subsequent story-related results, might indicate that the story was not appropriately adapted for Finnish pupils.

The third statement measured the players' immersion in the story as well as how well the story was able to have relevance in the players' minds and whether the story would have a chance to be remembered in the future in the context of fractions. Finnish pupils were negative about this, as 57 percent reported that they will not be thinking of leopards in their future fraction-related endeavors, and a further 24 percent offered no opinion. Most of the South African pupils (93%), on the other hand, reported that they would remember leopards in the future. This great difference between the two datasets confirms our previous observation that the story was not as immersive for the Finnish pupils as it was for the South Africans.

The fourth statement measured the pupils' willingness to use similar games to meet other animals and help them. The idea behind this statement is to see whether the pupils would be interested in using other perspectives and apply the experiences of UFractions to similar games relating to different areas (e.g., geometry). Additionally, this statement measures immersion in the story. The South African dataset gives high support (94%) for the idea of using other animals and their respective challenges. Finnish pupils, on the other hand, were not so eager (41% disagreed and 27% had no opinion). We consider these results as yet another indication that a learning tool cannot simply be (reverse) transferred without proper context adaptation or recontextualization.

The last statement on cultural context adaptation further measured the level of immersion in the story. In the South African dataset, 94 percent of the pupils agreed, thus we can again confirm that the story suited the South African pupils very well, but 46 percent of the Finnish pupils disagreed and 30 percent did not have an opinion. We can conclude that many Finnish students, due to lack of contextualization of the story, may have not entered the flow at all.

One of the key findings regarding cultural context adaptation was that there was a significant difference in the level of immersion between the two groups. Deep immersion of the South African pupils can also be seen in their comments during interviews:

> [I] would want to go on and on . . . and just never stop . . . like when you said that we have to stop I was so angry. (female, 13)
>
> It was like real, but I was using just imagination. (male, 14)
>
> Mother said that she needs help to raise the child, so I wanted to help to raise the child. (male, 13)
>
> It's perfect, I loved it. There are always some wrong things, but this one . . . I loved it. (female, 14)
>
> Are you still going to come again? (female, 14)

Possible reasons for the Finnish pupils' lack of immersion included questions being too easy, the story being uninteresting/too long and the game being too childish, and these were mentioned several times:

> The story could be shortened (male, 14)
>
> I would remove the leopard (male, 14)
>
> Better images, more action, more interesting story and characters (female, 14)
>
> That the game would not be so childish (female, 14)
>
> Not a game for 8th grade, the questions were too easy (female, 15)

These qualitative data support the findings from the quantitative statements related to cultural context adaptation, hence we can conclude that the game, culturally designed for South African pupils, does not work equally well for Finnish pupils of the same age.

PEDAGOGICAL CONTEXT ADAPTATION

The role of pedagogical context adaptation was evaluated by three statements that measured the comprehension of problems, the use of concrete manipulatives (Cuisenaire rods) in learning fractions, and the general effectiveness of UFractions as a learning tool (see Figure 14.8). These results relate to cultural context, and this relevance is analyzed below with the results.

From the pedagogical context perspective, the presented problems were considered easy to understand by both sets of students (Finland: 78%, South Africa: 94%). However, the data suggests that there is room for im-

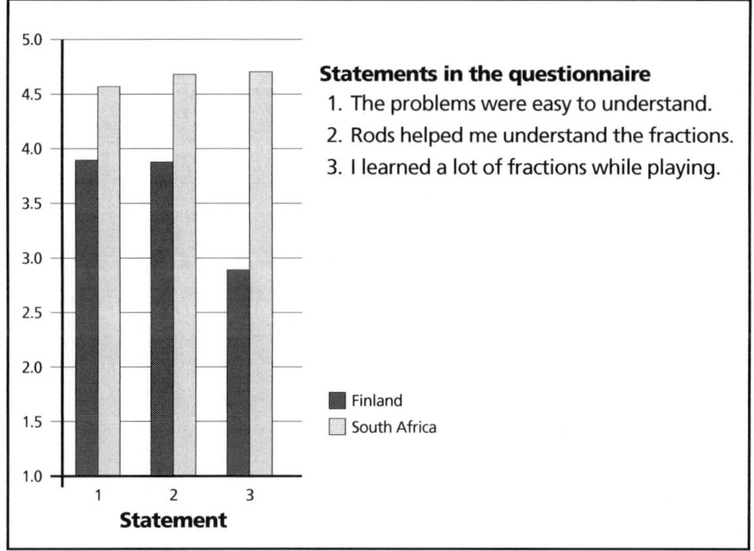

Figure 14.8 Evaluation of pedagogical context adaptation (1 = Strongly Disagree; 2 = Disagree; 3 = No opinion; 4 = Agree; 5 = Strongly Agree).

provement, especially in the Finnish version of the game (11% negatives, 12% no opinions). One explanation for this is that in the Finnish dataset, there were two pupils who reported their native language to be something other than Finnish—this relates to the cultural context adaptation where the game language was evaluated. Additionally, when translating the content from English to Finnish, the color codes were kept intact. This could also have caused confusion to some players, although we cautioned the pupils in the beginning to follow the color codes.

The second statement measured the importance of using concrete manipulatives to connect theory of fractions to physical objects. Again, this aspect of the game was highly valued by South African pupils as 96 percent of them considered the rods useful in learning fractions. The use of rods might have had novelty value for South African pupils, as several South African teachers reported that they had not used concrete manipulatives or games previously in the class. Most Finnish teachers, on the other hand, reported that they had been using either manipulatives or games or both in their mathematics classes. The rods helped a reported 74 percent of the Finnish pupils in understanding fractions, and 13 percent did not give an opinion. These results support the view that physical manipulatives may help the pupils to understand theoretical concepts better (Raphael & Wahlstrom, 1989; Sowell, 1989).

With the last statement, we investigated the educational value of the game by measuring how much the players felt that they learned fractions during the game session. This metric is far from comprehensive, but it might give an indication of educational effectiveness as well as the pedagogical suitability of UFractions to the target groups. The South African dataset revealed that 95 percent of the pupils reported that they learned while playing and 80 percent thought that they learned a lot (strongly agreed). On the other hand, only 33 percent of the Finns reported that they learned fractions while playing, 40 percent did not report any learning at all, and 28 percent had no opinion. These results indicate that the game and its challenges were useful in the South African context, and they were also useful for some of the Finnish pupils. As the cultural context adaptation results above suggest, the Finnish pupils were not immersed in the story as much as the South African pupils, hence rendering their learning processes less effective. Additionally, 51 percent of the Finnish teams played through at least two levels of the game, whereas in the case of South African teams, this figure was 19 percent, suggesting that the challenges were easy for at least some of the Finnish pupils, resulting in challenges being solved routinely.

The game was created for South African 8th graders to learn fractions. Positive learning experiences of South Africans can also be seen in qualitative data when we asked the pupils what they enjoyed about playing with the leopards. In these results, we observed several pupils reporting that they learned not only about fractions but also about leopards, and team play was appreciated too:

> I enjoyed learning how leopards survive in the wild and what they eat. (male, 14)

> I enjoyed playing with the Cuisenaire rods and solving the problems. It was also interesting to see how the leopards grow and how they take care of themselves. (female, 13)

> I liked everything because we were working together as a team. (female, 13)

> It exercises your brain. (male, 13)

Several Finnish pupils suggested that the game was not suitable for their skill levels, and some pupils suggested that parts of the problems were difficult to understand:

> I would give it for second graders. (female, 14)

> [The tasks] were a bit boring, too easy. (male, 15)

> Some questions were difficult to understand and there were too many intermediate explanations. (female, 14)

> Some tasks were very unclear. (female, 14)

TECHNOLOGICAL CONTEXT ADAPTATION

UFractions is not based on complex technologies. The only technologies that the players experience are the mobile device and the fraction rods, hence, in this section of the evaluation, we measured the motivation and ease of using these technologies (see Figure 14.9). The aim was to see how natural the use of integrated technology was to the pupils.

The first statement measures the motivation (fun factor) of using the mobile technology. The high positive ratings in both groups (Finnish: 78%, South African: 95%) suggest that the phone was received well as a platform for UFractions. In the Finnish dataset, 13 percent chose the "No opinion" option, whereas in the South African dataset, the value was only 3 percent. For some pupils, there might have been a degree of novelty value in using the phone for playing—to understand this factor better, we would need a longer-term investigation on phone usage as a learning tool.

The phone was considered to be an easy tool for playing in both datasets (Finland: 83%, South Africa: 93%). In the Finnish dataset, 10 percent of the pupils chose not to give an opinion. These figures indicate that the phone (hardware) and the game that was running on the phone (software) were functioning well enough so as not to disturb the pupils. In the Finnish dataset, the mobile phone ownership was 100 percent, whereas this number in the South African dataset was 63 percent. It is possible and even likely that

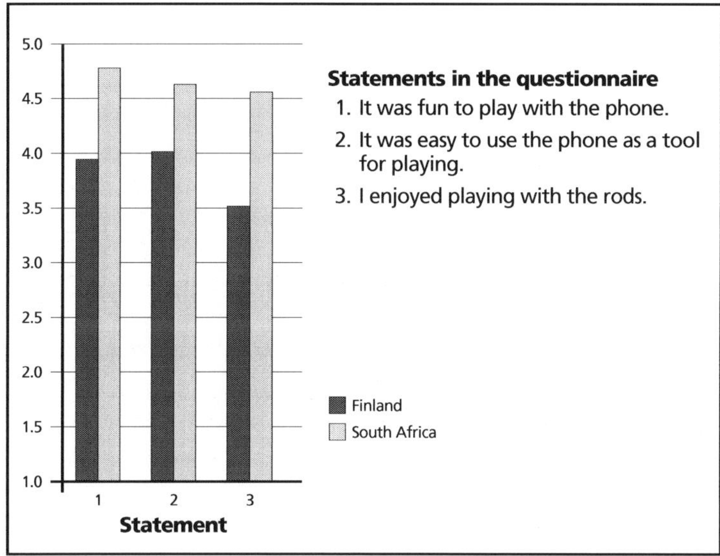

Figure 14.9 Evaluation of technology integration (1 = Strongly Disagree; 2 = Disagree; 3 = No opinion; 4 = Agree; 5 = Strongly Agree).

those South African pupils who do not own a mobile phone have been using one with their friends or at home.

In the third statement, we measured how much the pupils enjoyed using the rods during game play. In the Finnish dataset, rods were not appreciated as much as mobile phones were, as only 64 percent answered positively and 25 percent disagreed. On the other hand, South African pupils once again gave very high positive feedback (96%), but the number of "Strongly agrees" was lower than in the two previous statements, hence the lower overall score. These results indicate that in addition to mobile devices, fraction rods as a learning technology were enjoyed by most of the pupils.

The technological context adaptation results suggest that the technology worked well in both contexts. This follows the logic of reverse transfer: when a technology designed in a technology-alien context is brought to a technology-familiar context, it is likely that the users in the technology-familiar context will not experience problems with operating the transferred technology. In both South Africa and Finland, mobile devices are widely distributed, and especially in South Africa the mobile device can be seen as the main computing device in rural areas. The use of mobile technology and fraction rods was also reflected in pupils' comments from both countries.

> The game is very exciting and keeps your mind busy. It keeps your concentration on it. I think it is very good focus if we can have it on our mobile phones to keep us away from bad things. (female, 14, South Africa)

> It was nice to play around on a phone and getting educated at the same time. (female, 13, South Africa)

> The actual playing it on the phone, actually, that was the fun part. Because usually it's only a piece of paper and start writing. . . . For some children it's difficult to learn while they've been telling you or reading it. But it is on the phone now, something you're good at so you can just learn quickly instead of always being stressed after. (male, 13, South Africa)

> I enjoyed playing with rods the most. I enjoyed myself very much. (female, 13, South Africa)

> We never ever worked with the rods and this was my first experience with the rods and its really fun. (female, 14, South Africa)

> [I liked] that there were rods and fancy phones. (female, 14, Finland)

> Touch screen version would probably be better. (male, 14, Finland)

> [I liked] finding the sticks. (female, 15, Finland)

> It was nice to play with sticks. (female, 15, Finland)

> [I liked] calculating with the fraction rods and playing with them. (female, 14, Finland)

DISCUSSION

From the evaluation results, it is interesting to see that whereas South Africans were eager to choose "Strongly agree," Finns preferred to choose "Agree." Additionally, considerably more Finnish pupils chose "No opinion" (up to 30% in some statements), suggesting that the Finnish pupils may be more comfortable with withholding their opinions. These patterns partly explain why the Finnish pupils have lower mean values than South African pupils.

In several statements, standard deviation values differed substantially between the two datasets. The standard deviations for the Finnish dataset were generally higher than those for the South African dataset (the means being 1.07 and 0.69, respectively). We can think of two possible reasons for this: (a) given the high positive answers across the data, South African pupils might have tried to impress the authority (i.e., researchers) rather than disappoint them; and (b) English literacy levels of South African pupils are not as high as the Finnish language literacy of the Finnish pupils. This may lead to a situation where the pupils having the strongest English literacy skill help other team members to fill in the questionnaire. Without a focused study on this aspect, we cannot confirm these reasons.

One of the most significant results of the data is that when the UFractions game is contextualized properly to the cultural and pedagogical contexts, it is valued higher by the learners. In other words, when a ULS such as UFractions is badly contextualized (or not contextualized at all), its pedagogical and motivational values decrease. At the same time, the results support our view that the role of technology in reverse transfer is not as significant as when a technology developed in a technology-alien context is brought to a technology-familiar context—the users in the target context are able to use the technology because it is familiar to them. In case of UFractions, the mobile devices used (Nokia N95, N80) were already 3 to 4 years old when the tests took place, so the pupils in both contexts were used to them. Should the transfer have occured in the other direction, technology in context adaptation would be more important.

According to our definitions, UFractions as a ULS should, in an optimal situation, be able to adapt automatically to any context. Our evaluation results show that this is not the case for reasons of culture and pedagogy. A future solution would be to concentrate on increasing the context adaptivity of the story and the challenges, and introduce smart fraction sticks that can be used to detect the game's context and the players' actions more precisely (Smith & Laine, 2011).

FUTURE TRENDS

Since Weiser's prediction in 1991, ubiquitous technologies have developed significantly and today we can find affordable sensors, tags, and wireless communication devices all around us; familiar environments such as work, home, public transportation, cinemas and hospitals are becoming increasingly intelligent and are thereby able to provide us with more context-sensitive services. We expect this trend to continue as nano technologies are coupled with sensors, enabling new materials for building new services on. Body sensors will be increasingly available, and gathered data can be used to adapt services to users' body statuses. Needless to say, ethical concerns regarding the use of ubiquitous technologies increase as the technologies pervade our comfort zones.

In the future of ubiquitous learning, powerful mobile technologies with sensing capabilities will grant us new pedagogical possibilities to take learning from classrooms to the pockets of the learners while maintaining close links to the surrounding contexts. Mobile learning, as we know it today, will become more ubiquitous and pervasive, although we suspect that the term *m-learning* will remain in use. We envisage that mobile learners will become ubiquitous learners who use a general purpose ubiquitous learning tool to access various context-sensitive learning resources and activities as they traverse contexts in their everyday lives. The learning tool will be able to seamlessly adapt to new contexts and provide the learner with meaningful material and activities in a way that is the most comfortable for the learner. The adaptation is done based on various aspects of the surrounding context (e.g., physical, cultural, political, technological, social) and the learner's personal context (e.g., previous experiences, preferences). Following this idea, UFractions could develop into a tool that can be used for learning everyday mathematics by automatically adapting story and challenges to the surrounding context. Fraction sticks, for example, could then be replaced by real-world objects that are specific for a particular context (e.g., sticks in a forest, a cake in a bakery).

We see reverse transfer as a future trend of learning technology development where the core concept and technology are developed in a technology-alien context, and then recontextualized to suit the needs of a technology-familiar context. The advantage of this model is that the designers and developers must take into account serious challenges (e.g., pedagogical, technical) that they face in the technology-alien context. By meeting these challenges, the end product is likely to be more robust than in the case of an ordinary technology transfer. To investigate more on the effectiveness and the benefits of reverse transfer, we will continue developing technologies in places like South Africa and Tanzania, and then reverse transferring or recontextualizing them to technology-familiar contexts such as Finland.

CONCLUSIONS

We have analyzed how pupils from grade 8 use the ubiquitous mobile game UFractions in two different contexts, South Africa and Finland. The game was created in South Africa, and it was intended for learning fractions by solving problems encountered in a story line. The game makes use of manipulatives, called Cuisenaire rods, for concretizing the concept of fractions. The game was reverse transferred to Finland as such, only translated into Finnish.

The reverse transfer process, taking a technology from a context where the use of technology is on the average relatively low (South Africa) to a context with a high use of technology (Finland), helped us to focus our analysis on the role of the contextual factors for making functional use of technology for learning. In the conventional setting of transferring technology from the North to the South, it is hard to assess how much of possible obstacles to using technology are due to being not familiar with it rather than the cultural or pedagogical biases inherent in using a technology originated in a different context. Contrary to that, the reverse transfer process resulted in a scenario where pupils with a solid expertise in technology were given a technology with only cultural or pedagogical bias, not technical.

We were particularly interested in two aspects of the context: cultural and pedagogical. The results, obtained by questionnaires and interviews, indicated that the pupils in the Finnish context had significantly more problems or complaints in using the UFractions game than their South African counterparts. We interpret the results so that plain reverse transfer is not enough for a functional learning environment. Instead, a full recontextualization process is required, which covers at least the cultural and pedagogical aspects of the context of the users. With emerging ubiquitous technologies, part of this recontextualization process can be automated by the context-aware features of these technologies, assuming that appropriate knowledge architecture, for example ontologies, is established.

Although not investigated in the current study, the results also question the meaning of localization, especially if it is limited to content translation or transformation. Our results indicate that, whereas a story works in one context as a platform for learning content, a completely different type of platform might be needed for another context. Localization is insufficient to adapt such a story, and recontextualization is needed.

NOTES

1. The name Cuisenaire, as well as the special color sequence of the Cuisenaire Rods, are registered trademarks of ETA/Cuisenaire.
2. http://www.itnewsafrica.com/?p=2730 (accessed April 27, 2010)

3. http://en.wikipedia.org/wiki/sudoku (accessed April 27, 2010)
4. UFractions Web site: http://ubiquelab.joensuu.fi/ufractions (accessed April 28, 2010)

REFERENCES

Alessi, S. M., & Trollip, S. R. (2001). *Multimedia for learning: Methods and development* (3rd ed.). Boston: Allyn & Bacon.

Bada, J. K., Duveskog, M., Suhonen, J., & Sutinen, E. (2009, May 6–8). *Toward viable technology for HIV/AIDS education.* Proceedings of the IST Africa 2009 Conference, Kampala, Uganda.

Blignaut, A. S., & Els, C. J. (2010). Not yet where we want to be: South Africa's participation in SITES 2006. *US-China Education Review, 7*(2), 55–66.

Blignaut, A. S., Els, C. J., & Howie, S. J. (2010). Contextualizing South Africa's participation in the SITES 2006 module. *South African Journal of Education, 30*(4).

Botzer, G., & Yerushalmy, M. (2007, December 7–9). Mobile applications for mobile learning. In *Cognition & exploratory learning in digital age (CELDA).* Algarve, Portugal.

Brigham, F. J., Wilson, R., Jones, E., & Moisio, M. (1996). Best practices: Teaching decimals, fractions, and percents to students with learning disabilities. *LD Forum, 21*(3), 10–15.

Butgereit, L. (2007, April 18–20). Math on MXit: Using MXit as a medium for mathematics education. *Proceedings of the Meraka INNOVATE Conference for Educators, CSIR,* Pretoria, South Africa. (p. 13).

Butgereit, L., & Botha, R. (2010, January 21–23). Dr Math moves to C3TO: Chatter call center/tutoring online. *Proceedings of the Technology for innovation and education in developing countries,* Mozambique.

Cass, M., Cates, M. & Smith, M. (2003). Effects of manipulative instruction on solving area and perimeter problems by students with learning disabilities. *Learning Disabilities Research & Practice, 18*(2), 112–120.

Clements, D. H. (1999). Concrete manipulatives, concrete ideas. *Contemporary Issues in Early Childhood, 1*(1), 45–60.

Csikszentmihalyi, M., & Hermanson, K. (1995). Intrinsic motivation in museums: Why does one want to learn? In E. Hooper-Greenhill (Ed.), *The educational role of the museum.* (pp.110–117). London: Routledge.

Department Of Education. (2002). *Revised national curriculum statement for grades R-9: mathematics.* Pretoria, South Africa: Department of Education.

Department of Education. (2004). *White paper on e-education: Transforming learning and teaching through information and communication technologies (ICTs).* Retrieved July 26, 2006, from http://www.info.gov.za/whitepapers/2003/e-education.pdf

Dey, A. K. 2001. Understanding and using context. *Personal and Ubiquitous Computing Journal, 5*(1), 4–7.

Duveskog, M., & Sutinen, E. (2009, June 22–26). Enriching student HIV stories by the use of technology. In G. S. C. Fulford (Ed.), *World conference on educational multimedia, hypermedia and telecommunications 2009. AACE.* (pp. 3885–3892). Chesapeake, VA.

EDAC Wowe. (2008). *Progress in reading literacy study*. Retrieved May 15, 2009, from http://www.edacwowe.eu/en/frmShowGIW_SES?v_id=14

Eschenbrenner, B., & Nah, F. F. (2007). Mobile technology in education: Uses and benefits. *International Journal of Mobile Learning and Organisation, 1*(2), 159–183.

Finland Promotion Board. (2010). *This is FINLAND*. [Online]. Retrieved April 17, 2010, from: http://finland.fi

Finnish National Board of Education. (2010). *Education*. Retrieved April 17, 2010, from http://www.oph.fi/english/education

Gonzales, P., Guzmán, J. C., Partelow, L., Pahlke, E., Jocelyn, L., Kastberg, D. et al. (2004). *Highlights from the trends in international mathematics and science study (TIMSS) 2003*. Retrieved February 2, 2009, from http://www.colorado.edu/physics/phys4810/phys4810_fa08/refs/TIMMS_2003.pdf

International Telecommunication Union. (2008). *ICT-Eye: Telecommuniation/ICT statistics*. Retrieved April 27, 2010, from http://www.itu.int/ITU-D/ict/statistics/

Islas Sedano, C., Laine, T. H., Vinni, M., & Sutinen, E. (2007, November 15–17). Where is the answer?—The importance of curiosity in pervasive mobile games. *Proceedings of the Future Play Conference*, Toronto, Canada. ACM Press.

Kamii, C., Lewis, B. A., & Kirkland, L. (2001). Manipulatives: When are they useful? *Journal of Mathematical Behavior, 20*(1), 21–31.

Kankaanranta, M., & Puhakka, E. (2008). *Kohti innovatiivista tietotekniikan opetuskäyttöä; Kansainvälisen SITES 2006 -tutkimuksen tuloksia (The results of an international SITES 2006 comparison)*: University of Jyväskylä: Institute for Educational Research.

Kirriemuir, J. & McFarlane, A. (2004). Literature review in *Games and Learning*. NESTA Futurelab Series.

Laine, T. H., Islas Sedano, C., Vinni, M., & Sutinen, E. (2009, July 15–17). Uncovering the richness of an authentic living museum through pervasive learning environment. *Proceedings of ICALT 2009*, Riga, Latvia.

Laine, T. H., Vinni, M., Islas Sedano, C., & Joy, M. (2010). On designing a pervasive mobile learning platform. *ALT-J Research in Learning Technology Journal 18*(1), 3–17.

Law, N., Pelgrum, W. J., & Plomp, T. (Eds.). (2008). *Pedagogy and ICT use in schools around the world: Findings from the IEA SITES 2006 Study* (p. 296), Hong Kong: Springer and Comparative Education Research Centre, Universities of Hong Kong.

Lyytinen, K., & Yoo, Y. (2002). Issues and Challenges in Ubiquitous Computing. *Communications of ACM, 45*(12).

Maccini, P., & Gagnon, J. C. (2000). Best practices for teaching mathematics to secondary students with special needs. *Focus on Exceptional Children, 32*(5), 1–22.

Matthee, M., & Liebenberg, J. (2007, October 16–19). Mathematics on the move: Supporting mathematics learners through mobile technology in South Africa. *Proceedings of the 6th International Conference on Mobile Learning (MLearn 2007)*, Melbourne, Australia.

Michael, D., & Chen, S. (2006). *Serious games: Games that educate, train and inform*. Boston: Thomson Course Technology.

Ministry of Education and Culture. (2010). *Finland and PISA*. Retrieved March 27, 2011, from http://www.minedu.fi/pisa/?lang=en

Naismith, L., Lonsdale, P., Vavoula, G., & Sharples, M. (2004). *Literature review in mobile technologies and learning*. NESTA Futurelab Series.

Nestler, S., Echtler, F., Dollinger, A., & Klinker, G. (2008, May 31). Collaborative problem solving on mobile hand-held devices and stationary multi-touch interfaces. *Proceedings of the PPD 2008, Workshop on Designing Multi-Touch Interaction Techniques for Coupled Public and Private Displays.* Naples, Italy.

OECD (2007). *PISA 2006: Science Competencies for Tomorrows World.* Paris: OECD. Retrieved March 27, 2011, from http://www.tuac.org/en/public/e-docs/00/00/01/66/document_doc.phtml

OECD (2010). *PISA 2009 Results: Executive Summary.* Retrieved March 27, 2011, from http://www.tuac.org/en/public/e-docs/00/00/07/FB/document_doc.phtml

Piaget, J. (1969). *The child's conception of number.* London: Routledge & Kegan Paul Ltd.

Raphael, D., & Wahlstrom, M. (1989). The influence of instructional aids on mathematics achievement. *Journal for Research in Mathematics Education, 20,* 173–190.

Reilly, M. (Ed.). (1974). *Play as exploratory learning.* Thousand Oaks, CA: Sage Publications.

Scudder, K. V., Uttal, D. H., & Deloacher, J. S. (1997). Manipulatives as symbols: A new perspective on the use of concrete objects to teach mathematics. *Journal of Applied Developmental Psychology, 18*(1), 37–54.

Shin, N., Norris, C., & Soloway, E. (2006, June 27–July 1). Effects of handheld games on students learning in mathematics. *Proceedings of the 7th International Conference on Learning Sciences,* Bloomington, Indiana: International Society of the Learning Sciences (pp. 702–708).

Smith, A.C. & Laine, T.H. (2011). An intelligent fractions learning system: Implementation. Proceedings of the IST Africa 2011 Conference, May 11–13, Gaborone, Botswana.

South Africa Info. (2010). September 2007. South Africa: Fast Facts. *Gateway to the Nation.* Retrieved May 3, 2010, from http://www.southafrica.info/about/facts.htm

Sowell, E. J. (1989). Effects of manipulative materials in mathematics instruction. *Journal for Research in Mathematics Education, 20*(5), 498–505.

Statistics Finland. (2010). *Population in Finland 2010.* Retrieved March 27, 2011, from http://www.stat.fi/tup/suoluk/suoluk_vaesto_en.html

Statistics South Africa. (2009). *Mid-year population estimates.* Retrieved April 27, 2010, from http://www.statssa.gov.za/PublicationsHTML/P03022009/html/P03022009.html

Suomela, R., Räsänen, E., Koivisto, A., & Mattila, J. (2004, September 1–3). Open-source game development with the multi-user publishing environment (MUPE) Application Platform. *Proceedings of the Entertainment Computing – ICEC 2004* (pp. 308–320). Springer Berlin/Heidelberg.

Sutinen, E. (2010). Technology for losers: Re-equipping the excluded. *IEEE Communications Magazine, 48*(2) 120–124.

Trifonova, A. (2003). *Mobile Learning–Review of the Literature.* Informatica e Telecomunicazioni, University of Trento, Italy.

Turtiainen, E., Blignaut, S., Els, C., Laine, T. H., & Sutinen, E. (2009, August 21). Story-based UFractions mobile game in South Africa: Contextualization process and multidimensional playing experiences. *Proceedings of the 2nd Inter-*

national Workshop on Story-Telling and Educational Games (STEG'09) Aachen, Germany.

Vesisenaho, M. (2007). *Developing university-level introductory ICT education in Tanzania: A contextual approach*: Doctoral Dissertation, University of Joensuu, Finland.

Weiser, M. (1991). The computer for the 21st century. *Scientific American*, 94–104.

ABOUT THE AUTHORS

Teemu H. Laine is a PhD candidate at the University of Eastern Finland. After receiving the MSc Degree in software engineering at the University of Joensuu in 2007, Laine has concentrated his doctoral research on pervasive and mobile learning applications, models, and platforms. His other research interests are ubiquitous computing, software architectures, wireless sensors, digital games, and ICT for development. Laine has published and co-authored over 20 academic articles.

Eeva Nygren is a PhD candidate at the University of Eastern Finland. Nygren received an MSc Degree in mathematics in 2003 and postgraduate degree (Licentiate of Philosophy) from the University of Joensuu in 2005. Since then, she has worked as a mathematics teacher and vice principle in the Evangelical Folk High School of Kitee, Finland. Her main research interests are integrating educational technology into teaching, educational games, and tutoring systems.

Mike Joy received an MA degree in mathematics from Cambridge University, an MA degree in postcompulsory education from the University of Warwick, and a PhD degree in computer science from the University of East Anglia. He is currently associate professor at the University of Warwick. His research interests focus on educational technology and computer science education.

Erkki Sutinen is a professor and the leader of the Educational Technology Research group at the University of Eastern Finland. His research interests include using technologies for clearly defined needs for complex subject domains like programming in developing countries and within special education. The applied techniques cover visualization, information retrieval, data mining, robotics, and design models. He has co-authored and published over 100 academic papers.

Carolina A. Islas Sedano is completing her PhD at the University of Eastern Finland. She received an MSc in Communication and Media Engineering at the University of Applied Science in Offenburg, Germany, and her BSc is in Electronic Engineering and Communication Systems from the University Iberoamericana in Mexico City. Her research interests are in the conceptualization, development, and implementation of games with a bottom-up approach, involving the specific environment that surrounds the game play to promote informal learning experiences.

Seugnet Blignaut is a research professor in the School of Continuing Teacher Education, the Faculty of Education Sciences of the North-West University, Potchefstroom Campus. Her teaching expertise relates to teaching and learning with technology, and her research focuses is on the interaction in virtual learning communities, as well as ICT for Development. Seugnet Blignaut's research reflects numerous national and international research outcomes, which include articles in accredited journals, book chapters, conference papers, as well as the supervision of various master's dissertations and doctoral theses. In 2007, Seugnet obtained an NRF research rating and currently acts as the leader of the newly founded Research Niche Area for Educational Technology for Effective Teaching, Learning and Facilitation at NWU.

CHAPTER 15

CASE STUDY

Using Flickr in Design Education

Diane Robbie and Lynette Zeeng

ABSTRACT

This chapter describes a case study using u-learning for teaching and learning, specifically in a photographic subject in the design discipline. It details the adoption of the Web 2.0 social technology—Flickr—as a teaching methodology. This innovative pedagogy has captured the enthusiasm of students and teachers alike. The approach has inspired student learning in first-year design discipline photography units resulting in collaborative communities of design practice and discourse. This case study identifies how a change in the millennial student's educational, institutional, social, and economic environment impact on learning and teaching practice. Embracing the digital age and its expediential growth has encouraged student interaction, motivation, and peer learning.

INTRODUCTION

The introduction of Web 2.0 has had a profound effect on teaching and learning largely due to its communication tools that promote interaction,

Ubiquitous Learning, pages 283–298

collaboration, and information sharing facilitating ubiquitous engagement in the global community (Gray, Thompson, Sheard, Clerehan, & Hamilton, 2010; McLoughlin & Lee 2010; New Media Consortium 2008). Web 2.0 technologies also address contemporary models of higher education, constructed on principles of experiential and social constructivist learning (Kolb, 1984; Vygotsky, 1978) where learning is not limited to the classroom and involves building on existing knowledge, active learning experiences, reflection on experiences, and interactions with others in a social context. Additionally, Tutty and Martin (2009) suggest three dimensions for consideration using Web 2.0: collaborative/social, user-generated design, and knowledge management, as playing a fundamental role in learning and teaching in higher education. This case study substantiates an example of how these principles and dimensions can be applied using the Web 2.0 social networking tool Flickr.

Preparing students with professional skills for the 21st-century workplace environment has motivated teachers to review the curriculum and become more innovative in their delivery and teaching approach. The transformation from teacher-centered approaches characterized by presentations and information transmission has seen an increase in collaboration, creativity, information sharing, analytical and critical thinking, communication, student empowerment, and peer-to-peer learning (Bellanca & Brandt, 2010; Fisher, Higgins, & Loveless, 2006; New Media Consortium, 2008).

In this case study, embedding Flickr as a scholarly device creates an academic platform motivating students through progressive, constructive, and recorded peer and teacher review in a visually intensive and dynamic supportive learning environment. Students can freely share design skills, knowledge, and technical data, and keep records of their learning tasks and teacher feedback. Using u-learning for teaching and learning enables more flexibility for students to participate within their group cohort anytime, anywhere. This participation is conducive to student collaborative social interactions, building their design knowledge within university and working schedules. It also alleviates the need for expensive printing and use of chemicals, creating a sustainable and cost-free environment advantageous to the cash-strapped and time-poor student. U-learning further provides students the ability to access computers and the Internet at their place and pace of choice, becoming an essential ingredient in their learning. Juxtaposed to this, the Internet and online technologies are part of their daily lives. U-learning is an effective teaching tool, accessible to a vast amount of knowledge within a global community. Students appreciate the connectivity and fast response in a social and cost-effective milieu.

The Impact of Social Networking Tools for Teaching and Learning

Web 2.0 applications like wikis and blogs are currently used extensively in educational environments, yet social networks such as Flickr have not been as prevalent (Quereshi & Olla, 2009). The authors' appraisal of the literature on Web 2.0 in higher education indicates that Flickr is being used predominantly by educators as a means for sharing images, with occasional comments, but not as a platform for delivery in a design education context.

Prior to the implementation of this social networking tool, the potential impact was explored from four distinct viewpoints: innovative design education, student engagement, new technologies, and social networking. Implementing Flickr in the design discipline addressed these viewpoints through the following questions:

- How can we be innovative in design education without the constraints of existing text-based learning systems?
- How can we harness new ways of teaching to engage first-year design students, who are predominately digitally literate, and be creative in our teaching without compromising existing effective strategies?
- How can we address the needs of design students in an ever-changing technological world where collaboration and communication are available anytime and anywhere?
- How can we tap into the social network world of the "Netizen," coined by Hauben (1995) without the stigma of the "creepy treehouse" as defined by Stein (2008), where students see teachers as intruders in their private online spaces?

BACKGROUND

Design education is traditionally studio-based, with emphasis on communication. Within the studio, teachers critically analyze students' concepts and suggest the most effective plan of action within the confines of designated class time. Students are instructed to "pin-up" their work for critique and feedback in a series of presentations and information sessions. The critique is central to design education. Dialogue between teachers and students on "drafts" provide opportunities for improved practice, with suggestions that execute effective creative and aesthetically positive outcomes. Feedback is a pivotal element of the studio classes, teaching students to critically analyze the design process, improving their fundamental technical skills.

Teaching the basic elements of photography in the design context involves lectures and studio classes. Similarly, students bring printed versions of weekly learning tasks (images taken) to class and receive and give verbal critiques and feedback from teacher and peers. The verbal feedback is time-consuming and can be nonproductive, with students having limited memory of what was said. In many cases, work submitted was not referred to again nor reviewed by either teacher or students. Work was often forgotten, lost, not collected, or dispensed with. Learning tasks not completed or poorly executed required resubmission and further attention by the student and teacher in subsequent classes. This resulted in increased printing-related costs for students, who are often technically inexperienced and poor in both cash and time. With the massification of education, cohorts are larger, with a more diverse student population. Shorter studio times leave less time for critical, important, and immediate feedback, particularly when work requires reediting and reprinting. The more reticent student, who may not actively participate in class discussion, is likely to receive less feedback than others.

The photographic subject described in this case study received good feedback and high student satisfaction levels prior to 2006. The changing demographic of first-year undergraduates to a more diverse, more e-connected, cash-strapped and time-poor student body impelled changes in the nature of teaching photography for design. The first-year student experience research by Krause, Hartley, James, and McInness (2005); Yorke and Longden (2008); and Kift (2009) advocated that peer learning; early, prompt, and constructive feedback; and regular and timely contact with staff are essential elements for student retention.

Social networking embraces an integral part of a students' daily life. Its immediacy, connectedness, and collaborative sharing of information in the global social networking community provide a foundation for rethinking and creating a renewed learning environment. Introducing a new pedagogy, with students able to submit their work online anytime, anywhere, allows for regular, immediate, and effective feedback from teachers and peers. A visual and written record of their work as well as feedback given and received is now maintained indefinitely on the private Web site for review and reflection. Embracing Web-based technology in design classes has not only manifested stronger student involvement but has assisted in the achievement of substantially improved student outcomes.

Case Study: Photography in Design

In 2006, the potential of Web 2.0 educational technologies to enhance student learning was first explored by the authors (Robbie & Zeeng, 2008a). The social networking tool, Flickr, offered image exchange, collaboration, critical and analytical thinking, feedback of the visual image, and global perspectives. Flickr was chosen because it has a strong visual interface, supports interactive, collaboration, provides essential tools for 21st-century design students, and augments the critiquing capability in a virtual community of practice. The Flickr classroom enriches the learning and teaching environment and addresses the core elements of design education and supports first-year-experience research. The creation of the virtual learning classroom where students can collaboratively and independently build their knowledge and skills empowers learning.

Even in the course of teaching photography with new pedagogy, students still receive a basic photographic education in design. Students attend a 1-hour intensive weekly lecture, which describes and exemplifies photographic techniques and genres. Students also attend 2-hour studio classes where information discussed in the lecture is reinforced through a variety of learning activities. Students undertake practical application of the technical knowledge and further discuss expectations of the set tasks.

Completed student tasks are uploaded using Flickr. Once uploaded, the entire cohort of students and teachers can then critique and analyze student work. Assessment tasks require students to make three comments/critiques per week on the work of their peers. Students are encouraged to choose a variety of images, each from a different student and preferably images from students who are not in their studio classes. This increases their scope of potential inspiration, improves their critical and analytical skills, and makes them part of a broader community. They are expected to give constructive criticism, reflecting on the technical and aesthetic qualities of the image.

Implementing Flickr

Despite most students being computer literate, it was important to provide the skills for navigating through Flickr without compromising the teaching of photography. Well-planned teaching sessions and learning activities with explicit guidelines were developed. These were necessary in order to make the interactions and engagement with the lectures, studios, and online activities work successfully. Initially, students were guided in getting started, both with their cameras and setting up online sites, and in the procedures for undertaking out-of-class activities in face-to-face studio classes. These were supplemented by written instructions in the subject's Blackboard site, the learning management system used to access materials and resources. Flickr was used for uploading, discussing, and critiquing images. Studio time was then used to review and discuss students' images, critiques, and implement further photographic skills. As weekly tasks were completed and submitted in Flickr, the teachers reviewed and commented on students' work from technical and creative viewpoints. The teachers

1. Studio class learning activities

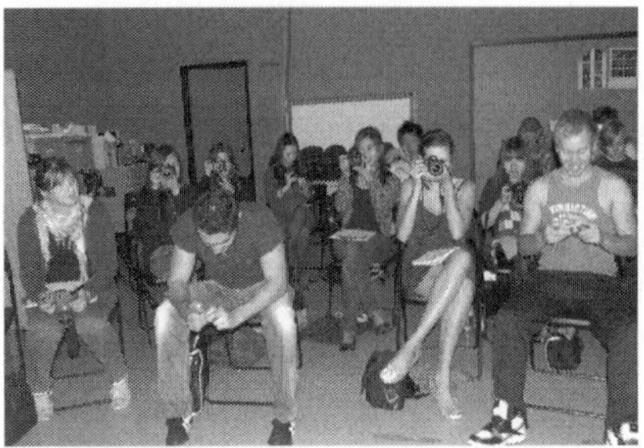

2. Practical application

3. Image uploaded to Flickr

4. Image sharing critique and feedback

Figure 15.1 The process.

contributed to student-generated discussion forums and communicated personally by private e-mail as needed.

By the end of the semester, the teachers had commented on the work of every student in studio classes and online. Not only did weekly critiquing by teachers and students provide immediate feedback, but it also assisted in keeping track of student performance. Figure 15.1 shows the process from studio class activities to practical application, and then image sharing and critique in Flickr.

Flickr Features

Adopting Flickr underpins the framework for design education facilitated by visual displays of work and active learning. Teacher feedback focuses on the technical, academic, and professional skills required to achieve proficient outcomes. Students receive feedback from teachers or peers on a

TABLE 15.1 Benefits of Using Flickr for Design Education

Teaching the Digital Student	What Flickr Web 2.0 Technology Provided
Strong visual orientation	• sharing of uploaded images • restricts amount of images, eliminating ill-considered image production • tags images, giving the teachers and students direct access to categories • metadata in the shooting process provides information on image quantity, quality, and time of uploading
Active learning and student centerdness	• opportunities for peer learning • ability to critique and analyze others and self • interaction between students • ownership of discussion forums • new topics can be posted or added to by anyone within the group • private and public communication
Engaging and supporting students	• use of social networks • commenting on any photograph by students and teachers • confidence through online voice for more reticent students • availability of 8 languages supported international students • constant and costly need for printing eliminated
Flexibility	• anytime, anywhere access • convenience without being restricted to timetabled class times. • immediacy of feedback
Sense of community	• accounts created within a private teaching space • student profiles showing name and portrait • identity, not anonymity • interaction across whole student cohort • exposure to a global society

Source: Robbie & Zeeng, 2008b

very regular basis, sometimes as soon as images are posted. Table 15.1 shows the benefits of using Flickr, which supports concepts instrumental in teaching photography in design.

Setting up the Flickr Classroom

1. The teacher creates a private Flickr group for the cohort of enrolled students and students ask to join.
2. Like on all social networks, students create their personal domain in Flickr. They then join the private Flickr group and upload a self-portrait as indicated in Figure 15.2.

   Whenever they interact within the group, add photographs, comment, or participate in discussions, their identity is included, eliminating anonymity in the large cohort of students. This sense of

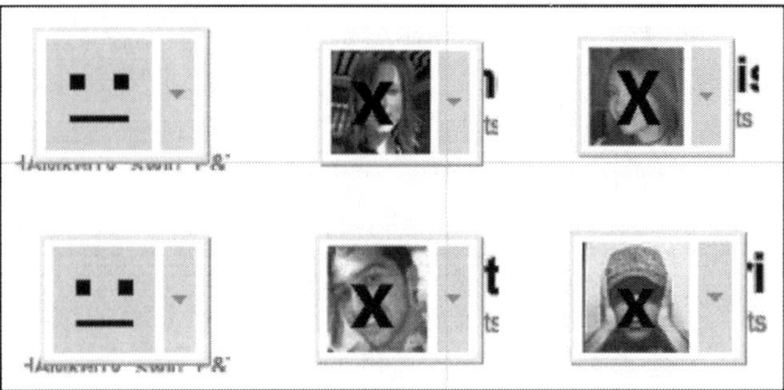

Figure 15.2 Student account.

belonging, an important part of the social network "connectedness" phenomena that students so readily engage in, is a vital component for participation in the subject.

3. Learning tasks are scaffolded on a weekly basis, building on photographic concepts discussed and practiced during studio sessions. Students' photographic resolutions to the task become part of a "pool" of images accessible to all students and teachers in the subject, not just in their smaller class groups. This approach has aided the learning potential of the cohort and allows for better understanding and broadening of their learning capacity. Figure 15.3 shows one example of a pool.
4. When submitted, students' work is displayed online for personal analysis and peer-to-peer critique, as shown in Figure 15.1. Students are encouraged to write brief critiques on a variety of images (a minimum of three per week), to make informed observations or constructive criticism, based on what they had learned about creative photography.
5. Students create a set of edited images for each specific task for the teacher to appraise. Once complete, the teacher comments on this work, and students can then review and revise their work (see Figure 15.4).
6. The gallery of best practice images (see Figure 15.5) is collated from the entire cohort of more than 240 on the teacher's site for further review by all students.
7. Discussions on Flickr form an important part of the program. Students or teachers may start a discussion on any topic. Students can seek help, make suggestions, or explore other photographic related topics. The discussions shown in Figure 15.6 further expand the curriculum, creating a lifelong learning arena.
8. At the conclusion of the semester, all students are expected to have posted a minimum of 100 images and made 33 comments on other

Figure 15.3 "Pool" of all student images.

A set created for appraisal.

The talk bubble icon shows that image has been commented on.

Figure 15.4 A completed task with a set of images for appraisal.

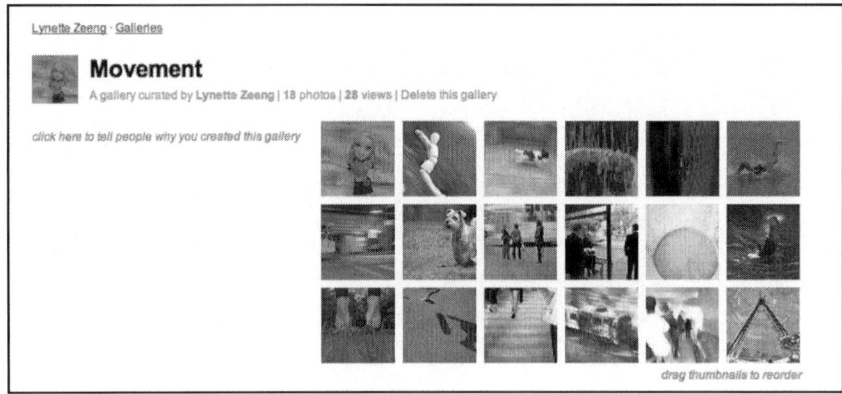

Figure 15.5 Gallery of best practice images.

Figure 15.6 Example of discussion topics.

students' work. They are also encouraged to contribute to at least one discussion. Being design students, they are asked to consider skills taught in other design classes, the application of photography in relation to other mediums, and design principles. All elements of design must be considered in the creation of their photographs.

Outcomes and Challenges of Flickr

Flickr has now been used successfully for 4 years in teaching photography to design students. This approach has contributed to large cohorts (240+)

of first-year students from design disciplines being motivated and inspired to learn.

Evaluation of this Web-based approach has highlighted the importance and acceptance of immediate, regular, and constructive feedback in the social network environment. This has manifested in stronger student involvement than previously and led to substantially higher levels of student satisfaction, as evidenced by student feedback surveys. Students have commented on the interactive and collaborative sharing of ideas, knowledge, and tasks as being key to their improved learning outcomes.

The affordances of Flickr have also offered unparalleled support for teachers who are able to observe discussions and interject professional judgment and knowledge as students engage in continual dialogue regarding photographic techniques and topics beyond the curriculum.

Additional feedback is given as technique improves and tasks become more difficult to resolve. Students' present performance is compared with their prior performance and assists in raising levels of confidence and aesthetic and technical competence. The students' complete body of work remains online where it can be referred to at anytime during the semester. This is vital in order to reflect on progressive improvement or resolving continuing problems, which all lead to better learning. Students can contact the teacher or each other for further clarification or direction, and use the discussion area to post questions or references, which is beneficial in resolving problems, assisting learning, and expanding their photographic knowledge.

This model has addressed a problem with digital photography where unlimited image capture can lead to indiscriminate shooting. Flickr restricts image number and size, forcing students to carefully consider composition and technique, which ultimately was time and effort, prior to submitting work for critique and assessment. This has facilitated the reinforcement of areas of the curriculum requiring students to begin personal critiquing and editing methods considering how, what, and why they were creating their work prior to submission. Through regular feedback and critiquing of images and creative processes, student learning has been stimulated. It has improved their skills through continual encouragement and support from teachers and peers. Students can also access a global community of experts promoting a large scope of creative influences and inspirations. The ability to be translated into other languages (currently eight) allows students to work in languages other than English, appealing to many of a diverse student cohort. Not only have students expressed high satisfaction levels of engagement, motivation, and curiosity in their learning but also improved skill level and application with increased confidence in taking photos, more creative use of the camera, and improved photographic skills.

The overall student learning experience has improved, providing students with a model that has captured their enthusiasm to exchange, review, and critique each others' work in a learning environment, which meets their desire for flexibility, networking, time and mode of access, and economic restraint. The flexibility of the online community has been instrumental in generating enthusiasm, establishing effective visual and analytical skills. This social dynamic has created a learning experience based on enjoyment and discovery of photography in the design disciplines.

Impact of Social Networking on Teaching, Student Motivation, and Learning Outcomes

Revisiting the four viewpoints considered prior to the implementation of Flickr, the impact on social networks for teaching and learning is evidenced through student feedback within classes and in universitywide surveys. This innovation in design education has been recognized by the faculty, university, and wider community. In 2009, photography received the highest aggregate student satisfaction level in the Faculty of Design, an Australian Learning and Teaching Council (ALTC) Award for Outstanding Contribution to Student Learning, invitations to present at conferences, and partnerships with local and international universities.

Students have responded positively to the dynamic interaction and immediate feedback with peers and teachers, keenly accepting this innovative teaching pedagogy as per the examples of student comments below.

> I think that this is a great way to learn. I could spend hours on here looking at everyone's photos. Because of Flickr, where we can access anyone's photos at any time, I'm learning from the people who are more advanced. Comments are always helpful because I'm getting feedback from someone else's perspective and they will notice things about the photo that I won't. (Student on Flickr Discussion Forum, 2009)

> It's a great way to view everyone's work, serving as a source of inspiration and provoking thought. I am always curious to see the variety of work being produced in Comm Design, but there are rarely opportunities to see pieces. From other people's ideas, thoughts, and criticisms I have been able to consider more in photography than I would've alone or by chance. (Student on Flickr Discussion Forum, 2007)

As indicated in the following comments, teachers have been encouraged and inspired by the students' engagement in the photographic community and the benefits associated with the online anywhere, anytime environment.

> As a sessional this is great as I can comment on the work almost daily. I can open the page to anyone's work at anytime and give them some feedback (Sessional teacher A, 2008)

> I can see all the metadata I need at any time that helps the students improve their skills and me to see how and when they are working. I no longer have to carry piles of photos, instead like the students I can work anywhere, anytime. As a sessional I can schedule my industry practice and teaching commitments. (Sessional teacher B, 2008)

Through their own self-evaluations, students have stated how their skills have continued to improve using the Flickr environment.

> At the beginning of this class all I did was point and shoot but now I focus, think... rethink, change balances consider all conditions and place and then maybe shoot... just maybe. There is no such thing as auto any more! (Online survey, 2007)

> I'm now able to compose much more dynamic and interesting images. (Online survey, 2007)

> I'd [sic] never been using my camera to the full potential before and the way the subjects [sic] been taught has helped me immensely [sic]. (Online survey, 2008)

> Its good uploading and commenting and all that in your own time and at your own pace. Getting comments and writing your own is a great way to improve your own photography and compare it with others.' (Online survey, 2007)

Students have responded positively to Flickr as a learning environment, for its environmental considerations and the recognition of them as having different needs and learning styles, as indicated in the following comments.

> No messing around with paper. Its clean, fast and easy, and saves money on printing costs each week!!!! (Student in Flickr Discussion Forum, 2008)

> Being a poorly uni student free = good so i think using flickr is an excellent choice because its free, easy to use and obviusly a popular site. Classes have been fun and informative too. (Student in Flickr Discussion Forum, 2009)

The "creepy treehouse" stigma has not been an issue, as students have willingly engaged in the Flickr community as a learning space, connecting with teachers, peers, and information in a global world.

CONCLUSION

This chapter showcases an example of implementing a social networking tool to enrich the design curriculum effectively with benefits for both teachers and students. Flickr has provided a visual environment essential in design education that has been significantly overlooked in many existing Web 1.0 text-based learning systems. The model adopted has now been expanded through partnerships with universities, internationally creating a global experience for teachers and students. Student learning activities are designed for various cohorts who now share the Flickr learning space created. The success of the model has also been instrumental in demonstrating and sharing across the university, leading to transferability to other design education disciplines.

While the photographic education principles remain the same, the introduction of Flickr has considered the digital technology age, the digital camera, the digitally aware student, and the diverse student demographic, and demonstrates a unique and effective model of student-centered learning (Biggs & Tang, 2007). The shift in teaching methodology from teacher- to student-centered, and the enhancement to improving critique and feedback have been a fundamental aspect of this new paradigm. Through ongoing evaluation, the new construct has contributed to cohorts of large groups of first-year design students being more motivated and inspired to learn.

ACKNOWLEDGEMENTS

The authors wish to acknowledge the students for their valued feedback and contributions

REFERENCES

Bellanca, J., & Brandt, R. (2010). *21st CENTURY Skills: Rethinking how students learn* (Leading Edge, Kindle Edition). Solution Tree Press.

Biggs, J., & Tang, C. (2007). *Teaching for quality learning at university: What the student does.* Maidenhead, UK: McGraw-Hill/Society for Research into Higher Education & Open University Press.

Fisher, T., Higgins, C., & Loveless, A. (2006). *Teachers learning with digital technologies: A review of research and project.* Future Lab Report 14. Bristol, UK: Future Lab.

Gray, K., Thompson, C., Sheard, J., Clerehan, R., & Hamilton, M. (2010). Students as Web 2.0 authors: Implications for assessment design and conduct. *Australasian Journal of Educational Technology, 26*(1), 105–122.

Hauben M. (1995). *Netizens: On the History and impact of Usenet and the Internet.* Retrieved April 2011, from http://www.columbia.edu/~hauben/netbook/

Kift, S. (2009). *Articulating a transition pedagogy: The first year experience and curriculum design.* Unpublished invited presentation, Swinburne University, Melbourne, Australia.

Krause, K., Hartley, R., James, R., & McInnis, C. (2005). *The first year experience in Australian universities: Findings from a decade of national studies.* Centre for Studies in Higher Education (CHSE), University of Melbourne.

Kolb, D. (1984). *Experiential learning.* Englewood Cliffs, NJ: Prentice Hall.

McLoughlin, C., & Lee, M. (2010). Personalised and self regulated learning in the Web 2.0 era: International exemplars of innovative pedagogy using social software. *Australasian Journal of Educational Technology, 26*(1), 28–43.

New Media Consortium. (2008). *The Horizon report: 2008 edition.* Austin, TX: New Media Consortium.

Quereshi E., & Olla, P. (2009). Incorporating Web 2.0 into education: Instructional design and pedagogical issues. In T. Kidd & I. Chen (Eds.), *Wired for learning: An educator's guide to Web 2.0* (pp.43–58). Charlotte, NC: Information Age Publishing.

Robbie, D., & Zeeng, L. (2008a). IT's evolving, they're changing, we're listening: Everybody's learning. In *Hello! Where are you in the landscape of educational technology? Proceedings of ascilite Melbourne, 2008.* Retrieved April 2011, from http// www.ascilite.org.au/conferences/melbourne08/procs/robbie.pdf

Robbie, D., & Zeeng, L. (2008b). Engaging student social networks to motivate learning: Capturing, analysing and critiquing visual image. *International Journal of Learning, 15.*

Stein, J. (2008). Defining "creepy treehouse." *Flexknowlogy.* (blog) Retrieved April 2011, from http://flexknowlogy.learningfield.org/2008/04/09/defining-creepy-tree-house/

Tutty, J., & Martin, F. (2009). User generated design: Teaching and learning with Web 2.0. In T. Kidd & I. Chen (Eds.), *Wired for learning: An educator's guide to Web 2.0* (pp.43–58). Charlotte, NC: Information Age Publishing.

Yorke, M., & Longden, B. (2008). *The first-year experience of higher education in the UK: Final report.* The Higher Education Academy.

Vygotsky, L. (1978). *Mind in society.* Cambridge, MA: Harvard University Press.

ABOUT THE AUTHORS

Diane Robbie is an academic developer in the Faculty of Design and Program Coordinator and teacher in the Graduate Certificate in Learning and Teaching (Higher Education) in Swinburne Professional Learning. She provides academic leadership in curriculum design, development, and improvement initiatives; reflective practice, inquiry and scholarship of learning, and teaching; and university-wide and faculty-based professional development. Diane collaborates with teaching staff to implement innovative teaching practices aimed at enhancing the student learning experience. Her research interests include exploring models of academic professional development, reflective scholarly practice in higher education, and innovative learning and teaching using educational technologies.

Lynette Zeeng is an experienced photographer and lecturer in the Communications Design Program. She obtained a Master of Arts (Visual Communication) from RMIT University. She is Program Coordinator of Communication Design in the Faculty of Design. and teaches students from a wide range of design disciplines including communication design, film and television, and multimedia. Lynette is involved in extensive research related to Web-based learning and its use in higher education. Her work in this area has been presented at education conferences both in Australia and overseas. She has received two teaching awards for her endeavors.

CHAPTER 16

GLOBAL PERSPECTIVES OF U-LEARNING

Dallas McPheeters

ABSTRACT

The trends for integrating technology in education point in the same direction around the world. However, the driving forces affecting those trends differ within each region, nation, and culture. Despite this complexity, the localized goal of each country remains the same; to ensure its constituents are globally competitive in order to maintain each country's fair share of global resources. But how can localized goals be reached without sacrificing global needs; and vice versa? Ubiquitous learning (u-learning) is a critical component needed to solve this complex puzzle because it offers the potential to flatten the dominant-versus-subordinate differences between economic regions. However, a global solution requires a global perspective, which has yet to congeal around a unified framework of understanding. This chapter explores the complexity that exists among the multitudinous perspectives toward education and identifies principle forces that affect the formation of a framework for unifying global perspectives of u-learning.

Ubiquitous Learning, pages 299–316

INTRODUCTION

Concerning our ability to know the past, the present, and the future of human experience, it is the *future* that is fundamentally unknown. Nevertheless, the human brain is able to contemplate the future. By anticipating possible outcomes of present actions based on past experiences, the human brain is able to predict future events with a certain degree of accuracy. When a pattern of changes is observed, we label it a *trend*. Researchers analyze the interplay between driving forces affecting trends and predict the most likely outcomes. This chapter examines how localized driving forces within both developed and developing nations can affect global trends toward ubiquitous learning. Ubiquitous Learning (u-learning) is approached differently by develop*ed* nations versus develop*ing* nations, despite the 10 driving forces that all nations face.

These 10 driving forces comprise Economic, Population, Societal, Labor, Family, Energy, Environmental, Terrorism, Institutional, and Technology developments (Cetron & Davies, 2010). These 10 forces, multiplied by the approximate number of countries on the planet today, create fertile soil for the interplay of conflicting pressures needed to drive u-learning innovation in innumerable directions by a factor of 195^{10}. We can simplify this factor by aggregating the countries according to the International Monetary Fund's (IMF) nine economic regions as follows: the United States and Canada, Western Europe, Industrial Asia, Emerging Asia, Latin America, Emerging Europe, Commonwealth of Independent States, Sub-Saharan Africa, and the Middle East. This simplification reduces the number of possible combinations of interacting forces to a factor of 9^{10}, still leaving more than 3 billion possible combinations of interplay at work.

Despite this complexity of forces, trends, and regions, the localized goal of each country remains the same; to ensure its constituents are globally competitive in order to maintain each country's fair share of global resources. So u-learning is a critical component needed to solve this complex puzzle because it offers the potential to flatten the dominant-versus-subordinate differences between economic regions. However, a global solution requires a global perspective, which has yet to congeal around a unified framework of understanding. This chapter explores the complexity that exists among the multitudinous perspectives toward education and technology integration therein. Also identified are the principle forces that affect the formation of a framework for unifying global perspectives of u-learning.

A clear understanding of the complexity of local driving forces affecting global trends will enable the reader to better appreciate the need for educators to impart a shared sense of values common to us all, regardless of our cultural heritage. Equally important, the reader of this chapter will better understand the need for future learning platforms to "model and facilitate the development of a shared cultural understanding and involvement in global issues through the use of contemporary communication and collaboration tools" (International Society for Technology in Education, 2009).

HISTORIC BACKGROUND

Since the time of early hunter-gatherer groups, human cultures have formed around available resources (Tattersoll, 1998). Hunter-gatherers migrated together *with* the animal herds they hunted. As societies grew more complex—due to factors such as the increase in populations, or tool and weapon innovations—specialization within societal roles emerged as well. First, increased complexity allowed hunting tasks to be assigned to a few rather than to all. This stratification of tasks can be likened to our present-day practice of assigning and promoting individuals based on their observed skills and abilities. Stratification allows the streamlining of group efforts by enabling individuals to focus on tasks for which they are particularly suited. Second, domestication of herds and crops evolved, thus simplifying an otherwise migratory lifestyle to a more sedentary one. Humans are social creatures and need to communicate. Travel for migration was no longer required, but this did not eliminate the need for travel altogether. Instead, as innovation grew, the purpose for travel was transformed from one of necessity to one of commerce and trade.

Thus, communities formed around resources and thrived by trading those resources with neighboring communities. This interaction served to increase complexity among community members as individual roles became more specialized. This cycle of development continued according to resource supply and community demand. However, supply and demand added pressures from more sides than merely supply *or* demand. In other words, development pressures were not simply a two-sided tug-of-war. For example, tribal conflict occurred as a result of pressure from forces outside the control of the community. Pressures from the population growth of domesticated herds increased the demand for grazing resources. Hence, the eventual encroachment on territory occupied by a neighboring community resulted in conflict. This conflict provided pressure to innovate protective technologies such as walls, barriers, and better weapons of defense. One cycle—human culture development—affected another cycle—technology innovation—which in turn increased specialization of assigned roles within each community. Technology innovations that ease demand and/or introduce new supplies, create paradigm shifts in our underlying assumptions about societal practices.

As an aside, it's important to note that paradigm shifts historically occur when supply limitations are met by rising demands, which produce the pressure needed to cause breakthrough research (Kurzweil, 2003). Following are some examples of such breakthroughs. Since whale oil was a principal supply for household oil lamps, 19th-century populations expected a forthcoming dark age as whale populations declined. Unexpectedly, the harnessing of electric powered lighting arrived just in time to avert the presumed imminent disaster. Another more recent example was the petroleum shortage of the early 1970s. The world's supply of petroleum was expected to be depleted within 25 years. Two innovations enabled the remaining supply to extend another 150 years; the ability to drill down below the Earth's surface twice as deep, and the introduction of more fuel efficient automobiles via the fuel injected engine (Pilzer, 1990).

In further support of our brief aside, many of us may recall a number of failed technology predictions such as Thomas Edison's claim that no one would ever use alternating current; or 20th Century Fox producer Daryl Zanuck predicting in 1946 that television would never capture the market because people would soon tire of staring at a plywood box every night (Failed Technology Predictions, 2007). Such naïve claims were based on the notion that what *exists* will be an ever-sufficient resource without regard for unexpected changes in demand.

Returning now to our historic narrative, as centuries passed, some cultures innovated more rapidly than others, and rapid modernization increased the need for additional resources to meet rising demands. Such modernization introduced colonization as a new way to harvest a neighboring country's resources. During this *colonial* period, for example, Europe's demand for salt and sugar motivated expansion to the Caribbean, where such resources could be harvested in abundance (Michener, 1989). Subsequently, slave labor was needed to mine the salt fields and work the sugar plantations. Protecting these valued resources required naval protection from piracy. Military protection added to the cost of supply. Conflicts ensued between the French, the English, and the Dutch as each nation fought to control the limited supply in order to profit from the growing demand. The ebb and flow of scarcity and abundance served to maintain the disparity between the *haves* and the *have-nots.* Nevertheless, innovation continued. The *haves* innovated to ease their role of dominance, while the *have-nots* innovated to ease their role of servitude.

Colonial innovations opened the door to the Industrial Age as populations moved from the fields of agriculture to the factories of the big cities. Automating human labor seemed the ideal way to reduce the pain of the poor while increasing resources for the many. However, the factories needed workers with new skills. Public education was invented to supply skilled workers to factories. Empirical knowledge was the base of education (Anglin, 1991). Prior to the Industrial Age, education involved teaching the younger generation the skills and values it should possess in order to survive and thrive. Individual apprenticeship has been the model for education as far back as 4th century BC China. However, the newly industrialized world required a mass-produced workforce. Therefore, education was systematized to meet this demand. Public education developed according to the new Industrial Age model. Rather than training individuals, public education sought new ways to mass produce workers for the Industrial Age. The new public education model used a standardized rather than individualized approach. Standardization was the goal of innovation during the Industrial Revolution. Machines were designed to *replicate* physical labor. Machines became larger, materials were made stronger, and output was more powerful, thus replacing human labor with more efficient machine labor.

A parallel exists between the Industrial Revolution of the past century and the technology revolution of the present. Technological innovation is designed to replicate the *mental* muscle of mankind just as the Industrial Age replicated the physical. Therefore, just as machines became larger and more powerful (more horsepower, more wattage, more speed), computer chips have become smaller and more nimble, enabling the simplest devices to manage billions of bits of data per second. Such data management speeds sound impressive, though it should be understood that present computer microprocessor speeds are closer to that of an insect's brain than that of a human brain (Kurzweil, 2006). Nevertheless, the computer's *precision* while organizing, storing, and retrieving information exceeds that of the human brain, and processing speeds are expected to match those of the human brain by 2025.

The goal of industrial standardization did not change with the technology revolution. However, advances in technology are affording society the power to personalize supply according to individual demand. Consequently, as industrial innovation saved the time human *labor* spent doing mundane, repetitive tasks (assembly-line work, etc.) in the same way, technological innovation is saving the time human *minds* spend on repetitive tasks (sorting, ranking, storing, searching, retrieving, etc.). And education serves to ensure the next generation will be able to maximize the advantages of emerging technological trends for the common good by empowering individuals according to their uniquely identified needs.

In keeping with this brief history, increase in production has been afforded by the electromechanical machines on behalf of the electrochemical humans. And all remains well so long as the end result is the necessary increase in consumable goods produced by the machines and required by the growing demand of the humans. Yet many unpredictable events can drastically change the direction and intensity of the driving forces affecting supply and demand. In times of abundance, we tend to focus on supply-side management: the distribution of resources. In times of scarcity, we tend to focus on demand-side management: the conservation of resources.

Pressure to innovate occurs when limits are reached on either side of the supply-versus-demand equation (Kruzweil, 2006). Thus, in a world where technology is eliminating many of the traditional space-time barriers of past centuries, the pressures that build in one region of the world more easily spill over to affect neighboring regions, further complicating the interplay of forces already at work.

For example, economic woes in the United States are forcing a burgeoning population of retirees to consider migrating to developing nations that offer a lower cost of living. If this trend continues, another 1 million retirees will move to developing nations, and their retirement income will be spent abroad rather than at home, further hindering recovery at home, while at the same time, becoming a boon to their newly adopted (and developing) retirement community. Such complexity of trends can be driven by economic fluctuations, as just illustrated, or by other forces such as terrorist attacks, natural disasters, trade legislation, and the like.

PREDOMINANT PERSPECTIVES BETWEEN DEVELOPED AND DEVELOPING NATIONS

Both developed and developing nations have their own context-specific perspectives (Preece, 2009), which this chapter addresses. However, it is increasingly difficult to label nations as *either* developed or developing because there is no consensus on what standards to measure. During the Cold War, nations considered developed were industrialized and exhibited economic and political stability. The post–Cold War NATO Treaty used the terms First, Second, and Third World to categorize nations as either industrialized, capitalist, democratic (First World), or communist-socialist (Second World), or neither (Third World). Global North and Global South are commonly used more recently to divide the wealthy developed countries from the poorer countries. The terms are not used geographically but socioeconomically and politically. Geographers generally use the labels MDC and LDC to identify More Developed Countries and Least Developed Countries. This chapter uses the terms *developed* and *developing* with the understanding that there are no universally agreed-upon standards by which countries are grouped.

The *developing* label presupposes a nation will become *developed*, generally through increased industrialization and the benefits of improved health and mobility such increase brings. However, it's interesting to note that broadband Internet use is appearing in many countries labeled *developing*, enabling those countries to advance while bypassing the assumed industrialization stages expected by the *developed* world. Asia is an example of this phenomenon of experiencing a booming economy through adoption of new technologies while bypassing older technology infrastructures altogether.

Developed nations tend to view trends and driving forces from an inside-out perspective. That is to say, they possess a dominant view that seems to state, "We innovate new technologies, therefore we own them and need to maintain control of them to remain competitive." On the other hand, *developing* nations tend to portray an outside-in perspective that says, in effect, "We don't have the newest innovations that we need to stay competitive. How can we access them in order to benefit?"

These predominant perspectives affect how a nation addresses its education needs. Both *developed* and *developing* nations wish to be sufficiently competitive to ensure their fair share of global resources. Both *developed* and *developing* nations value innovation as a means to ease their primary role within global society, whether dominant or subordinate. Yet the motives, the driving forces behind each perspective, are very different, and the outcomes *maintain* the socioeconomic disparities that exist today rather than eliminate them.

Another example of the conflict that differing perspectives can bring to the same driving force can be seen in the present sanctions imposed on Iran while they strive to join the nuclear-powered nations and achieve a globally competitive *developed* status. Iran is a modern country with a large, thriving youth culture and major universities lacking in nothing concerning mainstream, global educational offerings. However, imagine the complexity of tensions between various driving forces both inside and outside of Iran. Terrorism is a new part of today's global equation, with fear driving some nations to sanction against other nations. Such actions put unexpected economic pressures on families within those sanctioned countries who want their children to be educated and remain competitive within the global workforce. Thus, the pressures of sanctions from outside Iran have a ripple affect causing additional societal pressures inside Iran. This is one example of the difficult challenge before those seeking to provide ubiquitous learning solutions. No single solution can resolve the needs of every nation when global perspectives are divided. Rather, custom-tailored solutions are needed, which address the local needs, yet do so in light of a mutually shared global framework.

BARRIERS TO U-LEARNING: STRUCTURAL AND IDEOLOGICAL

The complexities afforded by multiple driving forces between differing perspectives impede the progress of u-learning. Next, we address structural and ideological barriers to u-learning. Research has identified a dozen common barriers to technology integration in education (Lumley & Bailey,

1993; Muilenberg & Berge, 2001). First, we begin with the obvious barriers, then proceed to the more subtle, hidden barriers.

The typical list of barriers to ubiquitous learning comprise computer hardware, application software, and broadband infrastructure. Computer hardware costs money. Application software must be updated, which in turn, requires upgraded hardware to meet the performance specifications of the software. Today's computer hardware *and* application software require broadband infrastructure to deliver the bandwidth upon which the newer technologies depend. It's interesting to note that both *developed* and *developing* countries struggle to overcome these three barriers, but for different reasons.

Again, we should not expect *developing* regions to follow the same linear pattern of industrial development experienced in the already *developed* countries. For example, in the United States, mainstream adoption of the telephone took approximately 70 years. The Internet took only 40 years to be adopted nationwide. Mobile phones required less than 10 years for mainstream adoption. This historic trend line is quite accelerated in the *developing* countries. When it comes to technology, *developing* countries are typically late adopters due to economic reasons, but fast adapters once a new technology is acquired. Even some transitional technologies are skipped altogether, such as landline telephones being bypassed for immediate broadband Internet access development.

Many *developing* countries today have adopted widespread usage of mobile technologies without fully integrating a landline predecessor. Infrastructure in *developing* countries prohibited the cost of adding physical telephone poles and hardwire across huge areas of undeveloped jungle, forest, and tundra, for example. However, microwave towers cost less to install, considering alternate technologies, such as transportation and computerization. Russia, Africa, and Haiti are just a few examples of the rapid adoption of mobile technologies over land-based technologies within *developing* countries.

Although mobile technologies have appeared in *developed* countries as a luxury at first, *developing* countries *require* mobile technology in advancing social services, such as health care and education. Many mobile technology manufacturers are working on solutions to the socioeconomic barriers preventing *developing* nations from widespread adoption of emerging technologies. Large organizations such as One Laptop Per Child (OLPC) have afforded innovation pressures seeking to produce laptop computers for under $100 or smartphones for under $12. The largest manufacturer of Windows mobile-enabled handsets in the world, High Tech Computer (HTC), has adopted the proposition that *developing* nations will primarily access the Internet via mobile handheld devices. *PC World* reported the following quote from HTC's CEO Peter Chou, during an interview (Nystedt,

2008), "We believe that going forward, this device [mobile phone] will be the main Internet device for the emerging market."

Bill Gates has announced, on a number of occasions, his firm belief that smartphones will be the principle computing device used by the poor for accessing the Internet. Nokia's chief echoed this conviction in a public speech given in January 2010. Intel announced in April of 2010 their "rugged" personal computer designed for the harsher environments encountered in developing countries. A quick Google search reveals pages of similar headlines announcing technology developments designed with the poorer nations in mind. The wheels of development are in motion, with a sharp focus on delivering affordable Internet access to developing countries to ensure their equal participation in the digital age.

Nevertheless, access to computer hardware, application software, and broadband infrastructure comprise only a few of the barriers to the global adoption of u-learning. Additional barriers remain and are detailed next and summarized in Table 16.1.

Lack of Expertise

One of the internal barriers nations face when it comes to preparing for ubiquitous learning is the lack of expertise needed to take advantage of emerging innovations in education. Teachers require an up-to-date understanding of how technology can be incorporated into the learning process. The lack of expertise within developing nations is a primary structural barrier. Due to lack of technology know-how, professional development focusing on technology integration is urgently needed. Consequently, many developing nations send students to the universities of developed nations for education. According to the Institute of International Education (2010), the United States enrolled nearly 700,000 students from abroad during the 2008–2009 academic year. Thus, needed expertise among developing nations is gradually being filled by training, which is provided in developed nations.

Consider the complex pressures this has caused globally. The former CEO of Intel, Craig Barrett (2008), speaking at the Aspen Institute, lamented that his best prospects for quality computer scientists increasingly resided in India, China, and Russia, among those previously educated in the United States. The developed nations, in an effort to share knowledge resources via education, may be losing their competitive advantage instead of maintaining it. Of course, this oversimplification illustrates once again the ebb and flow of driving forces and their complex interplay in global trends.

TABLE 1.16 Summary of Ideological Barriers to U-Learning

Barriers	Developed Regions	Developing Regions	Solutions
Lack of Expertise	Despite adequate infrastructure and equal access, when teachers lack expertise integrating technology and curriculum, students fall short of established technology standards. (McPheeters, 2009)	Developing nations send students to the universities of developed nations for education. Graduates often required to return to homeland where they are hired from abroad for lower wages.	Professional development focusing on technology integration is needed, as well as reforms that allow shared resources of expertise between developed and developing countries rather than exportation of expertise.
Resistance	Cultural and religious resistance may exist within ethnic neighborhood schools.	Some developing nations want the technology but not the culture that often comes with it.	Education that focuses on cultural awareness and appreciation of diversity is needed. Critical thinking skills are needed to reduce the fears that come with insecurity when confronted with uncharted ideological territory.
Tradition	Some education stakeholders remain entrenched in a 100-year-old industrial model of education with homogenized and standardized learning as the goal.	Cultural and religious traditions can preclude those of a certain race or gender from receiving the same educational opportunities as others.	Educating for cultural awareness and appreciation, as well as visionizing for a technologically rich future where a new breed of worker is needed, is required.
Lack of Research	Research often conducted by foreign students from abroad who are then required to return to their homeland after graduation.	Increasing research being conducted by those educated abroad.	New platforms of shared research are needed so knowledge is no longer proprietized nationally as a commodity to be sold and exported, but instead is open-sourced and made accessible for the common good.
Lack of Vision	Lack of global vision of interconnectedness through technology results in nationalized self-interest to hold a position of dominance.	Lack of global vision brings increasing disparity between socioeconomic classes.	Leadership is needed that models best practices and understands the new internetworked world.

Resistance

Cultural bias and ideological resistance to innovations can affect the interplay of driving forces. Certain religious groups in early American history were resistant to many of technology's modern conveniences. Recall how the Amish resisted the early adoption of electric appliances, or how Orthodox Jews avoid the use of certain technologies such as television, during their sabbath observance. More examples follow. Resistance within some cultures manifests its limiting quality by preventing access to education among a particular gender or within a certain ethnic group. This has been witnessed historically in South Africa's apartheid. Also, post–Civil War America was slow to reform education and allow former slaves to be educated. Even recent news headlines telling of China's Internet control policies opposing tech giant Google is yet another example of a resistance barrier. The China vs. Google incident demonstrates how resistance barriers can affect many aspects of life for the nation wherein it resides, as well as the economies of developed nations wishing to expand beyond their own borders. In other words, the interplay of localized resistance barriers affects the globally networked world.

Likewise, early Greeks feared the introduction of books would be a precursor to the inevitable decline in the human mental muscle that was required to memorize (Humphrey, Oleson, & Sherwood, 1998). Today, there are some who fear that computer technologies are weakening our critical thinking skills. They complain that the calculator prevents our need to memorize formulas; that Google leaves us free to look up information as needed rather than study it beforehand. Certainly our habits are changing due to rapid technology innovation. However, the time required to perform the old tasks is now available for new tasks. What will the new tasks be? Will the new tasks be self-serving and self-centered? Or will the new tasks be creative and socially concerned? Leadership that models sustainable best practices will decide the outcome.

Tradition

An example of a tradition barrier can be seen in developing nations that have not traditionally valued the education of women. A quick search on Google Scholar reveals a large number of recent studies on the topic of Muslim women and their culture's traditionally restricted access to education with the resulting social effects. The effects of such traditions are being eroded by the increased interaction of an emerging networked world.

Mobile technologies are widely opening the doors to previously closed segments of society. Isolated groups initially gain access to mobile technologies for communication purposes. In some areas of the world, economic needs are driving the increased use of mobile devices. Many people realize that Japan—a developed nation—enjoys the most advanced mobile technologies available on the planet today. However, not many people know that Africa—a developing nation—has the highest per-capita use of mobile phones. Internet access and usage is very low, but cell phone usage is high, including nearly 100 percent of youth. So, although Internet use is a weaker driving force of change, the strong mobile use is stirring up major structural changes within the economy already, such as remote banking and bill paying. Lateral adaptation of education follows easily along this mobile highway.

It is this type of driving force within the mobile technology arena inside developing nations that is driving companies like Motorola to develop the low-priced $12 smartphones mentioned earlier. Applying emerging mobile technology changes to create a ubiquitous education platform will most assuredly follow.

Lack of Research

The National Science Foundation (2009) reports an increasing 6-year rise in doctorate degrees awarded to temporary visa holders in the United States, many of whom have returned to their developing homeland after graduation and are now heading departments in their local universities or driving research and development divisions (R&D) for multinational companies that can hire them at lower wages. Research coming from developing nations such as India and China is expected to lead the world within the next 15 years (Cetron & Davies, 2010). An indicator of this trend is shown by the increasing number of published research papers. China alone has more than quadrupled its contribution of research papers in the past decade. With the increase in local research, local governments will more readily justify and adopt recommendations from their own national experts.

Lack of Vision

The self-absorbed nation remains isolated from the global perspective. Such isolation prevents its further advance in order to ensure its share of resources and maintain its competitive advantage. Countries that fall short of a global vision of their need to become technologically up-to-date will only increase the disparity. A global perspective of interconnectedness enables each nation to adopt, adapt, and integrate the emerging innovations. However, such perspectives must be taught in order to be learned. Instructional design experts make clear that in order to affect mindsets, three ingredients must be present in the educational environment. First, there must be someone who models the targeted behavior. Second, learners must be equipped with the vocabulary that is consistent with the targeted behavior. And third, learners must have the opportunity to rehearse the targeted behavior. For this reason, educational institutions provide professional development opportunities to their staff and faculty in hopes of producing such models equipped to pass on the needed vision.

WHAT SHOULD THE GLOBAL PERSPECTIVE BE?

After detailing the complexity of the u-learning challenge, it would seem irresponsible, if not ridiculous, to claim a simple solution. A shared global viewpoint among so many diverse cultural and ethnic traditions may not be possible. However, certain characteristics of a shared education framework can be agreed upon. Whereas historically, local communities have developed and guarded local resources, today's globally inter-networked resources cannot sustainably be used to leverage one nation against another. As Albert Einstein noted in 1921, "Nationalism is an infantile disease. It is the measles of mankind" (Calaprice, 1996). Self-preservation interests of individual nations are gradually giving way to globally shared needs due to the complex interplay of the 10 driving forces identified at the beginning of this chapter.

Apart from future innovations, the world's presently known resources are limited. As technology replaces the need for routine manual human skills and abilities, the essential need is to educate minds to best utilize existing resources while continuing to innovate new ones. Therefore, it is wise to ask ourselves, "What are the competencies of future innovators? How do we teach and train the next generation—regardless of homegrown perspectives—to be competent and skilled in their use of existing resources, yet innovative in their approach toward emerging ideas?"

Thus far, the pressures that drive every nation distill down to the 10 trends identified at the beginning of this chapter: Economic, Population, Societal, Labor, Family, Energy, Environmental, Terrorism, Institutional, and Technology developments (Cetron & Davies, 2010). However, to gather culturally different people around such driving forces with a unified concern requires a shared framework of values. Education is the optimum tool for social engineers interested in designing a sustainable future because education is based on and driven by society's values; u-learning ideally meets this need of increasingly globalized values. The renovation of old models will become unanimously adopted as no nation will be able to command a single resource to the extent that it can dominate and exclude that resource from others. The new model will be a confluence where driving forces converge to become nodes of influence both locally and globally.

This confluence of driving forces will create a world where individualized learning is available 24 hours a day, 7 days a week. Learning will become increasingly tailored to the individual. Location-aware applications will enable contextually relevant delivery of learning. Real-time and real-world scenarios will be accessible to everyone for continuous on-demand training. A major driving force in the direction of this confluence of forces can be seen in the economic trends within and among both developed and developing countries. Just as industrialization shaped public education in the 19th and 20th centuries, current business interests and demands for competent cloud workers are pressuring educational institutions into yet again *new* molds of instructional design for ubiquitous learning.

The spread of large multinational companies promotes what has been called by George Ritzer (1993), the McDonaldization of society. Multinational companies have an affect from *within* via their employees, and *without* via their customer base.

> By some counts, only half of the world's 100 largest economies are nation-states. The rest are multi-national corporations. Toyota alone has manufacturing or assembly plants in 22 countries. (Cetron & Davies, 2010, p. 36)

Multinational corporations understand the necessity of a shared vision among their employees. Driven by the need to deliver profits to shareholders, such corporations place strong emphasis on continuing education by way of training and customer influence by way of marketing, in order to maximize corporate efforts.

In addition, these global companies strive to unify markets in favor of their products. We shouldn't underestimate the sway that increasing international revenues have on the world at-large. The growth of international sales among the Standard and Poor's 500 economic index are outpacing domestic sales. The spread of market influences through such economical trends can flatten the sharp cultural differences between developed and developing countries. For example, consider the influence of free-trade introduced to former communist bloc countries like China and Poland. Such drastic changes affect the local societies both economically as well as culturally. Friedman (2007) details a recent example of this phenomenon as it relates to the technology revolution that touched the remote region of Bangalore, India's new "Silicon Valley."

IN SEARCH OF A UNIFYING FRAMEWORK

Physicists like Albert Einstein have been searching for a unifying theory that would accurately describe the state of being of all existing things. Education theorists are in search of a unifying theory that would accurately describe how we learn and the optimum way to deliver that learning for maximum results. Whether such a unifying theory exists within either domain remains a matter of debate, however a framework that provides a confluent view might be possible. Though driving forces might remain divergent according to local needs, global trends will continue to address basic human needs on a larger scale. The evolving theories, strategies, and methods have been blended into an interesting stew over the past 100-plus years. Yet much of our practice remains in the experimental stage, with localized needs taking precedence over global trends and immediate solutions targeted in place of long-range sustainability.

On the other hand, fears of a homogenized solution resulting from cloud standardization efforts of those valuing brand control (i.e., Google? Apple?), lead to a tug in the opposite direction to maintain localized variety (Leadbeater, 2010). Fears that corporate control might result in a kind of cloud monopoly are met by fears of government control based on perceived security threats. The tug-of-war between these two powerful players is felt abroad as an emerging cloud culture seeks to eradicate inequality by promoting an open web of democratic ubiquity.

Unique models of business and ownership are appearing on the Internet at an ever-increasing rate. Kiva.org is neither the result of corporate nor government planning, yet joins the resources of the developed countries with the needs of the developing countries. It is a crowd phenomenon, because change is induced by the loosely connected crowds of Internet users rather than the closely controlled institutions such as corporations or government. Likewise, Zerobaggage.com has appeared with a new model of shared ownership that meets the needs of the mobile generation already existing within developed countries and quickly emerging within the developing countries.

CONCLUSION

It has been shown that u-learning alone holds the greatest promise toward a unifying framework with which every culture views their place within global society, because u-learning equips individuals with the capacity to contribute and the recognition of the value of the contribution of others both locally and globally. This chapter details the complexity involved in determining the future of u-learning based on a host of driving forces affecting global trends in ways that are unique to local needs. Increased understanding of the issues surrounding new paradigms of community and identity results in participants becoming better equipped to impart common values to others (McPheeters, 2009). Throughout history, increasing complexity of community-role specialization augments mutual interdependence within local communities and exacerbates competition between neighboring communities. However, technological innovation is flattening the opportunity landscape and thereby making resources more widely available to all by reducing the space-time barriers of our constrained past.

Stakeholders interested in realizing broadscale democratic u-learning must provide for the smooth supply of global learning resources to meet the increased demand coming from the ever-flattening global community. Intercontributory communities result when individuals are equipped to participate and contribute regardless of their cultural context. Such participation and contribution is fostered by u-learning, creating communities of impact where members belong and have value and where the community itself reverberates beyond the borders of its membership. It is these communities that are sustainable and able to adapt to emerging trends. Because these communities impact global society synergistically, members connect to a value that is bigger than the individuals making up the community. Global knowledge resources are distributed by u-learning, thereby transcending mere local needs.

The trends for integrating technology in education point in the same direction around the world. However, the driving forces affecting those trends differ within each region, nation, and culture, and affect the rate at which emerging technologies are being adopted. Regardless, neither cultures nor nations need fear keeping up in this apparent technology race because we are on a collision course with u-learning. Our destiny lies in u-learning, which holds the promise for equipping humanity with a unifying framework of global understanding and cooperation.

REFERENCES

Anglin, G. (1991). *Instructional technology: Past, present, and future.* Englewood, CO: Libraries Unlimited.

Barrett, C. (2008, June). *Craig Barrett on technology: The human impact.* Retrieved from http://fora.tv/2008/06/30/Craig_Barrett_Technology_the_Human_Impact_2_of_2.

Calaprice, A. (1996). *The quotable Einstein.* Princeton, NJ: Princeton University Press.

Cetron, M. & Davies, O. (2010, May–June). Trends shaping tomorrow's world: Economic and social trends and their impacts. *The Futurist, 44*(3), 35–50.

Failed Technology Predictions. (2007). Top 30 failed technology predictions. *Listverse.* Retrieved May 19, 2010, from http://listverse.com/2007/10/28/top-30-failed-technology-predictions/

Friedman, T. (2007). *The world is flat: A brief history of the twenty-first century.* New York: Picador.

Humphrey, J., Oleson, J., & Sherwood, A. (1998). *Greek and Roman technology: A sourcebook: Annotated translations of Greek and Latin texts and documents.* New York: Routledge.

Institute for International Education (2008–2009). Foreign students studying in the U.S. Retrieved April 19, 2010, from http://www.iie.org/en/Research-and-Publications/~/media/Files/Corporate/Membership/IIE%20Naylor%20Advertising%20Kit%202010.ashx

International Society for Technology in Education. (2009). *National Education Technology Standards.* Retreived June 15, 2010, from http://www.iste.org/standards/nets-for-administrators/nets-for-administrators-sandards.aspx

Kurzweil, R. (2003). *Kurzweil's law (aka "the law of accelerating returns").* Retrieved May 19, 2010, from http://www.kurzweilai.net/articles/art0610.html?printable=1

Kurzweil, R. (2006). *Ray Kurzweil on how technology will transform us.* Retrieved January 22, 2009 from http://www.ted.com/index.php/talks/ray_kurzweil_on_how_technology_will_transform_us.html

Leadbeater, C. (2010). *Cloud culture: The future of global cultural relations.* London: The British Council.

Lumley, D., & Bailey, G. (1993). *Planning for technology: A guidebook for school administrators.* New York: Scholastic.

McPheeters, D. (2009). Cyborg learning theory: Technology in education and the blurring of boundaries. In T. Bastiaens et al. (Eds.), *Proceedings of World Conference on E-Learning in Corporate, Healthcare, and Higher Education 2009* (pp. 2937–2942). Chesapeake, VA: AACE.

Michener, J. (1989). *Caribbean.* New York: Random House.

Muilenburg, L. Y., & Berge, Z. L. (2001). Barriers to distance education: A factor-analytic study. *The American Journal of Distance Education, 15*(2), 7–24.

National Science Foundation. (2009, November). Numbers of U.S. doctorates awarded rise for sixth year, but growth slower. *National Science Foundation, Division of Science Resources Statistics Arlington, VA* (NSF 10-308). Retrieved April 19, 2010, from http://www.nsf.gov/statistics/infbrief/nsf10308/

Nystedt, D. (2008, June 6). HTC eyes market for smartphones in poor nations. *IDG News Service for PC World.* Retrieved May 16, 2010, from http://pcworld.about.com/od/mobilephones/HTC-Eyes-Market-for-Smartphone.htm

Pilzer, P. (1990). *Unlimited wealth: The theory and practice of economic alchemy.* New York: Crown Publishing Group.

Preece, J. (2009). Lifelong learning and development: A southern perspective. *Compare: A Journal of Comparative and International Education, 39*(5), 585–599.

Ritzer G. (1983). The McDonaldization of society. *Journal of American Culture. 6*(1), 100–107.

Tattersoll, I. (1998). *Becoming human: Evolution and human uniqueness.* New York: Harcourt Brace.

ABOUT THE AUTHOR

Dallas McPheeters is an award winning educational technologist, passionate about helping others feel at home with technology. His peer reviewed and published research focuses on the mashup generation of uncertainty facing an unknowable future and how to engage such minds as they prepare for tomorrow. Most recently, McPheeters received a Presidential Citation for his contribution to the field of education within multiuser virtual environments. Results from his research have been presented both nationally and internationally to educators and professionals interested in adapting emerging technologies to the next generation of learners and workers, whether face-to-face or in the cloud. McPheeters' work demonstrates how the elimination of space-time and identity barriers opens new avenues for learning previously unavailable in traditional venues. More about Mr. McPheeters can be discovered online at http://dallasmcpheeters.com

CHAPTER 17

THE FUTURE AS A UBIQUITOUS LEARNING OPPORTUNITY

Kay E. Strong and Peter C. Bishop

ABSTRACT

Human fascination with the future reaches back millennia, yet few people have engaged in the formal study of the nature and the origin of the future. The elements of change, how change unfolds and impacts the evolution of possible, plausible, and preferable future outcomes, are at the heart of futures studies. Futures studies is a field of inquiry open to ubiquitous learning. This chapter portrays those opportunities from two perspectives. The first is a linear view: *What Time is this Place?* teaches about the ubiquitous nature of change, and how we are all players in constructing (or destructing) the future. The second perspective is a complex view. Alternate-reality games that use the real world as a platform—a new context for informal ubiquitous learning—teaches players about unpredictability and uncertainty in complex environments.

Ubiquitous Learning, pages 317–327

INTRODUCTION

The arrival of the World Wide Web on the heels of the Internet opened whole new channels for communication and information delivery and retrieval. Social interactions need no longer be limited by physical proximity. Accessing information is no longer confined to local resources, and the 8-hour workday no longer constrains the learning environment. Advances in mobile devices nurture the development of ubiquitous learning.

It is no wonder then that educators are being drawn to new technologies as a way of expanding instructional options, engaging students in round-the-clock learning, and increasing interactivity outside the bounds of the traditional classroom. Students now engage formal learning opportunities at home, at work, and on-the-go. Some use automated Web sites without human interaction; others interact remotely through audio and video links, online discussion boards, e-mails, blogs, instant messages, chat rooms, texts, social networking sites, and even Twitter feeds. Of equal importance is the rise of informal ubiquitous learning opportunities; spontaneous or incidental learning occurring as the by-product of doing something else.

Advances in technology and the exponential growth of digital applications for learning have moved ubiquitous learning into the mainstream—anytime, anyplace, any topic, and any way accessible. Yet in spite of its timeliness and convenience, we believe that ubiquitous learning will never completely replace the traditional teacher-student classroom environment. Face-to-face interaction remains the most natural human interface, offering the highest bandwidth and, when done well, generates great satisfaction for teachers and learners alike. But the future of education clearly favors the growth of ubiquitous learning in both formal and informal contexts. Just as the Internet facilitates a global shopping experience, soon the world's best educational opportunities, content, teachers and degree programs will be but a few clicks away. Ubiquitous learning is truly revolutionizing the world of learning possibilities beyond the *status quo.*

The future is one field that lies outside the *status quo,* and that is open to the new possibilities of learning ubiquitously. This chapter describes two different approaches to enable learners to better understand the nature and the origin of the future. The first is an introductory approach using a linear view of the nature and origin of the future. The futures exercise, *What Time is this Place?* teaches about the flow of time. The second is a more complex approach, synthesizing systems principles, complexity, and social networking to explain the nature and origin of the future. Alternative-reality games—interactive narratives using multimedia and real life—teach important lessons about dynamics of connectedness and the possibility of co-creating a sustainable future ubiquitously.

A LINEAR APPROACH TO STUDYING THE FUTURE

The only constant is change, continuing change, inevitable change, that is the dominant factor in society today. No sensible decision can be made any longer without taking into account not only the world as it is, but the world as it will be.

—Isaac Asimov (1981)

Human fascination with the future reaches back millennia, but only since the late 20th century has the future been the focus of systematic studies. *On Thermonuclear War* (Kahn, 1960), perhaps the most controversial of books at its time, opened the floodgates to similar works such as the *Population Bomb* (Ehrlich, 1968), *Future Shock* (Toffler, 1970), and *Limits to Growth* (Meadows, Meadows, Randers, & Behrens, 1972). Each treatise exposed fresh opportunities and threats lying in the future and heightened public awareness about the longer-term consequences of collective behavior. As a result, a few academic courses and collegiate-level programs were founded to study the future. Sadly, the past 50 years has seen little growth in a field of study that holds such promise for humankind. Some would argue that the future is unpredictable, hence outside the reach of science and academic rigor. The argument contains a kernel of truth. Predicting the future, in the strong sense of "knowing what *will* happen," is a near impossibility. But that is not the goal of futures studies. Waldrop (1992) contends that the essence of any true science is comprehension and explanation, not prediction. Comprehension and explanation is the objective of futures studies. The methodologies and the tools of the futures field are time-tested, often leveraged by other professions. However, it is the study of the nature and the origins of the future that holds the greatest promise for improving humankind's collective future.

Isaac Asimov observed that change is the only constant, an observation that is valid throughout time, across cultures, and within our personal lives. The study of history provides a rear-view mirror look at change. Historians create narratives that identify a series of events, carefully manage their interactions, and narrowly infer their implications to produce a coherent story of what happened. This historical narrative then acts as a scaffold, bridging the past to our present.

The futurist, on the other hand, sees change as coming through the windshield—interpreting the unwinding dynamics and identifying potential implications that illuminate alternative futures, some probable, others plausible, and a few desirable. There is one facet, however, of studying the future to which history cannot lay claim, and that is its openness, of which Isaac Asimov observes, "No sensible decision can be made any longer without taking into account not only the world as it is, but the world as it will be" (Asimov on Science Fiction, 1981).

The origin of the future is born from the element of change, both change projecting from the past as trends and change materializing in the present as events. Trends are rooted in the past and represent a form of change evolved over relatively long periods of time. Adjustment to this form of change is frequent and ongoing. Events, on the other hand, represent abrupt, discontinuous breaks in the continuum of time. Our lack of preparation for discontinuous events makes us vulnerable to what happens next. Trends, events, and the execution of plans come at us from the world and affect the evolution of the future outside our immediate control. People and organizations have little hope of affecting the macroforces of the world, but actions and decisions made by individuals and organizations do impact their personal futures. Therefore, the future we actually experience is always a combination of inbound change (from the world) and outbound change (from ourselves). So, "we are neither hapless victims of change nor omnipotent dictators of the future" (Bishop & Strong, 2010).

A LINEAR LEARNING EXERCISE—*WHAT TIME IS THIS PLACE?*

Ubiquitous learning, as anytime, anyplace, any topic, any way accessible, creates a context for expanding formal learning opportunities. *What Time is this Place?* is an introductory exercise used in the master's program in futures studies at the University of Houston. It is a simple yet powerful way to experientially awaken students to the flow of time.

The first step in the exercise asks students to note the age and history of objects or structures in their immediate surroundings—neighborhoods, workplaces, or anywhere they happen to be. Students can visually capture images of their place of interest using an inexpensive digital camera or cell phone.

By consulting old newspapers or public records, students discover comparable pictures out of the past and read the public discourse concerning the pending changes. Interviewing individuals who have lived or worked in the surroundings puts the context of change into the first person.

The second step involves "time travel," taking students on a field trip to a neighborhood or a commercial site under construction or being considered for development. Students re-create the construction site by proposing images sketched by hand or computer-aided graphical tools.

In step three, students imagine the future of the site and write an illustrated story about events that might lead to other plausible futures or to their preferred future for the location. Many scenarios are possible, all of which demonstrate that the present is but one point on a forward moving continuum of time. Time changes all things, and the timeline branches, sometimes quite dramatically, after the present.

A simple exercise using one's everyday surroundings, *What Time is this Place?* teaches students important lessons about the flow of time, the ubiquitous nature of change, and how we are all players in constructing (or destructing) our world and the future.

A COMPLEX APPROACH TO STUDYING THE FUTURE

Although problems and catastrophes may be inevitable, solutions are not.
—Isaac Asimov (1975)

Hindsight is history's ally in describing how the future came to be. We unconsciously believe the past that did happen was the only outcome that could have happened, that it was inevitable, perhaps even predetermined. Duncan Watts, the author of *Six Degrees: The Science of a Connected Age,* observes that "we have a predisposition to believe that actual outcomes are somehow preferred over all other possibilities" (Watts, 2003, p. 245). "History has a tendency to ignore the things that *might* have happened but did not," adds Watts. The future, however, cannot ignore the things that might happen, though the possibilities are vast. The future will emerge where the myriad actions, dreams, policies, and ideas pulsing through the networks of living systems settle down to create the momentary present. Therefore, a more robust explanation of the nature and origins of the future is founded on concepts of systems-thinking supplemented with complexity and social networking theory.

Systems Principles

In a world given to analysis and reductionism, a systems perspective that emphasizes synthesis and holism seems counterintuitive. A system is a group of interconnected components that form a complex and unified whole (Anderson & Johnson, 1997). Systems are everywhere, some nested inside other systems and often operating on different time scales. Living systems of people and nature are dynamic, learning entities capable of producing complex behavior, that is, behavior greater than the sum of their simpler components. Systems engage in goal-seeking, self-preservation, and sometimes unexpected evolutionary behavior. It is information gathered about internal states and external influences that trigger behavioral changes in a system. Wheatley (2006) characterizes information as the creative energy of the universe, a form of "nourishment" *per se*: "for a system to remain alive, for the universe to keep growing, information must be continually generated" (p. 96). This ever-expanding universe of information weakens the sense of certainty about probable future outcomes in complex living systems.

Complexity Theory

Self-organization is the capacity of a system to structure itself, create new structure, and to learn and diversify; in essence, to become ever more complex. Axelrod and Cohen (2000, p. 7) define a system as complex "when there are strong interactions among the elements, so that current events heavily influence the probability of many kinds of later events" (p. 7). Coevolution is a feature of complex adaptive systems in which the rules of interaction between the components are in a state of constant flux. A change introduced by one part of the system or another system altogether is met with an adaptive response. These action-reaction volleys require updating ideas and a continual refreshing of the rules of the game. The future effects of the changes we make now are unpredictable, even in principle (Waldrop, 1992, p. 284).

Social Networking Theory

The great naturalist John Muir (1911) testifies that "when we try to pick out anything by itself, we find it hitched to everything else in the universe." Connection is a pervasive attribute of the world and of living systems. Social networks are a system, a structure of nodes (individual agents) connected through one or more links. The behavior of the network as a whole is determined almost entirely by the nature of the connections (Waldrop, 1992, p. 291). Social networks affect our lives in intimate ways. According to Christakis and Fowler (2009), "events occurring in distant others can determine the shape of our lives, what we think, what we desire, whether we fall ill or die. In a social chain reaction we respond to faraway events, often without being consciously aware of it" (pp. 304–305). Power resides in the connection (Waldrop, 1992, p. 292). Loosely connected networks encourage the inflow of new ideas, opportunities, and new membership, while connections to multiple networks expand access to a wider range of information. The introduction of new information opens the window to change, and change modifies the strength of the connection. In some instances, small change has the power to cascade through the connections of a system, unleashing unforeseen and major consequences. In other cases, strategic attempts by policymakers to introduce large-scale change are met with no discernible results. We are embedded in numerous social networks that both unite us as well as shape us. The future cannot help but be a co-production of a multitude of actors.

A COMPLEX LEARNING EXERCISE— ALTERNATE-REALITY GAMES

Alternate-reality games (ARG) are a growing genre of massively multiplayer online gaming (MMOG), which provide a new context for informal ubiquitous learning opportunities. An ARG is an interactive narrative using the real world as its platform. Employing various multimedia tools, players enter the game maintaining their own identity and work collaboratively to solve challenges. As such, ubiquitous, or incidental learning opportunities, are introduced. Through the dynamics of interaction, players' current understanding, knowledge, and worldviews (models) may be complemented, reinforced, or contradicted, and the learning may be additive or even transformative (Schugurensky, 2000). This form of MMOG is an ideal vehicle for revealing the richer dynamics of the nature and origins of the future, drawn from concepts of systems, complexity, and social networking theory. In some places, developmental costs and the lack of localized acceptance as a valid learning platform have deterred widespread classroom use of ARGs.

One professional futures research organization, the Institute for the Future (IFTF), has taken the lead in developing and launching spectacular futuristic games open to worldwide participation. Jane McGonigal, Director of Game Research and Development at the IFTF, claims that "reality . . . can only be fixed if we make the real world work like massive, multiplayer games" (Zetter, 2010). "Games—particularly alternate reality games—inspire large groups of people to pool their knowledge and skills to overcome obstacles, and this is precisely what's needed to tackle global social issues, such as poverty, hunger, disease and climate change, McGonigal says" (Zetter, 2010). The IFTF has fostered the development of three ARGs since 2007.

The IFTF's first ARG, *World Without Oil* (*WWO*), launched in 2007 (http://www.worldwithoutoil.org/), was co-produced with Ken Eklund, who worked for Strategic Simulations, Inc. on the role-playing game *Buck Rogers in the 25th Century: Countdown to Doomsday* in 1988. *World Without Oil* simulates 32 weeks of a major global oil crisis. Players in 12 countries reimagine the details of their personal life, bussing their children to school, or buying food in a world running short on oil. The game produced three noteworthy outcomes: (a) players learned about the importance of aligning thinking and action to the reality of a world without oil, (b) players developed new coping skills, and (c) players tested alternative conclusions. More than 1,800 people participated in *WWO*, using such multimedia tools as blogs, videos, e-mails, voicemails, and images.

In 2008, the IFTF followed *WWO* with *SuperStruct* (http://www.superstructgame.org/), the world's first massively multiplayer forecasting game. As the Web site states, "this is about more than just envisioning the future. It's about making the future, inventing new ways to organize the human race and augmenting our collective human potential." Players enter the world of 2019, a world plagued by superthreats: broken food chains, swarming climate refugees, and a pandemic outbreak of respiratory distress syndrome. To save the planet, players self-organize, work across traditional borders, and pool ideas to meet five intertwined challenges. A repository of solutions, identified as 21st Century Ideas, is housed at the game's Web site.

EVOKE, a social network game (http://www.urgentevoke.com/) released in early 2010, is a 10-week crash course in changing the world through innovation. McGonigal describes the objective:

> It's oriented toward young people in Africa primarily and more broadly to anyone in the world who wants to help solve problems in the developing areas. It's a crash course in how to start a venture, a business, that can tackle these problems [of poverty, disease, hunger] at a local level.... By the end of the game you have developed a real-world pitch for a venture [and] have acquired mentors to help you make it real. If you play the game you're connected to somebody in the real world who has entrepreneurial experience to mentor you; you've also developed skills to make you a better problem solver. (Zetter, 2010)

The game's goal is to "empower young people all over the world, and especially young people in Africa, to come up with creative solutions to our most urgent social problems" (http://blog.urgentevoke.net/2010/01/27/about-the-evoke-game/). Among the problems cited: food, water and energy security, disaster and poverty relief, and education. Unlike other MMOGs, *EVOKE* encourages collaborative interactions among players, and development of evoke powers such as vision, creativity, and local insight. The Web site states, "This is not a simulation. You are about to tackle real problems" (http://blog.urgentevoke.net/).

Alternate-reality games create high-end ubiquitous learning opportunities. Supported by global connectivity, ordinary individuals learn sophisticated ways to interact, to collaborate, and to contribute to the resolution of real-world problems. Asked whether evidence to support the claim that game-based learning translates into real-world learning, McGonigal responds,

> Yes. Many of the games I've done have triggered lasting change. With the *World Without Oil* project...we have followed [the players] for years now looking at what their everyday behaviors are like and overwhelmingly they report, three years later, having not only changed their own daily habits, but [they are] teaching friends, coworkers, family members, neighbors to adopt these

> habits as well. So at a micro level we can change people's behavior and show them it's possible to contribute to a better way of living on the planet and empower them to share that with other people. (Zetter, 2010)

By placing players in the driver's seat, ARGs teach important lessons about unpredictability and uncertainty in a complex interactive environment, the dynamics of connectedness, and the possibility of coevolutionarily producing a sustainable world and future ubiquitously. Players learn to imagine new possibilities, to interact across international borders, and to cooperatively create a better world—an outstanding way of engaging learning ubiquitously. While ARGs are exciting, they are also expensive to develop, and we can hardly expect teachers to take on the task of game developer. But teachers can help grow local acceptance of alternate-reality games as a viable learning platform by using high-end ARGs like those being developed by such leading research institutions as the IFTF in their classrooms.

CONCLUSION

In time, we believe most learning will be ubiquitous—outside the traditional confines of a formal classroom and rigid schedules. We will all need to become confident and comfortable with this emerging change. The movement toward ubiquitous learning will encourage teaching new things, one of which will be how to anticipate, manage, and live with change and how to collectively guide the future toward a more preferred outcome.

Change, the dynamics of change, and the long-term implications of change are at the heart of futures studies. This chapter examined the nature and origin of the future using two different, but complimentary perspectives. The *What Time is this Place?* exercise highlights the linear flow of time, the ubiquitous nature of change, and how we are all players in constructing (or destructing) the future. Alternate-reality games, like those produced by the IFTF, are a safe testing ground to ubiquitously learn important lessons about the complex nature of the future. ARGs challenge our perceptions about the certainty and predictability of the future in a world being co-created by billions of simultaneous players.

REFERENCES

Anderson, V., & Johnson, L. (1997). *Systems thinking basics: From concepts to causal loops.* Waltham, MA: Pegasus Communications, Inc.

Asimov, I. (1975). How to see the future. *Natural History* (April).

Asimov, I. (1981). *Asimov on science fiction.* Worchester, MA: Davis Publications Inc.

Axelrod, R., & Cohen, M. D. (2000). *Harnessing complexity.* New York: Basic Books.

Bishop, P. C., & Strong, K. E. (2010, Spring). Why teach the future? *Journal of Futures Studies.*

Christakis, N. A., & Fowler, J. H. (2009). *Connected: The surprising power of our social networks and how they shape our lives.* New York: Little, Brown and Company.

Ehrlich, P. R. (1968). *Population bomb.* Cutchogue, NY: Buccaneer Books, Inc.

Kahn, H. (1960). *On thermonuclear war.* Princeton, NJ: Princeton University Press.

Meadows, D. H, Meadows, D. L, Randers, J., & Behrens, W. W. (1972). *Limits to growth.* New York: Universe Books.

Muir, J. (1911). *My first summer in the Sierra.* New York, NY: Houghton Mifflin.

Schugurensky, D. (2000). The forms of informal learning: Toward a conceptualization of the field. New Approaches to Lifelong Learning–*NALL Working Paper 19/2000,* OISE-University of Toronto.

Toffler, A. (1970). *Future shock.* New York: Bantam Books.

Waldrop, M. (1992). *Complexity.* New York: Simon & Schuster Paperbacks.

Watts, D. J. (2003). *Six degrees: The science of a connected age.* New York: W.W. Norton & Company, Inc.

Wheatley, M. J. (2006). *Leadership and the new science: Discovering order in a chaotic world.* San Francisco: Berrett-Koehler.

Zetter, K. (2010). TED 2010: Reality is broken. game designers must fix it. *Wired.* Retrieved April 7, 2010, from http://www.wired.com/epicenter/2010/02/jane-mcgonigal/#ixzz0kQtR3TUv

ABOUT THE AUTHORS

Dr. Kay E. Strong, an associate professor of Economics at Baldwin-Wallace College in Cleveland, Ohio, was director of the Initiatives for the Future and facilitator of the IF Learning Community and "e-futuring" Learning Initiative at Bowling Green State University prior to taking professional leave to fulfill her master's degree in futures studies at the University of Houston. She has taught futures courses and developed a teacher's training workshop and a Summer Futures Camp for children. Dr. Strong has delivered future-based presentations in California, Chicago, and Texas. Dr. Strong received her doctoral degree in economics from Southern Illinois University.

Dr. Peter Bishop is an associate professor in the College of Technology and Coordinator of the graduate program in Futures Studies at the University of Houston. Dr. Bishop specializes in techniques for long-term forecasting and planning. He delivers keynote addresses and conducts seminars on the future for business, government, and not-for-profit organizations. Dr. Bishop is a founding board member of the Association of Professional Futurists and president of his own firm, Strategic Foresight and Development, which offers education and training to the corporate market. Dr. Bishop received his doctoral degree in sociology from Michigan State University.

ABOUT THE EDITORS

Terry T. Kidd, PhD, is an experienced academic with over 10 years of experience and expertise in faculty development, online learning, instructional design and technology support services, and in college teaching. His current research focuses on using methods of design science (e.g., as in human/computer interaction and computer-supported cooperative work), with critical theory/interpretive paradigms to study how ICT's, social media, eLearning, mobile learning, and u-learning may be used to support the goals and activities of a community.

Kidd has published and presented in the areas of educational technology, online learning, technology adoption, and faculty development and has collaborated with institutions such as Texas Southern University, the University of North Dakota, the University of Houston-Downtown, the National Cheng Kung University, and the University of Houston Main Campus. He is the author of *The Handbook of Research on Instructional Systems Technology*, *Social Information Technology: Connecting Society and Cultural Issues*; *Wired for Learning: An Educators Guide to Web 2.0*; and *Adult Learning in the Digital Age*, to name a few.

Irene Chen received her Doctor of Education in Instructional Technology from the University of Houston in 1998. Currently, she is an associate professor in the Department of Urban Education at the University of Houston-Downtown. Dr. Chen has diverse professional experiences. Previously, she was an instructional technology specialist, learning technology coordinator, and computer programmer/analyst. She has taught numerous graduate and undergraduate courses in instructional technology, curriculum and instruction, and delivered many K–12 in-service training, and professional development activities for university staff and faculty members.

Ubiquitous Learning, page 329

GLOSSARY OF TERMS

ABET: Accreditation Board for Engineering and Technology is a nonprofit accreditation organization for college and university programs in applied science, computing, engineering, and technology.

Academic development: Opportunities for staff to develop the links between pedagogical practice, research, and theory.

Active learning: In contract to passively listening to lectures, students actively participate in the learning process through talking and listening, reading, writing, and reflecting.

Alternative reality games (ARG): Interactive narratives using multimedia and real life to solve world challenges.

Assessment: Assessment is an ongoing inquiry process based on systematic collection, review, and use of information, which aims to improve student learning.

Back channel: Any technologically enhanced communications networks, such as Twitter or instant messenger, that enables students to discuss classroom work in real time without the approval of a teacher.

Coevolution: A feature of complex adaptive systems in which the rules of interaction are in constant flux.

Communication skills: Skills and/or mastery of imparting or disseminating information, thoughts and/or opinions, usually involving written, oral, and/or multimedia means of interchange.

Ubiquitous Learning, pages 331–337

Compendium (traditional definition): A collection of text, data, and software that allows the reader to reproduce the research that is presented in the document.

Compendium (new definition): A document with (open-access) references to (remotely) archived computations (including data, metadata, and software) that allows the reader to reproduce and reuse the underlying analysis.

Compendium platform: A system that facilitates the creation, maintenance, and permanent storage of statistical computation objects, which empowers authors to publish "compendia" of reproducible and reusable research through a series of Web services.

Context adaptation: The ability of a system to adapt automatically to diverse aspects of context (e.g., physical, cultural, political, technological, social) when the system is being transfered to a new context.

Context awareness: Relative to ubiquitous learning, applications, systems, and environments capable of sensing and incorporating user context into their functions.

Contextualization: A design principle that takes seriously the expectations, needs, and especially the strengths of the context that the proposed technology should serve.

Creepy treehouse: Inappropriate interaction and use of social networking tools by teachers to engage with students.

Cross-reality: The union of ubiquitous sensor/actuator networks positioned in the real world and shared online virtual worlds.

Dedicated device: Supporting device that is not portable. The size is generally big and not convenient to bring anywhere.

Design education: The teaching of theory and practice that applies to the design of services, products, and the environment.

Design critique: Collaborative dialogue between teachers and students discussing good and bad practice and principles of individual design outcomes.

Engaged learning: Learning that increases student interaction and collaboration using technology as a primary means of engagement.

Facebook: A social network site with over 400 million users, which can provide individual and group communication (www.facebook.com).

Facebook group: A focused community on Facebook, which may be open to all Facebook members or closed, which means one can join only via invitation.

Friending: Acknowledging a common bond between two social network users by creating an electronic link that permits sharing of data and communications.

Future studies: A study of how change impacts the development of possible, plausible, and probable futures.

Generation X: Persons born between 1965 and 1980; the successors to the baby boomers. Perceived to be the first generation exposed to technology from their early childhood and educational experiences through their adult lives.

Google Docs: A free, collaborative suite of tools including word processing, spreadsheets, and presentation software (http://docs.google.com).

Information residue: Forms of content and context information left in place as the result of a person's interactions and activities in that specific space.

Institute for the Future (IFTF): A nonprofit research center specializing in long-term forecasting and quantitative futures research methods.

Intercontributory community: Communities that exist because of the interdependence on member contributions.

Internet of Things: Embedding sensor, computational, and network hardware in everyday things, allowing them to communicate with users and other things and to interact within their environments.

Interplay: The way in which two or more things have an effect on each other.

Learning spaces: Physical and virtual, formal and informal places and spaces where learners can participate in learning activities.

Living-learning class: A classroom environment that allows students to aggregate knowledge using software tools, share information across semesters and years, and maintain communication between current and former classes.

Massively Multiplayer Online Games (MMOG): Digital-based games for teaching about the future.

Millennial generation: Persons born after 1980 and therefore the first generation to come of age in the new millennium.

Millennial students: The generation born in and after 1982. They are typically characterized as technologically savvy and prefer active experiential and collaborative learning.

MLE Moodle: A mobile plug-in for Moodle software that configures a Web-based Moodle site for mobile devices (http://mle.sourceforge.net).

MMS (Multimedia Messaging Service): Similar to SMS (Short Message Service), but includes the attachment and viewing of image and other multimedia files.

Mobile device: Pocked-sized computing device, like a PDA, a mobile phone, or a graphing calculator.

Mobility: The ability for students to participate in and link learning in a range of physical and virtual contexts.

Moodle (Modular Object-Oriented Dynamic Learning Environment): An open-source learning management system, originally developed by Martin Dougiamas. Moodle is used by thousands of educational institutions throughout the world (http://moodle.org).

Netizen: Active users of the Web for extended multiple purposes any time and anywhere.

Notebook: Portable computer.

Paradigm: An observed pattern.

PDA (Personal Digital Assistant): A mobile device that functions similar to a computer.

Personal computer: Desktop computer, which consists of a CPU, monitor, and other peripheral devices.

Perspective: A vantage point from which something is observed.

Pervasive learning space: A context-aware learning environment in which mobile and context-aware technologies are used to adapt learning experiences to a specific context. In other words, a pervasive learning space is designed for a specific context (e.g., a museum).

Physical mobile interaction (PMI): The use of mobile devices to physically interact with physical objects and places in a given context so as to facilitate access to associated information and services.

Photography in a design context: Teaching photography but taking into account the principles of design practice.

Podcasts: An audio file that can be easily or automatically downloaded from a Weblog to which an individual subscriber can download content on a regular basis. Podcasts can also be described as a series of digital media files (audio or video) that are released episodically and downloaded automatically through an automated feed with computer software like iTunes.

Posting: Copying or placing content on a social network site.

QR codes: A type of 2D code called Quick Response, supporting a dense data representation and associated application.

R framework: A set of software components that allows the user to compile and maintain Web-based software modules (so-called *R modules*) based on R code and a simple description of the user interface. The R framework ensures that there is a complete separation between user interface, storage, computing, and session management.

Read/write culture: Sometimes referred to as participatory culture, this is the idea that all media is meant to be both consumed and remixed.

Real Simple Syndication (RSS): Software that enables people to pull information from multiple Web sites into a single "reader," allowing for the aggregation of content and removing the need to visit Web sites.

Remote lab: Computer system that enables the use of real laboratory equipment through the Internet.

Reproducible computing: The use of computers and computer software in a manner that allows anyone else to replicate the results that are obtained at a later moment in time. In the traditional literature, researchers have almost exclusively used the term "Reproducible Research" instead of Reproducible Computing; this however may be confusing because the expression exclusively refers to the reproducibility of the computational aspects of research.

Reverse transfer: A process whereby a technology, designed for and within a technology-alien context, is transferred as such to a technology-familiar environment.

RFID/NFC (Radio Frequency Identifier/Near Field Communication): Technologies that support the identification and tracking of objects over short distances via radio waves.

RSS Feeds (Real Simple Syndication Feeds): The ability to subscribe to news content and have it automatically downloaded to your blog site so that you do not have to visit each news site separately.

RSS (Really Simple Syndication): Provides a helpful and easy way for users to subscribe to dynamic Web content through a feed reader. Instead of visiting a Web site to see if new information has been added, subscription to the site through a feed reader will provide this information. RSS began with blogs and is now a standard feature of many Web sites, audio, and video sites.

Rubric: A scoring tool that provides a detailed description on different levels of performance to assess and evaluate students' work.

Self-organization: The capacity of a system to structure itself, create new structure, and to learn and diversify; in essence, to become ever more complex.

Smart client application: A software application running on a mobile device under the operating system conditions.

Smartphone: A cell phone that has capability like a PDA or portable computer.

SMS (Short Message Service): A service for sending short text messages to mobile phones.

Social networking: The broad category of sites maintained by authors for the purpose of keeping in touch with friends and family, sharing pictures, and sharing invitations. Social networking can also be described as an online community of people who share common interests through discussion and image sharing.

Social networking site: An online or Web-based community with similar interests or activities.

Story stream: Bits of data and information collected by students, aggregated into public areas, and shared across semesters and years with other classes.

Supporting technology: Technology to support ubiquitous learning, which is embedded in the supporting device, for example, RFID and GPS.

Synergy: The whole is equal to more than the sum of its parts.

System: A group of interconnected components that forms a complex and unified whole.

Threaded discussion: A post that incorporates contributions and discussions from multiple users.

Trend: A measurable pattern of change observed over time.

Twitter: A microblogging service that allows the user to send short (up to 160 character) messages to people who follow them (http://twitter.com).

Twuffer: A Twitter scheduler that allows the user to schedule Twitter posts (tweets) at specific dates and times (http://twitter.com).

Ubiquitous learning space: A context-aware learning environment in which mobile and context-aware technologies are used to automatically adapt the learning experience to the learner's current context (context adaptation). In other words, ubiquitous learning space can seamlessly transfer across different contexts.

Ubiquitous learning: Accessing information from multiple sources, facilitated by multiple expert and nonexpert personnel and applied in multiple contexts by the learner. Ubiquitous learning can also be described as learning that is available at any time, at any place, from any location.

VARK Inventory: An assessment of learning tendencies developed by Neil Fleming, which categorizes learners according to their visual, auditory, read/write, and kinesthetic preferences.

Virtual lab: A computer system that simulates via software the behavior of certain laboratory equipment.

Web 2.0: All-encompassing term for blogging, RSS feeds, podcasts, and social networking sites.

WebLab: Online laboratory (both remote or virtual) accessible with a Web browser.

Weblog (blog): An electronic journal in which the author makes regular entries.

Wiki: Online encyclopedia with entries that can be contributed and edited by anyone on the Web, such as Wikipedia.

WordPress: A Web-based blogging software (http://wordpress.com).